However Blow the Winds

However Blow the Winds

An Anthology of Poetry and Song

From

Newfoundland & Labrador and Ireland

Edited by

John Ennis
Randall Maggs
and
Stephanie McKenzie

Scop Productions Inc.,
Centre for Newfoundland & Labrador Studies,
School of Humanities Publications,
Waterford Institute of Technology

We wish to acknowledge the generous financial assistance received towards the publication of this book from the Ireland Newfoundland Partnership and Foras na Gaeilge. For assistance with promotion, we thank the Ireland Business Partnership.

However Blow the Winds
First published in 2004 by

Scop Productions Inc., Waterford City, Ireland & Corner Brook, Newfoundland & Labrador and the Centre for Newfoundland & Labrador Studies, School of Humanities Publications, Waterford Institute of Technology.

Selection and Introduction. © John Ennis, Randall Maggs and Stephanie McKenzie, 2004. The appendices, beginning on page 553, form an extension of this copyright notice.

All rights reserved; no part of this book may be reproduced by any means, electronic or mechanical, except passages in a review to be printed in a newspaper or magazine or broadcast on radio or television.

Scop Productions Inc. and the Centre for Newfoundland & Labrador Studies acknowledge the financial assistance of the Ireland Newfoundland Partnership and Foras na Gaeilge in the publication of this book.

Set in Plantin.

Printed and bound in Ireland by eprint Limited, Dublin.

Book cover designed by Roger Cropera, lecturer in design at Waterford Institute of Technology.

National Library of Canada Cataloguing in Publication.

However Blow the Winds: An Anthology of Poetry and Song from Newfoundland & Labrador and Ireland / edited by John Ennis, Randall Maggs and Stephanie McKenzie.

Includes indices.

ISBN 0-9730945-3-2 (Canada)
ISBN 0-9540281-2-0 (Ireland)

1. Canadian poetry (English)—Newfoundland and Labrador. 2. English poetry—Irish authors. I. Ennis, John, 1944—II. Maggs, Randall, 1944—III. McKenzie, Stephanie, 1969—IV. Scop Productions Inc. V. Centre for Newfoundland & Labrador Studies, School of Humanities Publications, Waterford Institute of Technology.

PS8295.5 N4H69 2004   C811'.5408'09718   C2004-900800-5

In compiling this anthology, we wish to thank the following for their support and assistance:

In Newfoundland and Labrador:
Marilyn Thompson, Chair, and Colin Maddock, Director of International Development, of the Ireland Business Partnership; Philip Hiscock, Dept. of Folklore, Memorial University, for allowing us to reprint notes on several songs and offering us advice about authoritative versions; John Ennis, St. John's, for providing us with the epigraph; Anita Best, for her suggestions about which songs might be chosen; Obediah Payne, for sharing his expertise on west coast songs and for sending us selections; Tim Borlase, for sharing with us his knowledge about Inuit literature and making contacts; Pam Parsons and Pauline Hayes of Sir Wilfred Grenfell College; Elizabeth Behrens and Louise McGillis of the Ferriss Hodgett Library, Sir Wilfred Grenfell College; Wade Bowers, Professor of Environmental Science and Associate Vice Principal, and Adrian Fowler, Professor of English, Sir Wilfred Grenfell College; Debbie Edgecombe and Joan Ritcey, Centre for Newfoundland & Labrador Studies, Memorial University; Catharyn Anderson, Torngâsok Cultural Centre; editors, assistants, and permissions staff of the publishing houses by which we were facilitated; Hilda Lyall, Etienne Andrew, Helen Sylliboy, Bernie Francis, Brenda Jeddore, Chief Misel Joe, Marc Thackray, Holly Pike, Lois Sherlow, Donna Wells, Donna Hayes, Lauralee Earle, Benedict Hynes, Marni Van Dyk, Annie O'Dell, Caroline Crocker, Eric West, Pat Byrne, Mary Dalton, Nancy IKKusek, Rita Anderson, and a special thanks to Sir Wilfred Grenfell College and Anne Pinsent.

In Ireland:
Agnes Aylward, her board of directors at the Ireland Newfoundland Partnership; Deirdre Davitt and Foras na Gaeilge; Kieran R. Byrne, Director of Waterford Institute of Technology; Norah Fogarty, School of Humanities Administrator, Waterford Institute of Technology; Emanuele Sala, Centre for Newfoundland & Labrador Studies, Waterford Institute of Technology; Mary O'Brien and Martin Power, School of Humanities Administrative Staff, Waterford Institute of Technology; Dermot Aylward and Derek Sheridan of Educational Technology at Waterford Institute of Technology; Owen Davin, Finance Manager, Waterford Institute of Technology; Robbie Meredith, Literature and Languages Officer, The Arts Council of Northern Ireland; editors, assistants, and permissions staff of the publishing houses by which we were facilitated; colleagues Neil O'Flaherty, Marnie Carroll, Rachel Finnegan, Damian Harrington, Albert Keating, Colette Moloney, Christine O'Dowd Smythe, John Maher and David Rhodes; staff at College Street, including Larry Condon, Marc Jones and Edward Walsh; Liam Rellis, Alan Garvey, Tara Kelly and Jean Antoine Dunne. A special thanks to Nicholas Ó Carolan, Director, Irish Traditional Music Archive, and staff Maeve Gebruers and Orla Henihan for their invaluable assistance. Most of all, thanks to Barry O'Brien and Margaret Hamilton at eprint limited.

While every effort has been made to ensure that biographical and bibliographical details given in this work are accurate, the editors do not claim this work to be fully authoritative. The editors and publishers apologise to poets and their publishers for any errors or omissions in the acknowledgements and would be grateful to be notified of any corrections that should be incorporated into any future edition of this work. Most importantly, every effort has been made to trace the holders of copyright, but if copyright has been inadvertently breached in any case, copyright holders should contact the publishers.

The editors regret that it was not possible to include the poetry of James Joyce and Louis MacNeice in this anthology.

for all of those in Fiddlers' Green

Who would have thought that the storm blows
harder the farther it leaves Paradise behind?

                                        Benedict Anderson

William Ennis of Dublin 1796

William Ennis (or Ennes) was born in Lucan, a few miles from Dublin, about the years 1780. After he had been a few years at school, his father decided to move to Dublin; and together with his wife and three children, he settled down on the waterfront to congenial work that had been secured for him by an old friend, who in the days of prosperity had not forgotten him. It was a new life to the family and they were very happy in their healthful surroundings. The tang of the salt water of the Irish Sea and Dublin Bay had a large share in bringing back to Mrs. Ennis the health that had begun to fail her in Lucan; nor was it without a definite effect upon her boy William. It either created or awakened within him such a love for the sea that nothing less than association with it would satisfy him. Though his father and mother could not understand such love for the sea so mildly represented by Dublin Bay they made no attempt to oppose it, and when he told them that he had agreed to go to Newfoundland with Captain Cassin, on the brig, Lester, they gave their consent, and did all that was within their power to add to his bodily comfort during the voyage—on one condition—the promise that he would write to them at least once a year.

Within a few weeks of his 16th birthday, William Ennis landed in Trinity, Newfoundland, and such were the many good impressions made upon him during the voyage and after his landing in Trinity, that, with the Captain's permission, he offered his services to Mr. Garland, to whom the vessel had been consigned, to be trained as a fisherman in Trinity Bight. Mr. Garland was glad to have such a healthy, intelligent looking boy at his disposal, and after giving him a week to look around Trinity, and to enjoy the hospitality of his countrymen from Limerick and Waterford, he apprenticed him to Dennis Hone. Dennis Hone was born in Barnet Tree in the county of Waterford. He had come to Trinity some thirty years before, and at this time, he was the agent for the Garlands at their branch business at Salmon Cove, West, (now Champneys) near Trinity.

When William Ennis went to live with him, he had already two apprentices of William's age, in his care: viz: Gerald Keefe from Limerick and John Dolman from Dorset. The boys quickly became the best of friends, and with the kind care of Mr. and Mrs. Hone for their spiritual and temporal life; and with their daily work made as pleasant as it could be made, consistent with the practical training, they were as happy and contented as boys could be . . .

. . . The spring, summer, and fall work, followed each other in a more or less stereotyped way; and the netting of seals, and the duck shooting in the spring, the catching and curing of the codfish during the summer; and the shipping of it all in the fall; were carried on in such a well arranged sequence, that pleasure and profit were the results thereof. Their frequent visits to Trinity in the big seine skiff for supplies, and at fish shipping times, were days of special enjoyment and real sport. At such times they met with old friends; they brought gingerbread horses for the children; little trinkets for the girls; a kerchief or a pair of gloves for the mistress, and such things as they needed for themselves . . .

. . . Like as in all other conditions of life in which boys are bound to masters by apprenticeship, there have always been some hard and exacting masters, whose treatment of the boys entrusted to their care, made the boys' lives extremely hard; yet this was the exception in the training of youngsters in Newfoundland, and on the whole the boys were well treated; brought up largely as members of the family, and (as in the case of William Ennis) made members of the family themselves at the expiration of the apprenticeship . . .

. . . the following entry in the Old Church Register accounts for their [Hone's] other daughter, Mary:
'April 13th, 1801—Married: William Ennis of the city of Dublin, and Mary, daughter of Dennis and Elizabeth Hone of Salmon Cove in this district'.

from *The Evening Telegram* (St. John's, NL) 12 April 1924: 12.

Contents

Epigraph, William Ennis, 1796   vii

Introduction   xix

1

FOR TO FIT YOU OUT FOR SEA

Meshapush	Innu atanukan (Edward Rich, Narrator)	1
Giant Hare	Marguerite MacKenzie (Translator)	5
Wadhams Song	Wadham	9
The Cliffs of Baccalieu	Jack Withers	11
The Petty Harbour Bait Skiff	John Grace	12
The *Water Witch*	Trad	15
Lukey's Boat	Trad	18
The *Montague*	Trad	20
The Ryans and the Pittmans	H. W. Le Messurier	21
A Great Big Sea Hove in Long Beach	Trad	23
The Wave that Hit St. Brides	Daniel Payne	24
The Shoals of Herring	Ewan MacColl	26
Let Me Fish Off Cape St. Mary's	Otto Kelland	27
The Banks of Newfoundland	Trad	28
The Wreck of the Steamship *Ethie*	Trad	30
As: Eachtra Ghiolla an Amaráin / From: *The Adventures of a Luckless Fellow*	Donnchad Rua MacConmara	32
Eanach Dhúin / *Eanach Dhúin*	Antoine Ó Reachtabhra / Raifteirí	38
Caoineadh Athar / *A Father's Lament*	Seán Ó Muiríosa	43

2

A FINE PLANTATION

Donnchad Ruadh i dTalamh-an-Éisc / *Donnchad Ruadh in Newfoundland*	Donnchad Rua MacConmara	45
Carrickfergus	Trad	49
The Streams of Bunclody	Trad	50
The Prison of Newfoundland	Trad	51
Deep in the Canadian Woods	Timothy Daniel Sullivan	52
I Will Go With My Father A-Ploughing	Joseph Campbell	54

Tickle Cove Pond	Mark Walker	55
Pat Murphy's Meadow	John Devine	57
Home Free	Stephanie Payne	58
Jerry Ryan	Len Butt	59
Bucksaw Blues	Eugene Hutchings	61
Sliabh Geal gCua na Féile /		
Bright and Welcoming Mountain	Pádraig Ó Mileadha	62

3

THE RISING OF THE MOON

The Poet Egan O'Rahilly, Homesick in Old Age	Thomas Kinsella	65
Príosún Chluain Meala / The Jail of Clonmel	Trad	67
Na Connerys / The Connerys	Trad	70
The Rising of the Moon	John Keegan Casey	72
Boolavogue	P. J. McCall	73
Henry Joy McCracken	Trad	74
Rody McCorley	Trad	75
The Croppy Boy	William B. McBurney	77
De groves of de Pool	Dick Millikin	79
Dublin After the Union	Edward Lysaght	82
The Burial of Sir John Moore	Rev. Charles Wolfe	83
A Pastoral Ballad by John Bull	Thomas Moore	85
Caoineadh Baintrí / A Widow's Lament	Amhlaoibh Ó Súilleabháin	87
Annie Moore	Trad	91
Famine and Exportation	John O'Hagan	92
Siberia	James Clarence Mangan	94
Anti-Confederation Song	Trad	96
The Government Game	Pat Byrne and Al Pittman	97

4

WE LEFT THE BUNKHOUSE FEELING FINE

Finnegan's Wake	Trad	99
North Twin Lakes	Trad	101
The Kelligrews Soiree	Johnny Burke	103
Betsy Brennan's Blue Hen	Johnny Burke	105
Chrissey's Dick	Trad	108
Rubber Boots	Baxter Wareham	109
The Night Before Larry Was Stretched	J. P. Curran	111
Squid-jiggin' Ground	Arthur Scammell	113
The Pope	Trad	115
The Carrick Nine	Michael Coady	117

5

I SLEPT IN DUCK-DOWN / TILL NOONTIME CAME

As: Caoineadh Airt Uí Laoghaire /
From: *The Lament for*
Art Ó Laoghaire   Eibhlín Dubh Ní Chonaill   125
As: Cúirt an Mheán Oíche /
From: *The Midnight Court*   Brian Merriman   138
The Dark-eyed Sailor   Trad   144
The Tramway Line   Trad   146
Fanny's Harbour Bawn   Mark Walker   147
The Belfast Mountains   Trad   150
An Chúilfhionn / *The Cooleen*, or *Coolun*   Trad   151
A Sweet Little Song   James N. Healy   153
Mo bhrón ar an bhfarraige / *My grief on the ocean*   Trad   155
The Spinning Wheel   John Francis Waller   157
Brighid a Stóir / *Breed Astore*   Trad   159
Cailín Beag an Ghleanna / *Oh, Youth Whom I Have Kissed*   Trad   161
Éirigh Suas, a Stóirín / *Rise Up, My Darling*   Trad   163
Thugamar Féin an Samhradh Linn /   165
    We Brought the Summer With Us   Trad
Na Gamhna Geala / *The White Calves*   Trad   167
Cailín as Contae Lú / *A Lass From County Louth*   Trad   169
Dónall Óg / *Young Donal*   Trad   171
An Draighneán Donn / *The Dark Thorn Tree*   Trad   173
An cuimhin leat an oíche úd / *Remember that night*   Trad   175
Cradle Hill   Al Pittman   178

6

DEIRÍN DÉ

Deirín Dé / *Deirín Dé*   Trad   179
Surutsiutluta / *When We Were Children*   Sid Dicker   181
The Lord's Prayer (Mi'kmaw Translation)   Bernie Francis   183
A Mhuire na nGrás / *Blessed Mary*   Trad   184
Uvanga, Uvanga   Trad (Inuktitut)   186
Ag Críost An Síol / *To Christ The Seed*   Trad   187

7

THE BONE-AND-MARROW JUDGEMENT

R.M.S. Titanic	Anthony Cronin	189
The Ice-Floes	E. J. Pratt	200
From: *The Roosevelt and the Antinoe*		204
The Cleggan Disaster	Richard Murphy	219
Come Away, Death	E. J. Pratt	229
The Fog		231
The Ground Swell		232
Erosion		232
Come Not the Seasons Here		233
RosiaKKulak / *Beautiful Rose*	Joe K. Tuglavina	234
The Song of Wandering Aengus	W. B. Yeats	236
From: The Wanderings of Oisin		237
Down by the Salley Gardens		242
In Memory of Eva Gore-Booth and Con Markiewicz		243
Easter 1916		244
From: Meditations in Time of Civil War		247
The Wild Swans at Coole		252
Sailing to Byzantium		253
The Tomb of Michael Collins	Denis Devlin	255
From: *Missouri Sequence*:		
Nightfall, Midwinter, Missouri	Brian Coffey	258
Forget Me Not (1962)	Austin Clarke	264
The Snow Party	Derek Mahon	271
From: descending the mountain	Nick Avis	272
'after making love . . .'		
'we return . . .'		
'snowdrifts at my door . . .'		
'the village graveyard . . .'		
'the young plum pickers . . .'		
'a wedge of geese . . .'		

8

I HAVE LIVED IN IMPORTANT PLACES, TIMES

Epic	Patrick Kavanagh	273
The One		274
From: *The Great Hunger*		275
On Raglan Road		279

Dick King	Thomas Kinsella	280
Dínit an Bhróin / *Grief's Dignity*	Máirtín Ó Direáin	282
Cranna Foirtil / *Stout Oars*		284
Berkeley / *Berkeley*		286
Bogwood	Gregory Power	288
The Mummer	Tom Dawe	289
The French Shore Man		290
In Picasso's 'Madman'		292
Edwardians (Old Photograph)		294
The Veteran (1)		295
Daedalus		295
March 3, 1999—Notes on an upcoming anniversary	Des Walsh	298
On a train heading northeast		299
The triangle of the heart		300
Wednesday		301
My friend's death		302
The Launch, Trinity Shipbuilders, Trinity, June 24, 1995		303
On being Catholic and loving the treachery of winter		304
I love you more than any God, not falsely		305
Rosella and Bride	Mary Dalton	306
Bachelor Brothers		306
Brin		307
Mad Moll and Crazy Betty		308
Old Holly		308
Old Roman Candle		309
dead Indians		310

9

AN OLD GRAY TREE . . . IS TRANSFIGURED

Summer Solstice	Enos Watts	311
The Red-Throated Loon		313
Window		314
The Balcony Door		315
Cain		317
Confrontation		319
Yo-yo		320
Longliner at Sunset		321
Roses and Attic Throats		322
Waiting for Sunrise: Early December		323
Adhlacadh Mo Mháthar / *My Mother's Burial*	Seán Ó Ríordáin	324
Claustrophobia / *Claustrophobia*		328
Reo / *Freeze*		329
Fiabhras / *Fever*		330

Na Leamhain / *The Moths* 332
Othello's Own Brother David Elliott 334
Lighthouse 337
Frank 338
Mattie 339
Resonance 340
Talking to Trees 342
Magdalen at the Tomb 343

10

TOWARDS THE NEW OMAGH ROAD

The Route of *The Táin* Thomas Kinsella 345
From: *The Battle of Aughrim* Richard Murphy 348
Butcher's Dozen (1972) Thomas Kinsella 356
Hymn to The New Omagh Road John Montague 362
Clearances Seamus Heaney 367
From: *Sweeney Astray* 372
From: Sketches for an Elegy Julie O'Callaghan 377

11

NAMING THE ISLANDS

'Magic lantern'. (April, 1889) Michael Crummey 389
'The price of fish'. (September, 1887) 391
'Now in Africa among the Natives'. (1891) 392
'A narrow escape almost but saved'. (1892) 393
'Distance from Newfoundland. Northernmost 394
   grave in the world'. (1913)
'At home on a cold winter's night. 396
   The changing scenes of Life'. (1928)
'An old sailor's portion'. (1932) 398
Stones 399
Flame 400
Fog City 402
Naming the Islands 403
The Horses John Steffler 405
Saint Laurence's Tears 406
Boiler Room Men 407
The New Sled 408

From: *The Grey Islands*
'he's out there . . .'   409
'Nels and his wife . . .'   410
'they all save . . .'   411
'I thought I was headed . . .'   412
'when the rain comes . . .'   412
'on the bunk . . .'   414
'ducks swoop low . . .'   415
Nels: 'There was my great uncle . . .'   415
Nels: 'From the month of June . . .'   416
Nels: 'This one spring . . .'   417
Cedar Cove   418
Sour Fire   420
Smoke   422
Arriving in Russell   423
That Night We Were Ravenous   424
Bottled Rabbit   Ken Babstock   427
Drawing Skeletons   429
Bonavista   430

HOMECOMING

Do Jack Kerouac / *To Jack Kerouac*   Cathal Ó Searcaigh   433
Transubstaintiú / *Transubstantiation*   438
Dia: Nótaí Anailísí / *God: Analyst's Notes*   439
Haikú / *Haiku*   440
'Speal mo sheanathar . . .' / *'My grandfather's scythe . . .'*
'Dritheog nó dhó fágtha . . .' / *'An ember or two glow . . .'*
'Gealach na gcoinleach—' / *'Harvest moon—'*
'Oíche fhada gheimhridh— ' / *'Long Winter's night—'*
I gCeann mo Thrí Bliana, a Bhí Mé /   442
  When I Was Three
Ciréib / *Riot*   Gearóid Mac Lochlainn   444
Paddy / *Paddy*   448
The Green Shoot   John Hewitt   453
The Scar   454
A Belfastman Abroad Argues with Himself   455
Calling on Peadar O'Donnell at Dungloe   456
In recollection of Drumcliffe, September 1948   457
Eager Journey   458
Of Difference Does it Make   Tom Paulin   459
Desertmartin   460
Purity   461

A Nation, Yet Again		462
Telegrams	Bernard O'Donoghue	463
The Twisting of the Rope		465
Homecoming	Desmond O'Grady	466
The Butchers	Michael Longley	468
Wounds		469

13

SHE PUSHED HER SECRET OUT

From: The Bower	Vona Groarke	471
The Statue of the Virgin at Granard Speaks	Paula Meehan	475
If I Could Give You Now	Carmelita McGrath	478
Adam and Eve on a Winter Afternoon		480
For the First Time in Months, She Feels Her Feet		482
Breaking Ice		483
How She Had Her Nervous Breakdown		484
Touring the Manor Houses		486
Baked in Chocolate		487
Summer Night Heat		488
Peirsifine / *Persephone Suffering from SAD*	Nuala Ní Dhomhnaill	489
An Snag Breac / *Ten Ways of Looking at a Magpie*		491
River of January	Medbh McGuckian	494
Slieve Gallion		496
Hearing the Weather Fall		497
Gábhar Thobac / *Tobacco Shortage*	Seán Ó Duinnlé	499
Bean an Fhir Rua /	File Gan Ainm	500
The Red-Haired Man Reproaches His Wife		
Who Has Left Him		
Taisigh Agad Féin Do Phóg /		
Keep to Yourself Your Kisses	File Gan Ainm	503
The Second Voyage	Eiléan Ní Chuilleanáin	505

14

THE COST OF A GOOD CANOE

The Cost of a Good Canoe	Al Pittman	507
Gram Glover's Dream		509
Shanadithit		511
Kelly at Graveside		515
The Pigeon on the Gate		517
Living Alone		519

The Dandelion Killers		521
The Pink, White and Green		522
St. Leonard's Revisited		524
The Fish / *La pêche*	Michel Savard	525
The Second Coming	Kyran Pittman	531
Snipers in Derelict Houses	Alan Garvey	532

15

THAT YOU MIGHT REACH OUT

Incantata	Paul Muldoon	535
Early Christian Ireland Wedding Cry	Paul Durcan	547
Apoqnmuinen /		
Thank You Great Spirit	Morley Loon & Donna Augustine (Thunderbird Turtle Woman)	551

Appendices

Notes on Contributors (Newfoundland & Labrador)	553
Acknowledgements (Newfoundland & Labrador)	561
Notes on the Text (Newfoundland & Labrador)	567
Notes on Contributors (Ireland)	573
Acknowledgements (Ireland)	585
Notes on the Ballads and Songs of Ireland	591
Index of Poets	595
Index of Titles	597
Index of First Lines	605

Introduction

Complementing *The Backyards of Heaven* (2003), which featured contemporary verse, this new anthology is intended to provide a cross-section of poetry, song and verse written in Ireland and Newfoundland & Labrador over the past two hundred and twenty-five years or so.

However Blow the Winds commences with a traditional Innu story from Labrador, as well as ballads from both countries, and goes on to showcase the poetry of Donnchad Rua MacConmara (who lived and wrote in St. John's, Newfoundland in the eighteenth century), Eibhlín Dubh Ní Chonaill and Brian Merriman. The anthology features the work of poets, songwriters and ballad makers from Newfoundland & Labrador and Ireland. In the twentieth century, W. B. Yeats and E. J. Pratt figure strongly as does a range of important poets in both countries, including some not in the first volume.

However Blow the Winds explores related themes, while also adhering to a broad chronological line. A particular focus of the anthology is its exploration of the ballad, or folksong, genre, which is highly prized in Newfoundland, almost every bay having its own unique tradition in the history of song and writing.

This anthology also contains numerous examples of narrative poetry which has been, and continues to be, strong in both countries. Each country maintains its own distinct episodic structures, words and songlines, which make for considerable textual variety in one volume.

However Blow the Winds presents significantly fewer writers than *The Backyards of Heaven*, which was a book of contemporary introductions and shared visions. There is, therefore, a greater personal representation made possible for most poets in a bigger book. Of significance, too, is the greater number of original poems with translations. In the case of the Irish originals, translations span the stylistic distance between Douglas Hyde and Medbh McGuckian.

Sometimes writers from the two countries are aligned in the contents, as in the case of Enos Watts and Seán Ó Ríordáin, where related energies and a related poetic dynamic seem apparent. A further alignment is provided with the sequence which includes the poetry of Vona Groarke, Paula Meehan, Carmelita McGrath, Nuala Ní Dhomhnaill, Medbh McGuckian, Máire Mhac an tSaoi and Eiléan Ní Chuilleanáin.

More often, though, each country is facilitated to emerge uninterrupted over a span of space and time. It would be too facile, and too early, to generalise or talk extensively of shared affinities and parallels between two distinct traditions, where historical ties were once so strong and where contemporary partnerships can facilitate again a gradual and real commerce of hearts and minds.

Hopefully, what is clear from the poems, ballads and songs that we have been fortunate enough to display in this volume is a range of exciting work from artists who, well anchored in their own mores, communities and times, speak to us, nonetheless, of matters that are universal and related and of responses that accept, honour and transcend the immediate circumstances of the irritant that shapes the pearl of individual poem or song.

John Ennis
Randall Maggs
Stephanie McKenzie
March 2004

1

For to Fit you out for Sea

Meshapush

Eukuan tshe atanutsheian.

Ek^u anite etutet naneu, uapameu namesha, mishta-mitshetinua. Kuetu tutueu, apu tshi nipaiat. At tshikakuateu mani, mak^u apu tshi nipaiat. Ekue tshiuet.
 - Nukum, iteu, apu tshi nipaikau anite nameshat, mishta-mitshetuat.
 - Tau anite nussim, itiku, anapitsheu enik^u. Eukuan muk^u tepishkaniti ek^u ianapitshet. Apu tshi uapamakanit an ianapitsheti, tepishkaniti ek^u ianapitshet.
 - Nete nika natuapamau, iteu.
 - Tshika nipaik^u, itiku.
 - Mauat apu tshika tshi nipait.

Niatat, auennua uitshinua tapue. Uet unuiht ishkuessat.
 - Natuapamek^u uissitak^u, iteu uetakussinit. Eka uin peshuek^u uapushitak^u.
 - Eshe, itiku.

Tapue tshatuteht anitshenat ishkuessat, pietutaiaht nenua uissitakua. Ekute anite etat ne Uapush, nenua uissitakua. Katshi tshituteht, ekue anapitshet. Uiapamat ianapitsheniti tepishkanit.
Ek^u uenuipaniut.
  - Shash tshitshi tshissinuapamitin, iteu, etanapitshein, etapekaut tshitanapi.
  At ututamueu enik^u, apu katsheshtauat. Ekue unuipataniti. Tshauepatat ek^u.
  - Uashkashape, pishakanapi tuta, iteu ek^u ukuma.
  Ek^u uiashkashapepanit ne ishkueu, kukuminash. Katshi uashkashapet ne kukuminash, ekue anapitshet Uapush, anapitshepanu. Katshi anapitshet ekue nipaiat namesha tapue. Mishta-mitshetinua namesha nepaiat.
  - Apu takuak mukuman, iteu ne kukuminash. Tau anite kaiassikumanitshesht. Tshipa tshi minik^u natuenitamuti assikumana tshetshi mukumanitshein.
  - Eshe, iteu.

  Tshatshipatat tapue. Uiapamat auennua pemuteniti.
  - Peta ma, mini assikuman, iteu, nui mukumanitshen.
  Ekue minat ne kaiassikumanitshesht, papatshishekushinu nenu mineu. Ek^u tshauepatat. Ek^u apu tshi uinameshet eshk^u, usham papakashinu nenu, uakapissinam^u mani nenu at ua uinamesheti.
  - Mauat apu minuat au, iteu nenua ussima. Etatu menuanit kanuenitam^u an. « Apu minuat », tshe itat.
  - Eshe, itiku.
  Minuat tshatshipatat Uapush, niatat.
  - Apu minuat au ka minin, iteu, uauakapissipanu.
  - Apu tshi minitan minuat, itiku, nitapashtan au tanite nenua assikumana.
  - Eshe, iteu.
  Tshauet ek^u, ekue tshiuepatat nete kau. Ek^u anite ushpishkunnit uet natat, pemushinatauat, keutauat ne, uetshipitamuat nenu utassikumannu, tshauepatuat nenu menuanit, eukuannu tapue. Ek^u ne uiashkamenimut, apu takuannit nene utassikumanim ne kaiassikumanitshesht. Minuanu ek^u umukuman. Tutamupanu mukumannu, ek^u

uanameshet tapue. Katshi uinameshet, apu tshi piminuet ek^u, apu takuannit ishkutenu.
- Nika natshi-ishkutuen, iteu nenua ukuma.

Utanapia takuneu, ek^u anite etutet matshiteu, ek^u nekamut: « MISH-TA-A-ME-KU-TSHI-I-KU-MISH-TA-A-ME-KU-TSHI-I-KU-A-SHI-UA-KU-MU-U-KU-MISH-TA-A-ME-KU-TSHI-I-KU », itueu. Ekue ne ashakumuat tapue uapamekuat, ashakumuat neka ite akamit.

- Eka ui kassipishinan. Nika kutapaniunan uesh kassipishiati, iteu ne uapamek^u.
- Eshe, itiku.
Tapue teshkamipatat ek^u. Uauikuekashepaniu, tatakussepanishu anite. Nete tshekat nenua mashten kassipiteu ekue kutapaniuniti. Kutapaniunua ekue kapat nete. Eute ekuaukushit, akuaukushu anite uinipekut.

Anite tshimatenu mitshuapinu pessish, mishtikussuapinu, ek^u anite pepamuteht ishkuessat. Auennua uapameuat, akuaukunua nenua Uapusha, tshekat nipinua shash.
- Aaa, iteu, tshe metuatsheiak^u! Tshiuetaiatau!
Ek^u tshauetaiaht tapue nenua.
- Nuta, iteu, nipeshuanan ne aueshish. Nika metuatshenan.
- Mauat, nipaik^u anite, itiku nenua utauia. Meshapush an etshe.
- Namaieu an, iteu. Etatu an tshipa mishishtu Meshapush.
Ek^u tapue piashuaht anite, nete katshishapissiteshit pessish aneuat. Ek^u piashut ne Uapush. Tshek ekue nakataht anite e patshituaht. Nakateuat anite, shash aiatshishinua. Ek^u sheshkauat nenua utanapia. « Tshima pakushut nitanapi », itenimeu. Ek^u piakushuniti nenua utanapia, ute shekutikuameshu. Ekue ishkuteushiniti, uenuipatat.

Tshauepatat an. Tatakussepanu uapamekua, nenua ma mashten kassipiteu. Ekue kutapaniuniti kassinu etashiniti.
- Tshikassipitikunan! itakanu.
Eukueka kuetapaniuniti kassinu. Ekue kapapatat, tshiuepatuat nenu utishkutem.

- Shash nimishken ishkuteu! iteu ukuma.
Kuetuet ek^u, peminuet ek^u, mimimitshishu, matshishut ek^u Katshi mitshishut tapue ekuan, shash tanite utishkutemu an.

Eukuan uet takuak ne ishkuteu inanu, ne kassinu ishkuteu. Uapush nenu tutam^u. Apu ut takuak ute tshinanu ishkuteu ueshkat, muk^u nete katak^u takuanipan.

narrated by Edward Rich

Giant Hare

Now I will tell a legend.

Meshapush was walking along the shore when he saw some fish, a great many fish. He tried everything, but could not kill them. Even though he threw spears at them, he could not kill them. So he returned home.
— 'Grandmother', Meshapush said, 'I could not kill the fish over there, there were so many of them'.
— 'Over there my grandchild', she said to him, 'there is a spider who makes nets. But he only makes nets at night. He cannot be seen when he make the nets, as it is night when he weaves the nets'.
— 'I will look for him over there', Meshapush said to her.
— 'He will kill you', she replied.
— 'No, he will not be able to kill me'.

Meshapush went to look for the spider and someone was indeed living there. Some girls came out of the spider's house.
— 'You two go look for some rotted wood', the spider said to the girls that evening. 'Do not under any circumstances bring back hare-wood'.
— 'All right', they replied.
Sure enough, those girls went off and fetched the rotted wood. That is right where Hare was, in the rotted tree. After the girls had left, the spider wove a net. Meshapush watched him making the net during the night. Then Meshapush showed himself.
—'I have already learned what you were doing by watching you', Meshapush said, 'the way you were weaving a net, the way you weave your net'.
The spider began striking out at him but could not hit him. Then Meshapush ran outside. He ran back home.
— 'Cut some babiche! Make some cord!' Meshapush said to his grandmother.

So that woman, the old lady, started cutting the babiche. After the old woman had prepared the babiche, Meshapush wove a net. He made the net really quickly. After he had woven the net, then, indeed, he killed some fish. He killed a large number of fish.
— 'There is no knife', said the old woman. 'There is a metalworker over there. He would be able to give you some metal so you can make a knife, if you asked him for it'.
— 'All right', said Meshapush.

Then, indeed, Meshapush ran off. He saw someone walking along.
— 'Give me some metal', Meshapush said to him, 'I want to make a knife'.
So the metalworker gave him a very thin piece of metal. Meshapush ran home. But he could not clean the fish yet, because the metal was too thin; he kept bending it as he tried to clean the fish.
— 'No, this one is no good', she said to her grandson. 'He has a better one. 'It is no good', she would say to him.
— 'All right', he replied.
Again off ran Meshapush to see the metalworker.
— 'The one you gave me is no good', he said. 'It keeps bending'.
— 'I cannot give you anything else', the metalworker said to Meshapush. 'I am using these pieces of metal'.
— 'All right', said Meshapush.
So he went home, but then ran back again. He crept up behind the metalworker's back, threw something at him, knocked him down, grabbed his piece of metal and ran home with the good one. That is how it happened. When the metalworker woke up, his piece of metal was no longer there. Meshapush's knife was good. He fashioned a knife, and, sure enough, he cleaned the fish. After he had cleaned the fish, he was not able to cook them—there was no fire.
— 'I will go fetch fire', Meshapush said to his grandmother.

He took his net, walked over there to a point of land and sang: 'BIG WHALES, BIG WHALES, JOIN TOGETHER TO FORM A BRIDGE ACROSS, BIG WHALES', he sang. Then, indeed, the white whales formed into a group right across the water.
— 'Don't scratch us. We will dive underwater if you scratch us', the white whale told him.
— 'All right', said Meshapush.
Then, indeed, he ran across. He kept drawing his claws in and out as he stepped on each one there. He was almost on the last one when he scratched it, and under the water it went. It went underwater, and Meshapush fell off way over there. That's where he washed ashore. He was washed up over there in the salt water.

A house stood close by, a house built of wood, and there were girls walking around. They saw someone. It was Hare washed up over there, already nearly dead.
— 'Hey', said one, 'we can play with it! Let's take it home!' So indeed they brought it home .
— 'Father', she said, 'we brought home an animal. We are going to play with it'.
— 'No, kill it over there', their father said to them, 'it must be Meshapush'.
— 'No, it isn't', one said, 'Meshapush would be a lot bigger'. Then, indeed, they brought him inside there. They laid him way over there close to the stove. Then Hare dried out. They left him there when they went out to check their net. They left him there, but he was already starting to move around. He opened his own net with his feet. 'I wish my net would dry out', he thought to himself. And his net did dry out, tucked tightly here in his armpit. But the net caught fire and he ran outside.

Meshapush ran back home. He went pitter-patter across the white whales but scratched the last one. The whole lot of them dove underwater there.
— 'You are scratching us!' he was told.
There they all went underwater. Then he ran ashore and ran home with the fire.

— 'Now I have found fire!' Meshapush told his grandmother. He made a fire, then. He cooked, then. He ate and ate and ate, and, then, he ate some more. After he ate, that was it, for he already had fire.

That is why there is fire, it is said, all kinds of fire. Hare did it. In the old days, there never was fire here at our place; only over there, far away, did it exist.

Wadhams Song WADHAM

From Bonavista Cape to the Cabot Isles
The course is north full forty miles,
When you must steer away North East
Till Cape Freels, Gull Island bears West North West.

Then North, North West thirty-three miles,
Three leagues off shore lies Wadhams Isles;
Where of a rock you must beware,
Two miles Sou' South East from off Isle bears.

Then North West by West twelve miles or more,
There lies Round Head on Fogo Shore;
But Nor' Nor West, seven or eight miles
Lies a sunken rock near the Barrack Isles.

Therefore, my friend, I would you advise,
Since all these rocks in danger lies;
That you may never amongst them fall,
But keep your luff and weather them all.

As you draw near to Fogo Land,
You'll have fifteen fathoms in the sounding sand;
From fifteen to eighteen, never more,
And that you'll have close to the shore.

When you abreast of Round Head be,
Then Joe Batt's Point you'll plainly see;
To starboard then three or four miles
You'll see a parcel of damned rugged Isles.

When Joe Batt's Arm you are abreast,
Then Fogo Harbour bears due West;
But untold Fortune, unlucky laid,
A sunken rock right in the trade.

So West Nor' West you are to steer,
Till Brimstone Head doth plain appear;
Which over Pelley's Point you'll see,
Then of that danger you are free.

And as you draw within a mile,
You'll see a house on Syme's Isle;
The mouth of the channel is not very wide,
But the deepest water is on the larboard side.

When within Syme's Point you have shot,
Then three fathoms of water you have got;
Port hard your helm and take care,
In the mid channel for to steer.

When Pelley's Point you are abreast,
Starboard haul and steer Sou' Sou' West,
Till Pelley's Point covers Syme's stage,
Then you are clear I will engage.

Wadham
1756

The Cliffs of Baccalieu

JACK WITHERS

We were bound home in October from the shores of Labrador.
Trying to race a strong nor'easter and snow too;
But the wind came down upon us making day as dark as night,
Just before we made the land at Baccalieu.

We thought we'd make the island as we hauled her farther south,
As the gale from out the nor'east harder blew,
But the lookout quickly shouted, and there right dead ahead
Through the snow-squall loomed the land of Baccalieu.

It was hard down with the tiller and we struggled with the sheets,
Doin' our best to haul 'em in a foot or two,
And her deck soon sharply tilted 'till 'twas hard to keep your feet,
As we hauled her from the rocks of Baccalieu.

Oh, to leeward were the breakers and to win'ard was the gale,
The sleet and snow would cut you through and through;
With our lee-rail two feet under and two hands at the wheel,
We hauled her from the cliffs of Baccalieu.

The combers beat her under 'till we thought she'd never rise.
Our main-boom was buckling nigh in two,
And all hands clung to win'ard and stared with straining eyes
Down to leeward at the cliffs of Baccalieu.

Oh, we hauled her to the south'ard and our canvas stood the strain,
As the whistling snow-squalls from the nor'east blew,
But our hearts were beating gladly, for no longer could we gaze
Down to leeward at the cliffs of Baccalieu.

The Petty Harbour Bait Skiff

JOHN GRACE

Ye people all both great and small, I hope you will attend
To those few simple verses that I have lately penned.
They are concerning danger which our poor seamen stand,
While sailing on those stormy waves by the shores of Newfoundland.

This happened to be in the summertime in the lovely month of June,
When fields were green, fair to be seen, and valleys were in bloom;
When silent fountains do run clear that's sent by heaven's rain,
And the dewy showers they fall at night, to fertilize the plain.

We bid adieu unto our friends and those we held most dear,
Being bound for Petty Harbour in the springtime of the year;
The little birds as we sailed on sung o'er the hills and dales,
As Flora from her sporting groves sent forth a pleasant gale.

On Saturday we sailed away being in the evening late,
We were bound into Conception Bay all for a load of bait;
The sea-gulls flying in the air and pitching on the shore,
But little we thought 'twould be our lot to see our friends no more.

The weather being fine we lost no time until we were homeward bound,
The whales were sporting in the deep and swordfish swimming 'round;
Where Luna bright shone forth that night to calm amidst the sea,
And the stars shone bright to guide us right upon our rough pathway.

When we came 'round the North Head a rainbow did appear,
Every indication of a storm was drawing near;
Old Neptune riding on the waves to the wind'ard of us lay,
You'd think the ocean was on fire in Petty Harbour Bay.

We shook our reefs and trimmed our sails, across the Bay did stand;
The sun did rise all circlized with streams down o'er the land.
The clouds lay in the atmosphere for our destruction met,
As Boreas blew a heavy squall our boat was overset.

But Douglas Chafe that hero brave and champion on that day
He boldly launched his boat with speed and quickly put to sea;
He saved young Menchington from the wreck, by his undaunted skill.
His offers would be all in vain but for kind heaven's will.

When the sad news arrived next day to dear old St. John's town,
There was crying and lamenting on the streets both up and down;
Crying and lamenting, crying for those they bore,
In the bottomless waves they found their graves whom they never shall see no more.

Out of that fine young crew you know, there was one escaped being drowned,
He was brought to Petty Harbour where good comfort there he found;
He's now on shore and safe once more with no cause to complain,
He fought old Neptune up and down whilst on the stormy main.

John French was our commander, Mick Sullivan second hand,
All of the rest were brave young men, belong to Newfoundland;
Six brave youths to tell the truth were buried in the sea,
But Menchington spared by Providence to live a longer day.

Your heart would ache all for their sake if you were standing by,
To see them drowning one by one, and no relief was nigh;
Struggling with the stormy waves all in their youth and bloom,
And at last they sank to rise no more, all on the eighth of June.

The *Water Witch*   TRADITIONAL

Come all ye true-born fishermen and listen to my song,
I hope ye'll pay attention, I won't delay you long.
You all remember Pouch Cove and those true-born sons so brave,
Who saved the crew of the *Water Witch*, so near a watery grave.

On Christmas Eve that craft did leave when loud the wind did roar.
'Twas on a reef she came to grief not far from Pouch Cove shore,
A place they call the Horrid Gulch the schooner headed on,
And in the twinkling of an eye three poor, dear souls were gone.

Three seamen from the *Water Witch* leaped when they heard the shock;
The rest belong to that doomed ship were hurled on the rock,
To wait three hours in storms and showers, and loud the sea did dash;
They see their schooner breaking up, hard on the rocks did smash.

The Pouch Cove fishermen to a man turned out that cruel night.
For those who gazed on those poor souls, it was a doleful sight;
And for to make the scene much worse poor females numb with cold
Was waiting there to be relieved by those brave heroes bold.

Punts, rhodes and lanterns they were brought by kind and willing hands,
The shrieks of females in distress those fishermen could not stand.
And for to face the Horrid Gulch six hundred feet did go
To save those souls half-dead with cold who waited down below.

Brave Alfred Moore, a Pouch Cove man: 'I'll take the lead', he cried,
When around his waist strong hempen rope in double knots was tied;
And now strong men are on the top to lower him over the cliff
To dash our hero down below, in blinding snow and drift.

Three times they swung him in the dark in blinding drift and snow,
Before his foot could get a place to give him any hold;
At length he found one resting place close to a sheltered stone
Where he could see those souls below and hear their dismal moans.

Oh now to save this shipwrecked crew their hearts were filled with hope;
Six more brave Pouch Cove fishermen like heroes manned the rope.
And now some small handlines, like Moore, they managed for to lower
'Til all the *Water Witch's* crew were landed safe on shore.

Oh hark! another scream was heard—the people got a shock—
Another female left below to perish on the rock!
When Alfred made another dash, and loud the wind did roar,
And took the woman in his arms in safety to shore.

The news was soon in Town next day about the *Water Witch*,
The whole community got a shock, the poor as well as rich;
The Governor he sent home these words in letters bold and grand
To tell the pluck of these fishermen belong to Newfoundland.

The Humane Society of Liverpool, they very soon sent here
Gold medals to those fishermen who never knew no fear;
The Governor's lady pinned them on, those medals rare and rich,
To the Pouch Cove men who saved the lives aboard the *Water Witch*.

Oh here's success to those brave boys who risked in storm and breeze
Their precious lives to save those souls who ventured over the sea.
May peace and plenty be their lot, that gay and gallant band—
Brave Alfred Moore and all the rest belong to Newfoundland.

Lukey's Boat   TRADITIONAL

O, Lukey's boat is painted green,
  Aha, me b'ys,
O, Lukey's boat is painted green,
The prettiest little boat ever you seen.
  Aha me riddle I day.

O, Lukey's boat got a fine fore cutty,
  Aha, me b'ys,
O, Lukey's boat got a fine fore cutty,
And every seam is chinked with putty.
  Aha me riddle I day.

Lukey's boat got a high stopped jib,
  Aha, me b'ys,
Lukey's boat got a high stopped jib,
And a patent block to her foremast head.
  Aha me riddle I day.

'I think', said Lukey, 'I'll make her bigger'.
  Aha, me b'ys,
'I think', said Lukey, 'I'll make her bigger;
I'll load her down with a one-claw jigger'.
  Aha me riddle I day.

'And now', said Lukey, 'get aboard your grub'.
  Aha, me b'ys,
'And now', said Lukey, 'get aboard your grub;
One split pea and a ten-pound tub'.
  Aha me riddle I day.

Lukey's rolling out his grub,
  Aha, me b'ys,
Lukey's rolling out his grub,
A barrel and a bag and a ten-pound tub.
  Aha me riddle I day.

When Lukey come around the Bill,
   Aha, me b'ys,
When Lukey come around the Bill,
He spied his true love on the hill.
   Aha me riddle I say.

And when he was coming around the cape,
   Aha, me b'ys,
And when he was coming around the cape,
He spied old Jennie all on the flake.
   Aha me riddle I day.

His wife was dead . . .
   Aha, me b'ys,
'O', said Lukey, 'I don't care;
I'll have another in the spring of the year'.
   Aha me riddle I day.

The *Montague* TRADITIONAL

The *Montague* packet left Wexford at ten,
With a fine stock of cattle and a fine crew of men
   Hee Ho, Heave away, ho.

She sailed down the river so gay and so grand,
Till she came to the Dogger and stuck in the sand.
   Hee Ho, Heave away, ho.

Bob Kirwan cried out, Oh, what's to be done!
I've lost my fine cow that I bought in Taghmon.
   Hee Ho, Heave away, ho.

Jack Leary, six sheep and young Belton, a cow,
Nickie Byrne, a big goat, and Bob Brennan, a sow.
   Hee Ho, Heave away, ho. . . .

The Ryans And The Pittmans

H. W. LEMESSURIER

Chorus:
We'll rant and we'll roar like true Newfoundlanders;
We'll rant and we'll roar on deck and below,
Until we see bottom inside the two sunkers,
When straight through the channel to Toslow we'll go.

I'm a son of a sea-cook, and a cook in a trader;
I can dance, I can sing, I can reef the main-boom,
I can handle a jigger, and cuts a big figure
Whenever I gets in a boat's standing room.

If the voyage is good, then this fall I will do it;
I wants two pound ten for a ring and the priest,
A couple o' dollars for clane shirt and collars,
And a handful o' coppers to make up a feast.

There's plump little Polly, her name is Goldsworthy;
There's John Coady's Kitty and Mary Tibbo;
There's Clara from Bruley, and young Martha Foley,
But the nicest of all is my girl in Toslow.

Farewell and adieu to ye fair ones of Valen,
Farewell and adieu to ye girls in the Cove;
I'm bound to the Westward, to the wall with the hole in,
I'll take her from Toslow the wild world to rove.

Farewell and adieu to ye girls of St. Kyran's,
Of Paradise and Presque, Big and Little Bona,
I'm bound unto Toslow to marry sweet Biddy,
And if I don't do so, I'm afraid of her da.

I've bought me a house from Katherine Davis,
A twenty-pound bed from Jimmy McGrath;
I'll get me a settle, a pot and a kettle;
Then I'll be ready for Biddy—Hurrah!

I brought in the Ino this spring from the city
Some rings and gold broaches for the girls in the Bay;
I bought me a case-pipe—they call it a meerschaum—
It melted like butter upon a hot day.

I went to a dance one night at Fox Harbour;
There were plenty of girls, so nice as you'd wish,
There was one pretty maiden a-chawing of frankgum,
Just like a young kitten a-gnawing fresh fish.

Then here is a health to the girls of Fox Harbour,
Of Oderin and Presque, Crabbes Hole and Bruley.
Now let ye be jolly, don't be melancholy,
I can't marry all, or in chokey I'd be.

A Great Big Sea Hove In Long Beach   TRADITIONAL

A great big sea hove in Long Beach
Right fol-or-al Ta-deedle, I do.
A great big sea hove in Long Beach
And Granny Snooks she lost her speech.
To me right fol didy fol dee.

A great big sea hove in the Harbour,
Right fol-or-al Ta-deedle, I do.
A great big sea hove in the Harbour,
And hove right up in Keoughs' Parlour,
To me right fol didy fol dee.

Oh dear mother I wants a sack,
Right fol-or-al Ta-deedle, I do.
Oh dear mother I wants a sack
With beads and buttons all down the back,
To me right fol didy fol dee.

Me boot is broke, me frock is tore,
Right fol-or-al Ta-deedle, I do;
Me boot is broke, me frock is tore,
But Georgie Snooks I do adore,
To me right fol didy fol dee.

Oh, fish is low and flour is high,
Right fol-or-al Ta-deedle, I do;
Fish is low and flour is high,
So Georgie Snooks he can't have I,
To me right fol didy fol dee.

But he will have me in the Fall,
Right fol-or-al Ta-deedle, I do;
If he don't I'll hoist my sail
And say good-bye to old Cannaille,
To me right fol didy fol dee.

The Wave that Hit St. Brides

DANIEL PAYNE

Oh it's hard and unforgiving work
For those who fish the grounds
And when the wind comes in a gale
There's danger all around
For thirty years I worked the sea
The rolling waters wide
And in all my days ne'er faced a wave
Like the wave that hit St. Brides

The wave that hit St. Brides, me boys
The wave that hit St. Brides
And in all my days ne'er faced a wave
Like the wave that hit St. Brides

Oh the ocean crashed and foamed that day
As in our helpless view
Our boats behind the breakwater lay
And the gale stronger blew
Then like some ancient from the deep
It rose before our eyes
And took so much with just a touch
The wave that hit St. Brides

The wave that hit St. Brides, me boys
The wave that hit St. Brides
And took so much with just a touch
The wave that hit St. Brides

So here's to all the families
Who fish out of St. Brides
And all who lost both boats and gear
All in that awful tide
May the fates above look down on them
And be their watchful guides
And pray they meet no other wave
Like the wave that hit St. Brides

The wave that hit St. Brides, me boys
The wave that hit St. Brides
And pray they meet no other wave
Like the wave that hit St. Brides

The Shoals of Herring

EWAN MACCOLL

O, it was a fine and pleasant day,
Out of Yarmouth harbour I was faring
As a cabin boy on a sailing lugger
For to go and hunt the shoals of herring.

O, the work was hard and the hours were long
And the treatment sure it took some bearing;
There was little kindness and the kicks were many
As we hunted for the shoals of herring.

O, we fished the Sward and the Broken Bank
I was cook and I'd a quarter-sharing;
And I used to sleep standing on my feet
And I'd dream about the shoals of herring.

Well, we left the home grounds in the month of June
And to canny Shields we soon was bearing,
With a hundred cran of the silver darlings
That we'd taken from the shoals of herring.

Now you're up on deck, you're a fisherman,
You can swear and show a manly bearing;
Take your turn on deck with the other fellows
While you're following the shoals of herring.

In the stormy seas and the living gales
Just to earn your daily bread you're daring,
From the Dover Straits to the Faröe Islands
While you're following the shoals of herring.

O, I earned me keep and I paid me way,
And I earned the gear that I was wearing;
Sailed a million miles, caught ten million fishes—
We was following the shoals of herring.

Let Me Fish Off Cape St. Mary's

OTTO KELLAND

Take me back to my western boat,
Let me fish off Cape St. Mary's.
Where the hagdowns sail and the foghorns wail,
With my friends, the Browns and the Clearys.
Let me fish off Cape St. Mary's.

Let me feel my dory lift,
To the broad Atlantic combers.
Where the rip tides swirl and the wild ducks whirl.
Where old Neptune calls the numbers
'Neath the broad Atlantic combers.

Let me sail up Golden Bay,
With my oilskins all a-streamin'.
From the thunder squall when I hauled my trawl,
And my old Cape Ann a-gleamin',
With my oilskins all a-streamin'.

Let me view that rugged shore,
Where the beach is all a-glisten,
With the caplin spawn, where from dusk to dawn,
You bait your trawl and listen,
To the undertow a-hissin'.

When I reach that last big shoal
Where the ground swells break asunder.
Where the wild sands roll to the surges' toll,
Let me be a man and take it,
When my dory fails to make it.

Take me back to the snug green cove,
Where the seas roll up their thunder,
There let me rest in the earth's cool breast,
Where the stars shine out their wonder,
And the seas roll up their thunder.

The Banks of Newfoundland

TRADITIONAL

Now you may bless your happy lot that live secure on shore,
Safe from the tempest and the blast that round poor seamen roar.
It's little you know the hardships that we were forced to stand,
For fourteen days and fourteen nights on the banks of Newfoundland.

Our good ship never crossed before the stormy western waves;
The dashing seas came tossing down and broke her into staves.
She was built of green, unseasoned wood, and could but little stand,
The hurricane that met us on the Banks of Newfoundland.

We had Barney Lynch from Ballynahinch, Tim Sweeny and Mike Moore;
We pawned our clothes in Liverpool in Eighteen forty-four;
We pawned our clothes in Liverpool and sold them out of hand,
Nor thought of the cold nor'-wester on the Banks of Newfoundland.

The gale it blew from sunset till we sailed three mornings' dawn,
And when she fell to lee-ward two of our masts were gone.
We lashed ourselves to the mizen yards, and 'twas then we verily planned,
To show some signals of distress on the Banks of Newfoundland.

The ice fell down in torrents, from the time we left Quebec,
Unless we'd walk within our shoes we'd be frozen on the deck.
We were stout, hardy Irish boys that our good ship did man,
And the captain doubled each man's grub on the Banks of Newfoundland.

If you were to see us famishing, your heart would feel the pain;
For out of two and twenty, eleven did remain.
Some jumped in earnest in the seas and said they'd swim to land;
But alas, we were one hundred leagues from the shore of
  Newfoundland.

We fasted, boys, for five long days, our provisions being all out;
And on the morning of the sixth we cast the lot about.
The lot fell on the captain's son, but thinking relief at hand,
We spared him for another day on the Banks of Newfoundland.

No sail appeared next morning and the captain's son prepared;
We gave to him another hour, for to offer up a prayer,
When boundless Providence proved kind, and from blood saved
  every man;
An English vessel hove in sight on the Banks of Newfoundland.

When we were taken from the wreck, we were more like ghosts
  than men;
They fed us and they clothed us, and brought us home again.
And our dead friends, that lost their lives, they ne'er saw the Irish
  land,
For the raging waves roll o'er their graves on the Banks of
  Newfoundland.

'Twas on the seventh of January, this disaster it took place;
It would rend the heart of adamant, and of those that hear their
  fate.
For eleven of our gallant boys those hardships could not stand.
May Our Saviour's mercy reach their souls on the Banks of
  Newfoundland.

The Wreck of the Steamship *Ethie*   TRADITIONAL

Come all you true countrymen, come listen to me.
A story I'll tell you of the S.S. *Ethie*.
She being the steamboat employed on our shore,
To carry freight, mail and passengers down on the Labrador.

On the tenth of December as you all well may know,
In the year nineteen nineteen on her last trip did go;
Where she left Daniel's Harbour about four P.M.,
With a strong breeze from the south'ard, for Cow Head did steam.

The glass indicated a wild raging storm,
And about nine o'clock the storm did come on.
With the ship's husband on board, the crew had no fear;
Captain English gave orders straight for Bonne Bay to steer.

At first to the storm the brave ship gave no heed,
Until at length it was found she was fast losing speed,
And the great waves all round her like mountains did rise,
And the crew all stood staring with fear in their eyes.

The orders went round to preserve for their lives,
For the ship she is doomed and it's perish we might;
But still there is hope; there is one brave man on board
Who says he can guide her safely on to the shore.

Walter Young being our purser, as you may understand,
Volunteered for to guide her safely in to the land;
John Gullage, our first mate, bravely stood to the wheel;
Captain English gave orders and all worked with a will.

Up off Martin's Point about one o'clock,
Through bravery and courage, she escaped every rock,
And the people on the shore saw the ship in distress;
All rushed to the spot for to help do their best.

And then we were landed in a rude boatswain's chair,
Taken in by the people and treated with care;
We stayed on the point until the storm it was o'er,
And the brave little *Ethie* lay standing on shore.

O, what of the fright, the exhaustion and cold,
The depth of my story will never be told!
And all you brave fellows gets shipwrecked on the sea,
You think of the fate of the S.S. *Ethie*.

As: **Eachtra Ghiolla an Amaráin** DONNCHAD RUA MACCONMARA

....

Do chuir mé slán lém' cháirdibh in aenfheacht,
'Sag cuid nír fhágbhás slán le foiréigion,
Dá g-casfadh dam árthach d'fhághail in Éirinn,
Do rachainn tar sáile in áit nár bhaoghal dam
Bheith am' stróinse ag tarraint ar bhaile gach sméirle
Nó ag ól bhainne i d-tigh Mhaoilsheachlainn ui Mhaonaigh!

    Bíodh a fhios ag an talamh 'sag maithibh geal Paorach
A liacht beatha, min-earradh agus gréithre
Do thug an pobul i bhfochair a chéile
Chum mo chothuighthe i g-cogadh nó i spéirlinn—
Stór nach g-caillfeadh suim de laethibh,
As cófra doimhin a d-toillfinn féin ann;
Do bhí seacht bh-fichid ubh circe 'gus eunla ann
Le h-aghaidh a n-ithte chomh minic 's badh mhéin liom—
Cróca ime do dingeadh le saothar
As spólla soille ba throime 'ná déarfainn,
Bhí tuilleadh as naoi g-clocha de mhin choirce ghlain-
    chréitheartha ann
Re dríodar ná loisde 's iad croithte le chéile,
Lán an bharaille do b'fhearra bhí in Éirinn
De phrátaoibh dearga air eagla geur-bhruid'—
Do thugas cag leanna ann do lasfadh le séideadh
'S do chuirfeadh na mairbh 'na mbeatha dá mb'fhéidir—
Do bhí agam *jackets* chomh gasta le h-aen-neach
Agus léinteacha breaca go barraibh mo mheura,
Leaba 'gus clúda i g-ciumhais a chéile
Ceangailte ar dhróm mo thrónc le teudaibh—
Bhí bróga istigh ann, bhí *wig* as béabhar
Agus stór mar sin anois nach ndéarfad!

Go Port-láirge don stáir sin téidhim-se
Chomh farránta le Conán na Féinne,
Glacaim mo lóisdín, bórd bidh as feusta
A bhfochair na h'ógmhná ba chóraighe in Éirinn—
Do bhí sí fáilteach fáinneach, tréitheach,
Ba chaoin, deas, sásta an *drawer* le glaodhach í,
Gach sórt d'a d-tagadh a bhlaiseadh ní sheunfadh,
D'inneósadh eachtra, startha 'gus sceul duit,
Ní ghlacfadh sí fala ná fearg go h-eug leat
—Fad bhraithfeadh sí airgead agad ar aon chor!
'S i g-cúrsa mná ní thráchtaim féin air—
Acht cúis mo gháire fáth a sméide.
Do rinn' sí mo chlú da m'b'fhiu mo shaothar
Chuireadh sí am' chúl-sa púdar glé-geal—
Bhiodh deoch ar maidin 'smé am leaba d'á gleus dam
Ó bhonn go bathas 'sí dheasuigh go léir mé.
Ba mhór é m'iongantas a soineandacht féile
As cruas a muime chum pinginne d'éiliomh,
Ní mhaithfeadh a mághair cáirt ná braon dam
Acht chaithfeadh sí an táibhle d'fhághail gan phlé uaim!
  D'fhanas 'na bh-feighil sin suim de laethibh
Ag feitheamh ar loing dho raghach as Éirinn—
Bhí captaoin Allen, fear meanmnach aereach
Ag teacht fá'n mbaile, 's nír bh-fada gur reidheas leis.
Gleusaim orm go h-obann le féirsce
Mé féin as mo chostas ar sodar in aenfheacht.
Téidhim don Phasáiste ar ghearrán le cairréire
Agus ualach scadán am' mheadhachan ar thaobh de.
Do chuaidh mo chófra ar bórd go h-euscaidh
Bhí uaisle an phóirt ag ól gan traochadh ann,
Fiafruighid go h-aibigh an labhraim Beurla
Ar d'fheudas a bhfreagairt i Laidin air eigion.
Nír bh'fuláir dam m'ainm do thabhairt don chléireach
Ar Macnamara chuir tarsna 'san *daybook*—
Dob' éigean mo chófra sheoladh ar thaobh dhíom
'Smé ag déanadh ceoil as spóirt san *stateroom*.

Scaoiltear seolta ar nóin do Phoebus
Do bhí Aeólus leó agus Tétis—
Scinnid de phreab amach san treun-mhuir
Go ndruidid a-bhfad i d-teas na gréine.
Nír bh'fada gur ghoill ar chloinn sin Mhaoghnuis
An fhairge dhoimhin agus radharc na spéire—
Bhí beatha gan roinn ag Tadhg Ó Laoghaire
'Sní bhlaisfeadh se gréim le treighid ná braon dí,
Bhí Caoilte Ó Caoimh ag caoineadh a chéile,
'Sní bh-fuigheadh se saoiseamh ag caoi ar aon chor,
Bhí Peadar Ó Dubhda i g-cúinne 'na aonar
As é ag úrshlugan ar shúsa le Féidhlim,
Bhí Gearalt Ó Doghair as Flann dá d-taoscadh,
As Cathal as Conn a' planncadh a chéile—
Bhí Cairbre as Gearóid as Tiobóid ar saothar
Ag tarraing mo phlocóid' in onóir na scléipe!
Bhí Seaghan Ó Troighthigh san roide d'a thraochadh
As treaghaid 'na ghoile ag cur air le géire—
Do dhearbhuigh Diarmuid shar as faobhar air
Nach mairfeadh a d-trian le triall ar Éirinn!

. . . .

From: The Adventures of a Luckless Fellow
DONNCHAD RUA MACCONMARA

. . . .

Farewell I bid to my friends ere leaving,
—To some, I own, with no great grieving—
For once beyond the ocean landed
I'd feel no fear of e'er being branded
As idle wretch whose bitter pain is
To drink sour milk at Malachy Meany's!

   Throughout the five great Fifths of Erin
Let all men know the princely faring
The people gave me open-handed
To carry me o'er the sea till landed—
A store for a month—to me right pleasing!
A great deep chest I'd rest at ease in—
Of eggs, seven score it held, no boasting,
For frying or boiling, poaching, roasting—
A crock of butter packed full tightly,
A piece of bacon fine and sightly,
Nine stone of oatmeal clean-sifted,
No joke of a load for him who lifted—
A barrel there was of the best then growing
Of red potatoes, Munster's sowing,
A keg of good ale—all hail who brew so!
'Twould liven the dead, if aught could do so—
The neatest of jackets I had in plenty,
Of new check shirts I owned full twenty—
Good bedding, the best that Cork afforded,
On the top of my trunk securely corded—
I had shoes and wig and brand-new beaver,
With money *go leor*—I'm no deceiver!

For Waterford city I proudly started
Bold as a Fenian old, high-hearted,
My lodgings took at an inn most cosy
Where served a young maid bright and rosy,
Her ringlets fair, her face still fairer,
Pleasant she smiled when of liquor the bearer,
To sip she ne'er was loth, invited,
And many a tale for me recited,
Offence at jest she ne'er took gravely,
– At least while I was spending bravely!
Of a woman's ways I'll speak no longer—
Her love for me with time grew stronger,
I gained her heart, it seemed, completely—
She'd powder my hair each day so neatly—
A drink she'd bring before my rising,

E'en helped to dress me, more surprising!
But whilst I found her sweet and civil
Her mother for meanness beat the devil—
Each dram and drop she'd put in the statement,
And the score she'd have without abatement!

   With these I dwelt and in their caring
Awaiting a vessel would sail from Erin,
Till Captain Allen, so gallant and gracious,
Arrived in Waterford's harbour spacious.

To terms we came, I hurried *instanter*
And brought my baggage away in a canter
On a carman's *garran* I'd hired that morning—
A load of fresh herrings as balance not scorning—
My trunk being stowed quite to my thinking,
In cabin I found the gentry drinking—
'Do you speak English?' they asked me early,
And in Latin I managed to tell them fairly.
The clerk from me my name demanded
And wrote it down in style bold-handed,
And now I felt quite free and hearty,
I soon was happy amusing the party!

Our sails were spread, no ship went braver,
For wind and wave were both in our favour,
Over the sea our vessel now bounded
And soon had the isles of Carbery rounded.
Ere many days we'd passed on ocean,
These sons of Magnus felt dire commotion—
There was Theigue O'Leary with food untasted,
A colic severe his strength had wasted—
Keelty O'Keeffe in grief for Sheela,
Without relief crying 'Murder *as meela*!'
Peter O'Dowd from crowd retiring
On Felim's blanket sank as expiring,
Of sailing O'Dower felt sick in this one test,
While Cahal and Conn had a blackthorn contest—
Carbry and Garrett, my ale-keg hugging,
Had drawn my bung, and my beer were slugging!
Poor Shawn O'Trehy, to sickness sad victim—
His stomach's complaints did sore afflict him—
Old Dermot he groaned and moaned, despairing
That third of their number would ever see Erin!

. . . .

translated by Tomás Ó Flannghaile

Eanach Dhúin

ANTOINE Ó REACHTABHRA/RAIFTEIRÍ

Má fhaighimse sláinte beidh caint is tráchtadh
  ar an méid a báthadh as Eanach Dhúin,
's mo thrua amárach gach athair is máthair,
  bean is páiste 'tá ag sileadh súl.
A Rí na ngrása cheap Neamh is Parthas,
  nár bheag an tábhacht dúinn beirt nó triúr,
ach lá chomh breá leis gan gaoth ná báisteach,
  lán an bháid acu a scuabadh ar siúl.

Nár mhór an t-ionadh os comhair na ndaoine
  a bhfeiceáil sínte ar chúl a gcinn,
screadadh 'gus caoineadh a scanródh daoine,
  gruaig á cíoradh 's an chreach á roinn;
lár an fhómhair, daoine óga
  a bheith á dtórramh 's á dtabhairt go cill—
in áit a bpósta bheith gléasta i gcónra
  's a Rí na glóire nár mhór an feall.

Baile Chláir a bhí in aice láimhe
  níor lig an t-ádh dhóibh a dhul aníos,
bhí an bás chomh láidir nach dtugann cairde
  d'aon mhac máthar dár rugadh riamh.
Mura scéal a ceapadh dhóibh an lá seo a mbáite,
  a Rí na ngrása nár bhocht an ní!
Ach a gcailleadh uile gan loch ná sáile
  le seanbhád gránna 's iad láimh le tír.

A Thomáis Uí Fhearaíl, diomú Dé dhuit,
  's iomaí cailín spéiriúil a chuir tú chun báis
le do sheanbhád a bhí lofa pléascaith'
  ag dul go haerach go Cnoc an Duláin.
Briseadh an bád orthu 'gus scaip na daoine
  agus tugadh na caoire amach sa snámh;
gur tugadh abhaile iad 's go ndearnadh a síneadh—
  bhí aon fhear déag ann is ochtar mná.

A Sheáin Mhic Coscair, ba mhór an scéal thú
    gur sheas tú riamh i loing nó i mbád
 's a liachtaí coiscéim lúfar shiúil tú
    ó Londain anall go dtí Béal Trá.
Nuair a shíl tú snámh a dhéanamh,
    rug na mná óga ort abhus is thall,
 's gur shíl do mháithrín dá mbáití céad fear
    go dtabharfá an *sway* leat abhaile ag snámh.

D'éirigh mé féin go moch Dé hAoine,
    chuala mé an caoineadh 's an greadadh bos
ag na mná trom tuirseach de bharr na hoíche,
    gan ceo le déanamh acu ach ag síneadh corp.
A Dhia 's a Chríost a d'fhulaing íospairt,
    a cheannaigh fírinneach an bocht 's an nocht,
go Parthas naofa go dtugair saor leat
    gach créatúir dhíobhthu dár thit faoin lot.

Milleán géar ar an ionad céanna—
    nár lasa réalt ann 's nár éirí grian—
do bháigh an méid úd a thriall in éineacht
    go Gaillimh ar aonach go moch Déardaoin:
na fir a ghléasfadh cliath 'gus céachta,
    threabhfadh bréanra 'gus chraithfeadh síol
 's na mná dá réir sin a dhéanfadh 'ch aon ní,
    shníomhfadh bréidín is anairt chaol.

Tolladh cléibhe 'gus loscadh sléibhe
    ar an áit ar éagadar is milleán crua,
 's a liachtaí créatúir a d'fhág sé faonlag
    ag sileadh 's ag éagaoin gach maidin Luain.
Ní díobháil eolais a chuir dá dtreoir iad
    ach mí-ádh mór ar an gCaisleán Nua;
 's é críochnú an chomhrá gur báthadh mórán,
    d'fág ábhar dóláis ag Eanach Dhúin.

Eanach Dhúin ANTOINE Ó REACHTABHRA/RAIFTEIRÍ

While I keep my health, there'll be talk and discourse
 on the number drowned out of Eanach Dhúin,
and my grief tomorrow, each father, mother,
 child and woman with pouring eyes.
King, gracious Maker of Heaven and Paradise,
 of small account, maybe, two or three
—but a day so fine, with no rain or tempest,
 a full boatload to be swept away.

Great the wonder, before the people,
 to see them stretched with their heads laid back
—screams and wailing to affright the people,
 combing hair and the ruin shared out.
The height of Autumn and all these youngsters
 waked and brought to their burial place,
dressed not for marriage, but for the coffin.
 O King of Glory, was it not great wrong?

Baile Chláir, it was fast approaching,
 but their luck prevented to get so far,
and Death was strong, that gives no quarter
 to the woman's son that was ever born.
Unless 'twas fated that day to drown them
 was it not wretched, O King of Grace,
to lose them all, on no lake or ocean,
 in an old foul boat and they close to land?

Tomás Ó Fearaíl, God's blight upon you,
  so many bright girls you have done to death
with your ancient vessel, decayed and brittle,
  heading merrily for Cnoc an Duláin.
The boat dismembered, the people scattered,
  and the sheep were loosed out to swim away.
Home all were taken and stretched together
  —of men eleven, and of women eight.

Seán Mac Coscair, great the pity
  that you e'er set foot in a ship or boat,
and the many steps that you took with vigour
  back from London, to Béal Trá.
When you decided that you'd try swimming
  the young girls seized you on every side
—and your mother thinking, if a hundred foundered
  you'd be the winner that would swim ashore.

I arose myself on Friday early
  and heard the wailing and the beating palms
of women jaded by the nightlong labour
  —with stretching corpses their only task.
O God, O Christ Who suffered slaughter,
  O true Redeemer of the naked poor,
to holy Paradise bring safely with you
  all these poor creatures that were so despoiled.

A bitter curse on that same location,
  may star not shine there, may sun not rise
—to drown that number as they went together
  on Thursday early to the Galway fair,
men who would settle their ploughs and harrows
  and plough the stubble and shake the seed
and the women likewise, in all things expert,
  for weaving homespun and the linen thin.

Heart-impaling and mountain-burning
  on the place they died in, and hard reproach,
for the many creatures it left prostrated,
  crying and mourning each Monday morn.
Not faulty knowledge it was that strayed them
  but great misfortune at Caisleán Nua.
My story's ending: that many drownings
  left much affliction in Eanach Dhúin.

translated by Thomas Kinsella

Caoineadh Athar   SEÁN Ó MUIRÍOSA

Má théann tú amárach go dtí Tuar an Fhíona
gabh insa thimpeall go dtí an Buí-chnoc—
nach mó fear fionn a umhlóidh síos duit
agus bean faoi chlóca a phógfaidh ó chroí tú!
Má fhiosraíonn aoinne díot cér díobh tú
abair leo den chomhrá caoin
gur cailín breá tú le Seán Ó Muiríosa.

Tá tú ag dul amárach ag tógaint áras do leapa
san áit nach gá duit bheith ag rómhar ná ag grafadh,
san áit nach dtagann trálach i lámha na bhfear ann,
san áit nach gá duit bia ná éadach,
agus cuirfimid a chodladh le solas an lae tú.

Thabharfadh d'athair airgead agus ór duit,
thabharfadh d'athair macha breá bó duit,
rachadh sé abhaile le leaba do phósta,
rachadh sé abhaile le leaba do phósta
ach gur thóg tú de rogha Cathair na Glóire.

A Father's Lament   SEÁN Ó MUIRÍOSA

If you go tomorrow to Tuar an Fhíona
travel around it till you come to the Buí-chnoc;
many fair men there will do you honour
and women in cloaks give a heartfelt kiss.
If anyone asks you who are your people
give them an answer in gentle tones:
you are Seán Ó Muiríosa's handsome daughter.

You are going to make your bed tomorrow
where you'll never need to grub or dig,
where the hands of the men will get no cramps,
where you'll never want for food or clothing
and we'll put you to bed by the light of day.

Your father would give you gold and silver,
your father would give you a fine field of cows,
he would bring you home your marriage bed
—he would bring you home your marriage bed—
but you chose instead the Fort of Glory.

translated by Thomas Kinsella

A Fine Plantation

Donnchad Ruadh i dTalamh-an-Éisc
DONNCHAD RUA MACCONMARA

As I was walking one evening fair
   As mé go déidheanach i mBaile-Sheaghain
I met a gang of English blades,
   As iad d'a d-traochadh ag neart a námhad:
I boozed and drank both late and early
   With these courageous men of war—
'S gur bhinne liom na Sagsanaigh ag rith air éigion
   'S gan de Ghaedhil ann acht fír-bheagán.

I spent my fortune by being freakish
   Drinking, raking, and playing cards—
Gidh nach raibh airgead agam ná gréithre
   Ná rud san t-saogal acht nídh gan áird:
Then I turn'd a jolly tradesman,
   By work and labour I lived abroad—
Acht bíodh ar m' fhallaing gur mór an bhreug sin
   'S gur beag don t-saothar do thuit lém láimh!

Newfoundland is a fine plantation,
It will be my station until I die—
Mo chrádh, go mb' feárr liom a bheith in Éirinn
Ag díol gairtéiridhe ná ag dul fán gcoill:
Here you may find a virtuous lady
A smiling fair one to please your mind
An paca staigeanna as measa tréithe
Go mbeiridh mé 'shaoghal bheith as a radharc!

Come drink a health, boys, to Royal George
Our chief commander, nár órduigh Críost.
As bíodh bhur n-athchuingeadha chum Muire Mháthar
'E féin 'sa ghárdaidhe do leagadh síos!
We'll fear no arms nor war's alarms
While noble George will be our guide—
'Sa Chríost go bhfeicidh mé an bhrúid d'a chárnadh
Ag an mac so ar fán uainn thall san bhFrainc!

Donnchad Ruadh in Newfoundland
DONNCHAD RUA MACCONMARA

As I was walking one evening fair
  When I was lately in St. John's town,
I met a gang of English blades
  And jostled for six by the enemy
I boozed and drank both late and early
  With these courageous men of war—
How sweet to me, then, to see 'em on the run
  With just a few paddies on the scene.

I spent my fortune by being freakish
  Drinking, raking and playing cards—
Money I'd none, scarce trinkets either
  Nothing of value at all to my name:
Then I turned a jolly tradesman
  By work and labour I lived abroad—
Yet, on my very cloak, that's another lie
  For I never did a hand's turn.

Newfoundland is a fine plantation
  It will be my station until I die—
God no, I'd rather be back in Ireland
  Peddling garters or traipseing the woods:
Here you may find a virtuous lady
  A smiling fair one to please your mind
And gangs of informers the worst I've met.
  Commonsense whispers a clean pair of heels.

Come drink a health, boys, to Royal George
   Our chief commander, hardly crowned by Christ.
Let your prayers beseech our Blessed Mother
   Himself and his henchmen will be put down!
We'll fear no arms nor war's alarms
   While noble George will be our guide—
Christ, but I'd see the beast well pounded
   By that youngster exiled over in France!

lines in translation by John Ennis

Carrickfergus

TRADITIONAL

I wish I was in Carrickfergus
Only for nights in Ballygran
I would swim over the deepest ocean
Only for nights in Ballygran
But the sea is wide and I cannot swim over
And neither have I wings to fly
I wish I could find me a handsome boatman
To carry me over to my love and die.

My boyhood days bring back sad reflections
Of happy hours I spent so long ago
My boyhood friends and my own relations
Are all passed on now, like the drifting snow
But I'll spend my days, an endless rover
Soft is the grass I walk, my bed is free
Ah to be back in Carrickfergus
On that long road, down to the sea.

But in Kilkenny it is reported
There are marble stones there, as black as ink
With gold and silver I would support her
But I'll sing no more till I get a drink
I'm drunk today and I'm seldom sober
A handsome rover from town to town
Ah but I'm sick now and my days are numbered
So come all you young men and lay me down.

The Streams of Bunclody

TRADITIONAL

Oh were I at the moss house, where the birds do increase,
At the foot of Mount Leinster or some silent place,
By the streams of Bunclody, where all pleasures do meet,
And all I would ask is one kiss from you, sweet.

If I was in Bunclody I would think myself at home,
'Tis there I would have a sweetheart, but here I have none,
Drinking strong liquor in the height of my cheer,
Here's a health to Bunclody and the lass I love dear.

The cuckoo is a pretty bird, it sings as it flies,
It brings us good tidings, and tells us no lies,
It sucks the young bird's eggs to make its voice clear,
And the more it cries cuckoo the summer draws near.

If I was a clerk and could write a good hand,
I would write to my true love that she might understand,
I am a young fellow that is wounded in love,
That lived by Bunclody, but now must remove.

If I was a lark and had wings I could fly
I would go to yon arbour where my love she does lie,
I'd proceed to yon arbour where my true love does lie,
And on her fond bosom contented I would die.

'Tis why my love slights me, as you may understand,
That she has a freehold, and I have no land,
She has great store of riches and a large sum of gold,
And everything fitting a house to uphold.

So adieu, my dear father, adieu, my dear mother,
Farewell to my sister, farewell to my brother;
I am bound for America, my fortune to try,
When I think on Bunclody, I'm ready to die.

The Prison of Newfoundland

TRADITIONAL

Ye lads and lasses of Newfoundland, come listen to my sad tale,
While I relate the hardships that I spent in St. John's Jail.
Although I'm a prisoner in this land, I'll do the best I can
To relate the hardships I went through in the prison of
 Newfoundland.

On the twenty-first day of October to this country I first came,
On a British brig from Baltimore, the *Poregram* by name;
We were consigned to Harvey's wharf our cargo there to land,
Which causes me bitterly to regret my first voyage to
 Newfoundland.

The day all of my trial it would grieve your heart full sore,
When I thinks on Daniel Haggarty who falsely on me swore.
Judge Carter passed my sentence and this to me did say:
'Six months on hard bread and cold water in the penitentiary'.

O when my sentence it was passed then I was marched away,
Down to the penitentiary my winter there to stay;
Where I found comrades plentiful as you may understand,
To live on hard bread and cold water in the prison of
 Newfoundland.

My prison was situated by the side of a lonely pond,
Where oftentimes did I sit and sing like the mockingbird alone;
Watching the lads and lasses how they used to sport and play,
Through my iron-grated window in the penitentiary.

One night as I lay fast asleep in my lonely prison cell,
I dreamed I was back in old Ireland where once I used to dwell;
Those pleasant dreams disturbed my rest as you may
 understand,
'Twas there I awoke with a broken heart in the prison of
 Newfoundland.

Now to conclude and finish I mean to end my song,
Johnny O'Doyle it is my name and in old Ireland I belong;
I served my time in the Black Ball Line since ever I went to sea,
But now at last I am caught fast in the penitentiary.

I served my time in the Black Ball Line since ever I went to sea,
But very soon I'll be making tracks to the land of liberty.

Deep in the Canadian Woods

T. D. SULLIVAN

Deep in Canadian woods we've met,
   From one bright island flown.
Great is the land we tread but yet
   Our hearts are with our own.
And ere we leave this shanty small,
   While fades the autumn day,
We'll toast old Ireland, dear old Ireland,
   Ireland, boys, Hurrah!

We've heard her faults a hundred times,
   The new ones and the old,
In songs and sermons, rants and rhymes,
   Enlarged some fifty-fold.
But take them all, the great and small,
   And this we've got to say:—
Here's dear old Ireland! good old Ireland!
   Ireland, boys, Hurrah!

We know that brave and good men tried,
   To snap her rusty chain,
That patriots suffered, martyrs died,
   And all, it's said, in vain:
But no, boy, no: a glance will show
   How far they've won their way—
Here's good old Ireland! loved old Ireland!
   Ireland, boys, Hurrah!

We've seen the wedding and the wake,
   The patron and the fair,
And lithe young frames at the dear old games
   In the kindly Irish air,
And the loud 'Hurrah', we have heard it too,
   And a thundering 'Clear the way!'
Here's gay old Ireland! dear old Ireland!
   Ireland, boys, Hurrah!

And well we know in cool grey eyes,
   When the hard day's work is o'er,
How soft and sweet are the words that greet,
   The friends who meet once more:
With 'Mary Machree!' and 'My Pat, 'tis he!'
   And 'My own heart night and day!'
Ah, fond old Ireland! dear old Ireland!
   Ireland, boys, Hurrah!

And happy and bright are the groups that pass
   From their peaceful homes, for miles
O'er fields and roads, and hills, to Mass,
   When Sunday morning smiles!
And deep the zeal their true hearts feel
   When low they kneel and pray,
O, dear old Ireland! blest old Ireland!
   Ireland, boys, Hurrah!

But deep in Canadian woods we've met
   And we never may see again
The dear old isle where our hearts are set
   And our first fond hopes remain!
But come, fill up another cup
   And with every sup let's say:
'Here's loved old Ireland! good old Ireland!
   Ireland, boys, Hurrah!'

I Will Go With My Father A-Ploughing

JOSEPH CAMPBELL

I will go with my father a-ploughing
To the green field by the sea,
And the rooks and the crows and the seagulls
Will come flocking after me.
I will sing to the patient horses
With the lark in the white of the air,
And my father will sing the plough-song
That blesses the cleaving share.

I will go with my father a-sowing
To the red field by the sea,
And the rooks and the gulls and the starlings
Will come flocking after me.
I will sing to the striding sowers
With the finch on the greening sloe,
And my father will sing the seed-song
That only the wise men know.

I will go with my father a-reaping
To the brown field by the sea,
And the geese and the crows and the children
Will come flocking after me.
I will sing to the tan-faced reapers
With the wren in the heat of the sun,
And my father will sing the scythe-song
That joys for the harvest done.

Tickle Cove Pond MARK WALKER

In cuttin' and haulin' in frost and in snow
We're up against troubles that few people know
And only by patience with courage and grit
And eatin' plain food can we keep ourselves fit.
The hard and the aisey we take as it comes,
And when ponds freeze over we shorten our runs,
To hurry my hauling the Spring coming on,
Near lost me my mare on Tickle Cove Pond.

Chorus
Oh, lay hold William Oldford, lay hold William White,
Lay hold of the cordage and pull all your might,
Lay hold of the bowline and pull all you can,
And give me a lift for poor Kit on the pond.

I knew that the ice became weaker each day,
But still took the risk and kept hauling away,
One evening in April, bound home with a load,
The mare showed some halting against the ice road
And knew more than I did, as matters turned out,
And lucky for me had I joined in her doubt.
She turned 'round her head, and with tears in her eyes,
As if she were saying: 'You're risking our lives',

All this I ignored with a whip-handle blow,
For man is too stupid dumb creatures to know
The very next minutes the pond gave a sigh,
And down to our necks went poor Kitty and I.
For if I had taken wise Kitty's advice
I never would take the short cut on the ice
'Poor creature she's dead, and poor creature she's gone;
I'll never get my wood off Tickle Cove Pond'.

I raised an alarm you could hear for a mile
And neighbour turned up in a very short while
You can always rely on the Oldfords and Whites
To render assistance in all your bad plights.
To help a poor neighbour is part of their lives;
The same I can say of their children and wives.
When the bowline was fastened around the mare's breast
William White for a shanty song made a request.

There was no time for thinking, no time for delay.
So straight from his head came this song right away:
'Lay hold William Oldford, lay hold William White,
Lay hold of the hawser and pull all your might,
Lay hold to the bowline and pull all you can'
And with that we brought Kit out of Tickle Cove Pond.

Chorus

Pat Murphy's Meadow

JOHN DEVINE

The autumn days are here again, the night wind's chilly
   blow;
The woodland's turned to golden hue, and the harvest moon's
   aglow.
I dream again of days long past to come no more, I know,
When I mowed Pat Murphy's meadow in the sunny long-ago.

I see the blue of ocean, the distant sail afar,
As the maiden in the meadow strikes up 'Dark Lough na
   Gar'.
There was music soft and tender in winds that whispered
   low,
As I mowed Pat Murphy's meadow in the sunny long-ago.

Where are the boys and girls all who danced the gay
   quadrille,
And the singer warbling sweetly, 'The Burning Granite Mill';
To hear again at sunset, 'Where Sweet Afton Waters Flow',
When I mowed Pat Murphy's meadow in the sunny long-ago.

Those days are but a mem'ry, like the snows of
   yesteryear,
And when evening shades are falling, all alone I shed a tear.
On my cheek I feel the soft touch of winds that whispered
   low,
When I mowed Pat Murphy's meadow in the sunny long-ago.

Home Free

STEPHANIE PAYNE

I fished with my father when I was young
Rolling over the waves till our time it had come
To pack up our nets and go back to the shore
And dream about fish as we oft did before.

And as I grew older my father did too
And he said to me you know just what to do
When the fish are too small or your nets have been tore
You should never give up but try it once more.

Chorus
Cause we're home free, home free to live like we do taking fish from the sea
And we're home free, home free to live like we do taking fish from the sea.

My father passed on but I was old enough now
To fish for myself with my son at the bow
Who watched every wave rolling into the shore
And oft times had said I will go home no more.

And as I grew older my son he did too
And he said to me I know just what to do
When the fish are too small and my nets have been tore
I should never give up but try it once more.

Chorus

Now watching my Grandson play on the shore
I think of the train that has stopped at his door
Along with the fish that once danced with the sky
And I know he won't live like his father and I.

Chorus

Jerry Ryan

LEN BUTT

Now all you young men who go chopping,
Please listen awhile to my rhyme,
Concerning the year I was working
With the foreman, well-known Jerry Ryan.

We first met this man on the journey
Who promised us timber in store:
'Go up to the camp boys, to open,
And stay 'til the job it is o'er'.

We quickly agreed to his suggestion
And joined him in old Bishop Falls;
Being eager for work and employment so scarce,
Not knowing the wages were small.

We boarded the truck at the depot,
Our baggage went back in the rear;
'Twas little we thought as we journeyed along
Of the hardships you go through up there.

We passed by pine camps and still waters,
For our laughing and joking the while;
And Dan with a bound, he brought her around,
Saying: 'Boys, we are up thirty miles'.

Next morning all armed with equipment,
A bucksaw, an axe, and a rod;
With forty-nine men to make wages up there,
With only scrub spruce on a bog.

It is hard for a man to make money,
When it is only scrub spruce to be found;
And if you refuse a bad chance on a scale
The word is you've got to go down.

Seventy cents a day charged for your bucksaw,
And seventy cents a day for your board;
And then there's a fee for the doctor,
Comes out of one dollar and twenty a cord.

We found no complaint with this foreman,
I think he is honest and square;
But it fell to our lot, like cattle were bought,
And yoked to a bucksaw up there.

And when you lay down on your pillow,
No matter if you're asleep or awake;
You will think of the times you spent with Jerry Ryan,
On the borders of old Rocky Lake.

Bucksaw Blues   EUGENE HUTCHINGS

Come all ye young fellows, don't be in a hurry
To take hold the bucksaw for you know it's not fun;
Get your learning at highschool and then go to college;
Don't swing the bucksaw like we fools have done.

You go in the woods and swing the old bucksaw,
Four-fifty a cord in the blowdown, you see;
Swamp your own roads for the same amount of money;
That's where the contractors get it on we.

We pay our union four dollars yearly;
It be better for us if we spent it in beer,
For the tanglefoot blowdown with wages worked daily
We're frightened to kick but our union is there.

We stay in the bunkhouse and do all our talking,
Instead of getting the union to see;
But they'd rather save bus fare than make up the wages
That's where we lose and they gain in the fee.

We oft times wonder why people have money,
Especially those big shots and skippers like thee;
But the big shots are kicking from morning till evening,
And that's where they all get the better of we.

Sliabh Geal gCua na Féile

PÁDRAIG Ó MILEADHA

A Shliabh gheal gCua na féile, is fada uait i gcéin mé,
Im shuí cois cuain i m'aonar, go tréithlag faoi bhrón.
An tuile bhuí ar thaobh díom, idir mé agus tír mo chléibhe
Is a Shliabh gheal gCua na féile, nach géar é mo sceol.

Dá mbeinnse i measc mo ghaolta i Scéithín ghlas na séimh-
   fhear
Mar a scaipeann teas na gréine ó spéir gheal gan smál,
Nó dá mbeinnse ansiúd faoin réalta nuair a thiteann drúcht ar
   fhéar ann,
Ó a Shliabh gheal gCua nár dhéirc sin dá mb'fhéidir é a fháil?

'S é mo léan nach bhfuair mé tógáil le léann is mórchuid eolais,
I nGaeilge uasal cheolmhar ba sheolta mo bhéal,
Ó threabhfainn cuairt thar sáile is bhéarfainn bua thar barr
   chughat,
Mar, a Shliabh geal gCua, ba bhreá liom thú a ardú faoi réim.

Mo ghrása thall na Déise idir bhánta, ghleannta is shléibhte,
Ó shnámh mé anonn thar tréanmhuir táim tréithlag gan bhrí;
Ach ó thoiligh Dia mé a ghlaoch as, mo shlánsa siar go
   hÉirinn,
Agus slán le Sliabh na féile le saorghean ó mo chroí.

Bright and Welcoming Mountain

PÁDRAIG Ó MILEADHA

O bright and welcoming mountain, I'm far from you now overseas
Sitting alone by the harbour, weak these days and heavy hearted.
The brown fetid tide flows one side of me and between me, too, and my bosom home.
Dear welcoming mountain, my song's a bitter one.

Would that I were among my own, the gentle kindly people of the green fields of Scéithín:
Say, a day when the summer sun controls the cloudless sky,
Or out beneath the stars when a heavy dew drowns the meadows;
Dear Slieve gCua, that would be a charity if I could have it.

It's a grief to me I wasn't reared to the learning and scholarship,
The Irish that has become noble and lyrical on my tongue.
I'd plough the journey back to you, bring you the old palm of victory
Because, bright mountain, it is in my heart to do that for you.

My love, then, to the Deise, to its pastures, glens and mountains.
Since I swam over the wide bitter sea I'm so tortured, listless, down.
Yet, though it was God's will I came and, so, my farewell to Ireland
Dear mountain, my heart beats freer, stronger, toward you, even now.

translated by John Ennis.

The Rising of the Moon

The Poet Egan O'Rahilly, Homesick in Old Age
THOMAS KINSELLA

He climbed to his feet in the cold light, and began
The decrepit progress again, blown along the cliff road,
Bent with curses above the shrew his stomach.

The salt abyss poured through him, more raw
With every laboured, stony crash of the waves:
His teeth bared at their voices, that incessant dying.

Iris leaves bent on the ditch, unbent,
Shivering in the wind: leaf-like spirits
Chattered at his death-mask as he passed.

He pressed red eyelids: aliens crawled
Breaking princely houses in their jaws;
Their metal faces reared up, eating at light.

'Princes overseas, who slipped away
In your extremity, no matter where I travel
I find your great houses like stopped hearts.

Likewise your starving children—though I nourish
Their spirit, and my own, on the lists of praises
I make for you still in the cooling den of my craft.

Our enemies multiply. They have recruited the sea:
Last night, the West's rhythmless waves destroyed my sleep;
This morning, winkle and dogfish persisting in the stomach . . .'

Príosún Chluain Meala

TRADITIONAL

Ó, bliain 's an lá amárach
'sea d'fhágas an baile,
ag dul go hArd Pádraig
'cur lásaí lem hata:
bhí Buachaillí Bána ann
is rás acu ar eallaigh—
is mé go dubhach uaigneach
i bpríosún Chluain Meala.

Tá mo shrian is mo dhiallait,
ar iasacht le fada,
mo chamán ar fiaradh
faoi iarthar mo leapa,
mo liathróid á bualadh
ag buachaillí an ghleanna—
is go mbuailfinn poc báire
chomh hard leis na fearaibh!

A Chiarraígh, bídh ag guí liom,
is bog binn liom bhúr nglórtha
is beag a shíleas-sa choíche
ná fillfinnse beo oraibh—
's go mbeidh ár dtrí cinn-ne
ar thrí spící mar sheó acu,
faoi shneachta na hoíche
is gach síon eile 'á ngeobhaidh chughainn.

Go hUíbh Ráthach má théann tú,
beir scéala go dtí mo mhuintir
go bhfuilim daor ar an bhfód seo
is nach bhfuil beo agam ach go hAoine.
Bailídh gléas tórraimh
agus cónra bhreá im thimpeall—
sin críoch ar Ó Dónaill
is go deo deo bídh ag guí leis.

The Jail of Clonmel

TRADITIONAL

O it's one year tomorrow
my home I deserted
and went to Ard Pádraig
my hat done in laces.
The Whiteboys were there
tormenting the cattle
—now I'm grieving and lonely
in the jail of Clonmel.

My bridle and saddle
are loaned out a long time,
my hurley is slanted
in under the bed,
my ball hit about
by the boys of the valley
—I who'd hit a goal-puck
as high as the next!

Kerrymen, pray for me.
I love your soft voices,
nor thought I would never
return to you living.
But our three heads will soon
be on spikes for a show
in the snows of the night
and all weathers that come.

If you go to Uíbh Ráthach
take the news to my people
I'm condemned on this sod
and won't live beyond Friday.
Get the things for my wake
And a fine coffin round me
—here's an end of Ó Dónaill
and pray for him always.

translated by Thomas Kinsella

Na Connerys

TRADITIONAL

Tá jaicéid gairid á dhéanamh ó mhaidin dúinn, agus *trouser* dá réir—
Sin culaith farraige, ní nár chleachtamair i dtúis ár saoil.
Tá an chroch dá seasamh is an chnáibh dá casadh le bliain roimhré,
Is meireach feabhas ár gcarad bhí ár muinéal cnagtha, agus sinn go domhin sa chré.

A dhriothair m'anama, nach fada athá ár gcúis dá plé—
Óna sé ar maidin go dtí an dá uair dhéag?
Le linn na sagairt a bheith ag léamh an Aifrinn, cuirigí úr n'achainí chun Mac Dé
Chun na *Connerys* a thabhairt slán abhaile chughainn ós na *New South Wales*.

A Fhoghlú mhallaithe, guíme eascaine ort agus gráin Mhic Dé;
Agus Haicéad ós é a dh'iontaigh thú ar a dheisláimh fhéin.
Mar is sibh a dhearbhaigh i láthair Sasanach ar an dtriúr bocht sa mbréig
Chun na *Connerys* a chur thar farraige go dtí sna *New South Wales*.

An té a dhéanfadh machnamh ar ár gcúis le fada, agus í dá plé,
Is gur sheasaimh sí óna sé ar maidin go dtí an dá uair dhéag—
Le linn an dearbhaithe do chrith an talamh, is iad á dtabhairt sa mbréig—
Mo thrua-sa an t-anam bocht, tá sé damanta más fíor í an chléir.

Mo thrua-sa an t-athair bocht a thóig na macanna i dtúis an tsaoil,
Agus an bhanaltra a thál bainne orthu—tá sí go dúch ina ndéidh.
An téarma a gearradh dóibh, beidh sé caite acu bliain roimh naoi;
Agus beidh na *Connerys* ag teacht abhaile chughainn ós na *New South Wales*

The Connerys   TRADITIONAL

A short jacket is being made since morning for us, and a trousers accordingly, that is a sea-suit, something which we were not used to in the beginning of our life. The gallows is being erected and the hemp-rope is being twisted for a year beforehand. And if it were not for the goodness of our friends our necks would have been cracked, and we would have been deep in the clay.

O my dear brother, is not the discussion of our case taking a long time, from six in the morning until twelve o'clock? While the priests are reading Mass, beseech the Son of God to bring the Connerys safe home to us from New South Wales.

O cursed Foley, I pray a malediction on you and the hatred of God's Son; and on Hacket since it was he who betrayed you with his right hand. Because it was ye who swore falsely in the presence of Englishmen against the poor trio, to send the Connerys over the sea to New South Wales.

To consider for a long time our case while it was being discussed —it lasted from six in the morning until twelve o'clock. During the swearing the ground shook since they were taking the oaths falsely. Alas for the poor soul, it is damned if what the clergy say is true.

I pity the poor father who reared the sons in the beginning of their life, and the nurse who gave them milk—she is dejected after them. The term they were sentenced to will be served by them in a year less than nine, and the Connerys will be coming home to us from New South Wales.

translated by Dáithí Ó hÓgáin

The Rising of the Moon
JOHN KEEGAN CASEY

'O then, tell me, Shawn O'Farrell, tell me why you hurry so?'
'Hush, *mo buachaill,* hush and listen;' and his cheeks were all
   a-glow:
'I bear orders from the captain—get you ready quick and soon;
For the pikes must be together at the risin' of the Moon'.

'O then, tell me, Shawn O'Farrell, where the gath'rin' is to be?'
'In the old spot by the river, right well known to you and me;
One word more—for signal token, whistle up the marchin' tune,
With your pike upon your shoulder, by the risin' of the Moon'.

Out from many a mud-wall cabin eyes were watching through
   that night;
Many a manly heart was throbbing for the blessed warning light.
Murmurs passed along the valleys, like the *bean sighe's* lonely
   croon,
And a thousand blades were flashing at the risin' of the Moon.

There, beside the singing river, that dark mass of men was
   seen—
Far above the shining weapons hung their own beloved Green.
'Death to every foe and traitor! Forward! Strike the marchin'
   tune,
And hurrah, my boys, for freedom! 'tis the risin' of the Moon'.

Well they fought for poor old Ireland, and full bitter was their
   fate;
(O what glorious pride and sorrow fills the name of 'Ninety-
   Eight!)
Yet, thank God, e'en still are beating hearts in manhood's
   burning noon,
Who would follow in their footsteps at the risin' of the Moon!

Boolavogue

P. J. MCCALL

At Boolavogue as the sun was setting o'er the bright May
  meadows of Shelmalier,
A rebel hand set the heather blazing and brought the neighbours
  from far and near.
Then Father Murphy from old Kilcormac spurred up the rock
  with a warning cry:
'Arm! arm!' he cried, 'for I've come to lead you! For Ireland's
  freedom we'll fight or die!'

He led us 'gainst the coming soldiers. And the cowardly yeomen
  we put to flight.
'Twas at the Harrow the boys of Wexford showed Bookey's
  regiment how men could fight.
Look out for hirelings, King George of England. Search every
  kingdom where breathes a slave
For Father Murphy of County Wexford sweeps o'er the land like
  a mighty wave.

We took Camolin and Enniscorthy, and Wexford storming drove
  out our foes.
'Twas at Slieve Coilte our pikes were reeking with crimson
  blood of the beaten Yeos.
At Tubberneery and Ballyellis, full many a Hessian lay in his
  gore.
Ah! Father Murphy had aid come over, the Green Flag floated
  from shore to shore!

At Vinegar Hill o'er the pleasant Slaney, our heroes vainly stood
  back to back,
And the Yeos of Tullow took Father Murphy, and burnt his body
  upon the rack.
God grant you glory brave Father Murphy! And open heaven to
  all your men!
The cause that called you may call to-morrow in another fight
  for the Green again.

Henry Joy McCracken   TRADITIONAL

It was on the Belfast Mountains I heard a maid complain
   And she vexed the sweet June evening with her heart-broken strain,
Saying, 'Woe is me, life's anguish is more that I can dree,
   Since Henry Joy McCracken died on the gallows tree.

'At Donegore he proudly rode and he wore a suit of green,
   And brave though vain at Antrim his sword flashed lightning keen,
And when by spies surrounded his band to Slemish fled,
   He came unto the Cavehill for to rest a weary head.

'I watched for him each night long as in our cot he slept,
   At daybreak to the heather to MacArt's fort we crept,
When news came from Greencastle of a good ship anchored nigh,
   And down by yon wee fountain we met to say good-bye.

'He says, "My love be cheerful for tears and fears are vain",
   He says, "My love be hopeful our land shall rise again".
He kissed me ever fondly, he kissed me three times o'er,
   Saying, "Death shall never part us my love for evermore".

'That night I climbed the Cavehill and watched till morning blazed,
   And when its fires had kindled across the loch I gazed,
I saw an English tender at anchor off Garmoyle,
   But alas! no good ship bore him away to France's soil'.

Rody McCorley

TRADITIONAL

Come tender hearted Christians all, attention pay to me,
'Till I relate these verses great, these verses two or three,
Concerning of a clever youth who was cut off in his bloom,
And died upon the gallows tree near to the bridge of Toome.

The hero now I speak of, he was proper tall and straight,
Like to the lofty poplar tree his body was complete,
His growth was like the tufted fir that does ascend the air,
And waving o'er his shoulders broad the locks of yellow hair.

In sweet Duneane this youth was born and reared up tenderly,
His parents educated him, all by their industry,
Both day and night they sorely toiled for all their family,
Till desolation it came on by curséd perjury.

'Twas first the father's life they took and secondly the son,
The mother tore her old grey locks, she says 'I am undone
They took from me my property, my houses and my land,
And in the parish where I was born I dare not tread upon'.

'Farewell unto you sweet Drumaul, if in you I had stayed,
Among the Presbyterians I wouldn't have been betrayed,
The gallows tree I'd ne'er have seen had I remainéd there
For Dufferin you betrayed me, McErlean you set the snare.

'In Ballyscullion I was betrayed, woe be unto the man,
Who swore me a defender and a foe unto the crown,
Which causes Rody for to lie beneath the spreading thorn,
He'll sigh and say "Alas the day that ever I was born"'.

Soon young Rody was conveyed to Ballymena town,
He was loaded there with irons strong, his bed was the cold ground,
And there young Rody he must wait until the hour has come,
When a court-martial does arrive for to contrive his doom.

They called upon an arméd band, an arméd band came soon,
To guard the clever tall young youth down to the Bridge of
   Toome,
And when young Rody he came up the scaffold to ascend,
He looked at east and looked at west to view his loving friends.

And turning round unto the north he cried 'O faithless friend,
'Twas you who proved my overthrow and brought me to this
   end.
Since 'tis upon Good Friday that I'll executed be,
Convenient to the Bridge of Toome upon a Gallows Tree'.

The Croppy Boy   WILLIAM B. MCBURNEY

'Good men and true! In this house who dwell,
To a stranger *bouchal*, I pray you tell
Is the Priest at home? or may he be seen?
I would speak a word with Father Green'.

'The Priest's at home, boy, and may be seen;
'Tis easy speaking with Father Green;
But you must wait, till I go and see
If the holy Father alone may be'.

The youth has entered an empty hall—
What a lonely sound has his light foot-fall!
And the gloomy chamber's chill and bare,
With a vested Priest in a lonely chair.

The youth has knelt to tell his sins;
'*Nomine Dei*', the youth begins:
At '*mea culpa*' he beats his breast,
And in broken murmurs he speaks the rest.

'At the siege of Ross did my father fall,
And at Gorey my loving brothers all,
I alone am left of my name and race;
I will go to Wexford and take their place.

'I cursed three times since last Easter day—
At mass-time once I went to play;
I passed the churchyard one day in haste,
And forgot to pray for my mother's rest.

'I bear no hate against living thing;
But I love my country above my King.
Now, Father! bless me, and let me go
To die, if God has ordained it so'.

The Priest said naught, but a rustling noise
Made the youth look above in wild surprise;
The robes were off, and in scarlet there
Sat a yeoman captain with fiery glare.

With fiery glare and with fury hoarse,
Instead of blessing, he breathed a curse:—
'Twas a good thought, boy, to come here and shrive,
For one short hour is your time to live.

'Upon yon river three tenders float,
The Priest's in one, if he isn't shot—
We hold his house for our Lord and King,
And, Amen, say I, may all traitors swing!'

At Geneva Barrack that young man died,
And at Passage they have his body laid.
Good people who live in peace and joy,
Breathe a prayer and a tear for the Croppy boy.

De groves of de Pool

DICK MILLIKIN

Now de war, dearest Nancy, is ended,
    And de peace is come over from France;
So our gallant Cork city militia
    Back again to head-quarters advance.
No longer a beating dose rebels,
    We'll now be a beating de bull,
And taste dose genteel recreations
    Dat are found in de groves of de Pool.
        Ri fol didder rol didder rol, etc.

Den out came our loving relations,
    To see whether we'd be living or no;
Besides all de jolly ould neighbours,
    Around us who flocked in a row.
De noggins of sweet Tommy Walker
    We lifted according to rule,
And wetted our necks wid de native
    Dat is brewed in de groves of de Pool.
        Ri fol, etc.

When de regiment marched into de Commons,
    'Twould do your heart good for to see;
You'd tink not a man nor a woman
    Was left in Cork's famous city.
De boys dey came flocking around us,
    Not a hat nor wig stuck to a skull,
To compliment dose Irish heroes
    Returned to de groves of de Pool.
        Ri fol, etc.

Wid our band out before us in order,
  We played coming into de town;
We up'd wid de ould 'Boyne water',
  Not forgetting, too, 'Croppies lie down'.
Bekase you might read in the newses
  'Twas we made dose rebels so cool,
Who all tought, like Turks or like Jewses,
  To murther de boys of de Pool.
        Ri fol, etc.

Oh, sure dere's no nation in Munster
  Wid de groves of Blackpool can compare,
Where dose heroes were all edicated,
  And de nymphs are so comely and fair.
Wid de gardens around entertaining,
  Wid sweet purty posies so full
Dat is worn by dose comely young creaturs
  Dat walks in de groves of de Pool.
        Ri fol, etc.

Oh! many's de time, late and early,
  Dat I wished I was landed again.
Where I'd see de sweet watercourse flowing,
  Where de skinners dere glory maintain.
Likewise dat divine habitation,
  Where dose babbies are all sent to school
Dat never had fader nor moder,
  But were found in de groves of de Pool.
        Ri fol, etc.

Come all you young youths of dis nation,
  Come fill up a bumper all round;
Drink success to Blackpool navigation.
  And may it wid plenty be crowned.
Here's success to the jolly hoop-coilers,
  Likewise to de shuttle and de spool,
To de tanners, and worthy glue-boilers,
  Dat lives in de groves of de Pool.
    Ri fol, etc.

Dublin After the Union

EDWARD LYSAGHT

How justly alarmed is each Dublin cit,
　That he'll soon be transformed to a clown, sir!
By a magical move of that conjuror, Pitt,
　The country is coming to town, sir!
　　　Give Pitt, and Dundas, and Jenky, a glass,
　　　Who'd ride on John Bull, and make Paddy an ass.

Through Capel Street, soon, as you'll rurally range,
　You'll scarce recognize it the same street;
Choice turnips shall grow in your Royal Exchange,
　Fine cabbages down along Dame Street.
　　　Give Pitt, and Dundas, and Jenky, a glass,
　　　Who'd ride on John Bull, and make Paddy an ass.

Wild oats in the College won't want to be tilled,
　And hemp in the Four Courts may thrive, sir;
Your markets, again, shall with muttons be filled:
　By St. Patrick, they'll graze there alive, sir!
　　　Give Pitt, and Dundas, and Jenky, a glass,
　　　Who'd ride on John Bull, and make Paddy an ass.

In the Parliament House, quite alive shall there be
　All the vermin the island e'er gathers;
Full of rooks, as before, Daly's Club House you'll see,
　But the pigeons won't have any feathers.
　　　Give Pitt, and Dundas, and Jenky, a glass,
　　　Who'd ride on John Bull, and make Paddy an ass.

Our Custom House quay, full of weeds, oh, rare sport!
　But the Minister's minions, kind elves, sir,
Will give us free leave all our goods to export,
　When we've got none at home for ourselves, sir!
　　　Give Pitt, and Dundas, and Jenky, a glass,
　　　Who'd ride on John Bull, and make Paddy an ass.

Says an alderman, 'Corn will grow in your shops;
   This Union must work our enslavement',
'That's true', says the sheriff, 'for plenty of Crops,
   Already I've seen on the pavement!'
      Give Pitt, and Dundas, and Jenky, a glass,
      Who'd ride on John Bull, and make Paddy an ass.

Ye brave loyal yeomen, dress'd gaily in red,
   This Minister's plan must elate us;
And well may John Bull, when he's robbed us of bread,
   Call poor Ireland 'The land of potatoes!'
      Give Pitt, and Dundas, and Jenky, a glass,
      Who'd ride on John Bull, and make Paddy an ass.

The Burial of Sir John Moore   REV. CHARLES WOLFE

Not a drum was heard, not a funeral-note,
   As his corse to the rampart we hurried;
Not a soldier discharged his farewell shot
   O'er the grave where our hero we buried.

We buried him darkly at dead of night,
   The sods with our bayonets turning,
By the struggling moonbeam's misty light,
   And the lantern dimly burning.

No useless coffin enclosed his breast,
   Not in sheet or in shroud we wound him;
But he lay like a warrior taking his rest,
   With his martial cloak around him.

Few and short were the prayers we said,
   And we spoke not a word of sorrow;
But we steadfastly gazed on the face that was dead,
   And we bitterly thought of the morrow.

We thought as we hollow'd his narrow bed,
   And smooth'd down his lonely pillow,
That the foe and the stranger would tread o'er his head
   And we far away on the billow!

Lightly they'll talk of the spirit that's gone,
   And o'er his cold ashes upbraid him,—
But little he'll reck, if they let him sleep on
   In the grave where a Briton has laid him.

But half of our heavy task was done,
   When the clock struck the hour for retiring;
And we heard the distant and random gun
   That the foe was sullenly firing.

Slowly and sadly we laid him down,
   From the field of his fame fresh and gory;
We carved not a line, and we raised not a stone—
   But we left him alone in his glory!

A Pastoral Ballad
by John Bull
THOMAS MOORE

'*After the arrival of the packet bringing the account of the defeat of the Catholic Question, in the House of Commons, orders were sent to the Pigeon House to forward 5,000,000 rounds of musket-ball cartridge to the different garrisons round the country*'.

Freeman's Journal, *Dublin, March 12, 1827*

I have found out a gift for my Erin,
   A gift that will surely content her;—
Sweet pledge of a love so endearing!
   Five millions of bullet I've sent her.

She ask'd me for Freedom and Right,
   But ill she her wants understood;
Ball cartridges, morning and night,
   Is a dose that will do her more good.

There is hardly a day of our lives
   But we read, in some amiable trials,
How husbands make love to their wives
   Through the medium of hemp and of phials.

One thinks, with his mistress or mate
   A good halter is sure to agree—
That love-knot which, early and late,
   I have tried, my dear Erin, on thee.

While another, whom Hymen has bless'd
   With a wife that is not over placid,
Consigns the dear charmer to rest,
   With a dose of the best Prussic acid.

Thus, Erin! My love do I show—
Thus quiet thee, mate of my bed!
And, as poison and hemp are too slow,
Do thy business with bullets instead . . .

Caoineadh Baintrí
AMHLAOIBH Ó SÚILLEABHÁIN

26ú Meán Fomhair 1828

... D'éis imeacht ann cois na hAbha Bige, shíleas teacht abhaile slí níos díri níos réidhe.

Ghabhas chum lagbhotháin dearóil, cois na móna, ag fiafraí na slí. Tháinigh bean bhocht coslomnochta ard lántrua cheirteach chiarmhongach dheargshúileach ghruagstoitheach gan bairéad gan filléad, gan faice air a drom ach ceirt súichedhathach salach agus í ag gol go géar.

'Cá bhfuil an t-aicearra go Calainn?' ar mé féin.

'Taispeánfad féin sin duit agus céad mile fáilte' ar an bhean bhocht. 'Gluaiseam trés an ngarraí potátaí seo ar an gcosrán (.i. cosrian) se cois an chlaí fáis. Ba mise do chuir na potátaí se, ach bainfidh Páid Deibhriús iad'.

Ar ngabháil tré ghort cruithneachta, ar sí:

'Is iad mo chlannsa do chuir an síol, ach is é Páidín Deibhriús do bhain an Fómhar, mo mhallacht dó!'

Ar ngabháil trés an gclós:

'Ba liomsa na colúiríní coille se, ach is i bpota an Deibhriúsach fhiuchfaidh siad. Ba é m'fhearsa do thóg an tigh sin. Is mise do chuir súiche ar chleatha an tí ach bhain mac iníne Pháidín na gCeann an chomhla ón ursa, na tuislí de na bacánaibh. D'fhág sé an bothán gan doras, an fhuinneog gan gloine, an tinteán gan tine, an deatachán gan deatach, cró na muc gan cráin gan céis gan banbh gan collach gan muc, mór ná mion, méith ná trua.

'Ní chloisfead go brách arís búirthe mo bhó ar a lao ná ar a gamhain, ná siotrach mo láir ar a searrach ná ar a bromach ná méileach mo chaora ar a huan, ná meigeall mo ghabhair ar a mionnán, ná grágadaíl mo chirce dá heireoga ná dá gearrcacha, ná glao mo choiligh. Ní fheicfead mo lacha bhán ná mo bhardal breac ná mo ghé goir ná mo ghandal gléigeal. Ní fheicfead loch na móna. Ní chluinfead gáir an chort riasc, ná scréach an ghé fhiáin ná míog ón bpilibín míog, ná fead na feadóige ná meigeall an mhionnáin aeir. Ní chífead an duibhéan. Ní chloisfead plubarnaigh na circe uisce. Ní thráfad an linn don eascú ná don ghailliasc.

'Is fada uathu chuir fear mharfa Phog Ní tSéafra mé féin, is m'fhear bocht cráite is mo chlann bhocht chloíte. Ní fhásfad cartlainn chumhra an chinn bháin i móinéar cois linn ná an tseamróg bhán ná dhearg im mhóinéar tirim. Ní chuirfead an ros. Ní bhainfead an líon. Ní bháfad é sa linn. Ní bhainfead tointe óm thuran ná óm choigeal. Ní dhéanfad abhras. Tá mo thuran lín agus olainne sa díg, mo chófra i gclais na gainimhe, mo bhord ar an maolchlaí, mo phota sa bhfásach, mo chathaoir faoin bháisteach, mo shop leapan gan clúdach gan bráillín gan súsa, mo cheann gan caidhp, mo dhrom gan fallaing gan folach. Rug fear an chúlchíosa leis iad faraor crua cráite!'

A Widow's Lament

AMHLAOIBH Ó SÚILLEABHÁIN

26 September 1828

. . . As I had gone out by way of the Abha Bheag I decided to come home an easier, more direct way.

I went up to a miserable looking cabin at the edge of the bog to ask my way. A poor woman in her bare feet came out. She was tall and thin and red-eyed, in rags, with a mane of untidy black hair. She had neither bonnet nor scarf—nothing but a soiled and soot-stained rag. She was crying bitterly.

'I am looking for the short-cut to Callan', I said.

'I'll show it to you and welcome', the poor woman said. 'We can go through the potato field here, on the path along by the fence. Those potatoes: I planted them. But it is Páid Devereux will dig them'.

As we passed through a wheatfield she said:

'It was my family planted that seed but it was Páidín Devereux who reaped the harvest, my curse on him!'

As we passed through the yard:

'Those little woodpigeons used to belong to me, but they'll boil in Devereux' pot. It was my husband built our house—it was I sent the soot into the rafters—but Páidín na gCeann's grandson took the door off the jamb and the hinges off the hooks. He left the cabin without a door and the window without glass, the hearth without fire and the chimney without smoke, the pigsty without piglet or sow, young or old—without a pig or a boar, big or little, fat or lean.

'I'll never hear a cow of mine calling to her calf or young again, nor a mare of mine snorting to her foal or colt, nor sheep of mine baaing to her lamb, nor goat bleating to her kid, nor my hen clucking to her pullets and chickens, nor my cock crowing. And I won't see my white duck or my speckled drake again, or my hatching goose or my lovely white gander, nor the lake out on the bog. And I won't hear the crane calling in the marsh, nor the scream of the wild goose, or the marsh-plover piping or the moor-plover whistling or the bleat of the jacksnipe. I won't see the cormorant and I won't hear the moorhen bubbling. And I'll never drain the pool again for eel or pike.

'He has put me far from all that, that man who murdered Pog Ní tSéafra and my poor tormented husband and my poor ruined family. The sweet mint with the white tips won't grow again for me in the meadow by the pool, nor the white or red clover in the dry meadow. I'll plant no more flax-seed, nor lift the flax nor steep it in the pool. I'll never again draw the thread from the wheel or the distaff, or make any more yarn. The wheel for my flax and wool is in the ditch. My cupboard is out in the sandy trench, and my table out on the bare bank; my cooking-pot is on the waste ground and my chair is out in the rain; my bed-straw is coverless, without a sheet or a blanket. I've no cap for my head and no cloak or covering for my body. The rent collector took them with him for the arrears, o it's wretched hard . . .'.

translated by Thomas Kinsella

Annie Moore TRADITIONAL

As I roved out one evening in the month of sweet July
Through shady groves and valleys and streams as I passed by
The small birds they sat mourning on each green shady grove
They joined their notes all with that youth lamenting for his love.

He tore his hair distracted oft times his hands he wrung
The tears ran down his rosy cheeks like a watery stream
But still he cried my darling's gone the maid that I adore
By a sudden call to her long home—will I never see her more.

She was a proper tall young girl scarce seventeen years of age
And in no riotous company was ever she engaged
Her comrade girl asked her out a-walking for to go
She took her to that fateful spot which proved her overthrow.

It was on the twelfth day of July in the year of thirty-five
It ne'er shall be forgot by me as long as I'm alive
It was that day that very day my love was torn from me
She was the rose of Belfast town and the flower of this country.

It was on the twelfth day of July orange arches we did form
And Harvey and his cavalry thought to cut them down by storm
But all their efforts were in vain for we would not comply
And as we advanced 'No surrender' was our cry.

When riding forth to cut them down we received a mortal blow
You know a stone from David's sling did lay Goliath low
Then the Light Infantry got an order to fire a round of ball
It was at that fatal moment my true love she did fall.

A ball it entered in her breast and pierced her body through
And gently fell and waved her hand she could not bid adieu
As I held her milk white hand in mine my breast being filled with woe
To see those lips I oftimes kissed now whiter than the snow.

Annie Moore was my love's name of credit and renown
She was the flower of this country and the rose of Belfast town
The Protestant cause she dearly loved—William's sons she did adore
And round her neck even to the last she an orange ribbon wore.

The Protestants of Belfast turned out like heroes brave
To carry her remains to the cold and silent grave
And many of those heroes that day in tears were found
At the leaving of her residence convenient to the town.

Her dear friends and relatives their lost one they now deplore
Likewise her comrade girl was a-walking round the shore
Their many hearts are merry while my poor heart is dry
For it makes me sigh when I think of the twelfth day of July.

Famine and Exportation

JOHN O'HAGAN

During the last week the largest EXPORT OF GRAIN from Ireland to England, *ever known in one week*, took place—
London Paper, November, 1845.

Take it from us every grain,
We were made for you to drain;
Black starvation let us feel,
England must not want a meal!

When our rotting roots shall fail,
When the hunger pangs assail,
Ye'll have Irish corn your fill—
We'll have grass and nettles still!

We are poor, and ye are rich;
Mind it not, were every ditch
Strewn in Spring with famished corses,
Take our oats to feed your horses!

Heaven, that tempers ill with good
When it smote our wonted food,
Sent us bounteous growth of grain—
Sent to pauper slaves, in vain!

We but asked in deadly need:
'Ye that rule us! let us feed
On the food that's ours— 'behold!
Adder deaf and icy cold.

Were we Russians, thralls from birth,
In a time of bitter dearth
Would a Russian despot see
From his land its produce flee?

Were we black Virginian slaves,
Bound and bruised with thongs and staves
Avarice and selfish dread
Would not let us die unfed.

Were we, Saints of Heaven! were we
How we burn to think it—FREE!
Not a grain should leave our shore,
Not for England's golden store.

They who hunger where it grew—
They whom Heaven had sent it to—
They who reared with sweat of brow—
They, or *none*, should have it now.

Lord, that made us! what it is
To endure a lot like this!
Powerless in our worst distress,
Cramped by alien selfishness!

Not amongst our rulers all,
One true heart whereon to call;
Vainly still we turn to them
Who despoil us and contemn.

Forced to see them, day by day,
Snatch our sole resource away;
If returned a pittance be—
Alms, 'tis named, and *beggars*, we.

Lord! thy guiding wisdom grant,
Fearful counsellor is WANT;
Burning thoughts will rise within,
Keep us pure from stain of sin!

But, at least, like trumpet blast
Let it rouse us all at last;
Ye who cling to England's side!
Here and *now*, you see her tried.

Siberia   JAMES CLARENCE MANGAN

In Siberia's wastes
  The Ice-wind's breath
Woundeth like the toothèd steel.
Lost Siberia doth reveal
  Only blight and death.

Blight and death alone.
  No Summer shines.
Night is interblent with Day.
In Siberia's wastes alway
  The blood blackens, the heart pines.

In Siberia's wastes
  No tears are shed,
For they freeze within the brain.
Nought is felt but dullest pain,
  Pain acute, yet dead;

Pain as in a dream,
  When years go by
Funeral-paced, yet fugitive,
When man lives, and doth not live,
  Doth not live—nor die.

In Siberia's wastes
  Are sands and rocks.
Nothing blooms of green or soft,
But the snowpeaks rise aloft
  And the gaunt ice-blocks.

And the exile there
  Is one with those;
They are part, and he is part,
For the sands are in his heart,
  And the killing snows.

Therefore, in those wastes
  None curse the Czar.
Each man's tongue is cloven by
The North Blast, who heweth nigh
  With sharp scymitar.

And such doom each drees,
  Till, hunger-gnawn,
And cold-slain, he at length sinks there,
Yet scarce more a corpse than ere
  His last breath was drawn.

Anti-Confederation Song

TRADITIONAL

Hurrah for our own native isle, Newfoundland,
Not a stranger shall hold one inch of its strand,
Her face turns to Britain, her back to the Gulf,
Come near at your peril Canadian Wolf.

Ye brave Newfoundlanders who plough the salt sea,
With hearts like the eagle so bold and so free,
The time is at hand when you'll all have to say
If Confederation will carry the day.

Cheap tea and molasses they say they will give,
All taxes take off that the poor man may live:
Cheap nails and cheap lumber our coffins to make,
And homespun to mend our old clothes when they break.

If they take off the taxes how then will they meet
The heavy expense of the country's up-keep?
Just give them the chance to get us in the scrape
And they'll chain you as slaves with pen, ink, and red tape.

Would you barter the right that your fathers have won,
Your freedom transmitted from father to son?
For a few thousand dollars of Canadian gold
Don't let it be said that your birthright was sold.

The Government Game
PAT BYRNE AND AL PITTMAN

Come all you young fellows and list while I tell
Of the terrible misfortune that upon me befell.
Centralization they say was the name,
But me I just calls it the government game.

My name it don't matter, I'm not young anymore.
But in all of my days I'd never been poor.
I'd lived a right good life and not felt no shame,
'Till they made me take part in the government game.

My home was St. Kyran's, a heavenly place.
It thrived on the fishing of a good hearty race.
But now it will never again be the same,
Since they made it a pawn in the government game.

Sure the government paid us for moving away,
And leaving our birthplace for a better day's pay.
They said that our poor lives would ne'er be the same
Once we took part in the government game.

It's not many years now since they all moved away
To places more prosperous way down in the bay.
There's not one soul left now, not one who remains.
They've all become part of the government game.

Now St. Kyran's lies there all empty as hell,
Except for the graveyards where our dead parents dwell.
The lives of their children are buried in shame.
They lost out while playing the government game.

To a place called Placentia some of them went,
And in finding a new home their allowances spent.
So for jobs they went looking but they looked all in vain,
For the roof had caved in on the government game.

It's surely a sad sight their moving around,
Wishing they still lived by the cod fishing ground.
But there's no going back now, there's nothing to gain,
Now that they've played in the government game.

They tell me our young ones the benefits will see,
But I don't believe it, oh how can that be?
They'll never know nothing but sorrow and shame,
For their fathers were part of the government game.

And when my soul leaves me for the heavens above,
Take me back to St. Kyran's the place that I love.
And there on my gravestone, right next to my name,
Just say I died playing the government game.

4

We Left the Bunkhouse Feeling Fine

Finnegan's Wake TRADITIONAL

Tim Finnegan lived in Watling street,
A gentleman Irishman—mighty odd—
He'd a beautiful brogue, so rich and sweet,
And to rise in the world, he carried the hod.
But, you see he'd sort of a tipping way;
With a love for the liquor poor Tim was born,
And to help him through with his work, each day,
He'd drop of the craythir' every morn.

Chorus
Whack; fol-de-dooh-dah; dance to your partner
Welt the flure, yer trothers shake,
Isn't it the truth I've tould ye?
Lots of fun, at Finnegan's wake?

One morning, Tim was rather full;
His head felt heavy, which made him shake,
He fell from the ladder, and broke his skull,
So they carried him home a corpse to wake.
They rolled him up in a nice clean sheet,
And laid him out upon the bed,
With fourteen candles around his feet,
And a gallon of porter at his head.

Chorus

His friends assembled at his wake;
Missus Finnegan called for the lunch.
First they laid in tea and cake;
Then pipes and tobacky, and whisky-punch,
Miss Biddy O'Brien began to cry;
'Such a dacent corpse did ever you see?
Arrah! Tim avourneen, an' why did ye die?'
'Och, none of your gab', sez Billy Magee.

Chorus

Then Peggy O'Connor took up the job,
'Arrah! Biddy', says she, 'ye'er wrong, I'm shure',
But Biddy then gave her a belt on the gob,
And left her sprawling on the flure.
Each side in war did soon engage,
'Twas woman to woman and man to man,
Shillelah-law was all the rage—
An' a row an' a ruction soon began.

Chorus

Mickey Mulvaney raised his head
When a gallon of whiskey flew at him.
It missed him—and hopping on the bed,
The liquor scattered over Tim!
Bedad he revives! See how he rises!
An' Timothy, jumping from the bed
Cried, while he lathered around like blazes,
'In the name of the devil! D'ye think I'm dead'.

Chorus

North Twin Lakes   TRADITIONAL

There was a cook in a camp did dwell,
He had a keg o' beer he loved so well;
Finding it to his heart's delight,
He said call in all boys tonight.
To me we wack fi diddle aye gee-o,
To me we wack fi diddle aye gee-o.

It was proposed by every man
To play for mitts out of the van.
Everything was going fair,
Until they shouted for more beer,
To me we wack fi diddle aye gee-o,
To me we wack fi diddle aye gee-o.

Ten o'clock came to an end;
The mitts were won by the second hand;
He says now boys if you don't care,
We'll have another round o' beer,
To me we wack fi diddle aye gee-o,
To me we wack fi diddle aye gee-o.

We left the bunkhouse feeling fine,
He says now boys we'll make her shine
If we can start Jim Jesso's tongue,
We'll put the bunkhouse on the bum,
To me we wack fi diddle aye gee-o,
To me we wack fi diddle aye gee-o.

Ned Bursey from his bunk arose,
He said, 'John Bingo stole my clothes'.
John Bingo said it wasn't right
To blow the roast on him tonight,
To me we wack fi diddle aye gee-o,
To me we wack fi diddle aye gee-o.

Out in the middle of the row,
Across the alley our skipper did plow;
And as he entered the bunkhouse door,
He said now boys what caused this roar,
To me we wack fi diddle aye gee-o,
To me we wack fi diddle aye gee-o.

Jim Bingo said he didn't care,
He wouldn't get fired for drinkin' beer;
Come all young men a warning take,
No more beer on the North Twin Lake,
To me we wack fi diddle aye gee-o,
To me we wack fi diddle aye gee-o.

The Kelligrews Soiree

JOHNNY BURKE

You may talk of Clara Nolan's ball
Or anything you choose,
But it couldn't hold a snuff-box
To the spree at Kelligrews.
If you want your eyeballs straightened
Just come out next week with me
And you'll have to wear your glasses
At the Kelligrews Soiree.

Chorus
There was birch rine, tar twine,
Cherry wine and turpentine,
Jowls and cavalances, ginger beer and tea,
Pig's feet, cat's meat, dumplings boiled in a sheet,
Dandelion and crackies' teeth
At the Kelligrews Soiree.

Oh, I borrowed Cluney's beaver,
As I squared my yards to sail;
And a swallow-tail from Hogan
That was foxy on the tail;
Billy Cuddahie's old working pants
And Patsy Nolan's shoes,
And an old white vest from Fogarty
To sport at Kelligrews.

Chorus

There was Dan Milley, Joe Lilly,
Tantan and Mrs. Tilley,
Dancing like a little filly;
'Twould raise your heart to see.
Jim Brine, Din Ryan, Flipper Smith and Caroline;
I tell you boys, we had a time
At the Kelligrews Soiree.

Oh, when I arrived at Betsey Snooks'
That night at half past eight,
The place was blocked with carriages
Stood waiting at the gate.
With Cluney's funnel on my pate.
The first words Betsey said:
'Here comes a local preacher
With the pulpit on his head'.

Chorus

There was Bill Mews, Dan Hughes,
Wilson, Taft, and Teddy Roose,
While Bryant he sat in the blues
And looking hard at me;
Jim Fling, Tom King,
And Johnson, champion of the ring,
And all the boxers I could bring,
At the Kelligrews Soiree.

The Saritoga Lancers first,
Miss Betsey kindly said;
Sure I danced with Nancy Cronan
And her Grannie on the 'Head';
And Hogan danced with Betsey.
Oh, you should have seen his shoes,
As he lashed old muskets from the rack
That night at Kelligrews.

Chorus

There was boiled guineas, cold guineas,
Bullocks' heads and picaninies
And everything to catch the pennies,
You'd break your sides to see;
Boiled duff, cold duff, apple jam was in a cuff;
I tell you, boys, we had enough
At the Kelligrews Soiree.

Crooked Flavin struck the fiddler
And a hand I then took in;
You should see George Cluney's beaver,
And it flattened to the rim!
And Hogan's coat was like a vest—
The tails were gone you see.
Oh, says I 'the devil haul ye
And your Kelligrews Soiree'.

Betsy Brennan's Blue Hen JOHNNY BURKE

From the widow McKenny
I bought for a penny,
   To lay a few eggs when the berries are ripe;
But some dirty crawler
From the hen house did haul her
   My beautiful little blue hen did swipe.

May his whiskers turn green
When he eats a crubeen,
   And may pork fat and beans nearly make him insane;
May two dogs and a crackie
Eat all his tobaccy,
   The villain who stole my little Blue Hen.

Oh, this hen she had dozens
Of nephews and cousins.
   The world round I would roam for her sake;
But some wicked savage
To grease his white cabbage
   Walked off with my hen and my beautiful drake.

May her stockings fall down
When she goes out of town;
   May the hair on her crown she can't bob it and then;
May the girls from the Nor'ard,
Stick pins in her forehead,
   The villain who lifted my little Blue Hen.

I bought from Port Saunders
That hen and two ganders
   But some dirty clown from my hen house did steal;
My beautiful chicken
I would have for picken'
   On Christmas Day for to have a fine meal.

May the ravenous baste
Burst her blouse at the waist
   May she not get a taste of a dumplin' or cake;
May a man from Freshwater
Go back on her daughter,
   That lifted my hen and my beautiful drake.

I would search the seas over
From Boston to Dover
   To find out the rover and wouldn't stop then;
I would walk to Trepassey
To collar the lassie
   Who pilfered my dear little beautiful hen.

May the measles and gout
When he chance to go out
   On his double chain mouth, shove him down in the Pen;
By the curse of Belleoram
May he never stop roar'n
   The villain who lifted my little Blue Hen.

May his pipe never smoke;
May his tea pot be broke,
   And to add to the joke, may his kettle not boil:
May he burst on cauld tay
When he drinks any day
   And his ton of fox wishers may soon go to oil.

May his clothes be in rags
And his trousers bread bags
   May he stagger from jags if he goes round the lake;
And may he have bunions
As big as small onions
   The scoundrel who lifted my beautiful drake.

Chrissey's Dick   TRADITIONAL

O Chrissey went up to Aunt Margaret's to get a loan of her dick.
Says Mary Ann to Christopher: 'Be sure and do it quick!'
Says Mary Ann to Christopher: 'Be sure now don't you stop,
For you got plenty of bait today and you got to bait your pots'.

Chrissey went up to Aunt Margaret's and brought the dick down home:
'O isn't he a lovely bird, he's got a lovely comb.
Go in the house John Chesley and get 'en a piece of bread—
O isn't he a lovely bird, he's got the cutest head'.

The hens and chicks and all of them were feeded for the night,
When Chris got up in the morning, the dick he wasn't in sight;
Chrissey he jumped out of bed and stepped on Mary Ann's toes—
Says Mary Ann to Christopher: 'I thought I heard 'en crow!'

'It rained so very hard last night, why didn't you bar 'en in?
For going through the woods today, you'll get wet right through the skin'.
'Wet or dry', says Mary Ann, 'the dick you'll have to find—
Go on up to Aunt Margaret's, don't stop to look behind'.

Chrissey went up to Aunt Margaret's, the dick he wasn't there,
He felt so faint and frightened that he fell down on a chair;
He started off for home again not feeling very stout,
He fell down in a mud-hole and the mud ran in his mouth.

Chrissey jumped out of his breeches and tumbled to the door.
Says Mary Ann to Christopher: 'The dick is gone for sure.
Put on your clothes', says Mary Ann, 'and go and look for him,
For you'll get nothing to eat today unless you bring 'en in'.

He started off for Hay Cove, the dicky for to find,
But when he got about half ways over he heard 'en cry behind;
He looked around there he was not looking very warm—
He took the dick all by the tail and tucked 'en under his arm.

Says Mary Ann to Christopher: 'I'm glad you got 'en back,
For if we lost Aunt Margaret's dick, we'd have to pay a whack.
I'm gonna get some hens meself and raise our little chicks,
Then we won't have to bother Aunt Margaret for her dick!'

Rubber Boots   BAXTER WAREHAM

I'm a hardy old sailor from Newfoundland's shore.
I've fished for me livin' on the wild Labrador.
Now the fishin's all over, me work is all done,
And I'm goin' out tonight with me rubber boots on.

So I ate up me supper and I shaved off me beard,
For courtin' indeed I was highly prepared.
With the day's work all over and the night comin' on
I remember that night with me rubber boots on.

I knocked on her door and me knock it was low,
And out of her slumber my knock she did know.
She came to the door and said 'Is that you, Tom?'
'It is, love', said I, 'with me rubber boots on'.

She opened the door and invited me in,
And into her bedroom she invited me in.
She jumped on the bed with the blankets rolled on
And I hopped in beside her with me rubber boots on.

Well, daylight next mornin' with the sun in the sky,
I turned to me true love to say goodbye.
She said 'Don't you leave me, don't you know you done wrong,
For you slept here all night with your rubber boots on?'

I turned to me true love with a wink and a smile.
I said 'Nothing could happen in such a short while.
Whatever I did, love, I did it for fun'.
And I hopped out of bed with me rubber boots on.

It being nine months later I was summoned to court.
Ten shillings a week I was fined for me sport.
Ten shillings a week from a fisherman's son.
I regretted that night with me rubber boots on.

Ah, but now I'm back fishin', I'm happy for sure.
I'll make them ten shillings on the wild Labrador,
And when he gets bigger I'll take 'long me son,
And he'll catch those codfish with his rubber boots on.

The Night Before Larry Was Stretched

J. P. CURRAN

The night before Larry was stretched,
The boys they all paid him a visit,
  A bit in their sacks too they fetched,
They sweated their duds till they riz it;
  For Larry was always the lad
When a friend was condemned to the squeezer
  But he'd fence all the togs that he had,
To help a poor friend to the sneezer,
  And moisten his gob 'fore he died.

  'I'm sorry now Larry', says I,
'To see you in this situation;
  'Pon my conscience, my lad, I don't lie,
I'd rather it had been my own station'.
  'Och hone! 'tis all over', says he,
'For the neckcloth I'm forced to put on,
  And by this time to-morrow you'll see,
Your Larry will be dead as mutton,
  Because why, my dear, my courage was good.

  The boys they came crowding in fast,
They drew all their stools around about him;
  Six glims round his trap-case were placed,
He could not be well waked without them;
  I axed if he were fit for to die,
Without having duly repented?
  Says Larry, 'that's all in my eye.
It's only what gownsmen invented,
  To get a fat bit for themselves'.

The cards being called for, they played
Till Larry found one of them cheated,
   He made a smart stroke for the head,
(The boy being easily heated,)
   'Oh! By the holy, you thief,
I'll scuttle your nob with my daddle,
   You cheat me because I'm in grief,
But soon I'll demolish your noddle,
   And leave you your claret to drink'.

Then in came the priest with his book,
He spoke him so smooth and so civil,
   Larry tipped him a Kilmainham look,
And pitched his big wig to the devil.
   Then stooping a little his head,
To get a sweet drop of the bottle,
   And pitiful sighing, he said,
'Oh, the hemp will be soon round my throttle
   And choke my poor windpipe to death'.

So moving these last words he spoke,
We all vented our tears in a shower;
   For my part, I thought my heart broke,
To see him cut down like a flower.
   On his travels we watched him next day,
Oh the hangman I thought I could kill him,
   Nor one word poor Larry did say,
Nor changed till he came to King William.
   Then my dear his colour turned white.

When he came to the nubbling chit,
He was tucked up so nate and so pretty
   The rumbler jogged off from his feet,
And he died with his face to the city;
   He kicked too—but that was all pride,
For soon you might see 'twas all over,
   Soon after the noose was untied,
And at dark we waked him in clover,
   And sent him to take a ground sweat.

Squid-jiggin' Ground
ARTHUR SCAMMELL

Oh! this is the place where the fishermen gather,
   With oilskins and boots and Cape Anns battened down,
All sizes of figures with squid lines and jiggers,
    They congregate here on the squid jiggin' ground.

Some are workin' their jiggers while others are yarnin',
   There's some standin' up and some more lyin' down,
While all kinds of fun, jokes and tricks are begun
    As they wait for the squid on the squid-jiggin' ground.

There's men from the Harbour and men from the Tickle,
   In all kinds of motor boats, green, gray and brown;
There's a red-headed Tory out here in a dory,
    A runnin' down Squires on the squid-jiggin' ground.

There's men of all ages and boys in the bargain,
   There's old Billy Chafe and there's young Raymond Brown;
Right yonder is 'Bobby' and with him is 'Nobby',
    They're a-chawin' hard tack on the squid-jiggin' ground.

The man with the whiskers is old Jacob Steele;
   He's gettin' well up but he's still pretty sound;
While Uncle Bob Hawkins wears three pairs of stockin's
    Whenever he's out on the squid-jiggin' ground.

God bless my sou'wester there's Skipper John Chaffey.
   He's the best man at squid-jiggin' here, I'll be bound.
Hello! What's the row? Why, he's jiggin' one now—
    The very first squid on the squid-jiggin' ground.

Holy smoke! What a bussel; all hands are excited.
It's a wonder to me that nobody is drowned.
There's a bussel, confusion, a wonderful hussel;
   They're all jiggin' squid on the squid-jiggin' ground.

There's poor Uncle Billy, his whiskers are spattered
   With spots of the squid juice that's flyin' around.
One poor little boy got it right in the eye
   But they don't care a hang on the squid-jiggin' ground.

Says Bobby: 'The squid are on top of the water
   I just got me jigger about one fathom down'—
When a squid in the boat squirted right down his throat
   And he's swearin' like mad on the squid-jiggin' ground.

Now if you ever feel inclined to go squiddin'
   Leave your white shirt and collars behind in the town,
And if you get cranky without a silk hanky
   You'd better steer clear of the squid-jiggin' ground.

The Pope

A Bacchanalian Song TRADITIONAL

The Pope he leads a happy life,
No care has he nor wedded strife,
He drinks the best of Rhenish wine,
I would the Pope's gay lot were mine.
   He drinks the best of Rhenish wine,
   I would the Pope's gay lot were mine.

Yet all's not pleasure in his life,
He has no maid or wedded wife,
No child has he to bless his hope,
I would not wish to be the Pope.
   No child has he to bless his hope.
   I would not wish to be the Pope.

The Sultan better pleases me,
He lives a life of jollity,
He has wives as many as he will,
I would the Sultan's throne then fill.
   He has wives as many as he will,
   I would the Sultan's throne then fill.

Yet even he's a wretched man,
He must obey the Alcoran,
He dare not touch one drop of wine,
I would not change his lot for mine.
   He dare not touch one drop of wine.
   I would not change his lot for mine.

Then here I'll take my lowly stand,
And live in German father-land,
I'll kiss my maiden fair and fine,
And drink the best of Rhenish wine.
   I'll kiss my maiden fair and fine,
   And drink the best of Rhenish wine.

And when my maiden kisses me,
I'll fancy I the Sultan be,
And when my cheering glass I tope,
I'll fancy then I am the Pope.
   And when my cheering glass I tope,
   I fancy then I am the Pope.

The Carrick Nine   MICHAEL COADY

I

One pleasant morning in this new millennium
   The summer sun was beaming down,
As a hardy skipper and his companions
   Cast off and sailed out from Carrick town.
They embarked with no premeditation
   Or contemplation of piracy,
They were well-provisioned against dehydration,
   With no inclination to mutiny.

II

The tide was full and their craft was shipshape
   And decked out bravely in blue and white,
They little thought as they swung downriver
   That this June day wouldn't turn out right.
While other men were slaves to duty
   And tied down to production-lines,
They had the freedom of the river
   This Monday morning of their lives.

III

'Farewell', they cried, 'to Carrick Castle,
   The hill, the bridges and the town,
And *au revoir* to our wives and lovers,
   Expect us after the sun goes down.
The day is opening out before us,
   Who knows what's waiting around the bend?
The sky is blue and the birds are singing,
   Long enough we'll all be dead!'

IV

The lower Suir is a noble river,
　Broad and deep in each bend and reach.
They'd a skipper skilled in navigating
　Cross-currents where three counties meet.
They struck up shanties like 'Carrickfergus',
　'A Hard Day's Night' and 'Nancy Spain',
Helped on by copious draughts of cider
　That served to keep their spirits raised.

V

By Fiddown Bridge they were in fine fettle
　And there decided to sail on,
They throttled up for their destination—
　The Déise city of Waterford.
The Latin motto of that metropolis
　Means the city that was never sacked—
The Carrick Nine were set to challenge
　Its reputation as *urbs intact.*

VI

On they went by Rockett's Castle
　Then swung north in the Long Reach
Where they say a Viking longship
　Lies buried fifteen fathoms deep;
Past Grannagh Castle sacked by Cromwell
　Then east by the rock of Bilberry
Until standing high on the horizon
　Were Gracedieu and Mount Misery.

VII

When they reached the city all hands were famished
   With liquid rations almost drained,
Then their lookout spied upon the quayside
   A large consignment of kegs of ale.
The Nine were not men prone to plunder,
   They were no bloodthirsty privateers,
But that apparition was a fierce temptation
   To mortal men with a lust for beer.

VIII

They'd a keg on board and another hoisted
   When suddenly all hell broke loose;
That yard was under intense surveillance
   And a Garda squad car sped into view.
'Cast off me hearties!' the skipper shouted,
   'We'll quench our thirst on Tinhalla Quay,
Where our forefathers often landed salmon
   And brewed up gallons of strong black tea!'

IX

The Carrick Nine ploughed off upriver
   Thinking that they were safe afloat,
But the men in blue were out to get them—
   They straight-away commandeered a boat.
So here beginning was a chase most thrilling
   That would continue for several hours,
This naval tussle would test the muscle
   And sailing skills of the civil powers.

X

The pursuing Gardaí grew alarmed as
   The Carrick craft seemed to pull ahead;
They radioed for reinforcements
   And declared a high security alert.
They suspected big-time operators
   Dealing in cargoes of contraband—
These fleeing raiders must be captured
   And brought to justice upon the land.

XI

The Harbour Board was soon alerted
   And the South-East Fishery patrol,
An Slua Muirí and a helicopter
   Went on standby in Waterford.
Police were summoned from around the region
   With urgent orders to waste no time;
Thirty lawmen came swiftly speeding
   To meet the threat of the Carrick Nine.

XII

The wildlife never knew such action
   In the calm expanse of that waterway;
Swans and salmon were in a panic
   And trout were traumatized that day.
Boats came racing and making waves as
   Angry expletives were employed—
Words deleterious and names nefarious
   Flew fast and furious across the tide.

XIII

As the chase proceeded it became apparent
   There was no escape for the Carrick craft,
For it was trapped in a pincer movement
   With the Law advancing both fore and aft.
Boathooks were brandished at close quarters
   There were some dangerous attempts to ram,
One Garda tumbled into the river
   But happily came to no harm.

XIV

Pollrone's the place where the nine were captured
   It'll be remembered forevermore;
Statements were taken and charges drafted—
   This escapade would end up in court.
The Carrick Nine made their way homeward,
   Sick, sore and sorry to face their wives;
Their trip had ended in disaster
   But luckily with no loss of lives.

XV

When it came to court the lawyers wrangled
   About jurisdiction and piracy,
The saline content of river water
   And whether 'High Seas' embraced estuary.
Statutes were dusted dating back to
   The Great Armada and Francis Drake,
But the accused men pleaded the affair was simply
   A harmless spree and a big mistake.

XVI

In his summing up the judge was scathing
   About the waste of Garda time
And all the manpower that had been mustered
   To apprehend the Carrick Nine.
He imposed fines and applied probation,
   The sentences were rather light,
Since the only losses were a keg of Smithwick's
   And a sergeant's cap that sank out of sight.

XVII

Outside the court there was pandemonium
   And loud commotion as the men walked free.
The media went into feeding frenzy
   With microphones and photography.
There were mobiles trilling and reporters milling
   To grab some in-depth interviews;
This had the makings of a movie
   Or a Prime Time special after the News.

XVIII

The names of all could be related
   But I'll just mention their captain, Ben,
He made the papers and raised the flag for
   A famous family of fishermen.
Carrick people know their boatmen
   Are not found wanting when there's need,
They've often come to people's rescue
   In times of river emergency.

XIX

Fair play also for those who're sworn
   To be our guardians of the peace,
None of us could walk in safety
   Without their presence on our streets.
So spare a thought for those policemen
   Who were not trained for naval tasks,
And ne'er before set foot on water
   To apprehend a pirate craft.

XX

Now to conclude and close my story
   Concerning history and river lore,
God's blessing on our intrepid mariners
   Who boldly went where none did before.
Their dash and daring was quite amazing
   As delineated in these lines,
Sing on posterity to ensure longevity
   For the name and fame of the Carrick Nine.

5

I Slept in Duck-Down / Till Noontime Came

As: **Caoineadh Airt Uí Laoghaire** EIBHLÍN DUBH NÍ CHONAILL

Mo ghrá go daingean tu!
Lá dá bhfaca thu
ag ceann tí an mhargaidh,
thug mo shúil aire dhuit,
thug mo chroí taitneamh duit,
d'éalaíos óm charaid leat
i bhfad ó bhaile leat.

Is domhsa nárbh aithreach:
Chuiris parlús á ghealadh dhom,
rúmanna á mbreacadh dhom,
bácús á dheargadh dhom,
brící á gceapadh dhom,

rósta ar bhearaibh dom,
mairt á leagadh dhom;
codladh i gclúmh lachan dom
go dtíodh an t-eadartha
nó thairis dá dtaitneadh liom.

Mo chara go daingean tu!
is cuimhin lem aigne
an lá breá earraigh úd,
gur bhreá thíodh hata dhuit
faoi bhanda óir tarraingthe;
claíomh cinn airgid,
lámh dheas chalma,
rompsáil bhagarthach—
fír-chritheagla
ar námhaid chealgach—
tú i gcóir chun falaracht
is each caol ceannann fút.
D'umhlaídís Sasanaigh
síos go talamh duit,
is ní ar mhaithe leat
ach le haon-chorp eagla,
cé gur leo a cailleadh tu,
a mhuirnín mh'anama . . . .

Mo chara thu go daingean!
is nuair thiocfaidh chugham abhaile
Conchúr beag an cheana
is Fear Ó Laoghaire, an leanbh,
fiafróid díom go tapaidh
cár fhágas féin a n-athair.
'Neosad dóibh faoi mhairg
gur fhágas i gCill na Martar.
Glaofaid siad ar a n-athair,
is ní bheidh sé acu le freagairt . . . .

Mo chara thu go daingean!
is níor chreideas riamh dod mharbh
gur tháinig chugham do chapall
is a srianta léi go talamh,
is fuil do chroí ar a leacain
siar go t'iallait ghreanta
mar a mbítheá id shuí 's id sheasamh.
Thugas léim go tairsigh,
an dara léim go geata,
an tríú léim ar do chapall.

Do bhuaileas go luath mo bhasa
is do bhaineas as na reathaibh
chomh maith is bhí sé agam,
go bhfuaras romham tu marbh
cois toirín ísil aitinn,
gan Pápa gan easpag,
gan cléireach gan sagart
do léifeadh ort an tsailm,
ach seanbhean chríonna chaite
do leath ort binn dá fallaing—
do chuid fola leat 'na sraithibh;
is níor fhanas le hí ghlanadh
ach í ól suas lem basaibh.

Mo ghrá thu go daingean!
is éirigh suas id sheasamh
is tar liom féin abhaile,
go gcuirfeam mairt á leagadh,
go nglaofam ar chóisir fhairsing,
go mbeidh againn ceol á spreagadh,
go gcóireod duitse leaba
faoi bhairlíní geala,
faoi chuilteanna breátha breaca,
a bhainfidh asat allas
in ionad an fhuachta a ghlacais.

. . . .

Mo chara thu is mo thaitneamh!
Nuair ghabhais amach an geata
d'fhillis ar ais go tapaidh,
do phógais do dhís leanbh,
do phógais mise ar bharra baise.
Dúraís, 'A Eibhlín, éirigh id sheasamh
agus cuir do ghnó chun taisce
go luaimneach is go tapaidh.
Táimse ag fágáil an bhaile,
is ní móide go deo go gcasfainn'.
Níor dheineas dá chaint ach magadh,
mar bhíodh á rá liom go minic cheana.

Mo chara thu is mo chuid!
A mharcaigh an chlaímh ghil,
éirigh suas anois,
cuir ort do chulaith
éadaigh uasail ghlain,
cuir ort do bhéabhar dubh,
tarraing do lámhainní umat.
Siúd í in airde t'fhuip;
sin í do láir amuigh.
Buail-se an bóthar caol úd soir
mar a maolóidh romhat na toir,
mar a gcaolóidh romhat an sruth,
mar a n-umhlóidh romhat mná is fir,
má tá a mbéasa féin acu—
's is baolach liomsa ná fuil anois . . . .

Mo ghrá thu is mo chumann!
's ní hé a bhfuair bás dem chine,
ná bás mo thriúr clainne;
ná Dónall Mór Ó Conaill,
ná Conall a bháigh an tuile,
ná bean na sé mblian 's fiche
do chuaigh anonn thar uisce
'déanamh cairdeasaí le rithe—
ní hiad go léir atá agam dá ngairm,
ach Art a bhaint aréir dá bhonnaibh

ar inse Charraig an Ime!—
marcach na lárach doinne
atá agam féin anso go singil—
gan éinne beo 'na ghoire
ach mná beaga dubha an mhuilinn,
is mar bharr ar mo mhíle tubaist
gan a súile féin ag sileadh.

Mo chara is mo lao thu!
A Airt Uí Laoghaire
Mhic Conchúir, Mhic Céadaigh,
Mhic Laoisigh Uí Laoghaire,
aniar ón nGaortha
is anoir ón gCaolchnoc,
mar a bhfásaid caora
is cnó buí ar ghéagaibh
is úlla 'na slaodaibh
'na n-am féinig.
Cárbh ionadh le héinne
dá lasadh Uíbh Laoghaire
agus Béal Átha an Ghaorthaigh
is an Gúgán naofa
is ndiaidh mharcaigh na ré-ghlac
a níodh an fiach a thraochadh
ón nGreanaigh ar saothar
nuair stadaidís caol-choin!
Is a mharcaigh na gclaon-rosc—
nó cad d'imigh aréir ort?
Óir do shíleas féinig
ná maródh an saol tu
nuair cheannaíos duit éide.

. . . .

Mo ghrá go daingean tu!
's nuair théitheá sna cathracha
daora, daingeana,
bíodh mná na gceannaithe
ag umhlú go talamh duit,
óir do thuigidís 'na n-aigne
gur bhreá an leath leaba tu,
nó an bhéalóg chapaill tu,
nó an t-athair leanbh tu.

Tá fhios ag Íosa Críost
ná beidh caidhp ar bhaitheas mo chinn,
ná léine chnis lem thaoibh,
ná bróg ar thrácht mo bhoinn,
ná trioscán ar fuaid mo thí,
ná srian leis an láir ndoinn,
ná caithfidh mé le dlí,
's go raghad anonn thar toinn
ag comhrá leis an rí,
's mura gcuirfidh ionam aon tsuim
go dtiocfad ar ais arís
go bodach na fola duibhe
a bhain díom féin mo mhaoin . . . .

Mo ghrá thu agus mo rún!
Tá do stácaí ar a mbonn,
tá do bha buí á gcrú;
is ar mo chroí atá do chumha
ná leigheasfadh Cúige Mumhan
ná Gaibhne Oileáin na bhFionn.
Go dtiocfaidh Art Ó Laoghaire chugham
ní scaipfidh ar mo chumha
atá i lár mo chroí á bhrú,
dúnta suas go dlúth
mar a bheadh glas a bheadh ar thrúnc
's go raghadh an eochair amú.

A mhná so amach ag gol
stadaidh ar bhur gcois
go nglaofaidh Art Mhac Conchúir deoch,
agus tuilleadh thar cheann na mbocht,
sula dtéann isteach don scoil—
ní ag foghlaim léinn ná port,
ach ag iompar cré agus cloch.

From: The Lament for Art Ó Laoghaire EIBHLÍN DUBH NÍ CHONAILL

My steadfast love!
When I saw you one day
by the market-house gable
my eye gave a look
my heart shone out
I fled with you far
from friends and home.

And never was sorry:
you had parlours painted
rooms decked out
the oven reddened
and loaves made up
roasts on spits
and cattle slaughtered;
I slept in duck-down
till noontime came
or later if I liked.

My steadfast friend!
It comes to my mind
that fine Spring day
how well your hat looked
with the drawn gold band,
the sword silver-hilted,
your fine brave hand
and menacing prance,
and the fearful tremble
of treacherous enemies.
You were set to ride
your slim white-faced steed
and Saxons saluted
down to the ground,

not from good will
but by dint of fear
—though you died at their hands,
my soul's beloved . . . .

My steadfast friend!
And when they come home,
our little pet Conchúr
and baby Fear Ó Laoghaire,
they will ask at once
where I left their father.
I will tell them in woe
he is left in Cill na Martar,
and they'll call for their father
and get no answer . . . .

My steadfast friend!
I didn't credit your death
till your horse came home
and her reins on the ground,
your heart's blood on her back
to the polished saddle
where you sat—where you stood . . . .
I gave a leap to the door,
a second leap to the gate
and a third on your horse.

I clapped my hands quickly
and started mad running
as hard as I could,
to find you there dead
by a low furze-bush
with no Pope or bishop
or clergy or priest
to read a psalm over you
but a spent old woman
who spread her cloak corner
where your blood streamed from you,
and I didn't stop to clean it
but drank it from my palms.

My steadfast love!
Arise, stand up
and come with myself
and I'll have cattle slaughtered
and call fine company
and hurry up the music
and make you up a bed
with bright sheets upon it
and fine speckled quilts
to bring you out in a sweat
where the cold has caught you.

. . . .

My friend and beloved!
When you left through the gate
you came in again quickly,
you kissed both your children,
kissed the tips of my fingers.
You said: 'Eibhlín, stand up
and finish with your work
lively and swiftly:
I am leaving our home
and may never return'.
I made nothing of his talk
for he spoke often so.

My friend and my share!
O bright-sworded rider
rise up now,
put on your immaculate
fine suit of clothes,
put on your black beaver
and pull on your gloves.
There above is your whip
and your mare is outside.
Take the narrow road Eastward

where the bushes bend before you
and the stream will narrow for you
and men and women will bow
if they have their proper manners
—as I doubt they have at present . . . .

My love, and my beloved!
Not my people who have died
—not my three dead children
nor big Dónall Ó Conaill
nor Conall drowned on the sea
nor the girl of twenty six
who went across the ocean
alliancing with kings
—not all these do I summon
but Art, reaped from his feet last night
on the inch of Carriginima.
The brown mare's rider
deserted here beside me,
no living being near him
but the little black mill-women
—and to top my thousand troubles
their eyes not even streaming.

My friend and my calf!
O Art Ó Laoghaire
son of Conchúr son of Céadach
son of Laoiseach Ó Laoghaire:
West from the Gaortha
and East from the Caolchnoc
where the berries grow,
yellow nuts on the branches
and masses of apples
in their proper season
—need anyone wonder
if Uíbh Laoghaire were alight
and Béal Átha an Ghaorthaigh
and Gúgán the holy
for the fine-handed rider

who used tire out the hunt
as they panted from Greanach
and the slim hounds gave up?
Alluring-eyed rider,
o what ailed you last night?
For I thought myself
when I bought your uniform
the world couldn't kill you!

. . . .

My steadfast love!
When you walked through the servile
strong-built towns,
the merchants' wives
would salute to the ground
knowing well in their hearts
a fine bed-mate you were
a great front-rider
and father of children.

Jesus Christ well knows
there's no cap upon my skull
nor shift next to my body
nor shoe upon my foot-sole
nor furniture in my house
nor reins on the brown mare
but I'll spend it on the law;
that I'll go across the ocean
to argue with the King,
and if he won't pay attention
that I'll come back again
to the black-blooded savage
that took my treasure.

My love and my beloved!
Your corn-stacks are standing,
your yellow cows milking.
Your grief upon my heart
all Munster couldn't cure,
nor the smiths of Oileán na bhFionn.
Till Art Ó Laoghaire comes
my grief will not disperse
but cram my heart's core,
shut firmly in
like a trunk locked up
when the key is lost.

Women there weeping,
stay there where you are,
till Art Mac Conchúir summons drink
with some extra for the poor
—ere he enter that school
not for study or for music
but to bear clay and stones.

translated by Thomas Kinsella

As: **Cúirt an Mheán Oíche**

BRIAN MERRIMAN

I

Siúlann an file amach dó féin maidin shamhraidh agus castar spéirbhean air . . .

Ba ghnáth mé ag siúl le ciumhais na habhann
ar bháinseach úr 's an drúcht go trom,
in aice na gcoillte, i gcoim an tslé',
gan mhairg, gan mhoill, ar shoilse an lae.
Do ghealadh mo chroí nuair chínn Loch Gréine,
an talamh, 's an tír, is íor na spéire;
taitneamhach aoibhinn suíomh na sléibhte
ag bagairt a gcinn thar dhroim a chéile.

Do ghealfadh an croí bheadh críon le cianta,
caite gan bhrí, nó líonta de phianta,
an séithleach searbh gan sealbh gan saibhreas
d'fhéachfadh tamall thar bharra na gcoillte
ar lachain 'na scuainte ar chuan gan cheo
's an eala ar a bhfuaid 's í ag gluaiseacht leo;
na héisc le meidhir ag éirí in airde,
péirse im radharc go taibhseach tarrbhreac,
dath an locha agus gorm na dtonn
ag teacht go tolgach torannach trom.
Bhíodh éanlaith i gcrainn go meidhreach mómhar
is léimneach eilte i gcoillte im chóngar,
géimreach adhairce is radharc ar shlóite,
tréanrith gadhar is Reynard rómpu.

Ar maidin inné bhí an spéir gan cheo,
bhí Cancer ón ngréin 'na caorthaibh teo,
is í gofa chun saothair t'réis na hoíche,
is obair an lae sin raeimpi sínte.
Bhí duilliúr craobh ar ghéaga im thimpeall,
fiorthann is féar go slaodach taoibh liom,
glasra fáis is blátha is luibheanna,
scaipfeadh chun fáin dá chráiteacht smaointe.
Bhí mé cortha is an codladh am thraochadh,
shín mé thoram ar cothrom sa bhféar glas
in aice na gcrann, i dteannta trínse,
taca lem cheann, is mo hanlaí sínte.
Ar cheangal mo shúl go dlúth le chéile
greamaithe dúnta i ndú-ghlas néallta,
is m'aghaidh agam foilithe ó chuilibh go sásta
i dtaibhreamh d'fhuiling mé an chuilithe chráite
do chorraigh, do lom, do pholl go hae me,
im chodladh go trom, gan mheabhair gan éirim . . . .

II

Labhraíonn bean óg le maithe na cúirte i dtaobh a cuid trioblóidí:
í ag lorg céile i dtír nach bhfuil na fir óga ag pósadh.

'Is dearfa bhím am shíorthaspánadh
ar mhachaire mhín gach fíoriomána,
ag rínce, báire, rás is radaireacht,
tínte cnámh is ráfla is ragairne,
aonach, margadh is Aifreann Domhnaigh
ag éileamh breathnaithe, ag amharc 's ag togha fir.
Chaitheas mo chiall le fiach gan éifeacht,
dhalladar riamh mé, is d'iadar m'ae ionnam,
t'réis mo chumainn, mo thurraing 's mo ghrá dhóibh,
t'réis ar fhulaing mé d'iomada cránais,
t'réis ar chaitheas le caitheamh na scálaí,
béithe balbha, is cailleacha cártaí.

Níl cleas dá mbéidir léamh ná trácht air
le teacht na ré nó t'réis bheith lán di,
um Inid, um Shamhain, ná ar shiúl na bliana
ná tuigim gur leamhas bheith ag súil le ciall as!
Níorbh áil liom codladh go socair aon uair díobh
gan lán mo stoca de thorthaibh fém chluasa,
is deimhin nárbh obair liom troscadh le cráifeacht,
is greim ná blogam ní shlogainn trí trátha;
in aghaidh na srotha do thomainn mo léine
ag súil trím chodladh le cogar óm chéile;
is minic do chuaigh mé ag scuabadh ón stáca,
m'ingne is gruaig fán luaithghríos d'fhágainn,
chuirinn an tsúist fá chúl na gaibhle,
chuirinn an ramhan go ciúin fán adhart chugham,
chuirinn mo choigeall i gcillín na hátha,
chuirinn mo cheirtlín i dtiníl Rághnaill,
chuirinn an ros ar chorp na sráide,
chuirinn sa tsop fúm tor gabáiste.
Níl cleas acu súd dá ndúras láithreach
ná hagrainn cúnamh an Deamhain 's a bhráithre!
'S é fáth mo scéil go léir a bhrí dhuit
—táim gan chéile t'réis mo dhíchill,
fáth mo sheanchais fhada, mo phian-chreach!
Táim in achrann daingean na mblianta,
ag tarraing go tréan ar laethaibh liatha,
is eagal liom éag gan éinne' om iarraidh . . . .'

. . . .

From: The Midnight Court

BRIAN MERRIMAN

I

The poet walks out on a summer's morning, and encounters a vision woman....

By the brink of the river I'd often walk,
on a meadow fresh, in the heavy dew,
along the woods, in the mountain's heart,
happy and brisk in the brightening dawn.
My heart would lighten to see Loch Gréine,
the land, the view, the sky horizon,
the sweet and delightful set of the mountains
looming their heads up over each other.

It would brighten a heart worn out with time,
or spent, or faint, or filled with pain
—or the withered, the sour, without wealth or means—
to gaze for a while across the woods
at the shoals of ducks on the cloudless bay
and a swan between them, sailing with them,
at fishes jumping on high for joy,
the flash of a stripe-bellied glittering perch,
the hue of the lake, the blue of the waves
heavy and strong as they rumble in.
There were birds in the trees, content and gay,
a leaping doe in the wood nearby,
sounding horns, a crowd in view,
and Reynard ahead of the galloping hounds.

Yesterday morning the sky was clear.
The Sun was in Cancer, a blazing mass,
just setting to work as the night was ending,
the task for the day stretched out before it.
Foliage branched on the boughs above me,
the grasses close at hand were dense
and verdant growth and flowers and herbs
to drive all careworn thoughts away.
Weary I was, sleep bore me down,
and level I stretched in the verdant grass
not far from the trees, in a handy hollow,
and propped my head and stretched my limbs.
I firmly fastened shut my eyes,
securely fixed and locked in sleep,
my face contentedly covered from flies,
when I suffered in dream a swirling torment
that stripped and racked me and pierced my heart
in a heavy swoon, as I lost my wits . . . .

II

A young woman tells the court of her trouble in finding a husband in a country where the young men refuse to marry.

'I'm certainly always on display
at every field where the game's fought hard,
at dances, hurling, races, courting,
bone-fires, gossip and dissipation,
at fairs and markets and Sunday Mass—
to see and be seen, and choose a man.
But I've wasted my sense in the hopeless hunt;
they deceived me ever and wrung my guts
after my wooing and lapse and love
and all I've suffered of awful anguish,
and all I spent on tossing the cups,
on muttering women, and hags with cards!

There isn't trick you can hear or read of
when the moon is new, or reaches the full,
at Shrovetide, Samhain—the whole year through—
but I've found it silly to seek for sense in it.
I never could settle me down to sleep
without fruit in a sock beneath my ear;
I found it no trouble to fast devoutly
—three vigils I'd swallow no bite or sup;
I'd rinse my shift against the stream
for a whisper in dream from my future spouse;
many a time I have swept the corn-stack,
I've left my nails and my hair in the ash,
I'd place the flail behind the fork
and peacefully under my pillow, a spade;
in the kiln by the ford, I'd place my distaff,
in Raghnall's lime-kiln, my ball of thread,
out in the street, a seed of flax,
and under my bedding a head of cabbage.
There isn't a trick I have just related
but I prayed of the Devil and all his brethren!
But the point and purpose of my tale
is I've done my best and I've still no man;
hence, alas, my long recital!
In the knot of the years I am tangled tight,
I am heading hard for my days of grey
and I fear that I'll die without anyone asking . . . .'

. . . .

translated by Thomas Kinsella

The Dark-eyed Sailor

TRADITIONAL

It's about a maiden was young and fair,
Walked out one evening to take the air;
She met a sailor all on the way,
And she paid attention,
And she paid attention to hear what he did say.

Said Willie: 'Maiden, why roam alone?
The night is coming and the day far gone'.
She said while tears from her eyes did flow:
'It's my dark-eyed sailor—
It's my dark-eyed sailor is the cause of all my woe.

It's six long years since he left this land,
A gold ring he took from off my hand;
Broke it in two, left a part with me,
Whilst the other lies rolling—
Whilst the other lies rolling in the bottom of the sea'.

Said Willie: 'Drive him far from your mind,
A better sailor than him you'll find;
Love turns aside and cold do grow,
Like a winter's morning—
Like a winter's morning when the hills are clad with snow'.

O this did her fond heart enflame.
She said; 'On me you won't play no game;
A man he was, not a rat like you
To advise a maiden—
To advise a maiden to slight her jacket blue.

His tarry trousers I'll never disdain,
But I will always treat him the same;
To drink his health, here's a piece of coin
For that dark-eyed sailor—
For that dark-eyed sailor still claims the heart of mine'.

Then half the ring did young Willie show,
She fell distracted amidst grief and woe.
'You're welcome Willie, I have land and gold
For my dark-eyed sailor—
For my dark-eyed sailor so manly, true, and bold'.

Now in a cottage down by the sea,
They're joined in wedlock and do agree.
So maids be true whilst your love's away,
For a cloudy morning—
For a cloudy morning brings forth a pleasant day!

The Tramway Line

TRADITIONAL

Kind gents list with polite attention
   Pray listen to my song
About the work that's in Belfast
   That's going on so strong
The men are toiling night and day
   To get it done in time
Till the people get a penny trip
   Upon the Tramway Line.

Chorus
Pipe it, twig it, it is a gorgeous show
   Here and there and everywhere
It's through the streets they go.
   Red Roger he's to be a guard
In a box he'll sit behind
   To keep people from falling out
Upon the Tramway Line.

It was on the eighth of August
   That every one does know
Lord Lurgan and Lord Lieutenant
   Went to the Cattle Show
They walked about and indulged themselves
   Till they felt inclined to dine
And they took a bird's-eye view
   Upon the Tramway Line.

Chorus

There is a girl in Belfast
   In Ann Street she does dwell
She wears a hat and a feather
   And cuts a pretty swell
She says she knows Red Roger
   And she will speak in time
That she may get a ticket
   Upon the Tramway Line.

Chorus

Fanny's Harbour Bawn
MARK WALKER

As I roamed out one evening,
In the lovely month of May,
Those verdant hills I rambled
To view the distant bay;
The craft were flocking down the shore,
And pleasant looked the day;
To my surprise a pair I spied
Which caused me to delay.

'Twas then I saw a young man
Embracing fondly
The person of a fair one
That once was loved by me;
My heart with jealous notions
Felt eagerly the wrong,
Which caused this fearful contest
On Fanny's Harbour Bawn.

I there addressed this young man,
And unto him did say,
'Are you from Bonavista
Or are you from the Bay?
I think you are a Northern man,
A Bayman, I presume,
So I pray to be gone all from this Bawn,
Or I'll boot you in your bloom'.

He quickly made an answer,
And this to me did say,
'I'm not from Bonavista,
But I am from the Bay;
I do reside where storms and tide
Have swept down buildings strong,
Here in full glee from T. and C.
To meet you on the Bawn'.

I stood no hesitation,
But struck immediately.
This damsel mild stood like a child,
To witness the affray;
A pain then in my chest he rose
Before 'twas very long,
My person pucked and darling,
Took on Fanny's Harbour Bawn.

He skinned my nose down from my face
As I instantly did rise,
And soon unto my regal brow
He joined a bunch of fives;
He left me there prostrated
Quite lifeless on the Bawn,
And when I came to my senses,
This Bayman he was gone.

Now when you meet with Northern men,
You'll think they're somewhat green
You'll treat them with a scornful look
As unfit to be seen;
You'll scoff them and rebuke them
All with a scolding tongue,
Till you enrage, in a fight engage,
Then from Baymen you will run.

I will not fail to tell the tale,
Nor yet my true love's name,
Her name is Catherine Murphy,
And she dwells in Roger's Lane;
And I'm a youth from Carbonear,
Once loved by her, I know
My curse attend that Northern man
That proved my overthrow.

Now to conclude these painful lines,
From courting I'll refrain,
And the rest of my companions,
I hope they'll do the same,
For in courting there's great jealousy,
And likewise envy strong,
Which caused my claret free to flow
On Fanny's Harbour Bawn.

The Belfast Mountains TRADITIONAL

Being on the banks of Clady, I heard a maid complain,
Setting forth her lamentations down by yon purling stream,
Saying, 'Here I lie confined in the constant bands of love,
All by a British sailor lad that did inconstant prove'.

Chorus
It's O! you Belfast mountains, can you bring me no relief,
Have you got no tongue to flatter with, or to ease me of my grief?
Have you got no tongue to flatter with, or to ease me of my pain?
For it's hard to love an old sweetheart and not be loved again.

She twined her arms around my neck, just as we were going to part,
She twined her arms around my neck, saying 'You're my old sweetheart'.
She twined her arms around my neck, like the branches of yon vine,
Saying, 'Jamie, cruel Jamie, you have broke this heart of mine'.

Chorus

O! may you never prosper, nor may you never thrive,
In any job you take in hand as long as you're alive;
On the very ground whereon you stand may the grass refuse to grow,
For you're the whole occasion of my sad grief and woe.

Chorus

An Chúilfhionn TRADITIONAL

Ceó meala lá seaca, ar choilltibh dubha daraighe
A's grádh gan cheilt atá agam duit a bháin-chnis na
  ngeal-chíoch,
Do chom seang, do bheul tana, a's do chúilín bhí cas mín,
A's a chéad-shearc ná tréig mé, as gur mhéaduigh tu ar m'aicíd.

A's cia chidhfeadh mo ghrádh-sa ar cheart-lár an aonaigh,
'S gur marbhadh na mílte óganach le rósaibh a h-eudain.
A gruaidh mar an g-cocan, 's í budh bhreághtha ar domhan
  sgéimhe
A's gur dóigh le gach spriosán gur ab áilleán dó féin í.

An té chidhfeadh an Chúilfhionn 's í ag siúbhal ar na bántaibh
Ar maidin laé samhraidh 's an drúcht ar a brógaibh.
'S a liacht óganach súil-ghlas bhíos ag tnúth le na pósadh
Acht ní bhfághaidh siad mo rún-sa ar an g-cúntas is dóigh leó.

A Neilidh, mo ghrádh-sa, an dtiocfá liom faoi shléibhtibh.
Ag ól fíona a's bolcáin a's bainne an ghabhair ghlé-gil.
Ceól fada a's imirt do thabharfainn le d' raé dhuit,
A's cead dul a' codladh i mbrollach mo léine.

The Cooleen, or Coolun

TRADITIONAL

A honey mist on a day of frost, in a dark oak wood,
And love for thee in my heart in me, thou bright, white, and
  good;
Thy slender form, soft and warm, thy red lips apart,
Thou hast found me, and hast bound me, and put grief in my
  heart.

In fair-green and market, men mark thee, bright, young, and
  merry.
Though thou hurt them like foes with the rose of thy blush of the
  berry;
Her cheeks are a poppy, her eye it is Cupid's helper,
But each foolish man dreams that its beams for himself are.

Whoe'er saw the Cooleen in a cool dewy meadow
On a morning in summer in sunshine and shadow;
All the young men go wild for her, my childeen, my treasure,
But now let them go mope, they've no hope to possess her.

Let us roam, O my darling, afar through the mountains,
Drink milk of the goat, wine and bulcaun in fountains;
With music and play every day from my lyre,
And leave to come rest on my breast when you tire.

translated by Douglas Hyde

A Sweet Little Song

JAMES N. HEALY

Oh! a tall gangling lad had a boat on the Bandon,
   It's a sweet little song I have here for you now.
And a girl lived near by that he'd put a stray hand on,
   Oh! a sweet little song I have here for you now.

Chorus
'Martin, come on will you court with me, court with me',
Molly goes on with her squeezin' him, teasin' him;
Sandycove Harbour, tarum-te-diddle—
It's a sweet little song I have here for you now.

To the town of Kinsale Martin, sporting, is bound him,
   It's a sweet little song I have here for you now.
Before long he had twenty-two women around him,
   Oh! a sweet little song I have here for you now.

Chorus
'Martin, come on will you court with me, court with me'.
   Hear them go on with their squeezin' him, teasin' him;
Sandycove Harbour, tarum-te-diddle—
   It's a sweet little song I have here for you now.

But Molly arrived in a boat with her mother,
   It's a sweet little song I have here for you now.
And Martin was hooked, just like many another,
   Oh! a sweet little song I have here for you now.

Chorus
'Martin, come on will you court with me, court with me'.
Molly goes on, with her squeezin' him, teasin' him;
Sandycove Harbour, tarum-te-diddle—
It's a sweet little song I have here for you now.

If that tall gangling fellow from Bandon was able
  There's a sweet little song that he'd sing for you now.
But besides the two women there's the fill of a cradle,
  Oh! a sweet little song I have here for you now.

Chorus
'Martin, come on will you court with me, court with me'.
Molly has stopped all that squeezin' him, teasin' him;
Sandycove Harbour, tarum-te-diddle—
But the divil a sight does it see of him now.

Mo bhrón ar an bhfarraige

TRADITIONAL

Mo bhrón ar an bhfarraige,
is í atá mór,
's í ag gabháil idir mé
is mo mhíle stór.

Do fágadh sa mbaile mé
ag déanamh bróin,
gan aon tsúil thar sáile liom
choíche ná go deo.

Mo léan nach bhfuil mise
is mo mhuirnín bán
i gCúige Laighean
nó i gContae an Chláir.

Mo bhrón nach bhfuil mise
is mo mhíle grá
ar bord loinge
ag triall, go Meiriceá.

Leaba luachra
a bhí fúm aréir,
is chaith mé amach í
le teas an lae.

Tháinig mo ghrá-sa
le mo thaobh,
guala ar ghualainn
agus béal ar bhéal.

My grief on the ocean

TRADITIONAL

My grief on the ocean
it is surely wide
stretched between me
and my dearest love.

I am left behind
to make lament
—not expected for ever
beyond the sea.

My sorrow I'm not
with my fond fair man
in the province of Munster
or County Clare.

My grief I am not
with my dearest love
on board of a ship
for America bound.

On a bed of rushes
I lay last night,
and I shook it out
in the heat of the day.

My love came near
up to my side
shoulder to shoulder
and mouth on mouth.

translated by Thomas Kinsella

The Spinning Wheel

JOHN FRANCIS WALLER

Mellow the moonlight to shine is beginning,
Close by the window young Eileen is spinning;
Bent o'er the fire her blind grandmother, sitting,
Is crooning and moaning and drowsily knitting.

Chorus
Merrily, cheerily, noiselessly, whirring,
Swings the wheel, spins the wheel, while the foot's stirring,
Sprightly and brightly and airily ringing
Thrills the sweet voice of the young maiden singing.

'Eileen, a chara, I hear someone tapping',
''Tis the ivy, dear mother, against the glass flapping',
'Eily, I surely hear somebody sighing',
''Tis the sound, mother dear, of the summer winds dying'.

Chorus

'What's that noise that I hear at the window, I wonder?'
''Tis the little birds chirping the holly-bush under'.
'What makes you be shoving and moving your stool on?'
'And singing all wrong that old song of "The Coolin"?'

Chorus

There's a form at the casement, the form of her true love,
And he whispers with face bent 'I'm waiting for you, love'.
'Get up on the stool, through the lattice step lightly,
We'll rove in the grove while the moon's shining brightly'.

Chorus

The maid shakes her head, on her lips lays her fingers,
Steals up from her seat, longs to go and yet lingers;
A frightened glance turns to her drowsy grandmother,
Puts one foot on the stool, spins the wheel with the other.

Chorus

Lazily, easily, swings now the wheel round,
Slowly and lowly is heard now the reel's sound;
Noiseless and light to the lattice above her
The maid steps, then leaps to the arms of her lover.

Chorus

Slower, and slower, and slower the wheel swings,
Lower, and lower, and lower the reel rings;
Ere the reel and the wheel stop their ringing and moving
Through the grove the young lovers by moonlight are roving.

Brighid a Stóir TRADITIONAL

A Bhríghid a stóir ná pós an sean duine
Acht pós fear óg 's é d'oileadh leanbh duit,
Do shínfeadh síos go caoin ar leabhaidh leat
Do bhéarfadh póg no dhó ar maidin duit.

Is truagh a Bhríghid nach bás do fuaras
Sul a thug mé grádh chomh buan duit,
D'fhág tu m' inntinn claoidhte buaidhrighthe
Mar an crann críothain 's an ghaoth g'á luasgadh.

Dá mbeidheadh an tír seo mar bhudh chóir di
I g-caisleán aoibhinn do bheitheá do chómhnuidhe,
Bheidh' Gaill a's Gaodhail ag déanamh bróin tríot,
'S ni bhéidh mé féin ag plé níos mó leat.

Do gheall tu dhamh-sa, 's do rinn' tu breug liom,
Go mbeitheá liom-sa ag cró na g-caorach,
Do leig mé fead agus míle glaodh ort
'S ni bhfuaireas ann acht uain ag méidhligh.

'S do ghabh tu tharm go dorcha déigheannach
'S do ghabh tu tharm, a's solas an laé ann,
Dá dtiucfá [féin] asteach do m'fheuchaint
Deamhan fiarán (?) do bheidheadh agam féin leat.

Breed Astore TRADITIONAL

O Breed, astore, do not marry the old man,
But marry a young man 'tis he who would rear thee a child
Who would stretch softly on a couch beside thee;
Who would in the morning give thee a kiss or two.

'Tis a pity, O Breed, it was not death I found
Before I gave thee love so lasting.
Thou hast left my mind destroyed and troubled,
Like the aspen tree and the wind rocking it.

If this country were as it ought to be,
In a delightful castle thou wouldst be living;
Gall and Gael would be grieving, through thee,
And I, myself, shall not be pleading any longer with thee.

You promised me—and told me a falsehood—
That you would be with me at the pen of the sheep.
I let a whistle and a thousand shouts for you,
And I found nothing in it but the lambs a-bleating.

And you passed me by dark and late,
And you passed me by, and the light of the day in it.
If you would come in yourself to see me,
The demon a misunderstanding (?) I would have with you.

translated by Douglas Hyde

Cailín Beag
an Ghleanna
TRADITIONAL

A ógánaigh óig mar reultan tríd an g-ceó
  Do thugas-sa mo ghean go léir duit,
A's do gheall tu bheith rómham ag coill ghlais na g-cnó
  Go g-cuirfimís ár g-cómhairle i n-éinfheacht.
Tuig a mhíle stór nach bhfuil peacadh ar bith chomh mór
  Is measa agus is mó le deunamh
Ná maighdean dheas óg do mhealladh le (do) phóig
  Agus fealladh uirri go deó 'nna dhéigh sin.

A Radaighe (?) o a rúin an aitreach leat go buan
  Mar chuir tu le buaidhreadh an tsaoghail mé (?)
'S gur chuir tu do dhúil i n-airgiod 's i mbuaibh
  Agus i seafaideadhaibh dubha an tsléibhe.
B'fhearr liom go mór beith ar taoibh bhuachaill óig
  'Ná sealbhán bó ar taébh chnuic
'S é d'imeóradh (liom) air phean (?) agus cluithche cruaidh na ngeall
  Agus shiúbhalfadh an saoghal go réidh liom.

Ag dul 'nna luidhe do'n ngréin, mo chreach, mo dhith go geur!
  Is mise bhíos i bpéin an uair sin,
Go mbudh samhuil do m'ghné an té síneadh ann san gcré,
  'S a Mhic Mhuire nach mór an truagh sin!
Mo chairde uile go léir, an chuid aca nár eug
  Gur thugadar geur-fhuath dam,
Gan d'fhocal ann a mbeul, acht 'ó mhill tu thu féin
  Fulaing do réir sin buaidhreadh.'

Oh, Youth Whom
I Have Kissed
TRADITIONAL

Oh, youth whom I have kissed, like a star through the mist,
    I have given thee this heart altogether,
And you promised me to be at the greenwood for me
    Until we took counsel together;
But know, my love, though late, that no sin is so great
    For which the angels hate the deceiver,
As first to steal the bliss of a maiden with a kiss,
    To deceive her after this and to leave her.

And do you now repent for leaving me down bent
    With the trouble of the world going through me,
Preferring sheep and kine and silver of the mine
    And the black mountain heifers to me?
I would sooner win a youth to love me in his truth
    Than the riches that you, love, have chosen,
Who would come to me and play by my side every day
    With a young heart gay and unfrozen.

But when the sun goes round I sink upon the ground,
    I feel my bitter wound at that hour;
All pallid, full of gloom, like one from out a tomb,
    O Mary's Son, without power.
And all my friends not dead are casting at my head
    Reproaches at my own sad undoing.
And this is what they say, 'since yourself went astray,
    Go and suffer so to-day in your ruin'.

translated by Douglas Hyde

Éirigh Suas, A Stóirín

TRADITIONAL

Rachaidh mé amárach go haonach Chinn Trá,
An áit a bhfaighidh mé cuideacht' agus plé mór ar mhná,
Ní bheidh a'n duine liom ansin ach mé féin is mo ghrá,
Is a Bheití an chúil ómra, is tú 'tá mé rá.

Rise up, my darling, má tá tú 'do luí,
Foscail an doras is lig mé astoigh,
Tá buidéal i m'aice is drám fá bhean a' tí,
'Gus tá dúil agam nach ndiúlto(cha)idh sí mé fána níon.

Ná fágaigh *despond* orm chionn 's mé bheith gan mhaoin,
Bhéarfainn cupáin agus breacán duit is do sháith olann is lín,
Bhéarfainn sin agus tuilleadh duit is seascaireacht tí,
'Gus gruaim ar do mhalaidh, a ghrá, ní chuirfinn a choíche.

Chuirfinn bean a chodladh le ciúineas is ceol,
Agust bheinnse dá mealladh in ainneoin dá bhfuil beo,
Churifinn mo lámh ar a brollach agust bhéarfainn di póg,
Is cér mhiste don chailín sin, mise bheith 'g ól.

Nuair a éirímse amach ar maidin is amharcaim uaim,
Amharcaim insan taobh udaí a mbíonn mo ghrá ann,
Titeann no deora insna srathaí liom síos,
Agus nímse míle osna' bhíos cosúil le cumhaidh.

I ngleanntáin na coilleadh uaigní is lag brónach mar bhím,
Gach tráthnóna Dé Domhnaigh is ar maidin Dé Luain,
Is go mb'fhearr liom ar maidin is mé ag éirí amach 'mo shuí,
Dá bhfaighinnse mil ar chuiseoga ag bonn chnoc na sí.

Rise Up, My Darling

TRADITIONAL

I will go out tomorrow to Newry fair,
Where I will get company and much talk of girls,
There'll be no one along with me but my darling and me,
It's you whom I speak of my brown haired Betty.

Rise up, my darling, if you're lying down,
Open the door and let me come in,
I have a bottle beside me, a dram for your mother,
I hope she'll not refuse me the hand of her daughter.

Don't leave me despondent for having no wealth,
I'd give you cups and griddle bread, enough linen and wool,
I'd give you that and more and a sheltered house,
And bring a frown to your brow, love, I never would do.

I'd lull a woman to sleep with silence and song,
And I'd be enticing her in spite of them all,
I'd lay my hand on her breast and give her a kiss,
And me to be drinking, sure what odds to yon lass.

When I rise in the morning and look out beyond,
I look to the land where my true love lives on,
The tears from my eyes flow down in full stream;
I sigh a thousand times over, as if in melancholy.

In the lonely wooded glens I languish in pain;
Each Sunday evening and Monday at dawn,
I'd rather in the morning as I rise and go out,
To find honey on grasses at the fairy hill's foot.

translated by Pádraigín Ní Uallacháin

Thugamar Féin
an Samhradh Linn TRADITIONAL

Samhradh buí 'na luí ins na léanaí,
 thugamar féin a' samhradh linn;
Samhradh buí, earrach is geimhreadh
 is thugamar féin a' samhradh linn.

Cailíní óga, mómhar sciamhach,
 thugamar féin a' samhradh linn;
Buachaillí glice, teann is lúfar,
 is thugamar féin a' samhradh linn.

Bábóg na Bealtaine, maighdean a' tsamhraidh,
 suas gach cnoc is síos gach gleann,
Cailíní maiseacha, bángheala gléasta,
 is thugamar féin a' samhradh linn.

Tá an fhuiseog a' seinm is ag luascadh sna spéiribh,
 beacha is cuileóga(í) is bláth ar na crainn,
Tá an chuach is na héanlaith' a' seinm le pléisiúr,
 is thugamar féin a' samhradh linn.

Tá nead ag an ghiorria ar imeall na haille
 is nead ag an chorréisc i ngéagaibh a' chrainn,
Tá mil ar na cuiseóga(í) is fuiseoga(í) a' léimnigh,
 is thugamar féin a' samhradh linn.

Samhradh buí 'na luí ins a' léana,
 thugamar féin a' samhradh linn;
Ó bhaile go baile is go Lios Dúnáin a' phléisiúir,
 is thugamar féin a' samhradh linn.

We Brought the Summer with Us

TRADITIONAL

Golden summer, lying in the meadows,
    we brought the summer with us;
Golden summer, spring and winter,
    and we brought the summer with us.

Young maidens, gentle and lovely,
    we brought the summer with us;
Lads who are clever, sturdy and agile,
    and we brought the summer with us.

The May Doll, the summer virgin,
    up each hill and down the glen,
Beautiful maidens dressed in white clothes,
    and we brought the summer with us.

The lark is singing and swooping in the skies,
    bees and flies and blossom on trees,
The cuckoo and birds are singing with pleasure,
    and we brought the summer with us.

The hare has a nest at the edge of the cliff,
    the heron is nesting in the branches of a tree,
There is honey on grasses and larks leaping,
    and we brought the summer with us.

Golden summer, lying in the meadow,
    we brought the summer with us;
From home to home and to Lisdoonan of pleasure,
    and we brought the summer with us.

translated by Pádraigín Ní Uallacháin

Na Gamhna Geala TRADITIONAL

'Siad mo chuid gamhna, na gamhna geala,
Itheann siad an féar glas 's chan ólann siad an bainne,
Téann siad anonn a's anall thar a' bharra,
Is chan fhearr leo an trághadh ann nó barr a' láin mhara.

Mál álí aléo 's mo bhrónsa na gamhna,
Mál álí aléo sé mo bhrónsa na gamhna,
Maidin dhubh fhómhair nó coineascar a' tsamhraidh,
Is deas mar a sheolfainn na gamhna geala.

Is beag mo dhúil i gcupaí nó i gcártaí,
I bhfuinneogaí gloine nó i 'riúintí bána,
Míle uair go mb'fhearr liom agam cró beag sa tsamhradh,
Poll a bheith sna scrathaibh is mé 'g amharc ar na gamhna.

Dá mbeadh siad agam meadar nó buarach,
Cuinneog mhaith fhairsing 'na leapadh an t-uachtar.
Bheinn ag ga'áil eatarthu leis na buaibh tuata,
'S bheinn ag seoladh na ngamhna go gleanntán na luachra.

Bheirim mo mhallacht don tsagart a phós mé,
'S an darna mallacht don bhaile bhuí mhór seo,
Chan a' cur maoil ar chartaí a chleacht mé 'dtús m'óige,
Ach ag rinc' ar an tamhnaigh is na gamhna á seoladh.

Charbh fhearr liomsa flocas fúm ná 'n luachair,
Charbh fhearr liomsa ribíní bheith agam ná an buarach,
Ceoltaí 'n domhain dá seinnfí 'steach 'mo chluasaibh iad,
Och ba bhinne liomsa géimneach na ngamhna insa bhuailidh.

The White Calves   TRADITIONAL

My calves are the white calves,
They eat the green grass but they don't drink the milk,
They go back and forth across the sand bar,
And they'd rather the high tide to the ebbtide.

Mál-ál-aléo my sorrow the calves,
Mál-álí-aléo my sorrow the calves,
A dark autumn morning or a summer's evening,
How pleasantly I'd drive my bright calves.

I little care for cups and for quarts,
For glass windows and whitewashed rooms,
But I would a thousand times rather have a little bothy in the summer,
A hole in the thatch and me watching the calves.

If I had a bucket or spancel of my own,
A big broad churn where the cream would be slurping,
I would go at milking time with the dairy cows,
And drive the calves to the rushy glens.

My curse upon the priest who married me,
And may the second curse fall upon this old town,
It wasn't filling quarts that I spent my youth,
But dancing on the grassy uplands while driving the calves.

I'd rather the rushes than a bed of flock beneath me,
I'd choose a spancel than ribbons to have,
All the songs of the world if played in my ears,
Sweeter to me, in the booleys, is the lowing of the calves.

translated by Pádraigín Ní Uallacháin

Cailín as Contae Lú

TRADITIONAL

Bhí mé lá breá aerach ag dul bóthar a' Mhaighre,
Is chas domh spéirbhean as Contae Lú,
Is d'fhiafraíos féin di in eaglais Dé,
An bpósfadh sí gréasaí as Contae 'n Dúin?

Dúirt an spéirbhean go raibh mé a' pléadáil,
Is nár in mo leithéidse a chuir sí dúil,
Is dúirt sí 'na dhiaidh sin nár chleacht sé léi,
Gur mhíle b'fhearr léi bheith i gContae Lú.

A chailín tuatach de threibh na mbrúidéal,
Nach dtaithníonn súgradh leat is nach n-aithníonn greann,
Bíonn na doirse dúnta acu ar aghaidh aon siúiléara
Nuair a bhíonn(s) fáilte sa Dún do gach uile dhream.

Nach mbíonn úlla cumhra againn is mil is plúr ann
Nuair a bhíonn(s) mur gcrusta láidir teann,
Nach mbíonn sibh tuatach is mur ndoirse dúnta
Nuair a bhíonn(s) fáilte sa ghleann 'na bhfuil mise ann.

Cha raibh mise ach 'súgradh is chan olc liom diúltú,
Is a liacht sin cúileann deas thíos sa ghleann,
Nuair a bheas na doirse dúnta ar dhroim an diúltaithe,
Beidh fáilte dhúbalta síos fán Ghleann.

A Lass from County Louth

TRADITIONAL

One fine day I was going the Moyra pass,
And I met a fair one from County Louth,
I asked her myself, here in God's church,
Would she marry a shoemaker from County Down?

This fair maid said that I was jesting,
That it wasn't the likes of me that she desired,
She said as well that it wasn't her wont,
She'd a thousand times rather be in County Louth.

O lass from Louth, of the boorish people,
Who likes not sporting and knows not fun;
Your doors are shut in the face of each traveller,
When there's a welcome in Down for everyone.

Don't we have sweet apples, honey and flour,
When your crust of bread there is hard and firm?
Aren't you boorish with your closed doors,
When there's a welcome in the glen where I am in?

I was only sporting and I don't mind refusal,
And the many fair, fine women down by the glen,
When your doors will be closed after the refusal,
There will be a double welcome in the Glen.

translated by Pádraigín Ní Uallacháin

Dónall Óg TRADITIONAL

Shúd é an Domhnach a thug mé grá dhuit:
An dara Domhnach roimh Dhomhnach Cásca—
An sagart ar a ghlúine is é ag léamh na Páise—
Bhí mo chroí agus m'intinn ag leaghadh le grá dhuit.

Bhain tú thoir díom is bhain tú thiar díom;
Bhain tú gaoth agus bhain tú grian díom;
Bhain tú aoireacht na mbó fín sliabh diom;
Agus siúd is dóigh liom gur bhain tú Dia dhíom.

Dúirt tú liomsa, agus dhein tú bréag liom,
Go mbeifeá romham aige cró na gcaorach;
Scaoil mé fead agus dhá chéad glao ort,
Is ní bhfuaireas romham ann ach drúcht is féar glas.

Chonaic mé uam tú is mé sa ngairdín
I measc na gcrann is na *lilies* bhána;
Chrom tú do cheann is níor dhein tú gáire,
Agus ansúd a dh'aithin mé ná rabhais i ngrá liom.

Tá mo chroí istigh chomh dubh le háirne,
Nó le gual a dhófaí i gceárta,
Nó le bonn seana-bhróige a bheadh ar bharr fallaí bána
Tríd an mbuachaill donn deas a chuaigh thar sáile.

Young Donal

TRADITIONAL

That was the Sunday that I gave you love: the second Sunday before Easter Sunday. The priest was on his knees reading the Passion. My heart and my mind were melting with love for you.

You took the east from me and you took the west from me; you took the wind and you took the sun from me; you took the herding of the cows to the mountain from me; and I am of the opinion that you took God from me.

You said to me, and you told me a lie, that you would be waiting for me at the sheep fold. I whistled, and called you two hundred times; and I found nothing there before me but dew and green grass.

I saw you a distance from me when I was in the garden between the trees and the white lilies. You bowed your head and you didn't laugh, and it was there I realised you were not in love with me.

My heart within me is as black as a sloe, or as coal which would be burned in a forge, or as the sole of an old shoe on the top of white walls, because of the nice brown-haired boy who went overseas.

translated by Dáithí Ó hÓgáin

An Draighneán Donn
TRADITIONAL

Síleann céad fear gur leo féin mé nuair a ólaim leann;
Ní airím iad nuair a smaoiním ar a chomhrá liom.
Com is míne ná an síoda athá ar Shliabh na mBan bhFionn;
Is tá mo ghrá-sa mar bhláth na háirne ar an draighneán donn.

Is, a Dé dhil, cad a dhéanfainn má imíonn tú uaim?
Cá bhfaighidh mé eolas chun do thí-se má théim ar cuairt?
Sneachta síolmhar a bheith dá shíorchur agus mé faoi ghruaim—
Mná na hÉireann ag déanamh géim díom is mo ghrá i bhfad uaim.

Más ag imeacht ataoi, beir mo bheannacht leat is go dté tú slán;
Mar is baileach do shladais an croí as mo lár,
Níl coite agam a leanfadh tú, long ná bád—
Sin í an fharraige ina tuiltibh eadrainn, is ní heol dom snámh.

The Dark Thorn Tree

TRADITIONAL

A hundred men think that I belong to them when I drink ale. I do not hear them when I think of his conversation with me. A waist more tender than the silk which is on Slievenamon—and my love is as the blossoming of the sloe on the blackthorn tree.

And o dear God, what would I do if you leave me? Where will I get information as to where your house is if I come visiting? Abundant snow continually falling, and I am dejected—the women of Ireland making game of me and my love far away from me.

If you are leaving, bring my blessing with you and may you be safe; for you have definitely stolen the heart out of my breast. I have not a skiff to follow you, a ship or a boat—there is the sea in floods between us, and I don't know how to swim.

translated by Dáithí Ó hÓgáin

An cuimhin leat an oíche úd

TRADITIONAL

An cuimhin leat an oíche úd
  a bhí tú ag an bhfuinneog,
gan hata gan láimhne
  dod dhíon, gan chasóg?—
do shín mé mo lámh chughat
  's do rug tú uirthi barróg,
is d'fhan mé id chomhluadar
  nó gur labhair an fhuiseog.

An cuimhin leat an oíche úd
  a bhí tusa agus mise
ag bun an chrainn chaorthainn
  's an oíche ag cur cuisne,
do cheann ar mo chíocha
  is do phíob gheal á seinm?—
is beag a shíleas an oíche úd
  go scaoilfeadh ár gcumann.

A chumainn mo chroí istigh,
  tar oíche ghar éigin
nuair luígidh mo mhuintir
  chun cainte le chéile;
beidh mo dhá láimh id thimpeall
  's mé ag insint mo scéil duit—
's gurb é do chomhrá suairc mín tais
  a bhain radharc fhlaithis Dé díom.

Tá an tine gan coigilt
  is an solas gan múchadh,
tá an eochair faoin doras
  is tarraing go ciúin í,
tá mo mháthair 'na codladh
  is mise im dhúiseacht,
tá m'fhortún im dhorn
  is mé ullamh chun siúil leat.

Remember that night

TRADITIONAL

Remember that night
   and you at the window
with no hat or glove
   or coat to cover you?
I gave you my hand
   and you took and clasped it
and I stayed with you
   till the skylark spoke.

Remember that night
   when you and I
were under the rowan
   and the night was freezing?
Your head on my breasts
   and your bright-pipe playing. . .
I little thought then
   that our love could sever.

My heart's beloved
   come some night soon
when my people sleep,
   and we'll talk together.
I'll put my arms round you
   and tell you my story
—O your mild sweet talk
   took my sight of Heaven!

The fire is unraked
   and the light unquenched.
The key's under the door
   —close it softly.
My mother's asleep
   and I am awake
my fortune in hand
   and ready to go.

translated by Thomas Kinsella

From: *West Moon* AL PITTMAN

Jack: I don't think there'd be any harm in a song.

Ned: No harm at all.

Bill: Come on Ray, give us one, b'y.

Ray: I don't want my songs to get in the way of anything.

Maggie: So, who apart from Rose, got any objection?

Bill: What about 'The August Gale?'

Ray: Oh, that'd be too long Skipper. That's a long song, that one.

Bride: Bill always wants to hear 'The August Gale' just because he's into it.

Bill: I'm not the only one likes it.

Bride: What's that one you used to sing about Cradle Hill? That was a lovely song!

Aaron: That's where me and Donna done it for the first time. The first time for the both of us. Up there in the meadow on the side of Cradle Hill.

Ray: It's a long time since I sung that one.

Rose: Well, ye might as well get on with it. As far as I can see, some people are no better dead than alive. But I'll have nothin' to do with any of it. Either your songs or your sins. So, if you'll excuse me, I'll be at my prayers.

Cradle Hill

When the sun goes down on Cradle Hill
And darkness then fills up the sky
And memories fill up your mind
I hope you do not cry

I hope you do not weep for me
For I am always with you still
As on evenings long ago
We strolled up Cradle Hill

Oh do not weep my darling one
Oh no don't ever weep for me
For I'm far beyond the reach
Of the wild and the raging sea
For I'm far beyond the raging sea

Remember what it all meant then
The fragrant flowers blooming there
And birds whose summer song
Did fill the evening air

These are the things I keep with me
These are the constant joys of love
And they were ours and still will be
While stars shine up above

Oh do not weep my darling one
Oh no don't ever weep for me
For I'm far beyond the reach
Of the wild and the raging sea
For I'm far beyond the raging sea.

Aaron: Damn it! I wish I was still alive.

Deirín Dé

Deirín Dé
TRADITIONAL

Deirín dé, deirín dé,
tá an gabhar donn ag labhairt sa bhfraoch;
deirín dé, deirín dé,
tá na lachain ag screadaigh sa bhféith.

Deirín Dé, deirín dé,
gheobhaidh ba siar le héirí an lae,
deirín dé, deirín dé,
is rachaidh mo leanbh á bhfeighilt ar féar.

Deirín Dé, deirín dé,
éireoidh gealach is rachaidh grian fé;
deirín dé, deirín dé,
is tusa mo leanbh is mo chuid den tsaol.

Deirín Dé, deirín dé,
tá nead smólaí im chóifrín féin;
deirín dé, deirín dé,
tá, agus ór dom stóirín féin.

Deirín Dé, deirín dé,
ligfead mo leanbh ag piochadh sméar,
deirín dé, deirín dé,
ach codladh go sámh go fáinne an lae.

Deirín Dé

TRADITIONAL

Deirín dé, deirín dé,
the brown goat calling in the heather,
deirín dé, deirín dé,
the ducks are squawking in the marsh.

Deirín dé, deirín dé,
cows go West at dawn of day,
deirín dé, deirín dé,
and my babe will mind them on the grass.

Deirín dé, deirín dé,
moon will rise and sun will set,
deirín dé, deirín dé,
and you are my babe and share of life.

Deirín dé, deirín dé,
a thrush's nest in my little press,
deirín dé, deirín dé,
yes, and gold for my little darling.

Deirín dé, deirín dé,
I'll let my babe out picking berries,
deirín dé, deirín dé,
if he'll just sleep sound till the round of day.

translated by Thomas Kinsella

Surutsiutluta SID DICKER

UnikkausiKatlapungâli surutsiunigilauptaptinik
komut aitsainalaupogut iKaluganniaKaptatluta
Illannâoka ilagivlugit ukuangulautsimajugut
Jerry Sillett, George Dickerilu, Jontân Green, Albert Ford,
  Tikkimilu

AsiujiKattalauppugulli Kalliptinik kamittinilu
Kimminut nigijauKattatlutik ulitjauKattatlutalu
Illannâka ilagivlugit ukuangulautsimajugut
Jerry Sillett, George Dickerilu, Jontân Green, Albert Ford,
  Tikkimilu

Anggagiamik kiappiasuKattalauttugut
pijautlanialigapta alingigunnalaungilaguli komut aitsainatluta
Illannâka ilagivlugit ukuangulautsimajugut
Jerry Sillett, George Dickerilu, Jontân Green, Albert Ford,
  Tikkimilu.

Mânnali ittoligama ikKaumatuinnappunga
Kânuk piusiKalaumangâpta taipsumani surusiutluta
Illannâka ilagilautaka tamanegaluattuli suli
Jerry Sillett, George Dickerilu, Jontân Green, Albert Ford,
  Tikkimilu.
Jontân Green, Albert Ford, Tikkimilu.

When We Were Children   SID DICKER

I have many stories to tell about our childhood.
We always went to the brook to go after small trout.
I went with my friends, who were
Jerry Sillett, George Dicker, John Green, Albert Ford and Dick.

We used to lose our pants and boots.
Dogs would take away our clothes, and the water would rise on us.
I went with my friends, who were
Jerry Sillett, George Dicker, John Green, Albert Ford and Dick.

We used to be afraid to go home because we would get jawed,
But we kept going back to the brook anyway.
I went with my friends, who were
Jerry Sillett, George Dicker, John Green, Albert Ford and Dick.

Now I'm getting old, I am just reminiscing about the things we did that time when we were children.
I went with my friends, who were
Jerry Sillett, George Dicker, John Green, Albert Ford and Dick.
John Green, Albert Ford and Dick.

The Lord's Prayer

Wujjiek Wa'so'q epin, ktuisunm mkite'tasij, ika'j kteleke'wa'kim eimek, na'te'l wa'so'q teli-sqatulk elt wskitqamu'k tli-sqatulkij.

Nilu'nen ta'n i'-nkutikisknewey kiskuk pneknmuin aq ki'l tettulekl kas-wi'kmuinen teli kas-wi'kmaqajl ta'nik tettuinamijl, aq mukk la'linen ta'n winsutiktuk ela'luek, katu kesinukwa'luekl winjikl tuaqtuin. Tliaj

translated into Mi'kmaw by Bernie Francis

A Mhuire na nGrás   TRADITIONAL

A Mhuire na ngrás
  's a mháthair Mhic Dé,
go gcuire tú gach tráth
  ar mo leas mé.

Go sábhála tú mé
  ar gach uile olc,
go sábhála tú mé
  idir anam is chorp.

Go sábhála tú mé
  ar muir is ar tír,
go sábhála tú mé
  ar lic na bpian.

Glór na n-aingeal os mo chionn,
  ola Chríost ar mo chorp,
Dia romham agus Dia liom
  's duitse, a Íosa, m'anam bocht.

Blessed Mary

TRADITIONAL

Blessed Mary
   mother of God
direct me always
   toward my good.

Rescue me
   from every ill
rescue me
   both body and soul.

Rescue me
   on land and sea
rescue me
   from the slab of pain.

Voice of angels overhead
   oil of Christ upon my body
God before me, God beside me,
   my poor soul, Jesus, here it is.

translated by Thomas Kinsella

Uvanga, Uvanga TRADITIONAL INUKTITUT SONG

This is a song sung by someone who thinks he or she is bad, will never amount to anything and wonders how to get to Heaven.

The song is best sung with a pause (an anacrusis on 'Uvanga') to give it real emphasis.

Uvanga, uvanga piungitoalujunga
uvanga, uvanga piungitoalujunga
uvanga naminik Kunutsainatunga
Kanulli Kilangmut itittosauvingâ.

editorial note by Tim Borlase

Ag Críost An Síol TRADITIONAL

Ag Críost an síol, ag Críost an fómhar;
   in iothlainn Dé go dtugtar sinn.

Ag Críost an mhuir, ag Críost an t-iasc;
   i líonta Dé go gcastar sinn.

Ó fhás go haois, ó aois go bás,
   do dhá láimh, a Chríost, anall tharainn.

Ó bhás go críoch nach críoch ach athfhás,
   i bParthas na ngrás go rabhaimid.

To Christ The Seed TRADITIONAL

To Christ the seed, to Christ the crop,
   in barn of Christ may we be brought.

To Christ the sea, to Christ the fish,
   in nets of Christ may we be caught.

From growth to age, from age to death,
   Thy two arms here, O Christ, about us.

From death to end—not end but growth—
   in blessed Paradise may we be.

translated by Thomas Kinsella

7

The Bone-and-Marrow Judgement

R.M.S. Titanic   ANTHONY CRONIN

I

Trembling with engines, gulping oil, the river
Under the factories glowering in the dark
Is home of the gulls and homeless; cold
Lights on the sucking tideway, scurf and sewage,
Gobbets of smoke and staleness and the smell,
The seaweed sour and morning smell of sea.

Here in the doss the river fog is dawn.
Under the yellow lights it twists like tapeworm,
Wreathes round the bulbs and, with the scent of urine,
Creeps down the bare board corridors, becomes
The sour, sweet breath of old men, sleepless, coughing.

Lights on the glistening metal, numinous
Feathering to mist, thin garlands hung
On the wet back of the Mersey. Out to sea
A great dawn heaves and tugs the tide past Crosby.

II

On the bog road the blackthorn flowers, the turf-stacks,
Chocolate brown, are built like bricks but softer,
And softer too the west of Ireland sky.

Turf smoke is chalked upon the darker blue
And leaves a sweet, rich, poor man's smell in cloth.
Great ragged rhododendrons sprawl through gaps
And pink and white the chestnut blossom tops
The tumbled granite wall round the demesne.
The high, brass-bound De Dion coughing past,
O'Connor Don and the solicitor,
Disturbs the dust but not the sleeping dogs.

Disturb the memories in an old man's head.
We only live one life, with one beginning.
The coming degradations of the heart
We who awake with all our landfalls staring
Back at us in the dawn, must hold our breath for.
The west is not awake to where Titanic
Smokes in the morning, huge against the stars.

III

No one spoke of this in the parlour bookcase.
R. M. Ballantyne held no hint of chaos.
There was no astonishing ship in the morning sky,
Slanting and falling in appalling ruin.
There was only the deliberate enunciation of an April Sunday
Announcing twelve o'clock:
A bobbined green cloth on the parlour table,
The prolonged anticipatory pleasure of a boy's boredom,
Churchbells and baking smells, the buff and throaty hens.
A Protestant hymn vibrates in the musty sunlight,

Nearer my God to Thee, nearer to thee.
O nothing so huge and wonderful as disaster
(Fenimore Cooper could have foretold that,
Or all of the foolish liars in the bookcase
Prognosticated something of the kind
In terms of a boy's heroics,
The long, gashed hull, the officers, the boats)
But led by a cyclopedia to the slaughter,
Expecting a world of fountain pens and clippings;
And led like a romantic to the slaughter,
Imagining voices in the song-washed dusk—
O who in that bookcase foretold the derisive laughter?

IV

Those who lately took the notion
To cross the rolling and roaring Atlantic Ocean
Where the dead of the coffin-ships once washed
To and fro on the shingle, shoals of corpses,
Ocean dividing the parishes of Bertraghboy and Boston,
Are battened now beside the pounding engines,
Oil and varnish floating on the darkness,
While she wanders like a headland through the North Atlantic,
Or like a city oscillating across a landscape
Into whose basements the emigrants are crowded with their worries.
It is impossible not to feel for the poor of this nation
Sentiments of companionship and love,
For although the forgiving of misfortune is among the most dangerous of human operations,
In the alleyways of our need we turn for help
Not to those who judge but to those who do not care,
Companions now under the naked bulbs
In the communal forgetting of drunken consociation
Where the lies are allowed for an hour between one day and another.

V

Now Lightoller sees with pride the order of reasonable
    magnitude
Bulking and glistening round him, metallic, echoing,
As he stands on his bridge over vibrating darkness,
A capable man and therefore entitled to pride,
And truly also neither a bore nor a prig;
Or at least on this April night of nineteen twelve,
Standing decent and quiet under the towering smokestacks,
While the great ship, lighted like late-night London,
Moves towards a rising and falling horizon over the respiring
    ocean
Into disaster he cannot foresee, has no reason to inquire
Into the truth he might not be able to endure.
Mr. Lightoller, last of a line, now, let us take you, of likeable men,
As you move through the cloud of the night with a cap set square
    on your head
And your responsibilities shouldered,
For it is possible that there were such simplicities,
A schoolboy autumn order with no rot at the core,
Without the knowledge of interior and exterior degradations,
The cracked voice, the face crumbling into that of a fool or a
    bully
And already that of a bore:
But there will soon in the habited world be only the blind and the
    ruined,
The active who, claiming to be just, are devoid of compassion
    and self knowledge,
And those who will never act again, who tremble with disgust,
The half men and the crippled, neither good,
Who demand from omnipotent god excluding dispensations,
Or at best meet together in an obscene embrace
Like the criminal and the boyish police.
The limited man may act and judge, Mr Lightoller,
But prepare to incur some contempt.

VI

Down underneath the Irish poor are singing
Their songs of Philadelphia in the morning,
Brotherly and romantically clinging
To those whom they would murder without warning.
A warm frieze crowd where every eye is crying
And all the songs are always of misfortune,
Inured to the snug, cosy slop of dying
They watch the grey rats creeping to the ocean.
Down here no one will judge and all's forgiven.
Every man loves the thing he kills and, slowly,
With many a tear, the smiler does the knifing.
Down here the failure to redeem is holy.
Their songs of loss, of exile, desolation
Hang in the wide, still night. They shout of loving.
Each heart is full of black midnight emotion
And will create a sorrow for its proving.

Surely among the rich men's snowy linen
The dignified and decent can be found
The stainless, crystal, cut-glass attitudes
And mouths shut on the boy's need to impress,
Instead of the hysterical moist palm,
The smiling urgencies of need and love,
The trader's charm, the clever one's reply,
Familiarities of skin and cloth
Clinging in fecundation to the sweat,
What won't wash out, the bit of shit on shirt,
The fungoid socks, the broken shoe, skinned heel,
The hanging round for hours, the aptly named
Indeed intrusive, hand on shoulder touch—
Surely the rich, who know the tiny shiver
Caressing the dry, lonely selfish skin
Contrive to keep some attitudes intact,
Reptiles who change, three times a day, their cloth?

Sick in the bilboes of the world the poor
Cling to each other but the rich cling more
Closely to the cruelty that prevents
The dissolution of the modelled stance,
The waxwork melting of the features down,
The blubber sympathy when sorrows drown.
O if this face concealed great pain we might
Call it necessity and concede its right,
But multiplied in the racing mirrors here
The eyes of money, vacantly severe,
The polished surfaces, the silver knives,
The gorgon heads which model the good lives
Presume a reckoning from the weak, the odd,
The young to proffer to a glutton god—
The face of justice does not mask its grief
But emptiness and greed and disbelief,
A solemn bully's face, pretentious, grave,
Loathing the brother that it fears to save
Lest money and attendance might not get
Their due reward, their prior claims be met.
To all the decent scriveners it lied
Who bit upon that coin before they died
And found it hollow and who took the blame,
Bearing their own, their sons' and fathers' shame.

VII

A tragedy is only one mistake
Or the last in a series, making all irretrievable.
The tragic accident is the one which leaves
The knowledge that a desired possibility has been finally
    destroyed
By neglect, foolishness or bad luck.
When the shock ran back along the narrow alleys
The lights were suddenly darkened,
Bringing the consciousness of error.
But although the voices rose again after the silence
The lights did not fully recover.

Then the engines stopped,
For now they were in the interval between two events,
The irretrievable mistake in the past,
And the inevitable consequence in the future.
And as knowledge of the nature of the mistake grew in each mind
So did the penalty loom clearer out of the small hours.

VIII

Who can make plausible what happens?
Only the inexplicable rules
Over the worst of our lives,
The intimate degradations,
The inconsequent punishments
For the trivial mistakes.
Loud in the echoless night
Titanic is not alone,
Also enclosed by the sky
The Californian's lights
Deny necessity
And dignity to her fate.
Around her boarded decks
Fear infects the dark,
Slowly her floors slop down
Into the freezing peace
Of the calm and ridiculous sea.
Lightoller clings to the real,
The world that cannot be regained,
And those lustrous lights shine on
Like the ordinary overheard
After the end of the world.
They call out for help, they wait
For the casual world to reply,
But the Californian's lights,
Cosy in great, cold dark,
Simply inform the damned
The households are happy and safe.
Over and over again

Their rockets flare through the cold
But no answer at all returns
As from an inanimate phone
Incredibly ringing on
While the seconds expand in the head.
They stare at a shocking thing,
Mankind untouched by their fear,
The Californian's lights
Like a pierhead glistening there.
Nothing can ever explain
This further grotesque mischance,
Redeem with cause and effect
Their aloneness inside the vast
Cloud which obscures the real,
Which makes their voice unheard,
Their foghorn shaking the stars,
Their rockets shocking the dark,
Their courage, their casual jokes,
Their anxious ordinary talk.

Many at home will awake
To find this gigantic ship
Has sailed into the bay
Whose waves lulled them to sleep,
Preternaturally great,
Obscuring most of the sky,
While the darkness spreads overhead
As the great ship comes close,
The appalling shape in the bay
Towering over the house.

IX

Inpenetrably cold and dark the sea
Sucks down Titanic as the hiss of steam
Dies over empty distance. The boats gaze
On what was home, eleven storeys high,
Commotion crowding on her decks, her lights
Tilting above them as the band plays on.

Is Horatio Bottomley who climbs now by the stairs
To the sliding platforms of the ship
Strength or weakness? Are the deceptions the late king practised,
Flitting between the cabins, dishonour?

The freezing sea heaves slowly as it sinks
Into a tidal wave as high as it
Which licks the stars. The screaming rich sucked under
And the poor cry in that icy darkness
One last time, and then the cowering boats
Are hoisted up among the stars themselves.
The great ship gone the lucky count their loss
And search and search again to find the gain,
What guttered in the darkness of that wave,
For why else may the living not believe
The lies that served the first-class passengers
As passports to redemption from the dirt?

Under soft showers of April lies the west,
Belled, washed-out skies, the angelus, drenched birds.
Before our fathers stretches nineteen twelve,
The cloudy evenings and the river pools.
The freemen's journals soon will tell the story
And life rub in the lesson day by day.
There is no decency except a lie.

X

The hot breath of the brass, the drum's insistence,
Tar-barrels flaming in the market square,
And then the declinations of the heart.
Troubled by drums and scent the blood is trembling,
And caverned under canvas, taunting, white
The girls twist, sensuously touched by light.

Rain beats on the branches, scattering
Debris of April, blossoms and leaves on the ground.
Petals and twigs afloat on the sky in the roadway,
Deciduous stonework black as the big house crumbles,

The roofs with afterglow of rain still bright,
Auguring autumns to come in a cold light.

We live by living, survive by mere surviving.
Stubborn beyond our stubbornness or strength
Our virtues, like our weaknesses, prevail.
A man may suffer goodness like a growth
Intimate with his life. See, in his face
His gentleness encounter its disgrace.

XI

The dreams born in the mists of autumn evenings,
Cold, blue, tingling leaf-falls after rugby
With lights in passing buses; promises;
Remembrances of wrongs in mothers' eyes;
Money's smooth hum; migrating newspapers
Flocking across the skies; the cameras purring
On whores' ecstasies of self possession;
Insane and fearful punctualities
Will keep the bands still playing, the great ship
Towering above the roadsteads of the world.
And they will bless the Pope this time in building
It in a Belfast of exorbitant virtue
Bound still by decent business's iron tramlines.

As the world drifts with dismal Sunday bells
Into an April half a century on,
Sweating awake, their skin next to the blankets,
Many reflect on how their lives were not
As once imagined. Sepia photographs
Whose background was a swathe of shimmering sea,
Gone, with the cupboards, washstands, bedroom ceilings
Under which decencies perished hour by hour,
The patterns made by sunlight on those ceilings,
The German band tromboning on the corner
Fading laments for Genevieve and June,
Damp smells, diplomas, cobwebs, cindered yards,
Lugubrious moustaches, high-winged collars,

Tied bundles of old newspapers and books
On esperanto, self-help, concentration,
The wastages of effort and of love.

Coughing and spitting by the radiator
The old men listen to the wireless now
The world has turned into a coalyard where
Life which had died in shame is reborn free.
These years that saw declensions of the heart
Unguessed at on assistants' summer evenings
When ghostly skirts were whispering in the dark,
Saw also freedoms, huge across a sky
Grimy with blood and fire against which foundered
Towering gasometers, crossed girders, gantries.
Disgust itself is freedom, as is fear.
What steers us to destructions has released
Many from corridors, the servant's guile,
The clerk's reliable deft-fingered grace,
Imperial mirrors cracked across the smile
Of duty on the dowager's creamed face.
A daily drudgery of approximate justice
Is incumbent yet upon the brave who crouch
Still over tasks upon the drumming floor.
But the eyes of survivors will ask both more and less.
And no one now need ever fear a disgrace.
The responses the night is listening to are aware
Of the irrelevant ignobility of distress.

The Ice-Floes

E. J. PRATT

Dawn from the Foretop! Dawn from the Barrel!
  A scurry of feet with a roar overhead;
The master-watch wildly pointing to Northward,
  Where the herd in front of *The Eagle* was spread!

Steel-planked and sheathed like a battleship's nose,
She battered her path through the drifting floes;
Past slob and growler we drove, and rammed her
Into the heart of the patch and jammed her.
There were hundreds of thousands of seals, I'd swear,
In the stretch of that field—'white harps' to spare
For a dozen such fleets as had left that spring
To share in the general harvesting.
The first of the line, we had struck the main herd;
The day was ours, and our pulses stirred
In that brisk, live hour before the sun,
At the thought of the load and the sweepstake won.

We stood on the deck as the morning outrolled
On the fields its tissue of orange and gold,
And lit up the ice to the north in the sharp,
Clear air; each mother-seal and its 'harp'
Lay side by side; and as far as the range
Of the patch ran out we saw that strange,
And unimaginable thing
That sealers talk of every spring—
The 'bobbing-holes' within the floes
That neither wind nor frost could close;
Through every hole a seal could dive,
And search, to keep her brood alive,
A hundred miles it well might be,
For food beneath that frozen sea.
Round sunken reef and cape she would rove,
And though the wind and current drove
The ice-fields many leagues that day,
We knew she would turn and find her way
Back to the hole, without the help

Of compass or log, to suckle her whelp—
Back to that hole in the distant floes,
And smash her way up with her teeth and nose.
But we flung those thoughts aside when the shout
Of command from the master-watch rang out.

Assigned to our places in watches of four—
　Over the rails in a wild carouse,
　Two from the port and starboard bows,
Two from the broadsides—off we tore,
In the breathless rush for the day's attack,
With the speed of hounds on a caribou's track.
With the rise of the sun we started to kill,
A seal for each blow from the iron bill
Of our gaffs. From the nose to the tail we ripped them,
　And laid their quivering carcasses flat
On the ice; then with our knives we stripped them
　For the sake of the pelt and its lining of fat.
With three fathoms of rope we laced them fast,
　With their skins to the ice to be easy to drag,
With our shoulders galled we drew them, and cast
　Them in thousands around the watch's flag.
Then, with our bodies begrimed with the reek
　Of grease and sweat from the toil of the day,
　We made for *The Eagle*, two miles away,
At the signal that flew from her mizzen peak.
And through the night, as inch by inch
　She reached the pans with the 'harps' piled high,
　We hoisted them up as the hours filed by
To the sleepy growl of the donkey-winch.

Over the bulwarks again we were gone,
With the first faint streaks of a misty dawn;
Fast as our arms could swing we slew them,
Ripped them, 'sculped' them, roped and drew them
To the pans where the seals in pyramids rose
Around the flags on the central floes,
Till we reckoned we had nine thousand dead
By the time the afternoon had fled;

And that an added thousand or more
Would beat the count of the day before.
So back again to the patch we went
To haul, before the day was spent,
Another load of four 'harps' a man,
To make the last the record pan.
And not one of us saw, as we gaffed, and skinned,
And took them in tow, that the north-east wind
Had veered off-shore; that the air was colder;
   That the signs of recall were there to the south,
The flag of *The Eagle*, and the long, thin smoulder
   That drifted away from her funnel's mouth.
Not one of us thought of the speed of the storm
   That hounded our tracks in the day's last chase
(For the slaughter was swift, and the blood was warm),
   Till we felt the first sting of the snow in our face.
We looked south-east, where, an hour ago,
   Like a smudge on the sky-line, someone had seen
The Eagle, and thought he had heard her blow
   A note like a warning from her sirene.
We gathered in knots, each man within call
   Of his mate, and slipping our ropes, we sped,
Plunging our way through a thickening wall
   Of snow that the gale was driving ahead.
We ran with the wind on our shoulder; we knew
That the night had left us this only clue
Of the track before us, though with each wail
That grew to the pang of a shriek from the gale,
Some of us swore that *The Eagle* screamed
Right off to the east; to others it seemed
On the southern quarter and near, while the rest
   Cried out with every report that rose
   From the strain and the rend of the wind on the floes
That *The Eagle* was firing her guns to the west.
And some of them turned to the west, though to go
   Was madness—we knew it and roared, but the notes
Of our warning were lost as a fierce gust of snow
   Eddied, and strangled the words in our throats.
Then we felt in our hearts that the night had swallowed

All signals, the whistle, the flare, and the smoke
To the south; and like sheep in a storm we followed
Each other; like sheep we huddled and broke.
Here one would fall as hunger took hold
Of his step; here one would sleep as the cold
Crept into his blood, and another would kneel
Athwart the body of some dead seal,
And with knife and nails would tear it apart,
To flesh his teeth in its frozen heart.
And another dreamed that the storm was past,
And raved of his bunk and brandy and food,
And *The Eagle* near, though in that blast
The mother was fully as blind as her brood.
Then we saw, what we feared from the first—dark places
Here and there to the left of us, wide, yawning spaces
Of water; the fissures and cracks had increased
Till the outer pans were afloat, and we knew,
As they drifted along in the night to the east,
By the cries we heard, that some of our crew
Were borne to the sea on those pans and were lost.
And we turned with the wind in our faces again,
And took the snow with its lancing pain,
Till our eye-balls cracked with the salt and the frost;
Till only iron and fire that night
Survived on the ice as we stumbled on;
As we fell and rose and plunged—till the light
In the south and east disclosed the dawn,
And the sea heaving with floes—and then,
The Eagle in wild pursuit of her men.

And the rest is as a story told,
Or a dream that belonged to a dim, mad past,
Of a March night and a north wind's cold,
Of a voyage home with a flag half-mast;
Of twenty thousand seals that were killed
To help to lower the price of bread;
Of the muffled beat . . . of a drum . . . that filled
A nave . . . at our count of sixty dead.

From: *The Roosevelt And The Antinoe*

E. J. PRATT

Her high freeboard towering above the pier,
She lay beneath the lift of spars and blocks:
Her port life month by month and year by year
Knew nothing but the humdrum of the docks;—
The rumble of trucks along the warehouse floors,
The blare of sirens, shout of stevedores,
The play of tackle under the gruff mood
Of winches, clatter of hooks and booms, subdued
To the credit balance that must never fail
The ledgers of Hoboken Lines—so she,
Built for the tides of commerce on the sea,
Was under schedule in an hour to sail.

. . . .

Thursday morning rose without a sun,
Sleet in the air: the wind was westerly:
The river breeze of Wednesday had begun
To stiffen to a whole gale on the sea.
By noon the stations at the coast were flashing
Warnings, making smaller ships delay
Their date of sailing. Vessels under canvas,
Attempting shorter trips in gulf or bay,
Crawled back to harbour double-reefed, while others,
Still further to the east, that could not make
Return,—sails blown to ribbons from the gaskets—
Were forced to scud under bare poles to take
The luck ahead. Long threat lay in the signals.
The charts traced not a cyclone's come-and-go,—
The fury soon begun and as soon ended—
But those broad areas on which storms grow,
Northern and Oceanic, where each hour,
Feeding on the one before, transmits

In turn its own inheritance of power
Unto the next until the hammer hits
A hemisphere.

Along the eastern seaboard,
And inland to one-half the continent,
Thousands of dials in studio and station
Were 'off the air' by an ungrudged consent—
That the six-hundred-metre wave might keep
Upon the sea that night its high command
For the great business that was nigh at hand,
With deep already calling unto deep.

Friday evening, with Cape Race reporting
Big seas with thickening fog followed by snow,
Barometer still falling, very low.

Morning of Saturday! the gale now rising
To the dimensions of a hurricane,
With gusts that boxed the compass of a vane,
Sweeping around the headlands to contest
The arrogated highway from the West.

Evening again, and in its power to smite
The snowy cordon with its warning light,
The Cape's revolving beacon was as sick
As the guttering limit of a candle-wick.
And never—it was claimed—had tides so climbed
A slope of shoal from such a depth to feed
The tumult of the upper waves; so timed
Direction with their volume and their speed,
To meet both wave and wind that all might lock
In foam above so high a line of rock.

South of this Cape within these hours, the *Roosevelt*
Was driving East by North, with her decks stripped;
Her lower ventilator cowls unshipped,
The shafts plugged; battened and wedged the hatches;
Bell-mouths full-bore discharging from the bilge-pumps

Under the straining hull; thirty degrees
Measuring her roll within the heavier seas.
The facing of the 'midship house was spattered
At seventy feet. Captain and quarter-master
Saw nothing legible upon the face
Of day or night: the sextant in its case,
The navigators guessed the ship's position.

. . . .

Fried stepped inside the Pilot House to get
Another reading from the aneroid.
An hour ago the adjusting hand was set
At twenty-nine—the low foul weather mark,
And the indicator for that hour had stood
Directly underneath as though it were glued
To the card. He came nearer, full of dark
Conjecture, tapped the glass, and the hand fell,
The barest fraction but perceptible,
Entering by slow, inexorable rate,
The tragic ranges of the *twenty-eight.*
Later he returned; the oracle
Yielded this time a record to appal
The heart. Muttering '*twenty-eight (point) three*',
He shot a glance to the right where on the wall
He found, in confirmation, the line drawn
To the same level on the mercury.
'Twas four o'clock on a North Atlantic sea,
Three hours before a January dawn.
The wind having slipped the gale's leash was soon
To match the wing-shod speed of a typhoon:
The storm of nineteen twenty-six was on.

Somewhere far-off in that unwavering gloom,
Cramped in the quarters of a wireless room,
A boy was seated, tapping at a key.
Water ran along the floor: his knee

Was braced against a table to resist
The dangerous angle of a starboard list.
Upon his right a wireless log-chart lay
With many entries for so young a day.
He reached and pushed a button and the drone
Of a generator started. A switch thrown,
He rapped the key, then instantly transferred
To the receiving set; listened with keen
Thrust of his face; and with no answer heard,
Changed over, going through the same routine.

. . . .

The cabin of the *Roosevelt* radio!
Three dots, three dashes, and the dots again—
(The call sign) *British freighter, 'Antinoe'.*
Don't know position. Sixteen hours ago,
Rough latitude—North forty-six and ten,
Rough longitude—thirty-nine, five-eight.
Been hove-to ever since; the present rate
Of drift to East, two knots (approximate).
Fried took the message, reading nothing more
Than that a ship was sending out a call
For help, and that since noon the day before
She had not known her bearings. This was all
The cryptogram surrendered for a clue.
A fresh despatch was brought two minutes later,
The *Aquitania* calling—'*Which of two*
Should undertake location of the freighter?'
Their own positions given, 'twas agreed—
Cunarder farther off by hours, pressed
To the muzzle of the storm and moving West,—
The job might therefore be assigned to Fried.

Orders were given to the wireless chief
To bring the direction-finder into play,
Capture the signals and report at brief

Periods—and the ship was on her way.
Taking his station at the binnacle,
The head-phones on, he listened while he swung
The handwheel slowly to the right until
The loop above the Pilot House that hung
The wires came broadside to the signal cry.
The sounds grew fainter, faded out, came back
With further revolution but to die
Again with the reversal of the track.
Underneath, the hair-line on the face
Of the dummy compass card had kept its pace
With every move, faithful to every trial,
And like a dogma that might take denial
From neither sense nor reason, pointed *There*,
At a figure stamped in black upon the dial:
For when it moved to either side with the wheel,
It came back ever with the aerial square
To the source of the signal like a steadying keel
Demanding its position. How far? Where,
Along this line, now tossing like a chip
Upon those crests and hollows, lay the ship,
It could not tell—one hundred miles or two
It might have been for all the seamen knew.

Back in the wireless room the call came in
With the staccato of a bulletin;
Triads of notes spare and reiterant,
A whistle shot with burr and sibilant—
The international prelude which the sea
Beats out in storm from human veins to express
The fever pulses of its own distress.
Whether it was the sharp economy
Of pauses in the breaks, or some known trick
Of the ear to catch the timbre of a click,
A pressure or a crotchet in the tapping,
The operator felt someone was rapping
A message out with white intensity,
In life-death finger action on a key,
Within the cabin of the *Antinoe*.

Tarpaulins ripped. Another hatch let go.
Bad list. Grain swelling fast. Seams loosening now.
All life-boats gone from starboard davits. How
Many knots are you making? How far away
Do you reckon you are?
Ten knots: now eight:
Now ten—top speed allowed by sea.
                                        You say
That we sound nearer to you? Cannot wait
Much longer.
              Twelve.
                        Find it hard to steer,
Ice-chest has crashed into the steering gear.

. . . .

Eleven o'clock. Fried knowing that he neared
The ship's position by the growing power
Of the signals slowed the *Roosevelt* down to scour
The closer plotted area, fighting squall
On top of storm, boring through a pall
Of snow, till at the heart of the wave-zone,
With Jack reversed, the freighter like a lone
Sea-mallard with a broken wing was seen
Ahead, lee-rail awash, taking it green
At the bow.

            Do you wish to abandon?
                              Not just yet;
Endeavouring to fix steering gear, and get
Hatches secured. Water in stokehold. Grain
Cargo shifted. Trying to maintain
Sufficient steam to heave-to and survive
Till weather moderate. Crew twenty-five.
Can you spread oil to windward? Please stand-by.

But hard as the three engineers might try,
The leaks outraced the pumps. The daylight grew
To dusk, the hatches opened and the crew
Signalled for rescue. Fried, a quarter mile
To windward, poured his fuel oil on the sea,
Giving, that distance, what the *Roosevelt* lee
Afforded, edging in and backing while
He waited for a sign of the wind's subsiding,
Watching the scud of the waves, the darkening sky,
The drifting snow and the freighter heavily riding.

Then suddenly at nine as the squall increased,
With a smother of black hail the *Roosevelt's* light
Could not pierce through, the bridge look-out lost sight
Of the *Antinoe* and the wireless contact ceased.

Dead Slow! The *Roosevelt* took a risk as great
As if the air shook with the roar of reefs.
The wireless and the navigating chiefs
Fried summoned to the flying bridge to debate
The course. What with the hammer of the sea
To windward, and that anvil on the lee,
Judgment and will were warped by doubt. Suspend
Pursuit? Keep steerage-way and just hold on?
For at this hour with sight and hearing gone,
All felt within their blood they could depend
On nothing but an elemental trust
In bulkheads; in the physics of a dark
Equation, where with each remorseless thrust
Down to the starboard limits of the arc,
The ship should take under unheard commands
The port recoil, a pivoted keel, and then,
At the crux of the port roll find again
The firm up-heave of Atlantean hands.
On such a faith, borne in by night and snow,
Rested the riddle of the *Antinoe*.

. . . .

The ship with unremitting search despite
The chances stacked against her, steamed on far
Into the night, past midnight and the slow
Hours, blindly heading into snow;
Not a sextant reading off a star;
No radio now with subtle fingering
Untied the snarl of the freighter's wayward course.
Nothing but log and the dead reckoning,
And the *Roosevelt's* instruments stating the force
Of wind, direction and the tidal stress,
Nothing but these and the wheel's luck to trail her,—
Unless there might be added to the sum
Of them an unexplored residuum—
The bone-and-marrow judgment of a sailor.

. . . .

Feeling her shifted courses over-run,
And yet uncertain whether she should tack
Upon a chosen port or starboard track,
The baffled liner like a water-dog
Would dip her nose to the sea and then up-rear
Her head with black hawse nostrils keen to flair
A flying quarry covered by a fog.
Dawn and noon and now the afternoon.
'We picked her up'—so ran the captain's log—
'One point upon the starboard bow at four
O'clock, with nineteen hours of delay,
And sixty miles from her last known position'.
Her navigating bridge was swept away;
Flooded, steam off, lights out, a closing day,—
The time again awaited Fried's decision.
To pour fuel upon the sea to assuage
Its fury; make a high-decked vessel ride
Steady; maintain sufficient weather gage,
Four hundred tons of pressure at the side,
To avoid the crisis when a wave should toss

Her like a dinghy on the smaller ship,
Beam against beam, or stem to rail, to rip
The plates like cardboard to a double loss;
And yet mindful of this first charge, to crawl
Within a narrow margin to the hulk,
To take advantage of the liner's bulk,
As windbreak for a life-boat, and forestall
The second disappearance in a squall
Of the *Antinoe*;—in fine, to run a race
For a crew's life with the storm laps in advance;
To outstare Death to his salt countenance,
Made up the grim agenda on his face.

. . . .

At noon the starboard list began to assume
The final margin for the *Antinoe*,
The signal flags reporting that below
The sea was filling up the engine room.

The next attempt was with the Lyle gun.
Fried edged his vessel nearer to the wreck,
Trying for the safest, shortest run
To get a line across the after-deck.
But once again an adverse hand conspired
Against the chance, checkmated the design,
For at the muzzle as the gun was fired,
The steel projectile snapped the messenger line.
The second did the same, the third, and so
The fourth; the six succeeding carriers trailed
Their lines midway; the last, the eleventh, failed;
Only the iron passed the *Antinoe*.

The store of rockets next—but what availed
Their slender shafts and powder charges scaled
Against the weight of vapour, wind and snow?
An empty cask was lowered with the hope

The wind might carry it to the ship's side.
It sank beneath its sagging weight of rope.

Another stroke of rescue was devised.
A life-boat was trailed off without a crew;
It climbed, zigzagged and floundered, plunging through,
But pitched against the freighter and capsized.

Fried tried again, placing his ship to *looard*
Less than a hundred yards. The next boat moored
By a line rove through the high block of the kingpost
On the quarter-deck, was towed close to the stern
Of the *Antinoe*, but with the luff of the *Roosevelt*
To the weather side, the rope sagged at the turn;
Went underneath and fouled, and number three
Started to drift beyond recovery.

Another night, the third, confronted Fried,
When the last remnant of the sky was blown
Out, with the ocean like a pampas stirred
To the confusion of a great stampede—
Riot of lariat and hoof, of spurred
Horses, and the *Antinoe* a thrown
Spent rider overtaken by the herd.

Wednesday morning! and the twenty-five
Huddled on the aft deck—still alive.
One hundred hours had passed since the men had known
The wool-warmth of a bunk, or stood the cold
With nourished veins; and sleep had taken hold
Of tired bodies salt-drugged to the bone.
And in that hundred hours eternity
Had ticked its lazy seconds on the sea,
Timing the wind and surge and the defeat
Of day by night; of night by day; the slow
Unreasoned alternation of the sleet
With hurrying phantoms of the hail and snow,
The same rotation on the deck— the grey
Sterility of hope with each life-boat gone,

Dusk followed by the night, and every dawn
A slattern offering dust instead of day.

. . . .

And so the latter half of the fourth day
Came with the ocean well astride its prey:
The storm in front like a shifty pugilist,
Watching for some slight turn of luck to slay
The rescuer with an iron-knuckled fist.
'Twas useless for the *Roosevelt* to await
The issue of the struggle by debate,
For nothing in those skies favoured a sign
That by manoeuvre could the fight be won—
By floating cask or breeches-buoy or line,
Mere parleying with rockets and a gun.
The hour had called for argument more rife
With the gambler's sacrificial bids for life,
The final manner native to the breed
Of men forging decision into deed—
Of getting down again into the sea,
And testing rowlocks in an open boat,
Of grappling with the storm-king bodily,
And placing Northern fingers on his throat.

The call again, and number five was ready.
The men were chosen and the davits swung;
The boat moved outward easily and hung
Level and snug to leeward but unsteady
In the capricious pockets of the squall.
Another order and the falls began
To move—eight men inside her; Alfred Wall,
Araneda, Diaz, Albertz, Hahn,
Upton, Roberts, Miller in command.
The gunwale fended off with oar and hand
At every lurch, she managed luckily
To clear the steamer's side, covering the steep

Descent, and then undamaged took the sea.
Three oars aside and with a steering sweep,
The boat pulled out from the immediate lee
Into the eddies where the waters met
From stern and bow,—where the last ounces put
On the oars, even with the wind abaft, could yet
Advance them only by the inch and foot.
They followed down the beam-path of the searchlight,
The *Roosevelt* all the while manoeuvring,
Now drawing in, now clawing off, and now
Dead close, beam to the wind, just shadowing
The brute drive of the freighter, to allow
The boat with heavy lateral drift to steer
With wider berth into the wind and clear
The danger of the surge around the bow.
A swamping moment caught her, but each blade
Flexed to the curve of snapping, Miller made
The turn and came down sharp broadside to gain
A point amidships that he might obtain
Such shelter as this windbreak could afford.
But the wells were under water and the lee
Was like the surf of breakers, for the sea,
Contemptuous of this man-made sunken mole,
Threatened each time to hurl the boat aboard,
And reach the funnel with resurgent roll.
Escaping this disaster, Miller drew
His boat back in the sea, and tried to creep
Forward to higher freeboard where the crew
Near the First Hatch might have the shortest leap.
Backwatering and staving off the hull,
And crawling in again with a slight lull
Of the wind, or with recession of the surge,
He took three men who on the perishing verge
Of sleep fell from the rail to the thwarts and slumped
To the floor-boards. Out and back once more
With slow manoeuvring, and another four
Secure. Others of tougher sinew jumped
To the stern sheets from the rail. The task was done
With sudden moves and checks like a strange play

Which starts, is forced to stop, and then begun
Afresh on unknown ground but under sway
Of old Olympian rules. So one by one
The lives were scored and those who missed their aim,
And fell into the sea, were grabbed and pulled
Over the gunwale; counted with the same
Slow chalking up as of advances bulled
Out of the fiery scrimmage of a game.

Miller tried to close again but failed.
With water shipped as fast as it was bailed,
Seams leaking, twelve half-dead men barely stowed,
And with his crew of eight he did not dare
To give his boat a more unstable load;
So pushed away and with the wind and tide
In favour, forced her water-logged to where
The *Roosevelt*, now round to leeward, showed
A maze of lines and ladders on her side.
The first instalment of the crew too numb
To lay their hands on heaving-lines were placed
Within the cargo-nets and drawn up plumb;
The others taking ropes, with their feet braced
Against the hull went up with the sheer lift
Of their mates, till all were safe aboard, and now
The life-boat number five with damaged bow
And broken hoisting hooks was cast adrift.

The pitch of the storm, late night and still the snow,
Two hundred yards between of yawning space,
And thirteen sailors on the *Antinoe*.
Three nights upon the bridge behind the shield
Of the canvas dodger, his accustomed place,
Fried doubtful, peering with his blizzard face.
Now one o'clock, and a slight rift revealed
A spatter of light above the running seas—
The freighter's lantern jabbing out in Morse
That the ship's list had reached fifty degrees.
The last hour was on with no recourse
Except another summons to the crew.

Miller commanding for the third time drew
From the line-up of forty volunteers
Of every rank—deck-hand to passenger,
His four uninjured veterans and five new
Hands: Thomas Sloan, the third officer;
Reidel; Wilke; Deck Yeoman Wilson Beers;
And Caldwell, messman to the engineers.

The sixth life-boat was ready on the lee.
The others stood a moment in review;
Three hundred passengers, two hundred crew;
The cut was getting near the artery.
The men, lowered without mishap, once more
Brought round the boat to the lee bow of the freighter,
And ranged her off the First Hatch as before.
The risk this time for boat and ship was greater;
The growing list could take no steeper verge,
And all the boatmanship could not avail
At first against the backwash of the surge;
For there was peril in the sunken rail,
When at uncertain moments the ship tried
For balance, lifting up a wounded side
To ease a wave that struck amidships, cleaving
Her port; and peril in those hours of doubt
For strengthless men that watched their comrades leaving,
And long the galley fires had been out.
Fried shortened up his weather gage to try
To give a double shelter to the life-boat:
The message later read—*'Had to rely*
Upon the final power of my engines,
For had a revolution failed,—'twas either
"Roosevelt" or "Antinoe" with odds on neither'.
The revolution did not fail, and Miller
Secured his men, and though with cracked air-tank,
And all the spare oars rent in hull-collision,
The boat came down the wind to the lee flank
Of the liner where the remnant with their clothes
Sodden and shrunk were, like drowsed children, gathered
To the cargo hammocks, twelve of them, then Tose,

The captain, who had worn his buttons well.
His bread had now returned upon the waters,
For ten years back, as later stories tell,
He had while master of another vessel,
Rescued a Philadelphian bark in seas
And winds only less full of death than these.

Now open throttles! Now my lads, YOHO!
The *twenty-five*, by Neptune, every one!
Captain to deck-hand, every mother's son
Aboard! GOOD-BYE, GOOD-BYE, *THE ANTINOE!*
The sea had closed on forward deck and bow;
Let flag and mast and funnel settle now.
Frost-bitten, thinned in blood, gnarled to the bone,
But everyone surviving. All were brought
Below where ocean miracles are wrought,
Where the hearts' furnaces are stoked and blown,
Where men are shepherded in the old way
Of the sea, where drowned men come to life, they say.
Under such calls to breathe as never come
To those that roam the uplands of this earth:—
The hearty comradeship of a foc's'le berth,
With treble-folded blankets on their numb
Bodies, with balsam thawing out the brain,
Hot milk and coffee piping down their dumb
Constricted throats and mustard scattering pain,—
When cold half-foundered bellies steam again
Under the red authority of rum.

. . . .

The Cleggan
Disaster

RICHARD MURPHY

Off the west coast of Ireland in 1927

Five boats were shooting their nets in the bay
After dark. It was cold and late October.
The hulls hissed and rolled on the sea's black hearth
In the shadow of stacks close to the island.
Rain drenched the rowers, with no drying wind.
From the strokes of the oars a green fire flaked
And briskly quenched. The shore-lights were markers
Easterly shining across the Blind Sound.

Five pieces of drift-net with a mesh of diamonds
Were paid from each stern. The webbed curtains hung
Straight from the cork-lines, and warps were hitched
To the strong stems, and the pine oars boarded.
The men in the boats drew their pipes and rested.

The tide fell slack, all the breakers were still.
Not a flicker of a fish, only the slow fall
Of the ocean there drawing out the last drops of sleep.
Soon they could feel the effort of the ebb
Yearning at the yarn, twitching their mooring-stones
Stealthily seawards. Two boats began to haul.

From the bows of a boat in the centre of the bay
Concannon watched and waited. On each far wing
He heard them hauling. He held in his hand
The strong hemp rope which stretched from the cork-line
So that his fingers could feel the cord throb
If the shoal struck the nets. But so far, nothing.

Why had those others hauled? They were old
And experienced boatsmen. One man on the quay
At Bofin warned him, 'Sharpen your knife,
Be ready for trouble, cut away your nets.
Your crew is too young'. Were they going home?
Would the night not remain calm enough to fill
The barrels in their barns with food for the winter?

He had respect for the sea. He gave away
A share of his catch at the Cleggan market.
No one who asked for a feed of fish was refused.
On Bofin island, he loafed on land,
Dozed the sterile winter dreaming of boats,
And in summer wanted neither food nor sleep
While he gave his strength seriously to the sea.

He was sure of his boat, though small, well built.
Her ribs and her keel were adzed out of oak,
Her thole-pins were cut out of green holly,
And the grapnel was forged by the Cleggan smith.
Since the day she was launched, she had been lucky.

He was doubtful of his crew: three men and a boy
Who needed the money. Their land was poor,
But they had no heart for this work on water.
They helped each other. There were throngs of children
In thatched houses, whose lights they could see
Sparkling on the island, dim specks at Cleggan.
That night the best of boatsmen were on the bay
And many who wished they had waited by the fire.

In the dark before the moon rose, driftingly he smelt
Faintly on the water a floating oil
Bleeding from the nets where a blue-shark havocked
On the quivering tails of a mackerel shoal.
So he hauled until he reached the snarled threshes
Of the snapping shark, which he stunned across the rail
And clubbed with a foot-stick, bursting its blood.

Iron shouts clanged round the horseshoe bay
From the fetlock gap to the broad channel
As luck began to load the farthest nets,
And the green mackerel river raced through the water,
Crossed over the gunwales, and jetted fire
In the black braziers of the rolling bilges.

He thought, as the lucky stream continued to flow,
'There are three more pieces of net to be hauled.
If we're too greedy, we could sink the boat.
We have enough now to row home safely.
Cut them in time and return in the daylight.
Darker it's getting, with a north-west wind'.

The night was like a shell, with long sea surges
Loudening from afar, though no one was listening.
Quickly they folded the nets and heaped the fish.
The moon was kindling. The sky smouldered like soot.
Warm gusts of air floated by, moist with dew.
Mackerel flapped in the bilges. A woman was calling,
Crying from the beach. A shiver rippled the spine
Of the stony headland. Then, on the glistening gong
Of the sleeping sea, terrible hailstones hammered.

A storm began to march, the shrill wind piping
And thunder exploding, as lightning flaked
In willow cascades, and bayonets of hail
Flashed over craters and hillocks of water.
All the boats were trapped. None had reached the pier.
The target of the gale was the mainland rocks.

The men began to pray. Stack-funnelled hail
Crackled in volleys, with blasts on the bows
Where Concannon stood to fend with his body
The slash of seas. Then sickness surged,
And against their will they were griped with terror.
He told them to bail. When they lost the bailer
They bailed with their boots. Then they cast overboard
Their costly nets and a thousand mackerel.

She was drifting down the sound, her mooring-stone lifted
By the fingers of the tide plucking at the nets
Which he held with scorching hands. Over and over
He heard in his heart, 'Keep her stem to the storm,
And the nets will help her to ride the water;
Meet the force of the seas with her bows,
Each wave as it comes'. He'd use the knife later.

Down in the deep where the storm could not go
The ebb-tide, massive and slow, was drawing
Windwards the ninety-six fathom of nets
With hundreds of mackerel thickly meshed,
Safely tugging the boat off the mainland shore.
The moon couldn't shine, the clouds shut her out,
But she came unseen to sway on his side
All the waters gathered from the great spring tide.

As he slid from the cliff-slope of a heaped wave
Down the white and violet skin of turbulence
Into the boiling trough, he gathered in
Loose hanks of net, until the scalding rope
Steamed from his hands, the brittle boat, convulsed
By the far crest, shot through the spindrift safe.

The oarsmen were calling Concannon to let go,
Take it easy for a while. Let the boat drift
To the Cleggan shore, down wind, till they touch land.
Even there, if they died, it would be in a bay
Fringed with friends' houses, instead of in the open
Ocean, where the lost would never be found,
Where nothing is buried, no prayers are said.
Concannon silenced them, and stiffened his hold.

Twice the lightning blinked, then a crash of thunder.
Three cliffs of waves collapsed above them, seas
Crushed in his face, he fell down, and was dazed.

The wind began to play, like country fiddlers
In a crowded room, with nailed boots stamping
On a stone cottage floor, raising white ashes.
The sea became a dance. He staggered to the floor
As the music unleashed him, spun in a circle.
Now he was dancing round the siege of Death:
Now he was Death, they were dancing around him,
White robed dancers with crowns and clubs,
With white masked faces, and hands like claws
Flaying his eyes, as they clinched and swung.
He was holding the rope as the dance subsided.

While he lay there stunned, he remembered the sea
In tar-melting sunlight, dry weed on the thwarts,
The gills of mackerel tight in the meshes,
Hot stench of dead fish in the bailer,
Planks gaping wide, and thole-pins screeching,
The lines like lathes grooving the gunwales
While the depths yielded up the sacred John Dory.
He would never say, like that cripple on the quay,
He wished he had not wasted his life on the sea.

He knelt against the stem, his hands bleeding,
His eyes, scalded by the scurf of salt,
Straining to give shape to the shadows they saw
That looked like men in the milder water.
One of the crew said he heard his brother
Shouting for help, two oars away,
Yet when he hollowed, there was no reply.
In a lightning flash, a white hand rose
And rested on the gunwale, then slowly sank.

Down the valleys of this lull, like a black cow
In search of her calf, an upturned hull
Wallowed towards them. Her stem had parted.
All hands must have been lost. She lunged to his side
And almost staved him. Were the men inside?

Those who had thrown him his ropes from the quay?
The one who had warned him about his crew?
No help for them now. With his foot on her planks
He fended her off. As she bore away,
Her keel like a scythe cut a clear white swath
Through the gale's acres. Then a great sea crossed.
On the far side, as he nipped among white horses
Bolting towards him, under the streamers of manes
And the quick hoof-lash, he still headed the storm:
The chargers' lances hurtled with little harm
Through the icy air, while their hooves plunged on.

Now, though sea-boils encrusted his eyes,
He saw the Lyon Light, in spurts when they rode
Upon grey shoulders, flicker from white to red.
Lumps of water licked across tidal shallows.
They cantered at walls, and then faced hills.
The horses stampeded, as lanes closed ahead
In a white chalk-cliff. Rolled under horses
With manes in their mouths, their bones smashed,
Their blood washed away . . . Yet the cliff was passing.
The water rose to the thwarts. They went on bailing.

What were those lights that seemed to blaze like red
Fires in the pits of waves, lifted and hurled
At the aching sockets of his eyes, coals that lit
And expired in the space of a swell's slow heave?
'Am I going blind? *Am I going blind?*' he thought.
'Look at that wave. How it sharpens into a rock.
WATCH THAT ROCK. GET READY TO JUMP. It's gone.
Now *there's* a light . . . count the seconds: a slow pulse.
I can see that light from my own back door,
Slyne Head, never so high, such piercing brightness.
Where has it gone? Was it south of us it shone?
Lucky the keepers are safe. What a lonely life.
Lamps on the headlands have all been snuffed
By smothering waves. What weak pulse in the stars.
If I knew how to read them, we were saved'.

Lights flickered and vanished. Like a grey seal
Blinded by shot, he clung to the stem, his eyes closed.
The boy cried out: 'There's rocks to leeward'.
'What rocks do you think?' another asked.
'Dog Rock, I think, I fished here last summer'.
Concannon opened his knife: 'I'm cutting the nets'.
Piece by piece he slashed, but he had to tear
The clinging hanks with his finger bones, at last
He severed the rope, their guide on that dire sea-road,
And sank to his knees. The boatsmen rowed,
Backwards, falling away, her stem still to the storm,
With their eyes fixed on the faint lamps
That led across calm waters to Cleggan Quay.

It was three o'clock when she nudged the steps.
Safe on the stone bollards they fastened their ropes.
The full moon was whitening the ribs of hulks
In the worm-dark dock. The tide was flowing
As they trudged to the village. His crew helped him:
The sea had not claimed him, she had left him blind.

Lanterns shafted from the gates of the fish-store
Freshly that night cleaned for a *céilí*.
Bodies of fishermen lay on the floor on boxes,
Blood on their faces. Five had been found
By troops of searchers on shingle and sand.
Over the bier, with one hand cupping a flame,
An old man was looking at his drowned son.

As the day dawned, gap after gap was filled.
One of the boats was found on the beach at Letter
And floated off on the morning tide.

Only one body was got, the skull fractured:
Above high water mark he had crawled and died.
The walking-stick of a man who was lame
Was thrown in a heap of rods on a silver strand.
There was a king of the Mayo fishermen
Drawn from the sea in the chain of his own nets.
Of those who survived, a young one was seen
Walking at noon in the fields, clutching a bailer.

A sleep, cordoned by memories, calmed the sea.
Dead bracken was rusting the headlands,
The hills were flaked with hoarfrost, the sky marbled
Like mackerel netted in June water
When the men were returning home to the island.
Concannon felt his eyes like smithy troughs
Where hot harpoons are plunged, they boiled with pain.
Blindly he rowed, facing the hidden sun.

They passed the tower in the harbour's mouth
Snow-white on the gun rock, the two round towers
Touching each other on green fields, the castle
Of Cromwell's crimes full of screeching choughs.
Women in shawls on the quay were waiting.

The funeral boats brought over the bodies found,
But most were carried away on the great ebb tide.
From the village of Rossadillisk they lost sixteen
And from Bofin nine. One man above all was blind.

In a common grave that was dug in the sand dunes
Close to high water mark but leagues from low springs
They laid side by side the pinewood coffins
Lowering them on ropes, then shovelled the fine sand
Which whisperingly slid round their recent companions,
And sometimes the shovels met with a knelling clang
While in shifts they worked till the mound was raised.

After the prayers were said and the graveyard closed
Concannon was counting the fifty steps to his house,
Working out sounds, the sea-fall on the beach.
Would the islanders ever again dare to fish?
When he'd mastered this dark road, he himself would ask
To be oarsman in a boat, and mend the nets on land.
The croak of a herring gull tolled across the sky.
An oystercatcher squealed. Shoals broke on the bay.
The flood tide rose and covered the deserted strand.

    (YEARS LATER)

    Whose is that hulk on the shingle
    The boatwright's son repairs
    Though she has not been fishing
    For thirty-four years
    Since she rode the disaster?
    The oars were turned into rafters
    For a roof stripped by a gale.
    Moss has grown on her keel.

    Where are the red-haired women
    Chattering along the piers
    Who gutted millions of mackerel
    And baited the spillet hooks
    With mussels and lugworms?
    All the hurtful hours
    Thinking the boats were coming
    They hold against those years.

    Where are the barefoot children
    With brown toes in the ashes
    Who went to the well for water,
    Picked winkles on the beach
    And gathered sea-rods in winter?
    The lime is green on the stone
    Which they once kept white-washed.
    In summer nettles return.

Where are the dances in houses
With porter and cakes in the room,
The reddled faces of fiddlers
Sawing out jigs and reels,
The flickering eyes of neighbours?
The thatch which was neatly bordered
By a fringe of sea-stones
Has now caved in.

Why does she stand at the curtains
Combing her seal-grey hair
And uttering bitter opinions
On land work and sea fear,
Drownings and famines?
When will her son say,
'Forget about the disaster,
We're mounting nets today!'

Come Away, Death

E. J. PRATT

Willy-nilly, he comes or goes, with the clown's logic,
Comic in epitaph, tragic in epithalamium,
And unseduced by any mused rhyme.
However blow the winds over the pollen,
Whatever the course of the garden variables,
He remains the constant,
Ever flowering from the poppy seeds.

There was a time he came in formal dress,
Announced by Silence tapping at the panels
In deep apology.
A touch of chivalry in his approach,
He offered sacramental wine,
And with acanthus leaf
And petals of the hyacinth
He took the fever from the temples
And closed the eyelids,
Then led the way to his cool longitudes
In the dignity of the candles.
His mediaeval grace is gone—
Gone with the flame of the capitals
And the leisured turn of the thumb
Leafing the manuscripts,
Gone with the marbles
And the Venetian mosaics,
With the bend of the knee
Before the rose-strewn feet of the Virgin.
The *paternosters* of his priests,
Committing clay to clay,
Have rattled in their throats
Under the gride of his traction tread.

One night we heard his footfall—one September night—
In the outskirts of a village near the sea.
There was a moment when the storm
Delayed its fist, when the surf fell

Like velvet on the rocks—a moment only;
The strangest lull we ever knew!
A sudden truce among the oaks
Released their fratricidal arms;
The poplars straightened to attention
To the sound of a motor drone—
And then the drone was still.
We heard the tick-tock on the shelf,
And the leak of valves in our hearts.
A calm condensed and lidded
As at the core of a cyclone ended breathing
This was the monologue of Silence
Grave and unequivocal.

What followed was a bolt
Outside the range and target of the thunder,
And human speech curved back upon itself
Through Druid runways and the Piltdown scarps,
Beyond the stammers of the Java caves,
To find its origins in hieroglyphs
On mouths and eyes and cheeks
Etched by a foreign stylus never used
On the outmoded page of the Apocalypse.

The Fog

E. J. PRATT

It stole in on us like a foot-pad,
Somewhere out of the sea and air,
Heavy with rifling Polaris
And the Seven Stars.
It left our eyes untouched,
But took our sight,
And then.
Silently,
It drew the song from our throats.
And the supple bend from our ash-blades:
For the bandit,
With occult fingering,
Had tangled up
The four threads of the compass,
And fouled the snarl around our dory.

The Ground Swell

E. J. PRATT

Three times we heard it calling with a low,
   Insistent note; at ebb-tide on the noon;
      And at the hour of dusk, when the red moon
Was rising and the tide was on the flow;
Then, at the hour of midnight once again,
   Though we had entered in and shut the door
      And drawn the blinds, it crept up from the shore
And smote upon a bedroom window-pane;
Then passed away as some dull pang that grew
   Out of the void before Eternity
      Had fashioned out an edge for human grief;
Before the winds of God had learned to strew
   His harvest-sweepings on a winter sea
      To feed the primal hungers of a reef.

Erosion

E. J. PRATT

It took the sea a thousand years,
A thousand years to trace
The granite features of this cliff,
In crag and scarp and base.

It took the sea an hour one night,
An hour of storm to place
The sculpture of these granite seams
Upon a woman's face.

Come Not The Seasons Here

E. J. PRATT

Comes not the springtime here,
   Though the snowdrop came,
And the time of the cowslip is near,
   For a yellow flame
Was found in a tuft of green;
   And the joyous shout
   Of a child rang out
That a cuckoo's eggs were seen.

Comes not the summer here,
   Though the cowslip be gone,
Though the wild rose blow as the year
   Draws faithfully on;
Though the face of the poppy be red
   In the morning light,
   And the ground be white
With the bloom of the locust shed.

Comes not the autumn here,
   Though someone said
He found a leaf in the sere
   By an aster dead;
And knew that the summer was done,
   For a herdsman cried
That his pastures were brown in the sun,
   And his wells were dried.

Nor shall the winter come,
   Though the elm be bare,
And every voice be dumb
   On the frozen air;
But the flap of a waterfowl
   In the marsh alone,
Or the hoot of a horned owl
     On a glacial stone.

RosiaKKulak

JOE K. TUGLAVINA

RosiaKKulak RosiaKKulak
Naglinagunatuinavalulle
Akunialuk Inutlunga
TakuKattataga
NagligigasuKattatlugule
Akunile Inugama
Takunginatlugo
Inutsiavigigiatatagale

Kor
Rosiatsuga Rosiatsuga
Naglinagunatuinavalulle
Rosiatsuga Rosiatsuga
Naglinagunatsiamagikuluk

Inukulutuinaugama
Inukulugama
NagligigasuKattatagale
Akunile Inutlunga
Tamnasainautlunga
InukuluKattamigamale

Takunanginatlugule
RosiaKKulak
InutsiavigiKattatlugo
RosiaKKulak RosiaKKulak
Naglinagunatuinavalulle
RosiaKKulak RosiaKKulak
Nagligigajaksiamagittaga

Beautiful Rose

JOE K. TUGLAVINA

I

Beautiful Rose, beautiful Rose,
She is so sweet and lovable,
All of my life I see her around,
I see her all the time.
I've always tried to show her my love,
As long as I live,
I'll see her around,
I'll try to be so nice to her.

Chorus
Beautiful Rose, beautiful Rose,
She is so sweet and lovable,
Beautiful Rose, beautiful Rose,
She is so sweet and lovable.

II

I am only a human being
I am a human being.
I try hard to love her.
As long as I am alive
I am still me.
I am still a human being.

III

Often I look at her
Beautiful Rose,
I am friendly to her always
Beautiful Rose, beautiful Rose,
She looks so lovable
I will love her forever.

The Song of Wandering Aengus

W. B. YEATS

I went out to the hazel wood,
Because a fire was in my head,
And cut and peeled a hazel wand,
And hooked a berry to a thread;
And when white moths were on the wing,
And moth-like stars were flickering out,
I dropped the berry in a stream
And caught a little silver trout.

When I had laid it on the floor
I went to blow the fire aflame,
But something rustled on the floor,
And some one called me by my name:
It had become a glimmering girl
With apple blossom in her hair
Who called me by my name and ran
And faded through the brightening air.

Though I am old with wandering
Through hollow lands and hilly lands,
I will find out where she has gone,
And kiss her lips and take her hands;
And walk among long dappled grass,
And pluck till time and times are done
The silver apples of the moon,
The golden apples of the sun.

From: **The Wanderings of Oisin**

W. B. YEATS

. . . .

And then I mounted and she bound me
With her triumphing arms around me,
And whispering to herself enwound me;
But when the horse had felt my weight,
He shook himself and neighed three times:
Caoilte, Conan, and Finn came near,
And wept, and raised their lamenting hands,
And bid me stay, with many a tear;
But we rode out from the human lands.

In what far kingdom do you go,
Ah, Fenians, with the shield and bow?
Or are you phantoms white as snow,
Whose lips had life's most prosperous glow?
O you, with whom in sloping valleys,
Or down the dewy forest alleys,
I chased at morn the flying deer,
With whom I hurled the hurrying spear,
And heard the foemen's bucklers rattle,
And broke the heaving ranks of battle!
And Bran, Sceolan, and Lomair,
Where are you with your long rough hair?
You go not where the red deer feeds,
Nor tear the foemen from their steeds.

S. Patrick. Boast not, nor mourn with drooping head
Companions long accurst and dead,
And hounds for centuries dust and air.

Oisin. We galloped over the glossy sea:
I know not if days passed or hours,
And Niamh sang continually
Danaan songs, and their dewy showers
Of pensive laughter, unhuman sound,
Lulled weariness, and softly round
My human sorrow her white arms wound.
We galloped; now a hornless deer
Passed by us, chased by a phantom hound
All pearly white, save one red ear;
And now a lady rode like the wind
With an apple of gold in her tossing hand;
And a beautiful young man followed behind
With quenchless gaze and fluttering hair.

'Were these two born in the Danaan land,
Or have they breathed the mortal air?'

'Vex them no longer', Niamh said,
And sighing bowed her gentle head,
And sighing laid the pearly tip
Of one long finger on my lip.

But now the moon like a white rose shone
In the pale west, and the sun's rim sank,
And clouds arrayed their rank on rank
About his fading crimson ball:
The floor of Almhuin's hosting hall
Was not more level than the sea,
As, full of loving fantasy,
And with low murmurs, we rode on,
Where many a trumpet-twisted shell
That in immortal silence sleeps
Dreaming of her own melting hues,
Her golds, her ambers, and her blues,
Pierced with soft light the shallowing deeps.
But now a wandering land breeze came
And a far sound of feathery quires;
It seemed to blow from the dying flame,

They seemed to sing in the smouldering fires.
The horse towards the music raced,
Neighing along the lifeless waste;
Like sooty fingers, many a tree
Rose ever out of the warm sea;
And they were trembling ceaselessly,
As though they all were beating time,
Upon the centre of the sun,
To that low laughing woodland rhyme.
And, now our wandering hours were done,
We cantered to the shore, and knew
The reason of the trembling trees:
Round every branch the song-birds flew,
Or clung thereon like swarming bees;
While round the shore a million stood
Like drops of frozen rainbow light,
And pondered in a soft vain mood
Upon their shadows in the tide,
And told the purple deeps their pride,
And murmured snatches of delight;
And on the shores were many boats
With bending sterns and bending bows,
And carven figures on their prows
Of bitterns, and fish-eating stoats,
And swans with their exultant throats:
And where the wood and waters meet
We tied the horse in a leafy clump,
And Niamh blew three merry notes
Out of a little silver trump;
And then an answering whispering flew
Over the bare and woody land,
A whisper of impetuous feet,
And ever nearer, nearer grew;
And from the woods rushed out a band
Of men and ladies, hand in hand,
And singing, singing all together;
Their brows were white as fragrant milk,
Their cloaks made out of yellow silk,
And trimmed with many a crimson feather;

And when they saw the cloak I wore
Was dim with mire of a mortal shore,
They fingered it and gazed on me
And laughed like murmurs of the sea;
But Niamh with a swift distress
Bid them away and hold their peace;
And when they heard her voice they ran
And knelt there, every girl and man,
And kissed, as they would never cease,
Her pearl-pale hand and the hem of her dress.
She bade them bring us to the hall
Where Aengus dreams, from sun to sun,
A Druid dream of the end of days
When the stars are to wane and the world be done.

They led us by long and shadowy ways
Where drops of dew in myriads fall,
And tangled creepers every hour
Blossom in some new crimson flower,
And once a sudden laughter sprang
From all their lips, and once they sang
Together, while the dark woods rang,
And made in all their distant parts,
With boom of bees in honey-marts,
A rumour of delighted hearts.
And once a lady by my side
Gave me a harp, and bid me sing,
And touch the laughing silver string;
But when I sang of human joy
A sorrow wrapped each merry face,
And, Patrick! by your beard, they wept,
Until one came, a tearful boy;
'A sadder creature never stept
Than this strange human bard', he cried;
And caught the silver harp away,
And, weeping over the white strings, hurled
It down in a leaf-hid, hollow place
That kept dim waters from the sky;
And each one said, with a long, long sigh,

'O saddest harp in all the world,
Sleep there till the moon and the stars die!'

And now, still sad, we came to where
A beautiful young man dreamed within
A house of wattles, clay, and skin;
One hand upheld his beardless chin,
And one a sceptre flashing out
Wild flames of red and gold and blue,
Like to a merry wandering rout
Of dancers leaping in the air;
And men and ladies knelt them there
And showed their eyes with teardrops dim,
And with low murmurs prayed to him,
And kissed the sceptre with red lips,
And touched it with their finger-tips.

He held that flashing sceptre up.
'Joy drowns the twilight in the dew,
And fills with stars night's purple cup,
And wakes the sluggard seeds of corn,
And stirs the young kid's budding horn,
And makes the infant ferns unwrap,
And for the peewit paints his cap,
And rolls along the unwieldy sun,
And makes the little planets run:
And if joy were not on the earth,
There were an end of change and birth,
And Earth and Heaven and Hell would die,
And in some gloomy barrow lie
Folded like a frozen fly;
Then mock at Death and Time with glances
And wavering arms and wandering dances.

. . . .

Down by the Salley Gardens

W. B. YEATS

Down by the salley gardens my love and I did meet;
She passed the salley gardens with little snow-white feet.
She bid me take love easy, as the leaves grow on the tree;
But I, being young and foolish, with her would not agree.

In a field by the river my love and I did stand,
And on my leaning shoulder she laid her snow-white hand.
She bid me take life easy, as the grass grows on the weirs;
But I was young and foolish, and now am full of tears.

In Memory of Eva Gore-Booth and Con Markiewicz

W. B. YEATS

The light of evening, Lissadell,
Great windows open to the south,
Two girls in silk kimonos, both
Beautiful, one a gazelle.
But a raving autumn shears
Blossom from the summer's wreath;
The older is condemned to death,
Pardoned, drags out lonely years
Conspiring among the ignorant.
I know not what the younger dreams—
Some vague Utopia—and she seems,
When withered old and skeleton-gaunt,
An image of such politics.
Many a time I think to seek
One or the other out and speak
Of that old Georgian mansion, mix
Pictures of the mind, recall
That table and the talk of youth,
Two girls in silk kimonos, both
Beautiful, one a gazelle.
Dear shadows, now you know it all,
All the folly of a fight
With a common wrong or right.
The innocent and the beautiful
Have no enemy but time;
Arise and bid me strike a match
And strike another till time catch;
Should the conflagration climb,
Run till all the sages know.
We the great gazebo built,
They convicted us of guilt;
Bid me strike a match and blow.

Easter 1916

W. B. YEATS

I have met them at close of day
Coming with vivid faces
From counter or desk among grey
Eighteenth-century houses.
I have passed with a nod of the head
Or polite meaningless words,
Or have lingered awhile and said
Polite meaningless words,
And thought before I had done
Of a mocking tale or a gibe
To please a companion
Around the fire at the club,
Being certain that they and I
But lived where motley is worn:
All changed, changed utterly:
A terrible beauty is born.

That woman's days were spent
In ignorant good-will,
Her nights in argument
Until her voice grew shrill.
What voice more sweet than hers
When, young and beautiful,
She rode to harriers?
This man had kept a school
And rode our wingèd horse;
This other his helper and friend
Was coming into his force;
He might have won fame in the end,
So sensitive his nature seemed,
So daring and sweet his thought.
This other man I had dreamed
A drunken, vainglorious lout.
He had done most bitter wrong
To some who are near my heart,
Yet I number him in the song;

He, too has resigned his part
In the casual comedy;
He, too, has been changed in his turn,
Transformed utterly:
A terrible beauty is born.

Hearts with one purpose alone
Through summer and winter seem
Enchanted to a stone
To trouble the living stream.
The horse that comes from the road,
The rider, the birds that range
From cloud to tumbling cloud,
Minute by minute they change;
A shadow of cloud on the stream
Changes minute by minute;
A horse-hoof slides on the brim,
And a horse plashes within it;
The long-legged moor-hens dive,
And hens to moor-cocks call;
Minute by minute they live:
The stone's in the midst of all.

Too long a sacrifice
Can make a stone of the heart.
O when may it suffice?
That is Heaven's part, our part
To murmur name upon name,
As a mother names her child
When sleep at last has come
On limbs that had run wild.
What is it but nightfall?
No, no, not night but death;
Was it needless death after all?
For England may keep faith
For all that is done and said.
We know their dream; enough
To know they dreamed and are dead;
And what if excess of love

Bewildered them till they died?
I write it out in a verse—
MacDonagh and MacBride
And Connolly and Pearse
Now and in time to be,
Wherever green is worn,
Are changed, changed utterly:
A terrible beauty is born.

25 September, 1916.

From: **Meditations in Time of Civil War**

W. B. YEATS

II

My House

An ancient bridge, and a more ancient tower,
A farmhouse that is sheltered by its wall,
An acre of stony ground,
Where the symbolic rose can break in flower,
Old ragged elms, old thorns innumerable,
The sound of the rain or sound
Of every wind that blows;
The stilted water-hen
Crossing stream again
Scared by the splashing of a dozen cows;
A winding stair, a chamber arched with stone,
A grey stone fireplace with an open hearth,
A candle and written page.
Il Penseroso's Platonist toiled on
In some like chamber, shadowing forth
How the daemonic rage
Imagined everything.
Benighted travellers
From markets and from fairs
Have seen his midnight candle glimmering.

Two men have founded here. A man-at-arms
Gathered a score of horse and spent his days
In this tumultuous spot,
Where through long wars and sudden night alarms
His dwindling score and he seemed castaways
Forgetting and forgot;
And I, that after me
My bodily heirs may find,
To exalt a lonely mind,
Befitting emblems of adversity.

III

My Table

Two heavy trestles, and a board
Where Sato's gift, a changeless sword,
By pen and paper lies,
That it may moralise
My days out of their aimlessness.
A bit of an embroidered dress
Covers its wooden sheath.
Chaucer had not drawn breath
When it was forged. In Sato's house,
Curved like new moon, moon-luminous,
It lay five hundred years.
Yet if no change appears
No moon; only an aching heart
Conceives a changeless work of art.
Our learned men have urged
That when and where 'twas forged
A marvellous accomplishment,
In painting or in pottery, went
From father unto son
And through the centuries ran
And seemed unchanging like the sword.
Soul's beauty being most adored,
Men and their business took
The soul's unchanging look;
For the most rich inheritor,
Knowing that none could pass Heaven's door
That loved inferior art,
Had such an aching heart
That he, although a country's talk
For silken clothes and stately walk,
Had waking wits; it seemed
Juno's peacock screamed.

IV

My Descendants

Having inherited a vigorous mind
From my old fathers, I must nourish dreams
And leave a woman and a man behind
As vigorous of mind, and yet it seems
Life scarce can cast a fragrance on the wind,
Scarce spread a glory to the morning beams,
But the torn petals strew the garden plot;
And there's but common greenness after that.

And what if my descendants lose the flower
Through natural declension of the soul,
Through too much business with the passing hour,
Through too much play, or marriage with a fool?
May this laborious stair and this stark tower
Become a roofless ruin that the owl
May build in the cracked masonry and cry
Her desolation to the desolate sky.

The Primum Mobile that fashioned us
Has made the very owls in circles move;
And I, that count myself most prosperous,
Seeing that love and friendship are enough,
For an old neighbour's friendship chose the house
And decked and altered it for a girl's love,
And know whatever flourish and decline
These stones remain their monument and mine.

V

The Road at my Door

An affable Irregular,
A heavily-built Falstaffian man,
Comes cracking jokes of civil war
As though to die by gunshot were
The finest play under the sun.

A brown Lieutenant and his men,
Half dressed in national uniform,
Stand at my door, and I complain
Of the foul weather, hail and rain,
A pear-tree broken by the storm.

I count those feathered balls of soot
The moor-hen guides upon the stream,
To silence the envy in my thought;
And turn towards my chamber, caught
In the cold snows of a dream.

VI

The Stare's Nest by my Window

The bees build in the crevices
Of loosening masonry, and there
The mother birds bring grubs and flies.
My wall is loosening; honey-bees,
Come build in the empty house of the stare.

We are closed in, and the key is turned
On our uncertainty; somewhere
A man is killed, or a house burned,
Yet no clear fact to be discerned:
Come build in the empty house of the stare.

A barricade of stone or of wood;
Some fourteen days of civil war;
Last night they trundled down the road
That dead young soldier in his blood:
Come build in the empty house of the stare.

We had fed the heart on fantasies,
The heart's grown brutal from the fare;
More substance in our enmities
Than in our love; O honey-bees,
Come build in the empty house of the stare.

. . . .

The Wild Swans at Coole

W. B. YEATS

The trees are in their autumn beauty,
The woodland paths are dry,
Under the October twilight the water
Mirrors a still sky;
Upon the brimming water among the stones
Are nine-and-fifty swans.

The nineteenth autumn has come upon me
Since I first made my count;
I saw, before I had well finished,
All suddenly mount
And scatter wheeling in great broken rings
Upon their clamorous wings.

I have looked upon those brilliant creatures,
And now my heart is sore.
All's changed since I, hearing at twilight,
The first time on this shore,
The bell-beat of their wings above my head,
Trod with a lighter tread.

Unwearied still, lover by lover,
They paddle in the cold
Companionable streams or climb the air;
Their hearts have not grown old;
Passion or conquest, wander where they will,
Attend upon them still.

But now they drift on the still water,
Mysterious, beautiful;
Among what rushes will they build,
By what lake's edge or pool
Delight men's eyes when I awake some day
To find they have flown away?

Sailing to Byzantium

W. B. YEATS

I

That is no country for old men. The young
In one another's arms, birds in the trees
—Those dying generations—at their song,
The salmon-falls, the mackerel-crowded seas,
Fish, flesh, or fowl, commend all summer long
Whatever is begotten, born, and dies.
Caught in that sensual music all neglect
Monuments of unageing intellect.

II

An aged man is but a paltry thing,
A tattered coat upon a stick, unless
Soul clap its hands and sing, and louder sing
For every tatter in its mortal dress,
Nor is there singing school but studying
Monuments of its own magnificence;
And therefore I have sailed the seas and come
To the holy city of Byzantium.

III

O sages standing in God's holy fire
As in the gold mosaic of a wall,
Come from the holy fire, perne in a gyre,
And be the singing-masters of my soul.
Consume my heart away; sick with desire
And fastened to a dying animal
It knows not what it is; and gather me
Into the artifice of eternity.

IV

Once out of nature I shall never take
My bodily form from any natural thing,
But such a form as Grecian goldsmiths make
Of hammered gold and gold enamelling
To keep a drowsy Emperor awake;
Or set upon a golden bough to sing
To lords and ladies of Byzantium
Of what is past, or passing, or to come.

The Tomb of
Michael Collins

DENIS DEVLIN

To Ignazio Silone

I

Much I remember of the death of men,
But his I most remember, most of all,
More than the familiar and forgetful
Ghosts who leave our memory too soon—
Oh, what voracious fathers bore him down!

It was all sky and heather, wet and rock,
No one was there but larks and stiff-legged hares
And flowers bloodstained. Then, Oh, our shame so massive
Only a God embraced it and the angel
Whose hurt and misty rifle shot him down.

One by one the enemy dies off;
As the sun grows old, the dead increase,
We love the more the further from we're born!
The bullet found him where the bullet ceased,
And Gael and Gall went inconspicuous down.

II

There are the Four Green Fields we loved in boyhood,
There are some reasons it's no loss to die for:
Even it's no loss to die for having lived;
It is inside our life the angel happens
Life, the gift that God accepts or not,

Which Michael took with hand, with harsh, grey eyes,
He was loved by women and by men,
He fought a week of Sundays and by night
He asked what happened and he knew what was—
O Lord! how right that them you love die young!

He's what I was when by the chiming river
Two loyal children long ago embraced—
But what I was is one thing, what remember
Another thing, how memory becomes knowledge—
Most I remember him, how man is courage.

And sad, Oh sad, that glen with one thin stream
He met his death in; and a farmer told me
There was but one small bird to shoot: it sang
'Better Beast and know your end, and die
Than Man with murderous angels in his head'.

III

I tell these tales—I was twelve years old that time.
Those of the past were heroes in my mind:
Edward the Bruce whose brother Robert made him
Of Ireland, King; Wolfe Tone and Silken Thomas
And Prince Red Hugh O'Donnell most of all.

The newsboys knew and the apple and orange women
Where was his shifty lodging Tuesday night;
No one betrayed him to the foreigner,
No Protestant or Catholic broke and ran
But murmured in their heart: here was a man!

Then came that mortal day he lost and laughed at,
He knew it as he left the armoured car;
The sky held in its rain and kept its breath;
Over the Liffey and the Lee, the gulls,
They told his fortune which he knew, his death.

Walking to Vespers in my Jesuit school,
The sky was come and gone; 'O Captain, my Captain!'
Walt Whitman was the lesson that afternoon—
How sometimes death magnifies him who dies,
And some, though mortal, have achieved their race.

From: *Missouri Sequence*

BRIAN COFFEY

Nightfall, Midwinter, Missouri
To Thomas MacGreevy

Our children have eaten supper,
play Follow-my-Leader,
make songs from room to room
around and around;
once each minute
past my desk they go.

Inside the house is warm.
Winter outside blows from Canada
freezing rain to ice our trees
branch by branch, leaf by leaf.
The mare shelters in the barn.

On the impassable road no movement.
Nothing stirs in the sky against the black.
If memory were an ice-field
quiet as all outside!
Tonight the poetry is in the children's game:
I am distracted by comparisons,
Ireland across the grey ocean,
here, across the wide river.

★ ★ ★

We live far from where
my mother grows very old.
Five miles away, at Byrnesville,
the cemetery is filled with Irish graves,
the priest an old man born near Cork,
his bloss like the day he left the land.

People drifted in here from the river,
Irish, German, Bohemian,
more than one hundred years ago,
come to make homes.

Many Irish souls have gone back to God from Byrnesville,
many are Irish here today
where cedars stand like milestones
on worn Ozark hills
and houses white on bluegrass lawns
house people honest, practical and kind.

All shows to a long love
yet I am charmed
by the hills behind Dublin,
those white stone cottages,
grass green as no other green is green,
my mother's people, their ways.

France one loves with a love apart
like the love of wisdom;
Of England everyday love is the true love;
there is a love of Ireland
withering for Irishmen.

Does it matter where one dies,
supposing one knows how?

Dear Tom, in Ireland,
you have known
the pain between
its fruiting and the early dream
and you will hear me out.

★ ★ ★

Our children have ended play,
have gone to bed,
left me to face
what I had rather not.

They know nothing of Ireland,
they grow American.
They have chased snakes through the couch-grass
in summer, caught butterflies and beetles
we did not know existed,
fished for the catfish,
slept on an open porch
when Whip-poor-Will and tree-frog
work all night,
observed the pupa of the shrill cicada
surface on dry clay,
disrobe for the short ruinous day.
The older ones have helped a neighbour, farmer,
raise his field of ripe corn
in heat that hurt us to the bone,
paid homage to dead men
with fire-crackers in July,
eaten the turkey in November.
Here now they make their friendships,
learn to love God.

Yet we must leave America,
bitter necessity no monopoly
of Irish soil.
It was pain once to come,
it is pain now to go.

How the will shifts from goal to goal
for who does not freely choose.
Some choose, some are chosen
to go their separate paths.
I would choose, I suppose, yet would be chosen
in some equation between God's will and mine,
rejecting prudence to make of conflict
a monument to celtic self-importance.

The truth is, where the cross is not
The Christian does not go.

★ ★ ★

Return home takes on while I dream it
the fictive form of heaven on earth,
the child's return to motherly arms
for fright at frogs disturbed among iris leaves.

One poet I admire has written:
wherever the soul gives in to flesh
without a struggle is home.
Would one want home like that,
rest, supine surrender
to oneself alone,
flight from where one is?

There is no heaven on earth,
no facile choice for one
charged with care of others,
none for one like me
for whom no prospect opens
fairly on clear skies.

It grows late and winter
lays its numbing pall.
Doubts restless like what you see
when you lift a flat damp stone
exasperate my warring wishes
until wrenched apart by desperate extremes
I am back where I started.

Pain it was to come,
pain it will be to go.

★ ★ ★

Not just to go,
not just to stay,
but the act done in wisdom's way—
not impossible
if one is wise.

Our William Butler Yeats
made island flowers grow
that need as much
the local rain
as wind from overseas
to reach their prime.
He struggled towards the exact muse
through a sunless day.

No servant, the muse
abides in truth,
permits the use of protest
as a second best
to make clean fields,
exults only in the actual
expression of a love,
love all problem,
wisdom lacking.

★ ★ ★

How near the surface of the pool
sunfish play, distract
us from where down deep
real reasons impose their rule.

The room is filled with children's lives
that fill my cares who turn again
to sudden starting words
like birds in cages.
Without all is silent,
within I have no peace at all,
having failed to choose
with loving-wise choice.

Midnight now.
Deepest winter perfect now.
Tomorrow early we shall make lunches
for the children to take to school,
forgetting while working out the week
our wrestling with the sad flesh
and the only Ireland we love
where in Achill still
the poor praise Christ aloud
when the priest elevates
the Saviour of the world.

. . . .

Forget Me Not (1962)

AUSTIN CLARKE

Up the hill,
Hurry me not;
Down the hill,
Worry me not;
On the level,
Spare me not,
In the stable,
Forget me not.

Trochaic dimeter, amphimacer
And choriamb, with hyper catalexis,
Grammatical inversion, springing of double
Rhyme. So we learned to scan all, analyse
Lyric and ode, elegy, anonymous patter,
For what is song itself but substitution?
Let classical terms unroll, with a flourish, the scroll
Of baccalaureate.
     Coleridge had picked
That phrase for us—*vergiss-mein-nicht*, emblem
Of love and friendship, delicate sentiments.
Forget-me-nots, forget-me-nots:
Blue, sunny-eyed young hopefuls! He left a nosegay,
A keepsake for Kate Greenaway.

      Child climbed
Into the trap; the pony started quick
As fly to a flick and Uncle John began
Our work-a-day, holiday jingle.
      Up the hill,
 Hurry me not.
    Down the hill,
 Worry me not.
     Verse came like that, simple
As join-hands, yet ambiguous, lesson
Implied, a flower-puzzle in final verb

And negative. All was personification
As we drove on: invisibility
Becoming audible. A kindness spoke.
Assumed the god; consensus everywhere
In County Dublin. Place-names, full of Sunday,
Stepaside, Pass-if-you-can Lane, Hole in the Wall.
Such foliage in the Dargle hid Lovers Leap,
We scarcely heard the waters fall-at-all.
Often the open road to Celbridge: we came back
By Lucan Looks Lovely, pulled in at the Strawberry Beds,
Walked up the steep of Knockmaroon. Only
The darkness could complete our rounds. The pony
Helped, took the bit. Coat-buttoned up, well-rugg'd
I drowsed till the clatter of city sets, warning
Of echoes around St. Mary's Place, woke me;
But I was guarded by medal, scapular
And the *Agnus Dei* next my skin, passing
That Protestant Church. Night shirt, warm manger, confusion
Of premise, creed; I sank through mysteries
To our oblivion.
                  Ora pro nobis
Ora pro me.
                  'Gee up', 'whoa', 'steady', 'hike',
'Hike ow'a that,' Rough street-words, cheerful, impatient:
The hearers knew their own names as well. Horses,
Men, going together to daily work; dairy
Cart, baker's van, slow dray, quick grocery
Deliveries. Street-words, the chaff in them.
Suddenly in Mountjoy Street, at five o'clock
Yes, five in the evening, work rhymed for a minute with sport.
Church-echoing wheel-rim, roof-beat, tattle of harness
Around the corner of St. Mary's Place:
Cabs, outside cars, the drivers unranked in race
For tips; their horses eager to compete,
With spark and hubbub, greet with their own heat
Galway Express that puffed to Broadstone Station.
They held that Iron Horse in great esteem
Yet dared the metamorphosis of steam.
Soon they were back again. I ran to watch

As Uncle John in elegant light tweeds
Drove smartly by on his outside car, talking
Over his shoulder to a straight-up fare
Or two, coaxing by name his favourite mare;
The best of jarvies, his sarcastic wit
Checked by a bridle rein; and he enlarged
My mind with two Victorian words. Grown-ups
Addressed him as Town Councillor, Cab
And Car Proprietor!

                Horse-heads above me,
Below me. Happy on tram top, I looked down
On plaited manes, alighted safely, caught
Sidelong near kerb, perhaps, affectionate glance
As I passed a blinker. Much to offend the pure:
Let-down or drench, the sparrows pecking at fume,
The scavengers with shovel, broom. But, O
When horse fell down, pity was there: we saw
Such helplessness, girth buckled, no knack in knee,
Half-upturned legs—big hands that couldn't unclench.
A parable, pride or the like, rough-shod,
Or goodness put in irons, then, soul uplifted
Bodily; traffic no longer interrupted.
Strength broadened in narrow ways. Champions went by,
Guinness's horses from St. James's Gate:
Their brasses clinked, yoke, collar shone at us:
Light music while they worked. Side-streets, alleys
Beyond St. Patrick's, floats unloading, country
Colt, town hack, hay-cart, coal-bell. Often the whip-crack,
The lash of rein. Hand-stitch in the numb of pain
At school Religious orders plied the strap
On us, but never on themselves. Each day, too,
Justice tore off her bandage in Mountjoy Street.
The Black Maria passed, van o' the poor.
Weeks, months clung to those bars, cursed, or stared, mute.
Children in rags ran after that absenting,
Did double time to fetlocks. Solemnity
For all; the mournful two or four with plumes,

Hooves blackened to please your crape. The funerals
Go faster now. Our Christianity
Still catching up with All is Vanity.

Nevertheless,
Nature had learned to share our worldliness,
Well-pleased to keep with man the colours in hide,
Dappling much, glossing the chestnut, sunshading the bays,
To grace those carriage wheels, that *vis-à-vis*
In the Park. Let joy cast off a trace, for once,
High-stepping beyond the Phoenix Monument
In the long ago of British Rule, I saw
With my own eyes a white horse that unfabled
The Unicorn.

Mechanised vehicles:
Horse-power by handle-turn. My Uncle John
Lost stable companions, drivers, all. Though poor,
He kept his last mare out on grass. They aged
Together. At twenty-one, I thought it right
And proper.

How could I know that greed
Spreads quicker than political hate? No need
Of propaganda. Good company, up and down
The ages, gone: the trick of knife left, horse cut
To serve man. All the gentling, custom of mind
And instinct, close affection, done with. The unemployed
Must go. Dead or ghosted by froths, we ship them
Abroad. Foal, filly, farm pony, bred for slaughter:
What are they now but hundredweights of meat?
A double trade. Greed with a new gag of mercy
Grants happy release in our whited abbatoirs.
'Gentlemen, businessmen, kill on the spot! O
That', exclaim the good, 'should be your motto.
Combine in a single trade all profits, save
Sensitive animals from channelling wave,
Continental docking, knackering down.

We dread bad weather, zig-zag, tap of Morse'
Well-meaning fools, who only pat the horse
That looks so grand on our Irish half-crown.

I've more to say—

                Men of Great Britain
Openly share with us the ploughtail, the field-spoil,
Trucking in Europe what we dare not broil
At home.
         Herodotus condemned
Hippophagy.
              And Pliny, also.
                  Beseiged towns
Denied it.
              Stare now at Pegasus. The blood
Of the Medusa weakens in him.
                    Yet all the world
Was hackneyed once—those horses o' the sun,
Apollo's car, centaurs in Thessaly.
Too many staves have splintered the toy
That captured Troy. The Hippocrene is stale.
Dark ages; Latin rotted, came up from night-soil,
New rush of words; thought mounted them. Trappings
Of palfrey, sword-kiss of chivalry, high song
Of grammar. Men pick the ribs of Rosinante
In restaurants now. Horse-shoe weighs in with saddle
Of meat.
          Horseman, the pass-word, courage shared
With lace, steel, buff.
              Wars regimented
Haunches together. Cities move by in motor
Cars, charging the will. I hear in the lateness of Empires,
A neighing, man's cry in engines. No peace, yet,
Poor draggers of artillery.
                    The moon
Eclipsed: I stood on the Rock of Cashel, saw dimly
Carved on the royal arch of Cormac's Chapel
Sign of the Sagittary, turned my back

On all that Celtic Romanesque; thinking
Of older story and legend, how Cuchullain,
Half man, half god-son, tamed the elemental
Coursers: dear comrades: how at his death
The Gray of Macha laid her mane upon his breast
And wept.
                I struggled down
From paleness of limestone.
                            Too much historied
Land, wrong in policies, armings, hope in prelates
At courts abroad! Rags were your retribution,
Hedge schools, a visionary knowledge in verse
That hid itself. The rain-drip cabin'd the dream
Of foreign aid . . . Democracy at last.
White horses running through the European mind
Of the First Consul. Our heads were cropped like his.
New brow; old imagery. A Gaelic poet,
Pitch-capped in the Rebellion of '98.
Called this Republic in an allegory
The Slight Red Steed.
                            Word-loss is now our gain:
Put mare to stud. Is Ireland any worse
Than countries that fly-blow the map, rattle the sky,
Drop down from it? Tipsters respect our grand sires,
Thorough-breds, jumpers o' the best.
Our grass still makes a noble show, and the roar
Of money cheers us at the winning post.
So pack tradition in the meat-sack, Boys,

Write off the epitaph of Yeats.
                    I'll turn
To jogtrot, pony bell, say my first lesson:

> *Up the hill,*
> *Hurry me not;*
> *Down the hill,*
> *Worry me not;*
>
> *On the level,*
> *Spare me Not,*
> *In the stable,*
> *Forget me not.*
>
> *Forget me not.*

The Snow Party

DEREK MAHON

for Louis Asekoff

BASHŌ, coming
To the city of Nagoya,
Is asked to a snow party.

There is a tinkling of china
And tea into china,
There are introductions.

Then everyone
Crowds to the window
To watch the falling snow.

Snow is falling on Nagoya
And farther south
On the tiles of Kyóto.

Eastward, beyond Irago,
It is falling
Like leaves on the cold sea.

Elsewhere they are burning
Witches and heretics
In the boiling squares,

Thousands have died since dawn
In the service
Of barbarous kings—

But there is silence
In the houses of Nagoya
And the hills of Ise.

From: **descending the mountain**
NICK AVIS

after making love
we descend the mountain
　and its silence

　　　　　we return
　　　　　to the valley's warmth
　　　　　　　the smell of young leaves

　　　　　　　　　snowdrifts at my door
　　　　　　　　　a letter from an old friend
　　　　　　　　　　　never answered

　　　　　the village graveyard
　　　　　　one by one the headstones   lost
　　　　　in the ocean mist

　　the young plum pickers
breaking yet another branch
　　　　　late september winds

　a wedge of geese
　　　carries the last patch of sky
into the sunset

8

I Have Lived in Important Places, Times

Epic   PATRICK KAVANAGH

I have lived in important places, times
When great events were decided, who owned
That half a rood of rock, a no-man's land
Surrounded by our pitchfork-armed claims.
I heard the Duffys shouting 'Damn your soul'
And old McCabe stripped to the waist, seen
Step the plot defying blue cast-steel—
'Here is the march along these iron stones'
That was the year of the Munich bother. Which
Was more important? I inclined
To lose my faith in Ballyrush and Gortin
Till Homer's ghost came whispering to my mind
He said: I made the Iliad from such
A local row. Gods make their own importance.

The One

PATRICK KAVANAGH

Green, blue, yellow and red—
God is down in the swamps and marshes
Sensational as April and almost incred-
   ible the flowering of our catharsis.

A humble scene in a backward place
Where no one important ever looked
The raving flowers looked up in the face
Of the One and the Endless, the Mind that has baulked
The profoundest of mortals. A primrose, a violet,
A violent wild iris—but mostly anonymous performers
Yet an important occasion as the Muse at her toilet
Prepared to inform the local farmers
That beautiful, beautiful, beautiful God
Was breathing His love by a cut-away bog.

From: *The Great Hunger*

PATRICK KAVANAGH

. . . .

O the grip, O the grip of irregular fields! No man escapes.
It could not be that back of the hills love was free
And ditches straight.
No monster hand lifted up children and put down apes
As here.
        'O God if I had been wiser!'
That was his sigh like the brown breeze in the thistles.
He looks towards his house and haggard. 'O God if I had been
 wiser!'
But now a crumpled leaf from the whitethorn bushes
Darts like a frightened robin, and the fence
Shows the green of after-grass through a little window,
And he knows that his own heart is calling his mother a liar.
God's truth is life—even the grotesque shapes of its foulest fire.

The horse lifts its head and crashes
Through the whins and stones
To lip late passion in the crawling clover.
In the gap there's a bush weighted with boulders like morality,
The fools of life bleed if they climb over.
The wind leans from Brady's, and the coltsfoot leaves are holed
 with rust,
Rain fills the cart-tracks and the sole-plate grooves;
A yellow sun reflects in Donaghmoyne
The poignant light in puddles shaped by hooves.

Come with me, Imagination, into this iron house
And we will watch from the doorway the years run back,
And we will know what a peasant's left hand wrote on the page.
Be easy, October. No cackle hen, horse neigh, tree sough, duck quack.

II

Maguire was faithful to death:
He stayed with his mother till she died
At the age of ninety-one.
She stayed too long,
Wife and mother in one.
When she died
The knuckle-bones were cutting the skin of her son's backside
And he was sixty-five.

O he loved his mother
Above all others.
O he loved his ploughs
And he loved his cows
And his happiest dream
Was to clean his arse
With perennial grass
On the bank of some summer stream;
To smoke his pipe
In a sheltered gripe
In the middle of July—
His face in a mist
And two stones in his fist
And an impotent worm on his thigh.

But his passion became a plague
For he grew feeble bringing the vague
Women of his mind to lust nearness,
Once a week at least flesh must make an appearance.

So Maguire got tired
Of the no-target gun fired
And returned to his headlands of carrots and cabbage
To the fields once again
Where eunuchs can be men
And life is more lousy than savage.

III

Poor Paddy Maguire, a fourteen-hour day
He worked for years. It was he that lit the fire
And boiled the kettle and gave the cows their hay.
His mother tall hard as a Protestant spire
Came down the stairs bare-foot at the kettle-call
And talked to her son sharply: 'Did you let
The hens out, you?' She had a venomous drawl
And a wizened face like moth-eaten leatherette.
Two black cats peeped between the banisters
And gloated over the bacon-fizzling pan.
Outside the window showed tin canisters.
The snipe of Dawn fell like a whirring noise
And Patrick on a headland stood alone.

The pull is on the traces, it is March
And a cold old black wind is blowing from Dundalk.
The twisting sod rolls over on her back—
The virgin screams before the irresistible sock.
No worry on Maguire's mind this day
Except that he forgot to bring his matches.
'Hop back there Polly, hoy back, woa, wae',
From every second hill a neighbour watches
With all the sharpened interest of rivalry.
Yet sometimes when the sun comes through a gap
These men know God the Father in a tree:

The Holy Spirit is the rising sap,
And Christ will be the green leaves that will come
At Easter from the sealed and guarded tomb.

. . . .

On Raglan Road   PATRICK KAVANAGH

On Raglan Road on an autumn day I met her first and knew
That her dark hair would weave a snare that I might one day rue;
I saw the danger, yet I walked along the enchanted way,
And I said, let grief be a fallen leaf at the dawning of the day.

On Grafton Street in November we tripped lightly along the ledge
Of the deep ravine where can be seen the worth of passion's pledge,
The Queen of Hearts still making tarts and I not making hay—
O I loved too much and by such by such is happiness thrown away.

I gave her gifts of the mind I gave her the secret sign that's known
To the artists who have known the true gods of sound and stone
And word and tint. I did not stint for I gave her poems to say
With her own name there and her own dark hair like clouds over fields of May.

On a quiet street where old ghosts meet I see her walking now
Away from me so hurriedly my reason must allow
That I had wooed not as I should a creature made of clay—
When the angel woos the clay he'd lose his wings at the dawn of day.

Dick King

THOMAS KINSELLA

In your ghost, Dick King, in your phantom vowels I read
That death roves our memories igniting
Love. Kind plague, low voice in a stubbled throat,
You haunt with the taint of age and of vanished good,
Fouling my thought with losses.

Clearly now I remember rain on the cobbles,
Ripples in the iron trough, and the horses' dipped
Faces under the Fountain in James's Street,
When I sheltered my nine years against your buttons
And your own dread years were to come:

And your voice, in a pause of softness, named the dead,
Hushed as though the city had died by fire,
Bemused, discovering . . . discovering
A gate to enter temperate ghosthood by;
And I squeezed your fingers till you found again
My hand hidden in yours.

                I squeeze your fingers:

    Dick King was an upright man.
    Sixty years he trod
    The dull stations underfoot.
    Fifteen he lies with God.

    By the salt seaboard he grew up
    But left its rock and rain
    To bring a dying language east
    And dwell in Basin Lane.

By the Southern Railway he increased:
His second soul was born
In the clangour of the iron sheds,
The hush of the late horn.

An invalid he took to wife.
She prayed her life away;
Her whisper filled the whitewashed yard
Until her dying day.

And season in, season out,
He made his wintry bed.
He took the path to the turnstile
Morning and night till he was dead.

He clasped his hands in a Union ward
To hear St. James's bell.
I searched his eyes though I was young,
The last to wish him well.

Dínit an Bhróin   MÁIRTÍN Ó DIREÁIN

Nochtaíodh domsa tráth
Dínit mhór an bhróin,
Ar fheiceáil dom beirt bhan
Ag siúl amach ó shlua
I bhfeisteas caointe dubh,
Gan focal astu beirt:
D'imigh an dínit leo
Ón slua callánach mór.

Bhí freastalán istigh
Ó línéar ar an ród,
Fuadar faoi gach n-aon,
Gleo ann is caint ard;
Ach an bheirt a bhí ina dtost,
A shiúil amach leo féin
I bhfeisteas caointe dubh,
D'imigh an dínit leo.

Grief's Dignity MÁIRTÍN Ó DIREÁIN

I once had a glimpse
Of grief's great dignity
When I saw two women
Emerge from a crowd
In dark funereal garb,
Neither uttering a word:
Dignity departed with them
From the large and noisy crowd.

A tender was in
From a liner in the roadstead,
Everyone was scurrying around,
Hubbub and loud chatter;
But the silent couple
Who emerged on their own
In dark funereal garb,
Dignity departed with them.

translated by Douglas Sealy and Tomás Mac Síomóin

Cranna Foirtil
MÁIRTÍN Ó DIREÁIN

Coinnigh do thalamh, a anam liom,
Coigil chugat gach tamhanrud,
Is ná bí mar ghiolla gan chaithir
I ndiaidh na gcarad nár fhóin duit.

Minic a dhearcais ladhrán trá
Ar charraig fhliuch go huaigneach;
Mura bhfuair éadáil ón toinn,
Ní bhfuair guth ina héagmais.

Níor thugais ó do ríocht dhorcha
Caipín an tsonais ar do cheann,
Ach cuireadh cranna cosanta
Go teann thar do chliabhán cláir.

Cranna caillte a cuireadh tharat,
Tlú iarainn os do chionn,
Ball éadaigh d'athar taobh leat
Is bior sa tine thíos.

Luigh ar do chranna foirtil
I gcoinne mallmhuir is díthrá,
Coigil aithinne d'aislinge;
Scaradh léi is éag duit.

Stout Oars

MÁIRTÍN Ó DIREÁIN

Stand your ground, my soul;
Cleave to every rooted stock;
Don't behave like a callow youth
When your false friends depart.

You've often seen a redshank
Alone on a wet rock;
Though he drew no wealth from the wave,
His lapse incurred no censure.

From your dark realm you brought
No lucky caul around your head,
But the ritual wands were placed
To protect you in your cradle.

Useless sticks were placed around you,
An iron tongs above,
Beside you a piece of your father's clothing,
A poker placed in the fire.

Lean on your own stout oars
Against neap-tide and ebb,
Keep alight the coal of your vision;
To part with that is death.

translated by Douglas Sealy and Tomás Mac Síomóin

Berkeley

MÁIRTÍN Ó DIREÁIN

Ar charraig, a Easpaig Chluana,
A tógadh mise i mo ghasúr
Is bhí na clocha glasa
Is na creaga loma fúm is tharam,
Ach b'fhada uathu a mhair tusa,
A Easpaig is a fhealsaimh.

Swift féin an Déan mór
Níorbh ait fós má b'fhíor,
Gur fhág tú ar a thairsigh;
Comhla an dorais nár bhrionglóid
I do mheabhair de réir do theagaisc?
Is cad ab áil leis a hoscailt duit
Is gan ann ach a samhail?

An Dochtúir Johnson fós
Thug speach do chloch ina aice
Mar dhóigh go ndearna an buille
Ar an rud ionraic smionagar
De do aisling, a chuir i gcás
Gur istigh san aigne a bhí
Gach ní beo is marbh.

Ní shéanaim go raibh mo pháirt
Leis na móir úd tamall,
Ach ó thosaigh na clocha glasa
Ag dul i gcruth brionglóide i m'aigne,
Níl a fhios agam, a Easpaig chóir,
Nach tú féin a chuaigh air an domhain
Is nach iad na móir a d'fhan le cladach.

Berkeley

MÁIRTÍN Ó DIREÁIN

On a rock, Bishop of Cloyne,
I was reared as a boy
And the grey stones
And barren crags encompassed me,
But far from such you lived,
Bishop and philosopher.

Swift himself, the great Dean,
Was not mad, if it's true
He left you on his doorstep;
Was not the closed door a dream
In your mind, for thus you taught?
And why would he want to open it for you,
Since it was only a ghost of itself?

Dr. Johnson too
Kicked an adjacent stone
As if the assault
On the pure entity smashed
Your vision, and its implication
That in the mind was contained
All living substances and all inanimate matter.

I don't deny I agreed
With those great men for a while,
But since the grey stones began
To turn to dreams in my mind,
I do not know, my dear Bishop,
That you weren't the one who went on the deep
While the great men stayed on the shore.

translated by Douglas Sealy and Tomás Mac Síomóin

Bogwood

GREGORY POWER

The year we plowed the river field, we found
Deep in the silt, the warped and blackened bones
Of ancient trees; and most of them were sound,
Though every bit as heavy as the stones.
Among them there were ribs, backbones, and knees,
Thin fingers that had held green leaves, or fed
White blossoms to the wind, lost springs, when these
Made magic here. For days we harvested
These bones of trees from soft, black furrows where
The land was wet; and when the field was done
We left them in loose tangles, here and there,
To season in the summer wind and sun.

Around the coast, old custom sets a time
For certain work, and in our neighbourhood,
When April comes we tidy up and lime;
December is the month for getting wood.
So, while the meadows slept, benumbed and white,
And skies were little more than half-awake,
We cut them into junks and they were light
As feathers now, but hard enough to break
An axeman's heart. One bitter night we burned
This wood that time had tempered in the mire.
It charmed those hours of rest, when we concerned
Ourselves with dreams, and made a ghostly fire,
Beyond its blue, transparent flame, we saw
The heat waves dancing in a parched July;
Its light transformed by some enchanted law,
Was hoarded sunlight from an age gone by.

The Mummer

TOM DAWE

I was once the best mummer
in our cove.
I pleased the people
all the time.
And through the Christmas spell
I mummered by myself
across drifted fields
and tricky paths
above the cliffs
on raw nights
when sea voices whispered
in caves far below me.
I clutched my kerosene lantern
and felt my old accordion
wheeze against my ribs.
And in all those winter times
with my light coming to hers,
she always let me in,
though she never guessed me
and I did not lift my veil.
Not once did she guess
that all those tunes I played
of long-gone summer love
and never-forgetting
were just for her.
Though they danced and laughed
and shook the china on the shelves,
her youngsters could never know
how I played for mother alone.
Though they shone
with cake crumbs and syrup
on their happy faces,
I never played for them
in that salt-box house
where stove pipes cracked
and stars winked

on the snow outside.
And that big, lazy man she married . . .
least of all I played for him
snoring on the settle
in the chimney corner,
a red face so peaceful
with the tea-pot waiting
and long rubbers limp and steaming
by the blushing stove.
And in all those years
of forget-me-not tunes,
she never guessed me
and my veil stayed down.

The French Shore Man

TOM DAWE

Seems I can mind them
myself,
the French
along our coast,
and poor father
and his father before him
talking about the wonderful bread
those foreigners made
in beach-rock ovens
in the summertime.
That was well back
in the rowdy days
when they thought
this shore
belonged to them.
Sometimes they seemed pretty human
all the same,

giving you one
of their queer loaves
to go with your fish
when you crossed paths
on the water,
even though you were English
with wife and youngsters
on the shore.
It must have been hard
for them to accept defeat
and leave the coves
where they cured their cod.
I remember
poor grandfather grinning,
claiming he broke bread
with them one time
somewhere off the Grey Islands . . .

On raw days now
when the wind is in
and the sand taps
my window pane,
I can close my eyes
and see them
moving
in the landwash still . . .
Dreamy foolishness, I suppose,
for me with sixty summers notched.
But one day
six years ago,
I was digging a hole
to put the bark-pot on,
when all of a sudden,
my pick struck Frenchmen's bones.
Seems there were two of them
laid out there.
One had no teeth at all;
that devil yawned at everything.
The other had all his ivory,

no mistake about that,
and when I laid his skull
on a rock,
he seemed to stare
out over the water,
grinning at it all.

In Picasso's 'Madman'

TOM DAWE

Somehow, in Picasso's 'Madman',
I can see the four of them:

Uncle Henry Gaunt
just back from the Labrador,
bent over Aunt Carrie's grave,
crying in his big, cupped hands,
then stopping suddenly
to peer through knotty fingers
at aspen leaves
trembling on a white sky.

And my tired grandfather,
daydreaming in the landwash,
gazing through a web of caplin mesh
strung on his splayed fingers
in a moment
when he did not see me
watching him.

And poor Jenny Drake,
the war-bride
knitting by a kitchen window,
ignoring her baby's crying,
staring through the yarn-lines
in her thin fingers,
talking again of cowslip fields
and heather-slopes
across the sea.

And the retarded boy
who lived one time in Rampike Arm,
lying hidden under cherry-limbs,
talking to his contorted hands,
laughing excitedly
to himself
each time mosquitoes clustered
for his blood . . .

. . . Something of four people
I knew one time,
now glimmering
in Picasso's tattered 'Madman'
forever fascinated
with those invisible skeins
all tangled
in his scrawny hands.

Edwardians
(Old Photograph)
TOM DAWE

For them it is always Sunday afternoon:
six couples in the shade of a tree,
lounging in an English meadow.

They are blurred now:
sepia smokers in straw hats
lolling among wine bottles,
cake-baskets, clover.

They stare out at us:
lotus creatures, insolent somehow
in languid pose,
smug, sprawling, laid-back,
locked there in weekend.

Behind them, over daisy-dotted trench,
a jacket swings carelessly
on a strand of wire
dividing the property,

winding, coiling towards the Channel
perhaps, one inconspicuous,
barbed, metallic cord,
not really symbolic
in this landscape yet.

The Veteran (1)   TOM DAWE

I'll not forget that foreign scene,
and I just a frightened boy:
He tarried there in my rifle-sight,
So tall on the clearing sky.

I struggled to pull the trigger then,
For, just beyond his head,
Was a flash of something close to home,
Across those fields of the dead:

A wink of sea between two hills,
A gull's turn on the sky,
I stopped and put my rifle down
And let my man pass by.

Daedalus   TOM DAWE

Alone on the beach this morning
I catch myself
blaming the gods again
for this poised gull
against the sky,
mocking me now
as they did once
at my son's funeral
when a partridge laughed
from somewhere
in the grove.
I dream that day back
with gentle sea swell,
goats, green island,
the lip of a grave,

and sorrow planting me
like some tree
twisted
in sea wind.

On morning wings
across the sun
he comes before me,
there at the seabird's core,
my son,
the slave-girl's child,
that shadowy
all-too-human form,
five-pointed man
inside translucent feather.
Cruel are those gods
who coax
with sunshine!

Now I am forced
to see him
falling
once more,
clawing
the air
so far
beyond
my pleading.
And as he goes
by me,
one last
glimpse
of the slave
girl
free somehow
in frightened
contours
of his face.
And the mesmerizing

space
of it all,
the small flag
of a foot
disappearing
into the shimmer
of the herring
shoals.

And far away,
as if they know
about it already,
waiting, nodding,
placed there
for my returning,
sinewy, sunburned men,
like a chorus
of cormorants,
picking their snarled nets
along a sea-wall,
voicing their platitudes
against all heedless youth;
the mesh of an old hubris
closing in again.

March 3, 1999– Notes on an upcoming anniversary
DES WALSH

We are North Americans now
the same as those Pablo Neruda wearied of,
lulled into the same crimes,
the same culture-starved wanderings.
Fifty years ago we were Europeans,
singing stubbornly into the face of wind
cutting masts for schooners that would sail forever,
cutting pine for the churches of England.
Fifty years ago we were lean and sensual,
our mouths unhurriedly pressed into each other,
our tongues touched whatever God we wanted.
Before our glistening fish, salted for Portugal
and Spain, became the currency of theatre,
before being slaughtered in wars far from
the coves we wandered as children,
we pressed wild berries to our lips
and wiped the pungent juices from our mouths,
the blood red placenta of the promise of a healthy future.
And now, the disease spreading, we weep together,
collectively walking to every graveyard on every headland
and bury men and rodneys, women and knowledge.
We close the lodges and the halls, remove the steeples,
abandon the headstones, haul the doors of the trap, leave rosary
    beads
between stone and seaweed, leave saw blades to rust behind hills,
half-empty dippers of berries spilling into the mossy barrens,
    leave
our sensuality circling the tops of fog-wrapped fir trees.
And now, fifty years later, having done as we're told,
we are left to celebrate.

On a train heading northeast

DES WALSH

(from Cork to Dublin, October 18, 2000)

Outside the boundaries of ancient and formica
The rain-spattered train window
Allows me an image of cows, sheep and memory.
I leave Cork different than you, Thomas Walsh,
I move inland, my back to the harbour
While you, your eyes straining to see
Around the point in or about 1852,
Probably didn't suspect the shock
On turning your gaze back
To a disappearing headland,
Your last image of home.
What hills of these were yours I wonder
What myths did you carry with you
That now swirl inside me all these years later
When I too disappear into the arms of legend
Call the magpies by name and think of home,
Where sea foam tumbles over rocks and
Whispers to me that crows too have names
And every stone in Newfoundland has a reason
As perfect as the curved line of spruce
As perfect as all of us who come from that chosen ground.

The triangle
of the heart   DES WALSH
(for Thomas Walsh 1847-1952)

I will monitor the movement of tides
and wait anxiously for the shipping news
out of Trinity, where men mumble
among themselves and talk fairies and Greek legend.
It is said that Fahey's Point touches
the salt thighs of angels and that there,
my great-grandfather from Cork turned
his eyes to Ireland and wept for you,
one hundred and thirty-two years before you
ran your fingers along lime-washed picket fences
and bent slowly to kiss a stone. I am with him now.
We both walk the lanes of that place and watch
for any sign of you, each of us startled by the rush of
wings and the sensuous lapping of the ocean's cool, wet mouth.

Wednesday

DES WALSH

We watched it for ten days,
one lone trap-boat, its patterned rhythm
echoing off our hearts as it made its way
across the water and out through Trinity Harbour.
Each morning we followed its wake
and waited anxiously for evening's return . . .
the sound first, then the stem-head rounding the point.

It's almost light now, the lone hand is at the tiller and soon,
he will pass Hog's Nose and probably look up.
He will notice the empty window, no figures standing,
he will sense the emptiness of the house, once music-filled,
and know we're far away from the Trinity light
and sensing you without me,
know this has been the longest night of my life . . .
he will never pass that way without wishing the world felt the
  same,
wishing our embraces still disturbed Trinity doves
and we could watch him forever,
our lips smoothing the strongest of winds.

My friend's death
DES WALSH

(for Al Pittman, 1940-2001)

I can tell you, now that you're dead,
I'm sick too Al, my heart heavier than
all the flowers of Russia. I used to think
that I would live forever . . . I knew you
wouldn't, your eyes sunken from
the weight of lupins. I wanted to talk to you
about my illness, how the sadness sweeps
over me like broken glass, a small crack
and there it is . . . all has to be replaced.
But what now? The lupins by the chapel
in Trinity are bulldozed into the earth
just a week before you were sentenced,
the last ones harvested were those you
picked for Alfreda, when you stooped as you
stumbled in the road, and your music-filled
heart allowed you to bouquet your way
to Rocky's Place for another performance and another
poem. Are you closer to the moon now, can you
reach out and wrap lilacs around it? I hope so . . .
I can't, I'm sick . . . my heart heavier than all the
flowers of Russia, all the flowers of St. Leonard's,
that will never bloom again, now that you've
resettled and left them and they've no reason
to cry out and call your name.

The Launch, Trinity Shipbuilders, Trinity, June 24, 1995   DES WALSH

I was with men, women and children
who through their tears have
launched boats for generations,
whose fathers and mothers suffered
through seasons of 'low water, Sundays
and a ticking clock'. We launched
that boat (a membrane of new wood and
old history) in a harbour where my
great-grandfather would have
whistled his way over The Dock,
passed Green's Garden, and shielded
his life from the glimmering,
death-ridden sea. The boat in the cradle,
we wove along the fence-lined roads of Trinity
in a festive carnival toward the landwash.
My friend, Rocky Henry Pearce Johnson
was at the wheel, my heart was at the wheel.
Children peddled alongside in full participation,
for this was their boat too. Curtains were pulled open,
older women, their arms folded in salute
smiled alongside their fragile older men,
all of us were in love for that perfect moment,
all of us were home.

On being Catholic and loving the treachery of winter

DES WALSH

November winds move these leaves toward
insensible geographical landmarks where
people kneel and pray to be found.
Patrick Street is like that, the worthy and
the truthful have all lived there,
their voices singing over church spires,
both their tongues speaking to their own God.
I park my car next to what was always William's Grocery,
about twelve doors down and east of what was then the
Newfoundland Nail and Foundry, where galvanized
receptacles measured out a life's work in inches and pounds of
   metal.
I'll always stop and look at the tree where
he fell and died, frightened I'm told,
by the Wesley United Church Minister,
scolded for stealing chestnuts from the welcoming tree on
sacred property. And suddenly I'm reminded again that
down the street, St. Patrick's Church entertained no natural
   growth,
being housed only in stone, and that my love for you is its only
   salvation,
when snow crusts itself to the burning bark and God lets me
   touch you again.

I love you more than any God, not falsely

DES WALSH

I love you more than any God, not falsely,
for reasons that would dim the brightest star.
Your family knows this, they see it when
I genuflect as you pass. It isn't simply
how your hair falls across your eyes
or how your laughter subdues
the most anxious of moments
or even how your breasts lay beneath me,
it's the simple purity of love.
I know St. Jacques and the history
of where you're from, it's a French name.
Perhaps that's why foreigners circle you
like half-starved crows, thinking their
accents are enough to impress
the most wandering flower.
My family has a history as well,
we watch you everywhere.
Did you know there are Walsh's in Fleur de Lys?

Rosella and Bride   MARY DALTON

When they marched up from the cove to the Cross
They'd dazzle a blind horse with blinkers on—
Rosella and Bride rigged out in full sail—
In bright blue and yellow, red jumpers
Or green, rouged cheeks and the
Ear-rings as long as a jigger.
Sure when they laughed they lit up the very
Gravel on the road.
The women tsked. The men grinned.
A mile and a half of eyes behind curtains
As those two set off for the Shore.

Bachelor Brothers   MARY DALTON

They never were part of a crew—
Kept to themselves under the hill,
Kept up the peaked-roof house,
Set the small cabbage garden.
No marriage. Stubbly beards,
A raffish, ramshackle walk.
Mothers keeping their children in line:
The bogeymen will get you
If you don't be good.
One deaf. Or was he.
When they cross my mind's eye
Something of the terror of farms
And four green fields
Comes upon me.

Brin

MARY DALTON

Brin for a sack of coal.
Brin for a sack of salt.
Blubber in the tight brin bags—
Oil a-seep from the rotten livers.
A fisherman's bed:
Brin bag stuffed with straw.
And at the canning
All hands had a brin apron on.
Spuds in a brin bag.
Brin bag of oats on the horse's nose.
Salt beef junks in the brin bag.
Empt the beef
And fill her with birch junks.
To cure a broody hen
Stick her in a brin bag;
Plunge her in salt water.
The old brin bag after:
Washed and cut for a mat—
Sun, sky, stars, roses.

Mad Moll and Crazy Betty

MARY DALTON

We hated them mad rocks, yes,
Worse even than a hog's nose—
The saltwater hove up out of itself
Spinning out and up like a wild top—
Mad Moll and Crazy Betty,
Snaky with their sea-weed hair,
Slimy and slobbering,
With the water moving over their heads.
That lapping over and over.
A sea drooling for blood.

Old Holly

MARY DALTON

When the cliffs echo with shrieking, when fires hiss.
When the cowled figure wails, at night, on the mash.
A flutter of shawl, a sighing, she's gone.
When the fog-horn sounds out its story of doom.
When the wind keens, when the storm rises.
When the loon warns of the devil aboard.
When the drowned crew groans out its shanty.
The voice out of spume, out of rote, the old hag
And her choir of jinkers.

Old Roman Candle   MARY DALTON

That water-nipper hauled for us
All fall in the woods. Seventy and spry
As a kitten. He swung those buckets.
Spangles of water all over
His red bush of a beard.
And he'd a grand stock of them
Matches, the wait-a-minutes—
He'd scrape them right quick
On an ass of his pants, and
He fizz, and he fizz
And by and by he burn up
That brimstone and
He come to a flame.
Old Roman Candle, the cookee
Called him—he sure lit up
The woods that season.

dead Indians

MARY DALTON

dead Indians are safer—
in poems, museums,
archaeological pamphlets,
bone pendants and ochre—
lament, monographs,
no threat to our order

weeping walrus
we mourn the Beothuk
close the sky in
on Labrador Innu
the land wired
and caribou fled

9

An Old Gray Tree . . . is Transfigured

Summer Solstice
ENOS WATTS

Call it the solstice, call it
the longest day of the year
for a fisherman's wife,
the longest day in the life
of his just-married daughter

There are few who
could fail to recall
the pure flood
of his crude, gifted tongue
at the table
There were those
who remembered
his last, careless dance;
though no one saw him
sway down a lane,

with a rose in his coat,
to the landwash

But his bow
slapped water
some time before daybreak;
and few would publicly say
why they thought his boat
threw him,
how or why
it was beached
at full throttle

When the sun had finally
called it a day
there were voices, lights
on the harbour;
and two quiet women
who watched in the dark
knew it would never be over

The Red-Throated Loon

ENOS WATTS

(for the Koestlers who, aging and ill, chose the time and manner of their leaving)

The moon
wears a yellow veil
She is old; see how
she drags herself
across the sky
Snow sparkles
under the street lamps
Below the harbour ice
no-one can hear
the trapped tides

We are too tired
you and I, to deny
the myth of our madness
grasping the silver arrows
of easy sleep
Let no-one weep
for our leaving;
and as for the moon
there will be
seasons and seasons

Like those great boreal birds
also strange to their kind
we will course
the meridians south,
obeying something
unspoken, unsanctioned
to settle
to tremble alone
on a dark water

Window

ENOS WATTS

What we most fear
we fear most
for those we love

She will have this memory of him:
his back to her
at a window
the curtains slightly parted,
little to see
but a field and a clump of trees
They were prisoners,
he afraid to go out
keeping her in

Winter wasted him
Days on end he would watch
the wind take the field, send it
spinning into the trees;
then retreat
from the window
turn away from her, weeping

And she will remember
the nights
he woke wild-eyed and pale
wet with his fear,
nights of kindness and anger
when he was a child
and she raged
at the hounds of his sleep

Then one howling morning
he woke serene,
dressed for winter and wordless
walked out of his house
She couldn't see
the woods or the field
and she didn't move
from the window

The Balcony Door   ENOS WATTS

A white wind tore
out of the east
through the night
with gusts of 90
and more

And an old man turned
in his sleep, returned
to young summers,
where he saw himself noble
in carriage and power

while outside the dream
mercury climbed
out of season

The gale brought no dust
shooting off rooves, across
lawns and roads,
but snow had clung
to the walls and floor
of his fourth-story balcony
and thickened
his outward-opening door

By noon that day
he sensed the tapping drip
from his roof
slowing down—

(Earlier he'd watched
a youth swing a shovel
freeing his car, paid him;
then braved the stairs, paused
on the landings)

Now the balcony door
resisted his hands; only
his heavy battering feet
let daylight in
Outside
he attacked the sodden mass
with blind madness, heaving
heaped shovels
over the rail, ignoring
the ring tightening
round his head

Finally, like some old
world-weary monarch,
his subjects below him, but
far beyond the reach of his eyes,
he grasped a rail
at his legs' refusal and his right arm
arced up
as though he might have been waving—
before he sank back
to the hardening snow

Cain
for David Elliott

ENOS WATTS

Do you like this garden?
See to it that your children
do not destroy it!
          —Malcolm Lowry

Exiled from the sun
I am lost
amid charred ruins
stirring still-warm embers
faintly glowing
like wasted stars
abandoned by the gods
And the embers of faith
are dying . . .
Night's first threat
is nullity
the whispering void
I shall soon grope
blindly
welcoming pain
even my hands in fire

I wander east
through a maze of broken trees
pathetic ashes
of a majestic forest
lost like my father's garden
          a place of
               no returning

Still the outcast hears
the battered earth
its sullied stones:
a bleak
accusatory cry—
the voice of blood

The ophidian curse
uncoils
and should not harm me;
yet I bear
the scourge of memory
feel again
the sooty lash
across my brow
Against this shame
no talisman
can be found

I must seek the waters
of a new Eridanus
a sacred hope for me—
to run with the river
through labyrinthine caverns
      losing my way
      to find it
And the river
bearing darkness
will surge toward the sun
to merge with and at last
become the sea

Confrontation

ENOS WATTS

There'd seemed to be some justice
meeting him this way:
Newfoundland, neutral ground
light-years
from Babi Yar

He squints at the big Illyushin
floating out of the sun
fence wire cutting his face
wondering why he is there, wondering
why he should
brave the cold
waving a pitiful stick
just stripped of its message
by the capricious wind

The official party
moves toward the terminal
in animated dialogue
about the weather
and other weighty affairs . . .

And suddenly he is dancing
punishing the ground
like old Mattathias
gasping an ancient song that falls
inches from his face,
and shaking menacingly
his stick, a pennonless lance
at a man who could never
comprehend his dance,
a man who will never know
he was there

Yo-yo

ENOS WATTS

from a painting by Strombotne

The arc of the yo-yo
measures the distance
  between them

The old man
with sunburned bare legs
leers, his slack mouth
a chortle; uncertain,
he scratches his white
  infant's head

The young girl's free hand
rests on a hip
  thrust slightly forward

Dare to release them from this
safe frame; watch
the pendulum do
what pendulums
do

Longliner At Sunset   ENOS WATTS

I'd watch her each evening
the little longliner
inching above my horizon
and as if the whole scene
were orchestrated by Newton
she and the sun
would meet
one rising, the other descending
precisely
at my horizon

I would see around her
a slow dance of saddlebacks
riding the sun
soon to be left to its fate
in her wake below
my horizon

Then after scudding the shafts
from streetlamps across the harbour
she'd dock
in the cigarette glow of men
who'd been told by the gulls
there was fish

Roses And Attic Throats

ENOS WATTS

*What do the victims matter
provided the gesture is fine?*
            —*Laurent Tailhade*

He'd seen it before,
that cold grace:
her abstracted face
the fleeting tangency between
porcelain hands
and the reverent dark flesh.
He saw the rose
red near the Attic throat
and there was no
meeting of eyes
with those near the end of the line.

Avallanos moved
respectfully forward
his right arm stiff
as if in a splint.
He proffered the left.
'Signora', he said,
'it is nearer the heart'.

There was
a meeting of eyes
as the machete completed its arc.

That day Avallanos
danced his last dance;
but before the grace of his falling
a dream brought him
bandoliered women
and Zapata's ghost-stallion
waiting
restless at twilight.

Waiting for Sunrise: Early December

ENOS WATTS

I'm up early to catch
the still-hidden sun's
spreading glow
Down on the marsh
hoar-frost
silvers gray trees, the tufted
hollows, the sedge;
rooves of houses are
glittering argent
and the hydro cable above our fence
at the garden's east edge

Here and there curl
thin columns of smoke
in the still air, the quiet
broken only by
a distant dog barking, an occasional
whine of wheels
on the speedway

Three flags on a public building
sag, slightly sway

Now it appears
clears the rim of a hill;
hard silver
on eave, clothesline and cable
dissolves to droplets
of rainbow
trembling awhile
before letting go

And an old gray tree
on the fringe of the marsh is
transfigured

Adhlacadh Mo Mháthar

SEÁN Ó RÍORDÁIN

Grian an Mheithimh in úllghort,
　Is siosarnach i síoda an tráthnóna,
　Beach mhallaithe ag portaireacht
　　Mar screadstracadh ar an nóinbhrat.

Seanalitir shalaithe á léamh agam,
　Le gach focaldeoch dar ólas
Pian bhinibeach ag dealgadh mo chléibhse,
　Do bhrúigh amach gach focal díobh a dheoir féin.

Do chuimhníos ar an láimh a dhein an scríbhinn,
　Lámh a bhí inaitheanta mar aghaidh,
Lámh a thál riamh cneastacht seana-Bhíobla,
　Lámh a bhí mar bhalsam is tú tinn.

Agus thit an Meitheamh siar isteach sa Gheimhreadh,
　Den úllghort deineadh reilig bhán cois abhann,
Is i lár na balbh-bháine i mo thimpeall
　Do liúigh os ard sa tsneachta an dúpholl,

Gile gearrachaile lá a céad chomaoine,
　Gile abhlainne Dé Domhnaigh ar altóir,
Gile bainne ag sreangtheitheadh as na cíochaibh,
　Nuair a chuireadar mo mháthair, gile an fhóid.

Bhí m'aigne á sciúirseadh féin ag iarraidh
　An t-adhlacadh a bhlaiseadh go hiomlán,
Nuair a d'eitil tríd an gciúnas bán go míonla
　Spideog a bhí gan mhearbhall gan scáth:

Agus d'fhan os cionn na huaighe fé mar go mb'eol di
　Go raibh an toisc a thug í ceilte ar chách
Ach an té a bhí ag feitheamh ins an gcomhrainn,
　Is do rinneas éad fén gcaidreamh neamhghnách.

Do thuirling aer na bhFlaitheas ar an uaigh sin,
 Bhí meidhir uafásach naofa ar an éan,
Bhíos deighilte amach ón diamhairghnó im thuata
 Is an uaigh sin os mo chomhair in imigéin.

Le cumhracht bróin do folcadh m'anam drúiseach,
 Thit sneachta geanmnaíochta ar mo chroí,
Anois adhlacfad sa chroí a deineadh ionraic
 Cuimhne na mná d'iompair mé trí ráithe ina broinn.

Tháinig na scológa le borbthorann sluasad,
 Is do scuabadar le fuinneamh an chré isteach san uaigh,
D'fhéachas-sa treo eile, bhí comharsa ag glanadh a ghlúine,
 D'fhéachas ar an sagart is bhí saoltacht ina ghnúis.

Grian an Mheithimh in úllghort,
 Is siosarnach i síoda an tráthnóna,
Beach mhallaithe ag portaireacht
 Mar screadstracadh ar an nóinbhrat.

Ranna beaga bacacha á scríobh agam,
 Ba mhaith liom breith ar eireaball spideoige,
Ba mhaith liom sprid lucht glanta glún a dhíbirt,
 Ba mhaith liom triall go deireadh lae go brónach.

My Mother's Burial

SEÁN Ó RÍORDÁIN

June sun in an orchard, a rustle in the silk of evening, an ill-tempered bee droning like a scream renting the evening-cloth.

Reading an old soiled letter, and with every word-drink I sip, a sharp pain pierces my side, each word pressing out its own tear.

I remembered the hand that made the writing, a hand distinguishable as a face, a hand which bestowed old Bible kindness, a hand that was balsam when you were ill.

And June fell back into winter, the orchard became a white cemetery by a river and in the middle of the dumb whiteness around me the black hole shouted out loud in the snow.

The brightness of a young girl on her first communion day, the brightness of the host on a Sunday altar, the brightness of milk squirting, escaping from the paps. When they buried my mother, brightness of the sod.

My mind was scourging itself trying to fully taste the burial, when, gently through the white silence, a robin flew without confusion or fear.

And she stayed above the grave as if she knew the reason that brought her was hidden from all but the person waiting in the coffin, and I was jealous of the extraordinary intimacy.

The air of Heaven descended on that grave, there was a terrible saintly gaiety about the bird. A layman, I was kept apart from the mysterious business; the grave before me in the distance.

My lustful soul was bathed with the fragrance of sorrow, a snow of chastity fell on my heart. Now I will bury in the heart made upright the memory of the woman who carried me nine months in her womb.

The gravediggers came with the violent noise of shovels and they vigorously swept the earth into the grave. I looked the other way, a neighbour was wiping his knee. I looked at the priest, there was worldliness in his face.

June sun in an orchard, a rustle in the silk of evening, an ill-tempered bee droning like a scream renting the evening-cloth.

I'm writing small halting verses, I'd like to catch hold of a robin's tail, I'd like to banish the spirit of knee-wipers. I'd like to journey sadly to the end of day.

translated by Seán Dunne

Claustrophobia   SEÁN Ó RÍORDÁIN

In aice an fhíona
Tá coinneal is sceon,
Tá dealbh mo Thiarna
D'réir dealraimh gan chomhacht,
Tá a dtiocfaidh den oíche
Mar shluaite sa chlós,
Tá rialtas na hoíche
Lasmuigh den bhfuinneoig;
Má mhúchann mo choinneal
Ar ball de m'ainneoin
Léimfidh an oíche
Isteach im scamhóig,
Sárófar m'intinn
Is ceapfar dom sceon,
Déanfar díom oíche,
Bead im dhoircheacht bheo:
   Ach má mhaireann mo choinneal
   Aon oíche amháin
   Bead im phoblacht solais
   Go dtiocfaidh an lá.

Claustrophobia   SEÁN Ó RÍORDÁIN

Beside the wine there's a candle and terror, the statue of my Lord appears to be powerless. What will come of the night is like a crowd in the yard, the government of night is outside the window. If my candle is quenched later in spite of me, the night will leap into my lung; my mind will be taken over and terror will be made for me. A night will be made of me, I will be a living darkness. But if my candle survives one night, I will be a republic of light until day comes.

translated by Seán Dunne

Reo

SEÁN Ó RÍORDÁIN

Maidin sheaca ghabhas amach
Is bhí seál póca romham ar sceach,
Rugas air le cur im phóca
Ach sciorr sé uaim mar bhí sé reoite:
Ní héadach beo a léim óm ghlaic
Ach rud fuair bás aréir ar sceach:
Is siúd ag taighde mé fé m'intinn
Go bhfuaireas macasamhail an ní seo—
    Lá dar phógas bean dem mhuintir
    Is í ina cónra reoite, sínte.

Freeze

SEÁN Ó RÍORDÁIN

One frosty morning I roved out and a handkerchief was before me on a bush. I took it to put in my pocket but it slipped from me because it was frozen. It wasn't a living cloth that slipped from my grasp but a thing that died last night on a bush. And there I went searching in my mind until I found an equivalent for this event—a day I kissed a woman of my people when she lay in her coffin frozen.

translated by Seán Dunne

Fiabhras

SEÁN Ó RÍORDÁIN

Tá sléibhte na leapa mós ard,
Tá breoiteacht 'na brothall 'na lár,
Is fada an t-aistear urlár,
    Is na mílte is na mílte i gcéin
    Tá suí agus seasamh sa saol.

Atáimid i gceantar bráillín,
Ar éigean más cuimhin linn cathaoir,
    Ach bhí tráth sar ba mhachaire sinn,
    In aimsir choisíochta fadó,
    Go mbímis chomh hard le fuinneog.

Tá pictiúir ar an bhfalla ag at,
Tá an fráma imithe ina lacht,
Ceal creidimh ní féidir é bhac,
    Tá nithe ag druidim fém dhéin,
    Is braithim ag titim an saol.

Tá ceantar ag taisteal ón spéir,
Tá comharsanacht suite ar mo mhéar,
Dob fhuirist dom breith ar shéipéal,
    Tá ba ar an mbóthar ó thuaidh,
    Is níl ba na síoraíochta chomh ciúin.

Fever

SEÁN Ó RÍORDÁIN

    The mountains of the bed are rather high and sickness a heat in there, the floor a long journey, and miles, miles away, life's sittings and standings go on.
    We are in a place of sheets, we barely remember a chair. There was a time before we were a plain, in walking-times long ago, that we were tall as a window.

A picture swells on the wall, the frame has turned into liquid. Lacking faith we cannot stop it, things are moving towards me and I feel the world falling.

A place is travelling from the sky, a neighbourhood is settled on my finger, I could easily catch hold of a church. There are cows on the road to the North and the cows of eternity aren't as quiet.

translated by Seán Dunne

Na Leamhain SEÁN Ó RÍORDÁIN

Fuaim ag leamhan leochaileach, iompó leathanaigh,
Bascadh mionsciathán
Oíche fhómhair i seomra na leapa, tá
Rud leochaileach á chrá.

Oíche eile i dtaibhreamh bhraitheas-sa
Peidhre leamhan-sciathán,
Mar sciatháin aingil iad le fairsingeacht
Is bhíodar leochaileach mar mhná.

Dob é mo chúram lámh a leagadh orthu
Is gan ligean leo chun fáin,
Ach iad a shealbhú gan sárú tearmainn
Is iad a thabhairt chun aoibhnis iomlán.

Ach dhoirteas-sa an púdar beannaithe
'Bhí spréite ar gach sciathán,
Is tuigeadh dom go rabhas gan uimhreacha,
Gan uimhreacha na fearúlachta go brách.

Is shiúil na deich n-uimhreacha as an mearbhall
Is ba mhó ná riamh a n-údarás,
Is ba chlos ciníocha ag plé le huimhreacha,
Is cách ba chlos ach mise amháin.

Fuaim ag leamhan leochaileach, iompó leathanaigh,
Creachadh leamhan-scannán,
Oíche fhómhair is na leamhain ag eiteallaigh
Mór mo bheann ar a mion-rírá.

The Moths SEÁN Ó RÍORDÁIN

Sound of a fragile moth, turning of a page, bruising of small wings, an autumn night in the bedroom, a fragile thing is being tormented.

Another night in a dream I felt a pair of moth-wings. They were ample as an angel's wings, fragile as women.

It was my duty to touch them and not to let them go away, but to possess them without violating sanctuary and to bring them to full delight.

But I spilt the blessed powder that was spread on every wing and I realised I was without numbers, without the numbers of virility forever.

The ten numbers walked out of the confusion and their authority was greater than ever. And races were heard considering numbers and everyone was heard but me alone.

Sound of a fragile moth, turning of a page, ruining of the moth-film. Autumn night and the moths fluttering, I'm preoccupied with their minor uproar.

translated by Seán Dunne

Othello's Own Brother

DAVID ELLIOTT

Iago: I have seen the cannon
When it hath blown his ranks into the air,
And, like the devil from his very arm,
Puff'd his own brother.

I shall be a footnote and a reference,
But now I am a lieutenant to the famous Othello,
General of the Venetian armed forces,
And my own brother.
Our black faces lead those columns of white troops,
Ebony suns followed by silver moons.
Our grandfather was king in Mauretania.
How we got here is a long story.

We are arranged for battle
With Florence and Genoa. I am not sure which is which.
Othello knows, of course. He knows every detail of war.
I am really just a horseman,
Although I read a bit.
I find it is interesting that, according to prophecy,
Today sees my last battle.

Back home our mother had an Egyptian
Plot our horoscopes.

She said that I should be a soldier,
And when I came to battle on a green plain,
Overlooked by slender twin mountains, a stream flowing
   through,
It would be my last day.
She was vague about Othello.
I remember she gave my mother a handkerchief,
A kind of love charm.
Othello has it, I think.
Not that he needs it, he rarely has a girl.

He doesn't need anything to make him happy
Except a war.

Nothing disturbs him.
Anger, fear, jealousy, hate,
Those foes of our peace,
Do not attack him.

He seems to like Italy.
He forgets his blackness, as I never do mine.
And is really a Christian as I am outwardly one.
I don't know much about religion
Except that this religion
Seems more complicated than the one I was born to.

Well, to the battle.
Expectant vultures, the devil's Valkyries,
Flap overhead.
Those new-fangled cannon are arrayed against us.
I hate them, but Othello thinks of them
As war's orchestra.

If I fall, he will need a new lieutenant.
I wonder who?
Iago is most experienced, has fought in many countries,
And has been with Othello a long time.
He is brave, honest, quite skilled in battle,
But I doubt that he is much of a thinker.
I don't believe he could devise a complex plan
As war often demands.
Montano is worthy but ordinary.
Then there's Cassio, Othello's engineer,
Who has been on the outskirts of many battles.
He is doubtless clever, pleasant, likeable
And smooth as a greased sword.
I think, however, Iago would be best.
He is a real soldier, and the only man I know
Who can make Othello laugh, or, at least, smile.

Time to mount.
I must go to Othello for the accustomed ritual:
I stand beside him and he grasps my forearm.
Of course, I can't feel his touch through the armour,
But we have always done so.

His placidity would be proof against my death, but I know he loves me.

There go the guns, Genoese and Florentine.
What was it the English poet said? Something like
'Bounce, go the guns with a sulphurous huff puff and huff puff'.

That's close!
And huff—

Lighthouse

DAVID ELLIOTT

Everyone in the cove is sorry for me,
Because I live alone in the lighthouse.
On civil days they walk to the bill of the cape
For a torrent of talk, meaning to keep up my spirits.
Christ sake! I took the job to be alone,
Away from the giggling, gabbing, noisy cacklers
Who deafen the world. Weather keeps them away.
And yesterday there were sundogs,
And gulls swam with their tails to the wind,
Sure signs of a storm today, thank God.
Storms keep those chatterers away from me.
Roaring waves wash the cape clean
And level spray-drops fusillade the cove.
The opaque rain is a wall between me and the others.
Sometimes, of course, ships wreck on Charley's Rocks,
And bodies are battered ashore,
But I don't mind corpses—
They're so quiet.

Frank

DAVID ELLIOTT

for Adrian Fowler

The shrubs on Frank's grave have withered,
And snow sprinkles the lopsided mound
That covers his last bed.
He was only a cat,
But I am only a man.
I think of him,
Offering to share with everybody
Freshly-killed birds and mice,
Courteously obedient if the orders were reasonable,
Tolerant of kittens, children and other small animals,
Permitting his brother, Izzy, to romp with him,
Although Izzy bored him to pieces.
In his short old age he spent the days of summer,
Swaying in warm light on a branch of the poplar
At whose roots he now sleeps in cold darkness.

He looked like a miniature lion.

He could, all by himself, open the door to the garden.

Mattie

DAVID ELLIOTT

I was just thinking of Mattie
Who for twenty years ran a cathouse on Back Street.
She rose to whoremongering from whoring,
The only job she could get when young,
Country-fresh, innocent, unskilled to earn her bread.
She kept a good house, was just and forgiving to customers,
Clean, courageous, temperate, prudent,
Charitable from her heart,
Dispensing her gifts to the poor in handfuls of love.
But she thought of herself as a bad woman,
And despaired of forgiveness because of her job.
She died with the cries of grieving harlots in her ears
On the same day as the pious archbishop Gryphon.
I like to think of his face when he got to Heaven:
Saint Peter bowing, child-angels singing,
A whirl of dancing on the golden streets,
And the blazing of the horns of Paradise:
I bet he thought, at first, it was for him.

Resonance
DAVID ELLIOTT
After hearing Lorna Crozier read her poems

I

Yes, it's like that. Buffaloes whiten the moon,
And blossoms, bursting like rockets, fall on a faded house,
Where an old Ukrainian brings us soup if we are good.
The grouse, become the head of the corner,
Trapped in a cistern, dies in his winter clothes.
And foetus can dream now
Of breaking forth into a world
Where John Jameson smacks his bottom
And lets him take the first long sip
That will make it impossible for him
Ever to tell wind from sage.

II

Sometimes, bees yellow the air,
And blossoms burst like rockets to fall on a ragged house,
Where an ancient woman,
Startled by the soft patter on the wrinkled roof,
Looks up in fearful hope that something is changing.

Sometimes, the wounded partridge, caught by early winter,
Trailing exhausted wings, huddles in the cool drift,
Innocently letting the deadly snow
Seep into his blood.

Sometimes, the unborn child,
Writhing free from ontogeny
Kicks the world to pieces
And sets the cosmos rocking.

Sometimes, the sunrise trumpets wake me from my dream
Of sagging house and broken blossom,
Cringing hag and poisoned bird.

Sometimes, between the dreams, John Jameson
Rebuilds the house and heals the bird and soothes the crone.
Sometimes, between the dreams, John Jameson
Quiets the struggling child
Trapped in my heart.

Talking to Trees DAVID ELLIOTT

I like talking to trees
And they say they like talking to me.
Their speech delights me:
The heavy utterance of elms and pines,
The sensible remarks of maples,
The banter of birches,
Even the idle chatter of the giddy aspens.
There was an old spruce who taught me much poetry,
And in a far country an oak tree
Told me the meaning of patience.
But especially I loved the old poplars in my back garden.
How courteously they would interrupt their meditations
To answer my greeting.
I told them about us mobile folk,
And what strange lives the unrooted undergo.
They told me stories of air, wind, water,
And the slow riding of the midnight world
Toward the stars.
They died last winter.
This week I cut them down.
Some day, through various stages of ashes and dust,
We shall be back in earth together,
And resume our conversation.

Magdalen at the Tomb

DAVID ELLIOTT

One heavy cloud held back the lifting sun,
The wet trees quivered, every night-fast bloom
Unfolded its cold petals, one by one,
As Mary came to seek her master's tomb.
And when she saw the empty sepulchre
Gape in the light of hesitating day
A desolation swept the heart of her;
Blindly she looked, slowly she turned away,
Weeping she heard his voice, joyful she turned,
Forward she sprang the accustomed kiss to give:
Her outstretched arms and proffered lips he spurned
And said, 'Tell My disciples that I live'.
And as she numbly crossed the dawn-lit sod
She wept again because her man was God.

Towards the New Omagh Road

The Route of
The Táin
THOMAS KINSELLA

Gene sat on a rock, dangling our map.
The others were gone over the next crest,
further astray. We ourselves, irritated,
were beginning to turn down toward the river
back to the car, the way we should have come.

We should have trusted our book.
After they tried a crossing, and this river too
'rose against them' and bore off
a hundred of their charioteers toward the sea
They had to move along the river Colptha
up to its source.

            There:
where the main branch sharpens away gloomily
to a gash in the hill opposite.

then to Bélat Ailiúin
                by that pathway
climbing back and forth out of the valley
over to Ravensdale.

Scattering in irritation. Who had set out
so cheerfully to celebrate our book;
cheerfully as we made and remade it
through a waste of hours, content to 'enrich the present
honouring the past', each to his own just function.
Wandering off, ill-sorted,
like any beasts of the field,
one snout honking disconsolate,
another burrowing in its pleasures.

When not far above us a red fox
ran at full stretch out of the bracken
and panted across the hillside toward the next ridge.
Where he vanished—a faint savage sharpness
out of the earth—an inlet of the sea
shone in the distance at the mouth of the valley
beyond Omeath: grey waters crawled with light.

For a heartbeat, in alien certainty,
we exchanged looks. We should have known it by now
—the process, the whole tedious enabling ritual.
Flux brought to fullness; saturated;
the clouding over; dissatisfaction
spreading slowly like an ache;
something reduced shivering suddenly
into meaning along new boundaries;

through a forest,
by a salt-dark shore,
by a standing stone on a dark plain,
by a ford running blood,
and along this gloomy pass, with someone ahead
calling and waving on the crest
against a heaven of dismantling cloud,
transfixed by the same figure (stopped, pointing)
on the rampart at Cruachan, where it began.

The morning sunlight pouring on us all
as we scattered over the mounds
disputing over useless old books,
assembled in cheerful speculation
around a prone block, *Miosgán Medba*
—Queen Medb's *turd* . . .? And rattled our maps,
joking together in growing illness
or age or fat. Before us
the route of the *Táin*, over men's dust,
toward these hills that seemed to grow
darker as we drove nearer.

From:
The Battle of Aughrim

RICHARD MURPHY

. . . .

ST. RUTH

St. Ruth trots on a silver mare
Along the summit of the ridge,
Backed by a red cavalcade
Of the King's Life Guards.
He wears a blue silk tunic,
A white lace cravat,
Grey feathers in his hat.

He has made up his mind to put
The kingdom upon a fair combat:
Knowing he cannot justify
Losing Athlone
Before his Most Christian master,
He means to bury his body
In Ireland, or win.

The army commander only speaks
French and Italian:
His army speaks either
English or Irish.
When he gives an order
His jowls bleach and blush
Like a turkeycock's dewlap.

Lieutenant-General Charles Chalmont,
Marquis of St. Ruth,
The Prince of Condé's disciple
In the music of war,
Jerks with spinal rapture
When a volley of musket fire
Splits his ear.

Picture his peregrine eyes,
A wife-tormentor's thin
Heraldic mouth, a blue
Stiletto beard on his chin,
And a long forked nose
Acclimatized to the sulphurous
Agony of Huguenots.

He keeps his crab-claw tactics
Copied from classical books
An unbetrayable secret
From his army of Irishmen.
He rides downhill to correct
A numerical mistake
In his plan's translation.

He throws up his hat in the air,
The time is near sunset,
He knows victory is sure,
One cavalry charge will win it.
'*Le jour est à nous, mes enfants*',
He shouts. The next minute
His head is shot off.

THE WINNING SHOT

Mullen had seen St. Ruth riding downhill
And Kelly held a taper. 'There's the Frenchman!'
Trench laid the cannon, a breeze curved the ball.

The victory charge was halted. Life Guards stooped down
And wrapped the dripping head in a blue cloak,
Then wheeled and galloped towards the setting sun.

Chance, skill and treachery all hit the mark
Just when the sun's rod tipped the altar hill:
The soldiers panicked, thinking God had struck.

SARSFIELD

Sarsfield rides a chestnut horse
At the head of his regiment,
His mountainous green shoulders
Tufted with gold braid,
Over his iron skull-piece
He wears the white cockade.
A bagpipe skirls.

Last summer after the Boyne
When King James had run,
He smashed the Dutch usurper's
Waggon-train of cannon
Benighted at Ballyneety.
Patrick Sarsfield, Earl of Lucan
Commands the reserve today.

The saviour of Limerick knows
Nothing of St. Ruth's plan,
Not even that the battle
Of Aughrim has begun.
He has obeyed since dawn
The order to wait for further
Orders behind the hill.

He sees men run on the skyline
Throwing away muskets and pikes,
Then horsemen with sabres drawn
Cutting them down.
He hears cries, groans and shrieks.
Nothing he will do, or has done
Can stop this happening.

MEN AT THE CASTLE

Comely their combat
    amidst death and wounds,
Romantic their disregard
    for cosmic detail:
The wrong kegs of ball
    were consigned to the castle,
Irish bullets too large
    for French firelocks.
A great stronghold
    became a weakness.
Till sunset they loaded
    muskets with tunic buttons
To fire on cavalry,
    squadron after squadron
Crossed the causeway
    and flanked their front.
Heroic volleys
    continued until nightfall:
They fell with no quarter
    when the battle was lost.

LUTTRELL

Luttrell on a black charger
At the rear of his regiment
Stands idle in a beanfield
Protected by a tower.
He wears a dandy yellow coat,
A white-feathered hat
And a gilded sabre.

When he hears the word spread
Along the line, 'St. Ruth is dead',
He retreats at a trot:
Leading his priding cavalry
To betray the humble foot:
Ten miles to a dinner, laid
In a mansion, then to bed.

PRISONER

Night covers the retreat.
Some English troops beating a ditch for loot
Capture a wounded boy. 'Don't shoot!'

'What'll we do with him?'
'I'll work in the camp'. 'Strip him!'
Naked he kneels to them. They light a lamp.

'Pretty boy'. 'Castrate the fucker!'
'Let the papist kiss my flute'.
'Toss a coin for the privilege to bugger . . .'

He cries like a girl. 'Finish him off'.
'No, keep him alive to be our slave'.
'Shove a sword up his hole'. They laugh.

A tipsy officer calls out:
'You men be on parade at eight.
I want no prisoners, d'you hear me? Shoot

The crowd we took, when it gets light.
We've no more food. Good night.
God knows you all put up a splendid fight'.

4. AFTER

THE WOLFHOUND

A wolfhound sits under a wild ash
Licking the wound in a dead ensign's neck.

When guns cool at night with bugles in fog
She points over the young face.

All her life a boy's pet.
Prisoners are sabred and the dead are stripped.

Her ear pricks like a crimson leaf on snow,
The horse carts creak away.

Vermin by moonlight pick
The tongues and sockets of six thousand skulls.

*

She pines for his horn to blow
To bay in triumph down the track of wolves.

Her forelegs stand like pillars through a siege,
His Toledo sword corrodes.

Nights she lopes to the scrub
And trails back at dawn to guard a skeleton.

Wind shears the berries from the rowan tree,
The wild geese have flown.

She lifts her head to cry
As a woman keens in a famine for her son.

*

A redcoat, stalking, cocks
His flintlock when he hears the wolfhound growl.

Her fur bristles with fear at the new smell,
Snow has betrayed her lair.

'I'll sell you for a packhorse,
You antiquated bigoted papistical bitch!'

She springs: in self-defence he fires his gun.
People remember this.

By turf embers she gives tongue
When the choirs are silenced in wood and stone.

THE REVEREND GEORGE STORY CONCLUDES
An Impartial History of the Wars in Ireland

'I never could learn what became of St. Ruth's corpse:
Some say he was left stript amongst the dead,
When our men pursued beyond the hill;
And others that he was thrown into a Bog:
However, though the man had an ill character
As a great persecutor of Protestants in France,
Yet we must allow him to be very brave in his person,
And indeed considerable in his conduct,
Since he brought the Irish to fight a better battle
Then ever that people could boast of before:
They behaved themselves like men of another nation.

'But it was always the genius of this people
To rebel, and their vice was laziness.
Since first they began to play their mad pranks
There have died, I say, in this sad kingdom,
By the sword, famine and disease,
At least one hundred thousand young and old.
Last July alone, more execution was done
At Aughrim than in all Europe besides.
Seen from the top of the hill, the unburied dead
Covered four miles, like a great flock of sheep.

'What did the mere Irish ever gain
By following their lords into rebellion?
Or what might they have gotten by success
But absolute servitude under France?
They are naturally a lazy crew
And love nothing more than to be left at ease.
Give one a cow and a potato garden
He will aspire to no greater wealth

But loiter on the highway to hear news.
Lacking plain honesty, but most religious,
Not one in twenty works, the gaols are full
Of thieves, and beggars howl on every street.
This war has ended happily for us:
The people now must learn to be industrious'.

. . . .

Butcher's Dozen
(1972)
THOMAS KINSELLA

I went with Anger at my heel
Through Bogside of the bitter zeal
—Jesus pity!—on a day
Of cold and drizzle and decay.
A month had passed. Yet there remained
A murder smell that stung and stained.
On flats and alleys—over all—
It hung; on battered roof and wall,
On wreck and rubbish scattered thick,
On sullen steps and pitted brick.
And when I came where thirteen died
It shrivelled up my heart. I sighed
And looked about that brutal place
Of rage and terror and disgrace.
Then my moistened lips grew dry.
I had heard an answering sigh!
There in a ghostly pool of blood
A crumpled phantom hugged the mud:
'Once there lived a hooligan.
A pig came up, and away he ran.
Here lies one in blood and bones,
Who lost his life for throwing stones'.
More voices rose. I turned and saw
Three corpses forming, red and raw,
From dirt and stone. Each upturned face
Stared unseeing from its place:
'Behind this barrier, blighters three,
We scrambled back and made to flee.
The guns cried *Stop*, and here lie we'.
Then from left and right they came,
More mangled corpses, bleeding, lame,
Holding their wounds. They chose their ground,
Ghost by ghost, without a sound,
And one stepped forward, soiled and white:
'A bomber I. I travelled light

—Four pounds of nails and gelignite
About my person, hid so well
They seemed to vanish where I fell.
When the bullets stopped my breath
A doctor sought the cause of death.
He upped my shirt, undid my fly,
Twice he moved my limbs awry,
And noticed nothing. By and by
A soldier, with his sharper eye,
Beheld the four elusive rockets
Stuffed in my coat and trouser pockets.
Yes, they must be strict with us,
even in death so treacherous!'
He faded, and another said:
'We three met close when we were dead.
Into an armoured car they piled us
Where our mingled blood defiled us,
Certain, if not dead before,
To suffocate upon the floor.
Careful bullets in the back
Stopped our terrorist attack,
And so three dangerous lives are done
—Judged, condemned and shamed in one'.
That spectre faded in his turn.
A harsher stirred, and spoke in scorn:
'The shame is theirs, in word and deed,
Who prate of Justice, practise greed,
And act in ignorant fury—then,
Officers and gentlemen,
Send to their Courts for the Most High
To tell us did we really die.
Does it need recourse to law
To tell ten thousand what they saw?
The news is out. The troops were kind.
Impartial justice has to find
We'd be alive and well today
If we had let them have their way.
But friend and stranger, bride and brother,
Son and sister, father, mother,

All not blinded by your smoke,
Photographers who caught your stroke,
The priests that blessed our bodies, spoke
And wagged our blood in the world's face.
The truth will out, to your disgrace'.
He flushed and faded. Pale and grim,
A joking spectre followed him:
'Take a bunch of stunted shoots,
A tangle of transplanted roots,
Ropes and rifles, feathered nests,
Some dried colonial interests,
A hard unnatural union grown
In a bed of blood and bone,
Tongue of serpent, gut of hog
Spiced with spleen of underdog.
Stir in, with oaths of loyalty,
Sectarian supremacy,
And heat, to make a proper botch,
In a bouillon of bitter Scotch.
Last, the choice ingredient: you.
Now, to crown your Irish stew,
Boil it over, make a mess.
A most imperial success!'
He capered weakly, racked with pain,
His dead hair plastered in the rain:
The group was silent once again.
It seemed the moment to explain
That sympathetic politicians
Say our violent traditions,
Backward looks and bitterness
Keep us in this dire distress.
We must forget, and look ahead,
Nurse the living, not the dead.
My words died out. A phantom said:
'Here lies one who breathed his last
Firmly reminded of the past.
A trooper did it, on one knee,
In tones of brute authority'.
That harsher spirit, who before

Had flushed with anger, spoke once more:
'Simple lessons cut most deep.
This lesson in our hearts we keep:
You condescend to hear us speak
Only when we slap your cheek.
And yet we lack the last technique:
We rap for order with a gun,
The issues simplify to one
—Then your Democracy insists
You mustn't talk with terrorists.
White and yellow, black and blue,
Have learned their history from you:
Divide and ruin, muddle through.
We speak in wounds. Behold this mess.
My curse upon your politesse'.
Another ghost stood forth, and wet
Dead lips that had not spoken yet:
'My curse on the cunning and the bland,
On gentlemen who loot a land
They do not care to understand;
Who keep the natives on their paws
With ready lash and rotten laws;
Then if the beasts erupt in rage
Give them a slightly larger cage
And, in scorn and fear combined,
Turn them against their own kind.
The game runs out of room at last,
A people rises from its past,
The going gets unduly tough
And you have, surely, had enough.
The time has come to yield your place
With condescending show of grace
—An Empire-builder handing on.
We reap the ruin when you've gone,
All your errors heaped behind you:
Promises that do not bind you,
Hopes in conflict, cramped commissions,
Faiths exploited, and traditions'.
Bloody sputum filled his throat.

He stopped and coughed to clear it out,
And finished, with his eyes a-glow:
'You came, you saw, you conquered . . . So.
You gorged—and it was time to go.
Good riddance. We'd forget—released—
But for the rubbish of your feast,
The slops and scraps that fell to earth
And sprang to arms in dragon birth.
Sashed and bowler-hatted, glum
Apprentices of fife and drum,
High and dry, abandoned guards
Of dismal streets and empty yards,
Drilled at the codeword "True Religion"
To strut and mutter like a pigeon
"Not An Inch—Up The Queen";
Who use their walls like a latrine
For scribbled magic—at their call,
Straight from the nearest music-hall,
Pope and Devil intertwine,
Two cardboard kings appear, and join
In one more battle by the Boyne!
Who could love them? God above . . .'
'Yet pity is akin to love',
The thirteenth corpse beside him said,
Smiling in its bloody head,
'And though there's reason for alarm
In dourness and a lack of charm
Their cursed plight calls out for patience.
They, even they, with other nations
Have a place, if we can find it.
Love our changeling! Guard and mind it.
Doomed from birth, a cursed heir,
Theirs is the hardest lot to bear,
Yet not impossible, I swear,
If England would but clear the air
And brood at home on her disgrace
—Everything to its own place.
Face their walls of dole and fear
And be of reasonable cheer.

Good men every day inherit
Father's foulness with the spirit,
Purge the filth and do not stir it.
Let them out. At least let in
A breath or two of oxygen,
So they may settle down for good
And mix themselves in the common blood.
We all are what we are, and that
Is mongrel pure. What nation's not
Where any stranger hung his hat
And seized a lover where she sat?'
He ceased and faded. Zephyr blew
And all the others faded too.
I stood like a ghost. My fingers strayed
Along the fatal barricade.
The gentle rainfall drifting down
Over Colmcille's town
Could not refresh, only distil
In silent grief from hill to hill.

Hymn To The
New Omagh Road   JOHN MONTAGUE

As the bull-dozer bites into the tree ringed hillfort
Its grapnel jaws lift the mouse, the flower,
With equal attention, and the plaited twigs
And clay of the bird's nest, shaken by the traffic,
Fall from a crevice under the bridge
Into the slow-flowing mud choked stream
Below the quarry, where the mountain trout
Turns up its pale belly to die.

Balance Sheet

Loss

Item: The shearing away of an old barn
        criss-cross of beams where pigeons moan
        high small window where the swallow built
        white-washed dry-stone walls.

Item: The suppression of stone lined paths
        old potato-boiler full of crocuses
        overhanging lilac or laburnum
        sweet pea climbing the fence.

Item: The filling-in of chance streams
        uncovered wells, all unchannelled sources
        of water that might weaken foundations
        bubbling over the macadam.

Item: The disappearance of all signs
        of wild life, wren's or robin's nest,
        a rabbit nibbling a coltsfoot leaf,
        a stray squirrel or water rat.

Item: The uprooting of wayside hedges
        with their accomplices, devil's bit and pee the bed,
        prim rose and dog rose, an unlawful
        assembly of thistles.

Item: The removal of all hillocks
        and humps, superstition styled fairy forts
        and long barrows, now legally to be regarded
        as obstacles masking a driver's view.

Balance Sheet

Gain

Item: 10 men from the district being for a period of time fully employed, their ten wives could buy groceries and clothes to send 30 children content to school for a few months, and raise local merchants' hearts by paying their bills.

Item: A man driving from Belfast to Londonderry can arrive a quarter of an hour earlier, a lorry load of goods ditto, thus making Ulster more competitive in the international market.

Item: A local travelling from the prefabricated suburbs of bypassed villages can manage an average of 50 rather than 40 m.p.h. on his way to see relatives in Omagh hospital or lunatic asylum.

Item: The dead of Garvaghey Graveyard (including my grandfather) can have an unobstructed view—the trees having been sheared away for a carpark—of the living passing at great speed, sometimes quick enough to come straight in:

*Let it be clear
That I do not grudge my grandfather
This long delayed pleasure!
I like the idea of him
Rising from the rotting boards of the coffin
With his J.P.'s white beard
And penalising drivers
For travelling faster
Than jaunting cars*

II

From the quarry behind the school
the crustacean claws of the excavator
rummage to withdraw a payload,
a giant's bite . . .

'Tis pleasant for to take a stroll by Glencull Waterside
On a lovely evening in spring (in nature's early pride);
You pass by many a flowery bank and many a shady dell,
Like walking through enchanted land where fairies used to dwell.

Tuberous tentacles
of oak, hawthorn, buried pignut,
the topsoil of a living shape
of earth lifts like a scalp
to lay open

The trout are rising to the fly; the lambkins sport and play;
The pretty feathered warblers are singing by the way;
The black birds' and the thrushes' notes, by the echoes multiplied,
Do fill the vale with melody by Glencull waterside.

slipping sand
shale, compressed veins of rock,
old foundations, a soft chaos
to be swallowed wholesale,
masticated, regurgitated
by the mixer.

Give not to me the rugged scenes of which some love to write—
The beetling cliffs, o'erhanging crags and the eagle in full flight
But give to me the fertile fields (the farmer's joy and pride)
The homestead and the orchards fine by Glencull waterside.

Secret places
birds' nests, animal paths,
ghosts of children hunkering
down snail glistering slopes
spin through iron cylinders to
resume new life as a pliant stream
of building material.

These scenes bring recollections back to comrades scattered wide
Who used with me to walk these banks in youthful manly pride;
They've left their boyhood's happy homes and crossed o'er oceans wide
Now but in dreamland may they walk by Glencull waterside.

A brown stain
seeps away from where the machine
rocks and groans to itself, dis-
colouring the grass, thickening
the current of the trout stream
which flows between broken banks
—the Waterside a smear of mud—
towards the reinforced bridge
of the new road.

III

*My sympathy goes out to the farmer
who, mad drunk after a cattle mart,
bought himself a concrete swan
for thirty bob, and lugged it
all the way
home
to deposit it
(where the monkey puzzle was meant to grow)
on his tiny landscaped lawn.*

Clearances

SEAMUS HEANEY

in memoriam M.K.H., 1911-1984

She taught me what her uncle once taught her:
How easily the biggest coal block split
If you got the grain and hammer angled right.

The sound of that relaxed alluring blow,
Its co-opted and obliterated echo,
Taught me to hit, taught me to loosen,

Taught me between the hammer and the block
To face the music. Teach me now to listen,
To strike it rich behind the linear black.

I

A cobble thrown a hundred years ago
Keeps coming at me, the first stone
Aimed at a great-grandmother's turncoat brow.
The pony jerks and the riot's on.
She's crouched low in the trap
Running the gauntlet that first Sunday
Down the brae to Mass at a panicked gallop.
He whips on through the town to cries of 'Lundy!'

Call her 'The Convert'. 'The Exogamous Bride'.
Anyhow, it is a genre piece
Inherited on my mother's side
And mine to dispose with now she's gone.
Instead of silver and Victorian lace,
The exonerating, exonerated stone.

II

Polished linoleum shone there. Brass taps shone.
The china cups were very white and big—
An unchipped set with sugar bowl and jug.
The kettle whistled. Sandwich and tea scone
Were present and correct. In case it run,
The butter must be kept out of the sun.
And don't be dropping crumbs. Don't tilt your chair.
Don't reach. Don't point. Don't make noise when you stir.

It is Number 5, New Row, Land of the Dead,
Where grandfather is rising from his place
With spectacles pushed back on a clean bald head
To welcome a bewildered homing daughter
Before she even knocks. 'What's this? What's this?'
And they sit down in the shining room together.

III

When all the others were away at Mass
I was all hers as we peeled potatoes.
They broke the silence, let fall one by one
Like solder weeping off the soldering iron:
Cold comforts set between us, things to share
Gleaming in a bucket of clean water.
And again let fall. Little pleasant splashes
From each other's work would bring us to our senses.

So while the parish priest at her bedside
Went hammer and tongs at the prayers for the dying
And some were responding and some crying
I remembered her head bent towards my head,
Her breath in mine, our fluent dipping knives—
Never closer the whole rest of our lives.

IV

Fear of affectation made her affect
Inadequacy whenever it came to
Pronouncing words 'beyond her'. *Bertold Brek.*
She'd manage something hampered and askew
Every time, as if she might betray
The hampered and inadequate by too
Well-adjusted a vocabulary.
With more challenge than pride, she'd tell me, 'You
Know all them things'. So I governed my tongue
In front of her, a genuinely well—
Adjusted adequate betrayal
Of what I knew better. I'd *naw* and *aye*
And decently relapse into the wrong
Grammar which kept us allied and at bay.

V

The cool that came off sheets just off the line
Made me think the damp must still be in them
But when I took my corners of the linen
And pulled against her, first straight down the hem
And then diagonally, then flapped and shook
The fabric like a sail in a cross-wind,
They made a dried-out undulating thwack.
So we'd stretch and fold and end up hand to hand
For a split second as if nothing had happened
For nothing had that had not always happened
Beforehand, day by day, just touch and go,
Coming close again by holding back
In moves where I was X and she was O
Inscribed in sheets she'd sewn from ripped-out flour sacks.

VI

In the first flush of the Easter holidays
The ceremonies during Holy Week
Were highpoints of our Sons and Lovers phase.
The midnight fire. The paschal candlestick.
Elbow to elbow, glad to be kneeling next
To each other up there near the front
Of the packed church, we would follow the text
And rubrics for the blessing of the font.
As the hind longs for the streams, so my soul . . .
Dippings. Towellings. The water breathed on.
The water mixed with chrism and with oil.
Cruet tinkle. Formal incensation
And the psalmist's outcry taken up with pride:
Day and night my tears have been my bread.

VII

In the last minutes he said more to her
Almost than in all their life together.
'You'll be in New Row on Monday night
And I'll come up for you and you'll be glad
When I walk in the door . . . Isn't that right?'
His head was bent down to her propped-up head.
She could not hear but we were overjoyed.
He called her good and girl. Then she was dead,
The searching for a pulsebeat was abandoned
And we all knew one thing by being there.
The space we stood around had been emptied
Into us to keep, it penetrated
Clearances that suddenly stood open.
High cries were felled and a pure change happened.

VIII

I thought of walking round and round a space
Utterly empty, utterly a source
Where the decked chestnut tree had lost its place
In our front hedge above the wallflowers.
The white chips jumped and jumped and skited high.
I heard the hatchet's differentiated
Accurate cut, the crack, the sigh
And collapse of what luxuriated
Through the shocked tips and wreckage of it all.
Deep-planted and long gone, my coeval
Chestnut from a jam jar in a hole,
Its heft and hush become a bright nowhere,
A soul ramifying and forever
Silent, beyond silence listened for.

From: *Sweeney Astray*

SEAMUS HEANEY

Sweeney kept going until he reached the church at Swim-Two-Birds on the Shannon, which is now called Cloon-burren; he arrived there on a Friday, to be exact. The clerics of the church were singing nones, women were beating flax and one was giving birth to a child.

—It is unseemly, said Sweeney, for the women to violate the Lord's fast day. That woman beating the flax reminds me of our beating at Moira.
Then he heard the vesper bell ringing and said:
—It would be sweeter to listen to the notes of the cuckoos on the banks of the Bann than to the whinge of this bell tonight.
Then he uttered the poem:

> I perched for rest and imagine
> cuckoos calling across water,
> the Bann cuckoo, calling sweeter
> than church bells that whinge and grind.
>
> Friday is the wrong day, woman,
> for you to give birth to a son,
> the day when Mad Sweeney fasts
> for love of god, in penitence.
>
> Do not just discount me. Listen.
> At Moira my tribe was beaten,
> beetled, heckled, hammered down,
> like flax being scutched by these women.
>
> From the cliff of Lough Diolar
> up to Derry Colmcille
> I saw the great swans, heard their calls
> sweetly rebuking wars and battles.

From lonely cliff-tops, the stag
bells and makes the whole glen shake
and re-echo. I am ravished.
Unearthly sweetness shakes my breast.

O Christ, the loving and the sinless,
hear my prayer, attend, O Christ,
and let nothing separate us.
Blend me forever in your sweetness.

It was the end of the harvest season and Sweeney heard
a hunting-call from a company in the skirts of the wood.
—This will be the outcry of the Ui Faolain coming to
kill me, he said. I slew their king at Moira and this host is
out to avenge him.
He heard the stag bellowing and he made a poem in
which he praised aloud all the trees of Ireland, and
rehearsed some of his own hardships and sorrows, saying:

The bushy leafy oak tree
is highest in the wood,
the forking shoots of hazel
hide sweet hazel-nuts.

The alder is my darling,
all thornless in the gap,
some milk of human kindness
coursing in its sap.

The blackthorn is a jaggy creel
stippled with dark sloes;
green watercress in thatch on wells
where the drinking blackbird goes.

Sweetest of the leafy stalks,
the vetches strew the pathway;
the oyster-grass is my delight,
and the wild strawberry.

Low-set clumps of apple trees
drum down fruit when shaken;
scarlet berries clot like blood
on mountain rowan.

Brairs curl in sideways,
arch a stickle back,
draw blood and curl up innocent
to sneak the next attack.

The yew tree in each churchyard
wraps night in its dark hood.
Ivy is a shadowy
genius of the wood.

Holy rears its windbreak,
a door in winter's face;
life-blood on a spear-shaft
darkness the grain of ash.

Birch tree, smooth and blessed,
delicious to the breeze,
high twigs plait and crown it
the queen of trees.

The aspen pales
and whispers, hesitates:
a thousand frightened scuts
race in its leaves.

But what disturbs me
most in the leafy wood
is the to and fro and to and fro
of a oak rod.

★

A starry frost will come
dropping on the pools
and I'll be astray
on unsheltered heights:

herons calling
in cold Glenelly,
flocks of birds quickly
coming and going.

I prefer the elusive
rhapsody of blackbirds
to the garrulous blather
of men and women.

I prefer the squeal of the badgers
in their sett
to the tally-ho
of the morning hunt.

I prefer the re-
echoing belling of a stag
among the peaks
to that arrogant horn.

Those unharnessed runners
from glen to glen!
Nobody tames
that royal blood,

each one aloof
on its rightful summit,
antlered, watchful.
Imaging them,

the stag of high Slieve Felim,
the stag of the steep Fews,
the stag of Duhallow, the stag of Orrery,
the fierce stage of Killarney.

The stag of Islandmagee, Larne's stag,
the stag of Moylinny,
the stag of Cooley, the stag of Cunghill,
the stag of the two-peaked Burren.

*

I am Sweeney, the whinger,
the scuttler in the valley.
But call me, instead,
Peak-pate, Stag-head.

Then Sweeney said:

—From now on, I won't tarry in Dal-Arie because Lynchseachan would have my life to avenge the hag's.

So he proceeded to Roscommon in Connacht, where he alighted on the bank of the well and treated himself to watercress and water. But when a woman came out of the erenach's house, he panicked and fled, and she gathered the watercress from the stream. Sweeney watched her from his tree and greatly lamented the theft of his patch of cress, saying:

—It is a shame that you are taking my watercress. If only you knew my plight, how I am unpitied by tribesman or kinsman, how I am no longer a guest in any house on the ridge of the world. Watercress is my wealth, water is my wine, and hard bare tress and soft tree bowers are my friends. Even if you left that cress, you would not be left wanting; but if you take it, you are taking the bite from my mouth.

. . . .

From: **Sketches for an Elegy**

JULIE O'CALLAGHAN

*In memory of my father,
Jack O'Callaghan*

Jack and I are resting
under a weeping willow
beside the beach
I want to stop
asking silly questions
and talk about
important topics
such as
which colour he likes best

★

it could ruin
a person's outlook
on a jaunty
August morning
to wake up and hear
the Death March on WFMT
and then see
your ghostly bald father
facing the music
at the table
attempting to eat
a bowl of Cheerios

★

staring from his bed,
he asked, 'How long
did that doctor say?
Was it nine to ten months?
Or was it eight to twelve?'
when I told him six to eight
he shook his head
'Just look at that sky'

★

a cold start to the summer—
everything was haywire
mist all over the skyscrapers
and no customers
down at the beach

★

we stood in the park
looking for exotic migrating birds
resting on their way north
for the summer
yellow and blue and red birds
everywhere

★

sitting around
the chemotherapy room
for hours
I read all the magazines—twice
listening to the others
talk about the price of wigs
the great plumber
they had found

★

Sunday in August
nothing much doing
we go and get groceries
you need a bench to rest on
so we head for the beach
between the skyscrapers
once you feel better
we take off our shoes
and wade in the lake

*

a lunatic in the bank
telling the cashier
her life story
—poor bugger
you say

*

you pull me over and whisper
'See this guy. I've known him for years
—watch what happens when we pass by'
nothing
'Nobody recognizes me anymore'

*

he hears me arranging the flight
'Can't you stay another week?'
how was I supposed to know
he'd have only
three more of his own?

*

we let you go alone
to pick up
your camera lens downtown
but I worried
the whole time
what if you lost your balance
what if you couldn't walk any further

⋆

we're watching David Letterman
and you're paging through
the L.L. Bean summer sale catalogue
you see a shirt you like
and say, 'I won't need it
but one of the boys
could have it'

⋆

you lean forward
and I see a big
pillowy thing
protruding from your side
'It's my liver'

⋆

you have hand spasms
and you can't eat
you can't walk very far
you have no hair
but you can see the sky
the lake
the sunset to the west
so you're OK

⋆

you scratched your name
into cameras, pens, Swiss Army Knives
you etched your name
into sidewalks, kites, clouds, days

⋆

the monk eating pasta
in Dubuque Iowa
was the one I needed
to tell me something helpful
or at least not scary
—no use: he didn't have secrets
of the universe
just a plate of vermicelli

⋆

we were running
around the park
and down to the beach
picking up trash
the slobs
had left behind
hey slobs: no one's left
to pick up your garbage
why not go nuts

⋆

some were shocked
some looked away
others didn't recognise you
some got all teary
a few opted for chirpy
the doorman slapped your back
and said you looked great
on the bus
people stood up
to let you sit down

   ★

the last entire day
I will ever see you
is Chicago Air Show day
—for godsake
it isn't that often
you're having brunch
on the 22nd floor
and a Stealth Bomber
flies past the window
like a black triangle
from the planet Death

   ★

in that story
you're three or four
hanging out in the 1930s
in your Irish grandfather's room
he's sick and depressed
but you want him
to play with you:
you toss the rubber ball
in his direction
—as you're telling me
your voice changes
weeping, you say

'All I wanted
was for him to toss it back—
he wouldn't do it'

⋆

. . . .

the merchandise you ordered
arrived after you had died
we wondered
what it was
you felt you needed
in your last days
we tore it open
like a secret message
that would explain everything
you wanted us to know:
a tall white chef's hat

⋆

you tried to scribble
directions down for us nudniks:
taxes, good repairmen,
what to do
if the pipes froze,
how to apply
for a property assessment
pages and pages
on how to live

⋆

I wanted to belt
every person
who grabbed your arm

and put on a pitying voice
I wanted to guard you
from anyone shaking their head
dabbing their eyes
they could save their pity
for somebody else

⭐

sitting in the children's section
on a little chair
wearing your HANGTIME baseball cap
you page through a silly book
and nearly forget

⭐

there isn't much hope
80% are dead
within 16 months
but he'll try a few things
and see how it goes

⭐

driving you to chemotherapy
I realised I couldn't depend
on you anymore
my strong father

⭐

Miss You-Know-Who
wore skeleton earrings
with light-up red eyes
beneath a black cowboy hat
complementing her silver metallic
baseball jacket and knit mini-skirt
to your Memorial Service

—you would have been proud
of her genius at being insane

⋆

my meals boiled down
to microwave bowls and minutes
you would holler
from the bedroom
three minutes for peas
or seven for a potato
five minutes for fish
it didn't matter
gourmet wasn't called for
everything tasted like dirt

⋆

you still laughed at *Seinfeld*
and watered your plants
and read *The New Yorker*
and the Tuesday Science section
OK, it hurt a lot
and you said you'd never wear
your bike helmet again
but dying was easier
than I'd thought

⋆

when we were pretending you were OK
we planned a trip up the Missouri
like Lewis & Clark
what boat what route what time-frame
we studied *Undaunted Courage* for pointers
it would be great

⋆

. . . .

after everything
poison
scars
laser beams of radiation
he says the tumours
are bigger than ever
there is just one more thing
he can try
you asked how it would be
dying—talk me through it
then started painting a picture
of the red barn we saw near the Mississippi

. . . .

you didn't want to take the white stuff
but I made you do it twice a day
you complained
but you still drank it
how could you live without eating
that's what the white stuff did
it made hunger

      ★

Jack and me
on fold-up chairs
at the funeral parlour
my cousin's in that coffin
beside the flowers
relatives bending over
to talk to you
eyes everywhere noting
your ghostly appearance

      ★

would you do me
just one favour?
quit sitting like that
quit staring at the sky
don't sit and stare
you aren't the sit-and-stare type
go fix something
get out your tools
get busy and hammer

⋆

I'm blabbing away
about Irish people
you don't know
or houses
you'll never see
forgive me
it's just my way
of being inconsolable

⋆

remember how you told me
your mom used to
stroke your forehead and say,
'there, there' and how that
always made you feel better

⋆

what do I need to say about you
I didn't say before
you let me keep a horse in the city
—now that was nuts right there
you took me on a fossil-hunting expedition
and gave me Navajo earrings

⋆

when he was crying
he said, 'I'm not sad—
just sentimental'

⋆

the last page
about that summer
must be on the topic
of beaches
and how you loved them
and the machines which cleaned them
the police patrolling them
little old Russian ladies on the benches
the whackos dancing around on them
in the middle of the night
the boats floating on them
barges on the horizon
and the pier we walked down
to scatter your ashes

11

Naming the Islands

'Magic lantern'.
(April, 1889)   MICHAEL CRUMMEY

Bound for Great Britain and
beset by evening calm,
sails sheeted slack and lifeless;
the likeness of stars on the water,
hard yellow berries not ripe enough
to be gathered
Passengers and crew above decks
avoiding the breathless heat of their berths,
everyone wanting to be
anywhere but here

Brought out the magic lantern
and slides bought when I was last
in England, set it aboard a table
on the foredeck—
every head turning to
the breadth of the topmast
when the kerosene flame was lit
behind the lens,
the Tower of London standing
on the yellow canvas as if
we had dreamed it there
together

Flashed up the Crystal Palace,
Picadilly, the National Gallery,
then London Bridge,
the length of it shaken by
a rare gust of wind;
and the nearly-full moon rose
above the topyard,
the *Doune Castle* lying stilled
in its light like a photograph
projected on the water

'The price of fish'.
(September, 1887) MICHAEL CRUMMEY

I have had a fair trial on the fishing line now,
being 3 summers out from home, 2 summers on
the French Shore, 4 down on the Labrador,
and three trips this year to the Banks of Newfoundland,
and this is what I have learned to be the price of fish

Shem Yates and Harry Brown lost with the *Abyssinia*,
making through slack ice 60 miles NE of the Grey Islands
when the wind turned and she struck hard on a block,
the vessel split like a stick of frozen kindling—
May, 1886

Tom Viven out of Crow Head, his boat running
loaded down through heavy seas that opened her up forward,
going down just off Kettle Cove and a good trip of fish lost
   besides—
August, 1884

My last trip to the French Shore, Luke Brumley and Fred Strong
sent out to take in a trap set loose in a gale,
the rough weather filling their skiff with water
when they hauled up the span line, the two men
pitched under only a good shout from the *Traveller*
but neither one could swim a stroke—
June, 1882

Show me a map and I'll name you a dead man for
every cove between home and Battle Harbour

I am twenty four years old,
there is no guarantee I will ever see twenty five

'Now in Africa among the Natives'. (1891) MICHAEL CRUMMEY

In vain with loving kindness
the gifts of God are strown,
the heathen in his blindness
bows down to wood and stone.

Sketches in the old mission letters suggested
these people were grey, charcoaled,
unhappy shadows slumped and frowning.
I see now they are something altogether different—
skin the colour of stained wood
and teeth bright as the keys of a church organ;
hair as rich a black as peat moss, their voices
musical and muscular, echoing thunder and rain

God's will is God's will and if I once pretended to
comprehend a portion I have since given up the lie;
I've kept good company on Africa's shore,
on the white beaches of Brazil, in China and Ceylon,
it confuses me to have shared the kindness
of liquor and song with these when some
brought up under the sound of the Gospel would
see you dead before offering a drink of water

I thought the world would make me a wiser man,
but I am merely more perplexed—
I've learned to distrust much of what I was taught before
my travels showed me different;
the faces of Africa are as dark as a night without stars,
but they are not as blind as they are pictured

'A narrow escape almost but saved'. (1892) MICHAEL CRUMMEY

Aboard a Scotch boat shipping a cargo of
marble and alabaster across the Gulf of Lyons.
Three days out we came on a perfect gale,
the seas running above the mast heads
and the Captain had us clew up the topsails,
haul in the jibs and bring down the mainsail to reef it tight.
I was running out on the boom to make fast the outer jib
when the ship dropped away like a gallows door
and came up hard on a swell, chucking me
fifteen feet into the air and overboard;
I was lost but for falling into the outer jib whips
rolled four feet underwater by the gale,
like a dip net after capelin.
I hung fast to a rope as the ship rolled back,
got hold of the martingale whisker
and heaved myself in over the bowsprit to see the Captain
running about the deck with a life buoy
shouting he had lost a man.

We had a fine laugh about it afterwards—
when I climbed back aboard, they said my face was as white
as the 4 ton blocks of marble we had wedged in the hold.
But I don't remember being afraid when I fell,
only the certainty of knowing I was about to be drowned
a thousand miles from home,
and then the jib whip in my hands,
the peculiar darkness of discovering
there is nothing that is certain.

I came out of the water a different man than I had been
though I would be hard-pressed to say the difference.
The scar of that rope on my palms
for weeks after the storm had passed.

'Distance from Newfoundland. Northernmost grave in the world'. (1913)   MICHAEL CRUMMEY

A cairn of stones tells the story,
broken oar and a sledge runner
roughed into a cross
where the remains of George Porter lie,
the end of an expedition to Ellesmereland
1800 miles from St. John's harbour,
the vessel found wrecked
and nearly forgotten
on the Carey Islands.

I have travelled 12000 miles
to Van Dieman's Land,
crossed the line and lost sight
of everything I had looked upon,
the North Star put out like a pauper
when the Southern Cross
appeared in the sky;
the Water Bear, the Albatross,
the South Sea Seal guiding overhead,
so many strange things that seemed
strangely familiar
as if I was visiting an old city
I knew well from maps and stories.

In Constantinople I stepped into
the Dardanelles that drowned Leander
swimming for the light of Hero's torch;
I walked the streets of Salonica
where a seller of purple and fine linens
became Europe's first Christian,
a convert of shipwrecked–St. Paul,
the two of them praying together
among bolts of cloth, Lydia
was the woman's name.

George Porter lies under stone
only 1800 miles from Newfoundland
and almost further than a man could travel—
an initialled watch beside the cairn
where sailors stumbled upon it,
a notebook with the dead man's name,
how close he came
to being lost forever.

'At home on a cold winter's night. The changing scenes of Life'. (1928) MICHAEL CRUMMEY

November bluster,
the night sky obscured by cloud.

On the tall ships I was taught
to steer by the stars,
took them for granted,
like a portrait of grandparents
hung in the hallway before
you came into the world.

There is a telescope on Mount Wilson
in California whose lens
weighs 4 and one half tons
and measures 100 inches across—
they say it has mapped the heavens
for hundreds of millions of miles,
that the darkness is deeper than
we ever imagined.
New galaxies and constellations
discovered every day
and it is still only
the simplest things we understand.

The speed of light exceeds
eleven million miles a minute,
it travels through space
for thousands of years after
its star has collapsed;
it is possible
that all my life I have
taken my mark by
a body that does not exist.

A chunk of wood shifts in
the fireplace,
falls;
through the window I watch
winter clouds drift and gather.

Clotted field of stars beyond them,
light rooted hard in darkness.

'An old sailor's portion'. (1932)   MICHAEL CRUMMEY

I am an old man now
hard aground in Twillingate
and telling tales to skeptics,
my finger dipped in tea
to sketch a map across the table.

The young ones drop by with
whiskey to hear me talk,
I give them streets
cobbled with marble in Italy,
the long spiralling line of China's wall,
the songs I learned while drinking
with the darkies in Virginia,
those sounds as old as a continent . . .
I can tell they don't believe
the half of it.

It's an old sailor's portion
to be disbelieved so often
that he begins to doubt himself;
the best part of my life has passed
as a shadow, and shadows are what
I am left with—
perhaps every place I have ever been
is imaginary, like the Equator
or the points on a compass.

Don't ask me what is real
when you hear me talk,
I can only tell you
what I remember.

Look down at the table.
The map has already disappeared.

Stones MICHAEL CRUMMEY

A lot of it was learning to live with cruelty. To live cruelly.

We always had a couple of cats in the house, and the males you could do something with yourself. Father cut a hole in a barrel top, pushed the cat's head into it and had one of us hold its legs while he did the job with a set of metal shears. With females though, you had kittens to deal with once or twice a year. I drowned them in shallow water once, I didn't think it would make any difference, but I can still see that burlap sack moving like a pregnant belly only two feet out of reach; and I had to force myself to turn away. Those kittens were barely a week old but they took a long time dying.

The worst I ever saw was the horses. You'd get a strap around their waist with a ring underneath, and tie the fore and back legs to the ring with ropes. Then you'd back the animal up nice and slow so it would fall over in sections like a domino set, hind end first, then the belly, shoulders, head. Once it was on the ground you'd wash the bag with a bit of Jeye's Fluid, slit the sac open and snip the balls right off.

The cats bawled and screamed through the whole thing, but the horses never made a sound, they were too stunned I guess. Their legs made those ropes creak though, like a ship's rigging straining in a gale of wind. It would be a full day before they came back to themselves, standing out in the meadow like someone who can't recall their own name. Their wet eyes gone glassy with shock, as blind as two stones in a field.

Flame
Breen's Island, Labrador, 1944

MICHAEL CRUMMEY

When we came home from the Labrador in the fall, we'd take down the stage head and cutting room to save it from the ice that raked the shoreline over the winter. Next summer then, the first thing you'd want to do would be to get the stage head back up and ready to go. There wasn't much in the way of trees in the tickle though and we'd have to take the boat into the bay to cut some timber and firewood. All day in the woods then with an axe, and the flies after your eyes the whole time; if you opened your mouth to speak they were thick enough to choke you. Before we went in we'd douse our hands with gasoline and sprinkle a little on our hats, it helped keep them off a bit. All the same, when you came out of the bay there was a solid flame of blood across your forehead, behind your ears and along the back of your neck, as if someone had traced your hairline with a razor.

The year Mike Tobin was up with us he soaked himself before we went in, he couldn't stand those fucking flies. I'd say he had enough juice in his hair to send the boat down to Battle Harbour, you could see the fumes rising from his head like heat over pavement. We split up into pairs then and walked in.

Joe Crowley was with him, he says they stopped for a smoke after an hour and Mike reached up to scratch the back of his head still holding the cigarette. We heard the yelling, and then we could see a small fire tearing through the trees toward the bay. He stripped off his shirt as he ran and he looked like a big wooden match, his head in flames above the white skin of his chest, a tassel of black smoke trailing behind him. It was funny as hell to look at but we managed to hold off until we got him out of the water and saw that he wasn't hurt bad. The hair was mostly gone and what was left smelled like piss on fire, but that was the worst of it.

Mike would've preferred if we never said a word about it afterwards, but it was too good to pass up. And Joe was the hardest on him. Everytime he wanted a laugh that summer he'd take out a cigarette, wave it in Mike's direction and shout, 'Hey Tobin. Got a light?'

Fog City

MICHAEL CRUMMEY

Running the Quidi Vidi loop in mauzy weather,
alone on the trail but for the vague outline of
a retriever trotting ahead,
arc of the tail's baton marking time.
A ballgame on the diamond at Caribou Field,
gauzy park lights visible on the opposite shore—
blunted *chink* of the metal bat making contact,
muffled commotion as a pop fly
disappears into grey-mesh sky,
teammates calling advice on distance,
direction, index fingers extended
pointlessly toward absence.
The one silent player is the outfielder
judging the ball's arc by its trajectory
as it leaves the bat
and I can feel the contours of
his solitude clear across the lake,
a loneliness made worse by company,
by the encouragement of others.

That edgeless shape of a dog
steadily ahead on the trail
and not appearing to belong to anyone.

Naming the Islands

MICHAEL CRUMMEY

Inhabitants and Explorers
Iles des Esquimaux. Indian Island, Indian Bay, Indian Tickle.
Frenchman's Island. Cranford Head, Turner's Bight, Gilbert Bay.
Lac Grenfell, Tom Luscombe's Pond.
Cartwright, Cabot and Granby Islands.

No Comment Necessary
Island of Ponds, Bay of Islands.
Iles du lac, la Grande Ile.
Woody Point, Rocky Bay, Stoney Arm.
Fishing Ships Harbour.
Drunken Harbour Point.

You'll Know It When You See It
Table Island, Square Island, Narrow Island.
Saddle Island, Iles Crescent.
Chimney Tickle, Quaker Hat, Spear Point.
Castle Island.
Conical Island.

Tomayto/Tomahto
You say Napakataktalic I say Manuel Island
"   "   Tessiujalik   " " Lake Island
"   "   Nanuktok   " " Farmyard Islands
"   "   Wingiayuk   " " Lopsided Islands
"   "   Nunaksuk   " " Little Land Island

Mostly Wishful Thinking
Belle Isle. Bonne-esperance, Baie des belles amours.
Comfort Bight. New York Bay.
Paradise.

Abandon Hope All Ye Who Enter Here
Devil's Lookout, Black Tickle, False Cape, Bad Bay.
Savage Cove, Brig Harbour.
Battle Island, Cut Throat Island. Wreck Cove.
Pointe aux morts.
The Dead Islands.

Phallic and Phallocentric
Big Island and Long Island. Cox Head. Stag Island.
Halfway Island about 10 nautical miles from Entry Island.
The Shag Islands.
Snug Harbour.
The post-coital Tumbledown Dick.

All Creatures Great and Small
Porcupine Island. Crab Island, Caribou Run, Deer Island.
Iles aux chiens, Bull Dog Island.
Seal Bight, Capelin Bay, Partridge Bay Pond.
Goose Cove, Fox Cove, Hare Harbour.
Duck, Eagle, and Gannet Islands.
The Ferrets, the Wolves. Otter Bay.
Venison Island.
Snack Island in the mouth of Sandwich Bay.

Come Again?
Haypook Island. Horse Chops Island.
Bed Head. Separation Point.
The River S-t-i-c-k-s.
Nothing Bay.

The Horses

JOHN STEFFLER

now and then
do the horses still return to the old house
at night

as a child
when I slept out under the porch
and the damp fragrant darkness
went on and on
I strained in my socket of blackness
into the static ubiquitous chant of small creatures
and caught the quiet incisive cries
of the large ones near at hand

    a rustle and mutter
    the swish of a footstep
    and I could see the roundness
    swaying dark and shadowy
    under the shadows

in the first greyness I crept out
and saw them
gliding   turning   listening
up behind the garden
their thin black legs criss-crossing
silent and graceful
shuttering through the trees and fences in the mist

and as they vanished in the fields
their eyes flashed strangely young and milky
doe-like
almost tender in their dusky faces
but no never never of our world
and I wondered who should visit them upon us
and I wondered who they were

Saint Laurence's Tears

JOHN STEFFLER

No questions of falling then,
the August earth of Ontario under our backs—summer's
whole history we floated our small witnessing lives upon—
my sister and I in the star-showering night,
counting the quick silver scores
like lightning the crickets made
when their white-hot music built too intricate-tall
and fell, starting again.

No question of sinking
safe on the land that wanted us,
ocean of loam so many had sailed their houses on,
its slow cooperative swell thick with all it had borne,
gathered back: flints, coins, kitchen knives
in shallow constellations below,

the farm's old owners still setting
their lanterns down at the mouth of a stall,

harness riding into the strength it borrowed from.

Boiler Room Men JOHN STEFFLER

Boiler room men in their nests
of machinery under the underground parking lots, behind
steel doors, are all comfortable
cowards, wise *philosophes*

who slapped the gym mat frantically long ago in some
watershed wrestling match with the drafty
tumbledown world—and women what they are, clacking
around in their high heels overhead—gave up trying to
build some weather-tight enterprise of their own,
oh better,

much better to serve the big boys' corporate physical plant
like eunuch slaves at the emperor's bed,
maintaining the apparatus of power
from time to time,
their stocking feet propped otherwise on a steam pipe, the
hockey game yelping away on a small TV.

Even room for a cat down here
or at least a kettle for tea.

For Christ sake, who needs high pay

in a place as safe as this,
even taking into account the risk of explosion
which is kind of neat?

And it's as good as having money in the bank or jeans
the ladies can't take their eyes off, watching
the needle dials tremble, holding
the kilo-pascals, the obedient power that's really
all theirs,
that they didn't have to raise.

The New Sled

JOHN STEFFLER

The new sled
which the boy insists on calling
the GT Snowracer
and is no mere sled in his opinion
(the very word sled makes him laugh with brief
contempt as he pulls his woolen helmet on)
can swoop like an osprey
down the valley's white throat

can veer out of sight in the afternoon
which is only sky

and the boy, from a far speck,
against regrettable gravity, comes
wrestling his hawk-hearted companion back
to the father-held earth,
flame-faced and loud with something of what a hawk
must know.

From:
The Grey Islands   JOHN STEFFLER

he's out there the kids say pointing.
a little hut. the far end of a loose beaver dam.
Nels's stage.
must be so familiar to him and his family
they don't even see it anymore,
run, scramble sure-footed over the holes
and wobbles.

to me it's a jungle.
trip-vines, man-traps, where do you put your feet
for godsake, gaps, loose sticks teeter-totter,
water right under you.
hello!
I poke my head in the low door, rafters
dangling every kind of gaff and rusty implement.
an old man at the splitting table.
two boys perch watching him sharpen
squid jiggers with a file.

he shakes my hand, cautious,
feeling what kind of man.
traveller. landsman.
(salesman? missionary? taxman? crook?)
I want to get to the island I tell him,
hear he takes people out.

he spits. goes back to filing.

it spiles a day, he warns.

then flings out what it'll cost.
if we can go on the water.

I wait.

am I with the government?
no no! I'm (what'll I call myself?)

I just want to spend some time out there.
fish for trout

he cuts his price in half

★ ★ ★

Nels and his wife and half a dozen or so of their kids are loading empty barrels into a boat. 'Goin squiddin', Nels says.

I ask if there's room for me.

'Y'ever done it before?'

'Nope'.

'It's terrible dirty work', he warns, his eyes bright with glee.

I tell him that's okay, and he sends his youngest boy to find me a pair of rubber trousers.

I step into them, pull the braces up and grab a barrel to take aboard.

They do me the favour of letting me try to help.

Later Nels moves the barrel to where it was meant to be.

★ ★ ★

they all save one last squirt
till they're clear of the water,
black splats straight in the air,
up your sleeve, into your eye.

we sit tossing our jiggers,
ducking, chuckling, piling up squids
easy as pie.

'Take a chunk outa ya big as a dime',
Nels says, shaking one down that's
braided around his arm.

'Fall in there and they'd drown ya,
drag ya down'.

dark in the water long forms shoot criss-cross
like limbs of a sunken forest. strange.
not the same things we're pulling in,
stringy legs, flabby pouches.

coming up they ink wildly, puff like
parachutes. trying to put on the brakes.

dying they make small sunsets
with their bodies. glow blood-orange, freckle
like trout, huff, sigh. drain iridescent
green. lemon. white.

'Dry 'em on a line', Nels says. 'Wintertime,
put 'em in a toaster same as a slice a bread.
Sure! Better 'n potato chips!'

★ ★ ★

I thought I was headed for silence
but this island blares and bustles
as hard as any town

the sea slops and thumps
gurgles and knocks
suddenly loud
   (so close I turn expecting some
   person or creature climbing the bank)
suddenly muffled
steered away by the wind rustling
the grass, whispering up the wall

and the gulls
their single distant cries piercing
the shore's roar
their spiral bickering, jeers,
griefs, alarms
sharpen the air: salt
made audible.

even a bumble bee
touring slowly in at the door
and out
can make the cabin hum like a guitar.

★ ★ ★

when the rain comes and a cold wind
with it, it takes me by surprise:
no wood in the cabin. nothing to burn. but
I should have thought of this!
sunshine being the exception here.

I crouch shivering in front of the rusty
stove, trying the doors and vents,
not even sure if it's safe to use.

along the landwash some scattered
sticks, not too deeply soaked,
I split them, get them to burn
and then the real work starts:

braced against rain, I hack
at slippery boards all morning,
jump on them, break them
over my knee, the textbook
tenderfoot—foresight! foresight!—
scrambling now to save myself,
and hearing Nels's voice:

'When the wood's dry, *that's*
when ya cut it 'n stack it.
Not when it's soakin wet!'

'Good weather, plan for rain.
Gotta know what y're about b'y!'

arm-load by arm-load I stack my
soggy splits around the stove,
in the oven, up the wall,
keeping a careful relay:

burning wood. to dry wood.
to burn.

burning wood. to dry wood.
to burn.

★ ★ ★

on the bunk, behind the stove,
every bowl and pan catching
drips, I make my rounds as if
tapping a sugar bush, empty
them all in a pail and open the door
to pitch it—rain gusting in—
I stop. seeing the cabin's afloat
in a giant pool. mountain runoff
pouring under the back wall
gurgling out at the steps. I close
the door hearing my father's voice
his solid Ontario disbelief:
'they built it in the middle of a
bog for cats' sake! And the roof!
Man-oh-man'. (in real grief)
'The flashing's on *top* of the shingles!
All the rain goes *inside*!'

I stand listening like a boy
embarrassed
ashamed to have any connection
with such a place

having no excuse that would convince *him*
no practical explanation why
people here set so little store
in staying high and dry.

★ ★ ★

ducks swoop low over the
near beach as I breast the tall
weeds, stepping
carefully among the spiky planks
around these broken dwellings

no doors attached, no
glass in the windows, I look in
on fallen ceilings, iron beds, chairs
crushed under avalanches of lath.

where have they gone
the people who carved the air here
with their births and funerals
their scurried visits along the windy paths?

where have their children scattered to?

the grass still rustles with their parents' voices,
people who tried to balance their homes
between water and air.

★ ★ ★

Nels

There was my great-uncle Aaron Shale, one of the biggest fish-killers on the coast and a right hard man. The way a lot of 'em used to be.

He'd be out with his boy Clement—that woulda been my Uncle Clement—they'd be fishin with handlines together, and he expected the boy to jig just as many fish as he did, and as big too. He'd take a thick stick out in the boat with him, and if *he* jigged a fish and the boy didn't he'd give the boy a wallop with the stick. And not lightly neither I can tell ya. Or if *he* jigged a big fish and the boy only come up with a small one, he'd hit him for that. Oh yes sir! Catchin big fish was the sorta thing ya could do if ya had a mind to, accordin to Aaron Shale.

And by and by the boy learned, too. For a time there he could jig fish right alongside his old man.

★ ★ ★

Nels

From the month of June to the month of October, Aaron Shale never took his oilskins off. He never shifted out of 'em night or day for the whole fishin season. He was that hard at it. At eleven or twelve at night he'd come up from his boats and stores, lie down just like he was, and get up again at three in the mornin to pull his traps.

Nothin got in *his* way, my son.

And he *drove* his family, and them he had hired on, drove 'em just like he drove hisself. Never a minute's rest as long as the fish was runnin. He wouldn't so much as allow 'em to *speak* unless it had to do with the fish or the traps or what they needed to do. And he never opened his mouth hisself except to give orders, never even spoke to his wife for weeks on end. He'd come in dinner-time—and his food had to be ready, ready and waitin; she'd watch till he left the wharf, and get it all laid out hot before he opened the door—he'd walk across to his chair, sit down, eat, and walk out again without sayin a word, without even lookin at her while she stood there beside the stove.

The year his boy Clement died, the fish was some thick. They was bringin in three, four skiff-loads a day. And Aaron wouldn't take the time to put his son in the ground. He ordered the others to salt the boy, just like a fish, and he kept him like that out on his stage till the end of the season. Then they buried him. When the fish was done.

★ ★ ★

Nels

This one spring an iceberg come and set right on top of Aaron Shale's salmon net. He was in a state about that of course; but there wasn't a thing he could do. After a few days though, the berg foundered, turned bottom-up, and there was Aaron Shale's salmon net away up in the air, draped over the very tip of the thing.

When Aaron saw that he just turned around and went and got an axe. Then he rowed up to the berg all by hisself and climbed aboard of her. The other men were gathered around in their boats watchin—most of 'em scared even to go near the thing lest she broke or rolled again—and they watched Aaron Shale climb the side of that berg like a mountaineer, hackin out step after step for hisself as he went on up to the very pinnacle. Sixty feet over the water. And he unhooked his net and got it down out of there.

Cedar Cove

JOHN STEFFLER

If your wharf is washed away
it will come to Cedar Cove—
Wild Cove on the maps or
Capelin Cove. If your boat

goes down it will sail to Cedar
Cove piece by piece.
And your uncle, should he not come back
from his walk on Cape St. George,

will be found grinning among
the glitter of barkless roots
laths struts stays
stringers and frayed rope

in Cedar Cove, where no
cedars have ever grown,
but that's what the local people
call it. The water horizon

topples straight down
on Cedar Cove over
and over, box cars
falling, loads of TNT.

And the wind will not let you speak
in Cedar Cove, which could
be called Deaf Cove
or Lobotomy Cove, will not

let you think or stand straight;
the shrunk trees writhe
and have the wrong kinds
of leaves, but their roots spread

wide in Cedar Cove,
whose gravel is soft compared
to its air. We have come to Cedar
Cove overland, my love

and I, having been lost
at sea in another way.
All day we scatter
ourselves through the noise

and whiteness, learning the thousand
ways things can be taken
apart and reassigned—
the boot sole impaled on the shattered

trunk, the rust flakes,
the bone flakes encrusting a bracelet
of kelp—losing our pictures
of home, stick by stick.

After Cedar Cove,
how will we look?

Sour Fire

JOHN STEFFLER

Those determined middle-aged
men whose marriages have failed
and who've taken to the outdoors
and puff alone along trails
with their backpacks and their practical shapeless hats—
I do not want to be one of them.

I do not want to have everything I need
in a van,
drawers that open under the bed,
shelves that flop down.
I do not want to park on a wharf
eating my tin of stew.

Because he always yearned to go camping, but
the wife wasn't so keen (although she made an effort
and there are photos of her in a plaid shirt
drinking whisky from a mug near a lot of smoke),
and now she's left,
and I don't want this museum-house, each
item in it swollen with past,
tender, cut by the slightest glance, the memories
spurting—
her painted birds over the bed: they plucked
Ruth out of the air, but wherever they're flying
I'm still going down
down—
the masculine hinterland beckons.

But I don't want to join the trekkers trying
to repudiate houses and towns
and the work that creates them
as though they're all dedicated to women.

This man squatting alone by a sour fire,
bitten by flies,
telling himself he's getting close to the truth,
is not me.

Smoke

JOHN STEFFLER

To still be driving the familiar roads
when your family has gone—every object
gives off past like evening rocks
shedding their daytime heat. Mount Moriah,
Rattling Brook, Bottle Cove: encyclopaedias
opening at a glance. You ghost, you deep
sea diver. Every twig behind glass.
We all talked at once passing along
here, someone reaching into the back seat
for the thermos, someone clattering
in a bag of cassettes, streak of colours
left hanging over the pavement, old aviary
on wheels, travelling bonfire, smoke
you sniffing lost dog now pass through

Arriving in Russell   JOHN STEFFLER

When Cook came ashore here, his heart rose
and advanced like the boat that brought him,
riding on water so clear he might have been
sailing in sky, and the white sand he squinted at
and the green curls hanging plaited with red
hibiscus confirmed in his mind that God shared
his ideal of feminine beauty, since it burgeoned
forth in women and antelopes, fern-trees, even
in whole islands like this formed far from
jaded Europe in boundless blue. Having seen
the like in Tahiti and the many coral or smoking
islands on his way, he was already sure this
wasn't the southern continent. It rode too
lightly on the sea to carry massive commerce,
rivers of iron and brick, but then you never knew,
there might be gold, or wood to fashion ships
that wouldn't rot. And the excitement of Banks
and Solander, now crowding the dinghy's prow,
was always contagious; they had already spotted
birds they didn't recognise; would be in the water
before the boat touched land. No matter that
the natives, when they met them, would undoubtedly
be thieves, as proud of murder as of any art
they had, and that there would be venomous things
in the thickets; the world held marvels like
the legends said. By now he was mapping dreams.

That Night We Were Ravenous

JOHN STEFFLER

Driving from Stephenville in the late October
dusk—the road swooping and disappearing ahead
like an owl, the hills no longer playing dead
the way they do in the daytime, but sticking their black
blurry arses up in the drizzle and shaking themselves,
heaving themselves up for another night of
leapfrog and Sumo ballet—some

trees detached themselves from the shaggy
shoulder and stepped in front of the car. I swerved

through a grove of legs startled by pavement, maybe a
hunchbacked horse with goitre, maybe a team of beavers
trying to operate stilts: it was the

landscape doing a moose, a cow
moose,
most improbable forest device. She danced
over the roof of our car in moccasins.

She had burst from the zoo of our dreams and was
there, like a yanked-out tooth the dentist
puts in your hand.

She flickered on and off.
She was strong as the Bible and as full of lives.
Her eyes were like Halley's Comet, like factory whistles,
like bargain hunters, like shy kids.

No man had touched her or given her movements geometry.

She surfaced in front of us like a coelacanth, like a face
in a dark lagoon. She made us feel blessed.

She made us talk like a cage of canaries.

She reminded us. She was the ocean wearing a fur suit.

She had never eaten from a dish.
She knew nothing of corners or doorways.

She was our deaths come briefly forward to say hello.

She was completely undressed.

She was more part of the forest than any tree.
She was made of trees. The beauty of her face was bred
in the kingdom of rocks.

I had seen her long ago in the Dunlap Observatory.

She leapt from peak to peak like events in a ballad.

She was insubstantial as smoke.

She was a mother wearing a brown sweater opening her arms.

She was a drunk logger on Yonge Street.

She was the Prime Minister. She had granted us a tiny reserve.

She could remember a glacier where she was standing.

She was a plot of earth shaped like the island of
Newfoundland and able to fly, spring down in the middle of
cities scattering traffic, ride elevators, press pop-eyed
executives to the wall.

She was charged with the power of Churchill Falls.

She was a high-explosive bomb loaded with bones and meat.
She broke the sod in our heads like a plough parting the
earth's black lips.

She pulled our zippers down.
She was a spirit.

She was Newfoundland held in a dam. If we had touched her,
she would've burst through our windshield in a wall of blood.

That night we were ravenous. We talked, gulping, waving our
forks. We entered one another like animals entering woods.

That night we slept deeper than ever.

Our dreams bounded after her like excited hounds.

Bottled Rabbit   KEN BABSTOCK

A dream: of a stand of pole birch straight ahead
that drink into their moon-white trunks what little
light there is, then pose in stark relief to the darkening

beyond. The silence, though, is too complete, not right,
nothing shifts, whistles, or scuttles through the mess
of undergrowth. The effect, not of waking in the midst

of dark woods, the right road lost but the wringing
of phantom hands, a poverty of words, as the mind tries
to flush some authentic response to this charcoal study

by Cézanne. When waking comes it's to radio voices, a he
and a she, on about slips, snares, the gutting shed, and mason
jars. It's the CBC, in a town I didn't catch near Gander, doing

a segment, it seems, on the unusual folk dishes and dietary
habits of the ever-colourful Newfoundlander. '. . . bottled rabbit',
he's saying, 'today I'll show you how to make bottled rabbit, or

jarred rabbit, as it's called in other parts'. And as the host
gives a slowed-down translation that imparts a tut-tut sound
to all the *t's*, I'm seeing that reticent, cardiganed man in

the one-act by Pinter hauling up tiny masts on a glassed-in
schooner; only it's a matchstick bunny now, and he's trying to
attach the whiskers. 'You can see I've already skinned, cleaned,

and quartered this one' (the whiskers quiver, fall off, the ears
lie back. The man sighs, lights up, starts in again) 'and normally
   one
rabbit, quartered, 'll fit into each mason jar'. It's here the Pinter

set fades, morphs, becomes my great-aunt's kitchenette twenty
years ago; the margarine-coloured curtains are closed, so
the light takes on a clinical, formaldehyde glow, and two jars

are eased down from a shelved row of preserved I-didn't-know-
whats. A lid twists, its wax and rubber seal breaks with a sucking
sound, bits of white fatty pulp drop from the lip and she dunks

two fingers and thumb through the film for the pink-brown,
   naked
oblongs of meat. Perhaps we are what we remember we ate, but
I've no memory, now, of what that rabbit tasted like, though I'm

tempted to say it tasted like rabbit. The host, here, pipes in
unbelievably with 'Wow, it tastes like chicken. . . ' And thusly
a nation is born, I thought, or something fuzzier that meant

that, as I was still barely awake. But you were coming to, just
   then,
as they descended into clangorous cleanup noises, his water
audibly bubbling in the pan. I touched your forehead: 'What's
   real?'

Our aloe plant teetered on its chopstick struts, leaned over
its double crawling the bedcover. The word wore down, thinned
to a film on the air in the ear. Morning ate its hinge.

Drawing Skeletons
—for Kajin Goh

KEN BABSTOCK

Living in Cow Head, Newfoundland, you'd draw
bones, collecting them from
beaches and backyards of dead outports.

Skeletal frames of sheep, intact chain of
a seal's spine. The dried,
final frame from a wound up spool, shelved—

sketch the end then drift backward into
an idea of life. Nothing
lives if not in your mind . . .

mites tunnelling the porous bone, awash
in the light of a basement lamp.
You, huddled over a study of humpback's ribs as

a Gros Morne sun sifts through the crackling, black
and white speckled credits.

Bonavista

KEN BABSTOCK

1. From a Photo of My Grandmother

Out back of a house, the blue of a crib
or dorsal fin, the black dirt hoed into
lines, a garden plot big enough
for potatoes and not much else.

This was my grandparents' home, stitched curtains
waving each dawn in time to the tide pushing
out under dories. The men in oilskins,
hardtack between their boots, hack at the bay,
taking nips of good screech to taunt
the bad weather, bolster the guts.

I don't know this village, only its stories.
Did visit once. I was two
when both grandparents dropped
the cove a last grin, whistled
a humpback out of the depth,
and put their leather lives away.

Strongest memory now is a photo:
a two-year-old and his father's mother,
kerchief knotted round the salt straw
of her hair, and a pail
of capelin hinged to her hip.
Mud-caked wellies sunk ankle-deep, we're
spreading fish to rot in the furrows
then nourish the crop. The kid,
one hand splayed, is stumbling
on stubby legs, reaching for the soil
to prop his upper half,
staring the dead catch in the eyes.

2. Mainland Boy in Eastport

Yet when cocky men peered round the curtain of sky
there was no god and the mists came
—Paul Durcan

That cod had come up without effort.
Gavin had hooked its lower
lip and it swam with each hand-
over-hand. Hauling nylon
jig line over the gunnel, beads
of sea water raced away to plop
back into the black.
     Unimpressed, doubtful,
he kept muttering, *there's nothing on it*
and his uncle at helm, an eye
on the water's heave and give, swung
the boat around, *haul the friggin'*
thing in if ye felt a tug.

It split the surface and hung there
with the awful, ageless grin
of a bottom-dweller in a dinosaur book.
Gaping and dumb, its filmy eye rolled
then fixed on the jig's chrome flash
stuck through its chin. Gavin slid
fingers under gills, hoisted its cold
bulk over so it thudded on deck;
its white belly, porcelain-smooth,
bumped his boot-toe and expired.

    We tied up at Salvage and went
    home in the truck.
        At dinner,

squeaking his chair across lino,
a mainland boy fidgets while grace
is mumbled through, he's sneering
at the choral amen, at these supplicants,
their decorum, having seen what he'd
raised from the bottom.

3. Uncle in Eastport

Cap-beak smudged with engine
grease, stained denims that sagged
in the crotch. He'd pause, for effect,
then unleash a laugh that bugged
out the veins in his neck. He was all
wrinkles, all pipe smoke and
the same flappy ears as my father,
who he'd elbow with jokes for leaving the Rock,
for having come from away
with these sons who couldn't tell
tomcod from wet socks—

    I buried my fists
in my jacket, squinted into the wake-spray
as the bow banged down over breakers.
Licks of silver mist ribboned
out from the point and beyond that
a damp, blurry oatmeal of grey. Behind me,
he stayed drawn-lipped and hushed,
thick fingers twisting a tin thermos lid,
just doled out two cups—then,
heard through a wind, *I'se a ten week man . . .
two kids . . . I laughs when I can.*

12

Homecoming

Do Jack Kerouac CATHAL Ó SEARCAIGH
do Shéamas de Bláca

'The only people for me are the mad ones,
the ones who are mad to live, mad to talk,
mad to be saved, desirous of everything at
the same time, the ones who never yawn or
say a commonplace thing but burn,
burn like fabulous yellow roman candles'

Sliocht as *On the Road*

Ag sioscadh trí do shaothar anocht tháinig leoithne na cuimhne chugam ó gach leathanach.
Athmhúsclaíodh m'óige is mhothaigh mé ag éirí ionam an *beat* brionglóideach a bhí ag déanamh aithris ort i dtús na seachtóidí.
1973. Bhí mé *hookáilte* ort. Lá i ndiaidh lae fuair mé *shot* inspioráide ó do shaothar a ghealaigh m'aigne is a shín mo shamhlaíocht.

Ní Mín 'a Leá ná Fána Bhuí a bhí á fheiceáil agam an t-am adaí
   ach machairí Nebraska agus táilte féaraigh Iowa.
Agus nuair a thagadh na *bliúanna* arm ní bealach na Bealtaine a
   bhí romham amach ach mórbhealach de chuid Mheiriceá.
'Hey man you gotta stay high' a déarfainn le mo chara agus muid
   ag *freakáil* trí Chailifornia Chill Ulta isteach go Frisco an Fhál
   Charraigh.

Tá do leabhar ina luí druidte ar m'ucht ach faoi chraiceann an
   chlúdaigh tá do chroí ag preabadaigh i bhféitheog gach focail.
Oh man mothaím arís, na *higheanna* adaí ar Himiléithe na hóige:
Ó chósta go cósta thriall muid le chéile, saonta, spleodrach,
   místiúrtha;
Oilithreacht ordóige ó Nua-Eabhrac go Frisco agus as sin go
   Cathair Mheicsiceo;
Beat buile inár mbeatha. Spreagtha. Ag bladhmadh síos bóithre i
   gCadillacs ghasta ag sciorradh thar íor na céille ar eiteoga na
   mbennies.
Thrasnaigh muid teorainneacha agus thrasnaigh muid taibhrithe.
Cheiliúraigh muid gach casadh ar bhealach ár mbeatha,
   *binge*anna agus
bráithreachas ó Bhrooklyn go Berkeley, *booze, bop* agus
   Búdachas; Éigse na hÁise; sreangscéalta as an tsíoraíocht ar na
   Sierras; marijuana agus misteachas i Meicsiceo; brionglóidí
   buile i mBixby Canyon.

Rinne muid Oirféas as gach *orifice.*

Ó is cuimhneach liom é go léir, a Jack, an chaint is an cuartú.
Ba tusa bard beoshúileach na mbóithre, ar thóir na foirfeachta,
   ar thóir na bhFlaitheas.
Is cé nach bhfuil aon aicearra chuig na Déithe, adeirtear,
   d'éirigh leatsa slí a aimsiú in amantaí nuair a d'fheistigh tú úim
   adhainte ar Niagara d'aigne le *dope* is le diagacht.
Is i mBomaite sin na Buile gineadh solas a thug spléachadh duit
   ar an tSíoraíocht,
Is a threoraigh 'na bhaile tú, tá súil agam, lá do bháis chuig
   Whitman, Proust agus Rimbaud.

Tá mo bhealach féin romham amach . . . '*a road that ah zigzags all over creation. Yeah man! Ain't nowhere else it can go. Right!*'
Agus lá inteacht ar bhealach na seanaoise is na scoilteacha
Nó lá níos cóngaraí do bhaile, b'fhéidir,
Scroicfidh mé Crosbhealach na Cinniúna is beidh an Bás romham ansin,
Treoraí tíriúil le mé a thabhairt thar teorainn,
Is ansin, *goddammit* a Jack, beidh muid beirt ag síobshiúl sa tSíoraíocht.

For Jack Kerouac CATHAL Ó SEARCAIGH
for Séamas de Bláca

'*The only people for me are the mad ones,
the ones who are mad to live, mad to talk,
mad to be saved, desirous of everything at
the same time, the ones who never yawn or
say a commonplace thing but burn,
burn like fabulous yellow roman candles*'

On the Road

Thumbing through your work tonight the aroma of memories came from every page.
My youth rewoke and I felt rising in me the dreamy beat that imitated you at the start of the '70s.
1973. I was hooked on you. Day after day I got shots of inspiration from your life which lit my mind and stretched my imagination.
I didn't see Mín 'a Leá or Fána Bhuí then, but the plains of Nebraska and the grassy lands of Iowa
And when the blues came it wasn't the Bealtaine road that beckoned but a way stretching across America.
'Hey man you gotta stay high', I'd say to my friend as we freaked through California's Cill Ulta into Frisco's Falcarragh.

Your book lies shut on my breast, your heart beating under the skin cover in the muscle of every word.
Oh man I feel them again, those highs on youth's Himalayas from coast to coast we roamed together, free, wild, reckless:
A hitchhiking odyssey from New York to Frisco and down to Mexico City.
A mad beat to our lives. Crazed. Hurtling down highways in speeding cars, skidding over the verge of sanity on the wings of Benzedrine.

We crossed frontiers and we scaled dreams.
Celebrations at every turn of life's highway, binges and brotherhood

from Brooklyn to Berkeley; booze, bop and Buddhism; Asian verse; telegrams from a Sierra eternity; marijuana and mysticism in Mexico; frenzied visions in Bixby Canyon.

Orpheus emerged from every orifice.

O I remember it all Jack, the talk and the quest.
You were the wild-eyed poet walking free, searching for harmony, searching for Heaven.
And although it is said there's no shortcut to the Gods you opened one up now and then, harnessing your mind's Niagara with dope and divinity.
And in those rapturous moments you generated the light that you saw eternity by
And that guided you, I hope, the day of your death, home to Whitman, Proust and Rimbaud.

My road is before me 'a road that ah zigzags all over creation.
   Yeah man! Ain't nowhere else it can go. Right!'
And someday, on the road of failing sight and knotted limbs
Or a less distant day, perhaps
Death will face me at Fate's Crossroads
My gentle companion across the frontier
And then, goddamit Jack, we'll both be hiking across eternity.

translated by Sarah Berkeley

Transubstaintiú

do Vona Lynn CATHAL Ó SEARCAIGH

Idir an smaoineamh agus an briathar
tá dúichí oighir agus ceo.

Ach beidh mise le mo bheo
ag cascairt an tseaca, ag scaipeadh an cheo

ag gríosú is ag grianadh
le gaetha tintrí mo chroí

ionas go dtiocfaidh tú fós í mbláth,
tusa nach bhfuil ionat ach scáil.

Transubstantiation

For Vona Lynn CATHAL Ó SEARCAIGH

Between the thought and the word
are regions of ice and fog;

but all my life I'll be
shattering the frost, scattering the fog

stirring and sunning
with my heart's fiery rays

so that you'll flower one day
you that are only a shadow.

translated by Gabriel Fitzmaurice

Dia: Nótaí Anailísi

do Des Lynn CATHAL Ó SEARCAIGH

I dtráth agus in antráth
coinníonn sé súil ghéar ar ghairdín na n-úll.

Díbríonn sé a chlann ar shiúl
Ádhamh agus Éabha de bharr alpadh na n-úll.

Tá a chroí is cosúil
i bpióga úll. Tinneas an tsaoil nó saobhdhúil?

Tá sé doiligh a rá
mar nach gceadóidh sé scrúdú dochtúra

ná ceistiú go brách.

God: Analyst's Notes

for Des Lynn CATHAL Ó SEARCAIGH

From early hours to late
he keeps a sharp eye on Eden's gate.

He evicts his own Family,
Adam and Eve, because of what they ate.

His heart, it would appear,
Is lost to apple-tarts. Is he world-weary or somewhat queer?

Difficult to relate
since he refuses to be psycho-analysed

or scrutinized.

translated by Gabriel Rosenstock

Haikú

CATHAL Ó SEARCAIGH

do Mháirín Ní Dhubhchoin

Speal mo sheanathar
ag meirgiú sa scíoból—
clapsholas Fómhair

        Dritheog nó dhó fágtha
        I mbucóid luatha an tseanduine—
        grian na tseanduine.

Gealach na gcoinleach—
tá úll dearg san fhuinneog
is an dath ag siothlú as

        (I mo sheomra leapa)

        Oíche fhada gheimhridh—
        cumhaidh ar an chuileog fosta
        léi féin sa leabaidh

Haiku

CATHAL Ó SEARCAIGH

for Máirín Ní Dhubhchoin

My grandfather's scythe
Rusting in the barn—
harvest twilight

translated by Gabriel Fitzmaurice.

An ember or two glow
in the old man's ash bucket—
Winter morning sun

Harvest moon—
As red fades from the apple
Set in the window

(In my bedroom)

Long Winter's night—
the fly grieves too
alone in the bed.

translated by Gréagóir Ó Dúill

I gCeann mo Thrí Bliana a Bhí Mé CATHAL Ó SEARCAIGH
do Anraí Mac Giolla Chomhaill

'Sin clábar! Clábar cáidheach,
a chiuilcigh', a dúirt m'athair go bagrach
agus mé ag slupairt go súgach
i ndíobhóg os cionn an bhóthair.
'Amach leat as do chuid clábair
sula ndéanfar tú a chonáil!'

Ach choinnigh mé ag spágáil agus ag splaiseáil
agus ag scairtigh le lúcháir:
'Clábar! Clábar! Seo mo chuid clábair!'
Cé nár chiallaigh an focal faic i mo mheabhair
go dtí gur mhothaigh mé i mo bhuataisí glugar
agus trí gach uile líbín de mo cheirteacha
creathanna fuachta na tuisceana.

A chlábar na cinniúna, bháigh tú mo chnámha.

When I Was Three

CATHAL Ó SEARCAIGH

for Anraí Mac Giolla Chomhaill

'That's muck! Filthy muck, you little scamp',
my father was so severe in speech
while I was messing happily
in my mud-trench by the road.
'Out with you from that muck
before you freeze to death!'

But I continued shuffling, having fun,
all the time screaming with delight:
'Muck! Muck! It's my own muck!'
But the word was nothing in my innocence
until I felt the squelch of wellies
and, through the dripping wet of clothes,
the shivering knowledge of water.

Ah! Muck of destiny, you drenched my bones!

translated by Thomas McCarthy

Círéib GEARÓID MAC LOCHLAINN

(An lá ar saoradh Pte Lee Clegg)

I

Cúlaíonn beirt dhéagóirí, scairfeanna thar a mbéal,
an leoraí Bass trasna an bhóthair
sula gcuirtear na suíocháin stróicthe trí thine.
Léimeann siad anuas is cuirtear buama peitril tríd an fhuinneog.
Pléascann sé ina smionagar oighir ar an tarramhac te,
ag lonrú mar a bheadh i gcárta Nollag.
Doirteann scata amach as an *Beehive*, piontaí ina lámha
is seasann siad thart go balbh ag na soilse tráchta,
lucht féachana an *Mardi Gras* feirge.
Léimeann na páistí scoile
trí na boinn rubair dóite ina luí ar an bhóthar.
Screadann an fear líreacáin ar chluasa bodhra.
Tagann máithrín ina déaga
amach as siopa an bhúistéara le pram is earraí grósaera.
Trasnaíonn sí go cúramach le cuidiú fir óig
a stopann an trácht atá anois ag lúbadh
mar nathair mheicniúil ar an chosán,
exhausts ag siosarnach go mí-fhoighneach.

I bpreabadh na súl tá *dumper* buí nua
is tochaltóir JCB ón suíomh tógála
tóin le tóin le chéile i lár an bhóthair,
ainmhithe aisteacha éalaithe ón zú.
Tá beirt sheanbhan ina slipéir sheomra,
lámha crosáilte, ag croitheadh a gcinn.
—*Bloody ridiculous*, a deir siad
sula bhfilleann siad chun dinnéir.

II

Ní bheidh sé i bhfad go dtiocfaidh
iriseoirí nuachtán, grianghrafadóirí,
ina dhiaidh sin jípeanna le saighdiúirí, jípeanna le póilíní
is gunnaí, gunnaí, gunnaí, gunnaí,
ag screadaíl thar bráid trí na bladhmanna
faoi bháisteach chrua chloch is bhuidéal.

Tá an chíréib tosaithe
is ar feadh tamaillín,
tá na marbháin beo arís.

Riot
(for Karen Reilly)

GEARÓID MAC LOCHLAINN

I

Backing a *Bass Ireland* lorry across the road
before its razored seats are set alight,
two young bucks with scarves over their mouths.
As they hop clear, a petrol bomb smashes
the window into smithereens
that glitter the hot tarmac like ice on a Xmas card.
A table or two pile out of the *Beehive* with pints
and stand about mute at the traffic lights,
spectators at a bitter Mardi Gras.
School-kids hop-scotch through
smouldering tyres lying on the road
and turn deaf ears on the lollipop
man's tongue-lashing.
A teeny-mother wheels out of the butcher's
with a buggy-load of groceries
and crosses over carefully with the help of a youth
who stops the line of traffic now writhing up
onto the footpath like a mechanised boa.
Exhausts hiss and spit their impatience.

In no time, a yellow dumper
and JCB digger from the building site
stand arse to arse in the middle of the road
like exotic animals gone AWOL from the zoo.
Two old women in slippers stand
with folded arms, shaking their heads.
—*Bloody ridiculous*, they say
before turning back to their dinners.

II

It won't be long now
till the journalists come
with wide angle, zoom and digital.
After that, saracens of infantry,
then storm-troopers and Vaders
with guns and sabres
racing and screeching through tunnels of flame
under a hard rain of bottle, stone and grating . . .

The riot has just begun
and for a little while
the dead will flicker and stir.

translated by Frankie Sewell and Gearóid Mac Lochlainn

Paddy GEARÓID MAC LOCHLAINN

(i ndilchuimhne)

'Did ya hear about Donal's wee brother?'
a scairt Chips liom thar longbhá an tábla, callán an ghrúpa,
trí fhaobhair bhána *feedback* ón *Fender*,
an t-inneall toite is an smúit.
Mé ar seachrán, ag mairnéalacht,
smaointe místiúrtha faoi lánseol,
ag bádóireacht ar thonnta cordaí is *riff*eanna,
as mo cheann ar *Bush* is raithneach,
ag gig éigin, víbeanna ag bleaisteáil.

Is chuala mé do scéal, a Phadaí óig.
Thaibhsigh tú i gcuan cáiteach mo chuimhne
an oíche ólta sin,
le d'fholt dubh, tiubh, slíochta,
cíortha siar ó d'éadan muscach
inar neadaigh lonta dubha do shúl.

Padaí óg na *good looks*.
Gléasta i do chulaith fhaiseanta nua néata gan smál
a chuir poll i do phóca.

Wee Paddy a thug muid ort is tú thar sé throigh
nuair a lean tú lorg do dheartháireacha ba shine,
cárta bréagach aitheantais i do ghlac,
do phas go Kelly's, Lavery's, Robinson's,
le bheith ag guaillíocht leis na meisceoirí eile,
caillte i gcathair ghríobháin *round* síoraí.
Sa deireadh go Londain thall
ar lorg luach do shaothair,
pubanna is clubanna a d'oirfeadh don chulaith is úire,
d'acmhainn.

Londain thall. Súil na himpireachta.
Seanbhitseach sheargtha na gcíoch searbh.
Seanbhitseach na súl seachtantach,
na sciathán leathair
a eitlíonn go réidh i mbolg dubh an *underground*.
Seanbhitseach starrfhiaclach
ag súmaireacht ar fhuil an deoraí
faoi ghealacha *neon*acha.
Ríle, ríle, ráinne.
Seanbhitseach ghlic ag an choirnéal i Soho
a bhfuil a fhios aici '*What ya want. What ya need*'.
Cathair na mbréag. Cathair an chumha.
Cathair chruálach ag creimeadh croí Éireannach,
croí Iamácach, croí Indiach,
croí Giúdach, croí Albanach.
Triop treap triopaití treap.
Seanbhitseach shnoite ina luí ag fanacht
faoin droichead i gcathair chairtchláir.

Triop treap tripaití treap.
Seanbhitseach shnoite
a chreim do chroí Feirsteach amach
gur fágadh thú i do phuipéad. *Pinocchio* teipthe,
gan phíobaire teallaigh,
ag luascadh ó shíleáil, sreangaithe amach sa deireadh.
Plúchta. Múchta.
D'amhrán gafa go deo i do scornach,
gléasta i do chulaith ghorm is goirme.

Taibhsíonn tú i gcuan m'aigne anocht arís.
Stánaim, gan deoir, i lonta dubha do shúl,
scáth spíonta i do shuí os mo chomhair ag an tábla sa chistin,
mé ag éisteacht le víbeanna maithe ag preabarnach,
ag stealladh, ag doirteadh ina thonnta dorcha rithime ó shúile
    dubha
na *speakers* ar mo *ghetto blaster*,
an Sliabh Dubh lasmuigh den fhuinneog,
faoi fhial fearthainne,
ag déanamh faire fhoighneach ar chathair bhriste
Bhéal Feirste.

Cuirim CD ar siúl, ag bleaisteáil víbeanna
a chuireann na cupáin ag rocáil ar an tseilf.
Ardaithe i ndilchuimhne,
duitse, domhsa.
Briathra binne, beachta, cinnte
don neamhdhuine ina luí i ndoras siopa i Londain thall,
Linton Kwesi Johnson ag ceol fírinne,
a scaoileann sealán na croiche,
a shuaimhníonn an oíche seo,
a thugann bomaite eile beatha duitse, a Phadaí,
i dteach slán na cuimhne.

—*Inglan is a bitch*
dere's no escapin' it

Paddy

GEARÓID MAC LOCHLAINN

'Did ya hear about Donal's wee brother?'
cried Chips through the din of mates
manning the shipwreck-table,
the white noise of the band,
his mouthed words parrying blades
of cranked up *Fender* amp feedback,
cutting through the smoke
and fog machines.

We had spliced the mainbrace
and become unmoored with Bush and grass,
drifting over looped chords and sinnets of riffs.
It was some gig or other,
good vibes crackling through
the valves and leads.

And as I heard your story, Paddy,
you ghosted into the squally harbour of memory,
sleek dark hair combed off a dusky forehead
where your blackbird-eyes nested,
dressed in your latest slick-cut suit
that burned a hole in your pocket.

We called you wee Paddy
though you were over six feet
when you trailed us,
flashing phoney ID to the monkeys
on the doors of Kelly's, Lavery's, Robinson's,
where you'd go to rub shoulders with other mates
lost in the submarine labyrinth of an eternal round
and finally, fed up with it all,
to London.

London. Eye of the empire.
Old withered bitter-titted-bitch.
Bat-winged-bitch who flits in the whale-belly underground.
Wide-boy-bitch on Soho corner who
knows 'What ya want. Got what ya need'.
Fanged-bitch sucking exile blood
under neon-moons.
City of remorse.
Cruel city gnawing the heart-strings
of Irish, Jamaican, Jew, Scot.

Trip-trap-trippity-trap.
Haggard-old-bitch
slupping out of the Thames
to trawl beneath the bridge in Cardboard City.
Trip-trap-trippity-trap.
Mean-old-bitch who munched out your Belfast heart,
left you a puppet, Pinocchioed,
suspended, finally strung out.
Your swan song stilled.
Dressed in your newest and bluest of blue suits.

Tonight you drift again
into the mind's harbour,
a parched dust-devil.
I stare deep into your blackbird-eyes
across the kitchen table,
the room
immersed in waves of rhythm
that roll and lash
from the black-eye-speakers
on the ghetto-blaster.
The Black Mountain looms outside the window
under a dark veil of rain,
keeps patient vigil on *Béal Feirste cois cuain*.

I turn up the volume, pump it,
till it sets the cups jitterbugging on the shelf,
till the bind in me unravels.
I let it out,
soft sure words for the corpses washed up
in shopfronts. In London.
Linton Kwesi Jonson sings it true,
looses the noose,
soothes and smoothes away the night
and suddenly, Paddy, you catch your breath
in the safe-house of memory

—Inglan is a bitch
dere's no escapin' it
Inglan is a bitch fi true
a noh lie me a tell, a true.

translated by Gearóid Mac Lochlainn

The Green Shoot   JOHN HEWITT

In my harsh city, when a Catholic priest,
known by his collar, padded down our street,
I'd trot beside him, pull my schoolcap off
and fling it on the ground and stamp on it.

I'd catch my enemy, that errand boy,
grip his torn jersey and admonish him
first to admit his faith and, when he did,
repeatedly to curse the Pope of Rome;

schooled in such duties by my bolder friends;
yet not so many hurried years before,
when I slipped in from play one Christmas Eve
my mother bathed me at the kitchen fire,

and wrapped me in a blanket for the climb
up the long stairs; and suddenly we heard
the carol singers somewhere in the dark,
their voices sharper, for the frost was hard.

My mother carried me through the dim hall
into the parlour, where the only light
upon the patterned wall and furniture
came from the iron lamp across the street;

and there looped round the lamp the singers stood,
but not on snow in grocers' calendars,
singing a song I liked until I saw
my mother's lashes were all bright with tears.

Out of this mulch of ready sentiment,
gritty with threads of flinty violence,
I am the green shoot asking for the flower,
soft as the feathers of the snow's cold swans.

The Scar
JOHN HEWITT

for Padraic Fiacc

There's not a chance now that I might recover
one syllable of what that sick man said,
tapping upon my great-grandmother's shutter,
and begging, I was told, a piece of bread;
for on his tainted breath there hung infection
rank from the cabins of the stricken west,
the spores from black potato-stalks, the spittle
mottled with poison in his rattling chest;
but she who, by her nature, quickly answered,
accepted in return the famine-fever;
and that chance meeting, that brief confrontation,
conscribed me of the Irishry forever.

Though much I cherish lies outside their vision,
and much they prize I have no claim to share,
yet in that woman's death I found my nation;
the old wound aches and shews its fellow-scar.

A Belfastman Abroad Argues With Himself

JOHN HEWITT

Admit the fact, you might have stood your ground
and kept one corner clear for decency,
making no claims, but like a friendly tree,
offering shade to those who'd gather round.
You should have spoken when that evil man
first raised his raucous shout, to all who lied
given the lie direct, that little clan
who later marched for justice, joined with pride.

Now from safe distance, you assert your right
to public rage. This town is, after all,
where I was born and lived for fifty years.
I knew its crooked masters well by sight,
endured its venom and survived its sneers—
I scratch these verses on its flame-scorched wall.

Calling on Peadar O'Donnell at Dungloe   JOHN HEWITT

I remember striding through the August twilight
along a narrow lane from house to house;
a crowd of lads were hurling loud and shouting,
and once a black calf gave a mournful cry.

It seemed the long track round that we had taken
over a rough ground higher than the bog.
Three fields away foam topped the distant breakers.
Storm's opposition flogged us both dog-tired.

Then darkness dropped, and window after window
offered no trace of colour. We went on,
slow pacing now, and painfully admonished
by plaintive gulls above the ocean's din.

We reached the three small houses and the gate
which faced the place the drive swung to the right.
Now far too late to make our call we argued.
There was no blink of light in any room.

But halfway up the drive we glimpsed the writer
still working in the garden with his wife;
I shouted and he straightened up to answer,
and in the gloom his fine head glimmered white.

In recollection of Drumcliffe, September 1948

JOHN HEWITT

The years spin quicker since that day I stood
to watch the poet's coffin take to earth
a second time, in kinship's neighbourhood
which gave his proud imagination birth;
and my clenched homage knelt to cross and tower,
to those dark famous hills which, till time ends,
must wear the shapes conferred by vatic power,
the power that fleshed our legends and his friends.

Although I could not share his thoughts, and choose
instead a faith in man's progressive range,
finding his stance and temper alien,
I carry thence what I shall never lose,
his chanted cadence, and the right to change
the masks with which I face my fellowmen.

Eager Journey

JOHN HEWITT

My mother's father, when he came to die,
summoned his house to join him singing clear
his road to Glory: this, obediently,
they, with schooled voices, did, well versed in praise,
for Methodists were people without fear
of Hell, or doubt of Their Redeemer's Grace.

That first time it was difficult for them
to hold their grief in balanced harmony,
claiming death gate to joy's Jerusalem,
while their brave father struggled with his pain;
but, when the crisis ebbed, relieved to see
the steady breath restored, they wept again.

For days he wrestled, weakening, called for song
when the end beckoned, falling back in sleep
each time God failed to answer. Far too long
and pitiful a vigil for his kin;
a nurse was mustered, so that they might keep
some grip on time, some rhythm of discipline.

One afternoon, slipped down to fetch his tray,
quickly returned, she found him sprawling dead
athwart the tumbled blankets' disarray,
the man who never once had failed a friend,
alone now on that eager journey sped,
not one hosanna trumpeting the end.

Of Difference
Does It Make

TOM PAULIN

During the 51-year existence of the Northern Ireland Parliament only one Bill sponsored by a non-Unionist member was ever passed.

Among the plovers and the stonechats
protected by the Wild Birds Act
of nineteen-hundred-and-thirty-one,
there is a rare stint called the notawhit
that has a schisty flight-call, like the chough's.
Notawhit, notawhit, notawhit
—it raps out a sharp code-sign
like a mild and patient prisoner
pecking through granite with a teaspoon.

Desertmartin

TOM PAULIN

At noon, in the dead centre of a faith,
Between Draperstown and Magherafelt,
This bitter village shows the flag
In a baked absolute September light.
Here the Word has withered to a few
Parched certainties, and the charred stubble
Tightens like a black belt, a crop of Bibles.

Because this is the territory of the Law
I drive across it with a powerless knowledge—
The owl of Minerva in a hired car.
A Jock squaddy glances down the street
And grins, happy and expendable,
Like a brass cartridge. He is a useful thing,
Almost at home, and yet not quite, not quite.

It's a limed nest, this place. I see a plain
Presbyterian grace sour, then harden,
As a free strenuous spirit changes
To a servile defiance that whines and shrieks
For the bondage of the letter: it shouts
For the Big Man to lead his wee people
To a clean white prison, their scorched tomorrow.

Masculine Islam, the rule of the Just,
Egyptian sand dunes and geometry,
A theology of rifle-butts and executions:
These are the places where the spirit dies.
And now, in Desertmartin's sandy light,
I see a culture of twigs and bird-shit
Waving a gaudy flag it loves and curses.

Purity

TOM PAULIN

Perhaps a maritime pastoral
Is the form best suited
To a northern capital
With its docks and gantries,
An oil refinery on the salt marsh.

Far from the playful celebration
Of good manners on a green field
There is always that dream
Of duck-down and eider,
The lichened island whose sour light
Lets us be ourselves.

Those luminous privacies
On a bleached coast
Are fierce and authentic,
And some of us believe in them.
They are the polities of love.

But in the brilliant distance
I see a crowded troopship
Moving down the blue lough
On a summer's morning,
Its anal colours
Almost fresh in the sun.
Those black boots are shining.
There is only a pink blur
Of identical features.

A Nation, Yet Again

TOM PAULIN

after Pushkin

That kitsch lumber-room is stacked
with a parnassian dialect:
'love, hope, and quiet reputation
kissed us for a short season
and the gamey letters that we swopped,
in clipped verse, soon had to stop'.
No one, then, praised either side,
though some dipped down among the shades
to find Aeneas and to file
a delicate, a tough, new style
that draws the language to the light
and purifies its tribal rites.
I'm tense now: talk of sharing power,
prophecies of civil war,
new reasons for a secular
mode of voicing the word *nation*
set us on edge, this generation,
and force the poet to play traitor
or act the half-sure legislator.
No matter; there's a classic form
that's in the blood, that makes me warm
to better, raise, build up, refine
whatever gabbles without discipline:
see, it takes me now, these hands stir
to bind the northern to the southern stars.

Telegrams BERNARD O'DONOGHUE
for Mick Henry

I. TWIST AND BUST

End of a day in the wet trench,
you're all so tired you can hardly pull
the boots off, but you have to
before the pub will let you in.
Polite notice: site footwear
not admitted.

On the dark table,
inside the digs front door:
the buff envelope, face down.
Whose father, sister, brother, mother
this time? Come on; leave it. Eat first,
play a hand of cards in the *Bell*,
face it after closing-time.

II. DELIVERY BOYS

Fogarty's kept his usual station at the bar
all night, with a good view of the swing doors
in the mirror in front of him. Two more
and he'll be off himself to catch
the second-last bus to Camden Town.

And then he sees them coming: two
workmates from the old days in Bristol,
but wearing ties. 'I know what's bringing
ye fuckers, and I don't want to hear about it'.

III. SAILING TICKETS

In high summer when they all went home,
numbers on the mailboat were controlled
by the issue of ten-shilling sailing tickets.
No getting on without them: that is except
if you could show an Irish telegram
to the man at the barrier: 'I must get back
for the funeral, sir; my mother's passed away'.
Sometimes of course she had; more times she hadn't.

The Twisting of the Rope
BERNARD O'DONOGHUE

A man lived down by the castle
called Tim John Batt. His father was Batt Murphy
who delivered the post on foot and went by boat
every weekend to run in Wales and London,
so their long low farmhouse was filled with trophies.
His mother's people were poets from Kiskeam.

In the time when hay was drawn in by float,
Tim John was attended by a team of children.
To keep them safe, he'd punch an indentation
at the front of the big haycock and strap them down
with the hayrope he threw diagonally from the back,
pulled tight to stop the cleanings falling off.

Nearly fifty years on, I walk those fields again,
now to read the summer sky. At midnight
it's all under control: Vega blue in the heights;
the Plough's steady eyes upon its furrow.
But when I wake up in the early hours,
it's all gone haywire: the Triangle

has toppled westward; Orion's on his face,
his Dog above him, sniffing anxiously
for signs of life before it dawns. Later again,
the whole thing has gone, the Dog fading last,
his bark growing less audible until
in the end you can hardly even hear

the music of the spheres. Yes, many things
have changed since then, it's true. The corncrake's gone;
the cuckoo's on her way. Tim John, who'd forced
the jawing horse back towards the haybarn,
is now himself backing out of the picture,
twisting the long hayrope as he goes.

Homecoming

DESMOND O'GRADY

The familiar pull of the slow train
trundling after a sinking sun on shadowed fields.
White light splicing the broad span of the sky.
Evening deepens grass, the breeze,
like purple smoke, ruffles its surface.
Straight into herring-dark skies the great cathedral spire
is sheer Gothic; slender and singular,
grey as the slate at school when a child looking up—
a bottle of raspberry in one hand, a brown bag of biscuits in
   t'other—
Feathereye Mykie my uncle told me a man
shot down a hawk dead from the cross
with a telescope fixed to his rifle.

Pulling home now into the station. Cunneen waving
a goatskin of wine from the Spain he has never seen
like an acolyte swinging a thurible.
My father, behind him, as ever in clerical grey,
white hair shining, his hand raised,
preaching away to the Poet Ryan.
And after a drink at the White House—out home.

The house in bedlam. He's here says my father.
Sober? my mother. She's looking me over.
Bring out the bottle. Pull round the fire.
Talk of the journey, living abroad:
Paris and London, Rome and New York.
What is it like in an airplane? my sister.
Glad you could make it—my brother.
Everything here the same tuppence ha'penny—the neighbours;
just as you left it; the same old roast chestnut.
After the songs, the one for the road,
the last caller gone—up to my room.

As I used find it home for the Christmas from school.
The great brass bed. The box still under it full
of old prayerbooks, assorted mementos,
the untouched bundle of letters mottled with mould.
Now it's a house of doorways and walls
and no laughter. A place for two old people
who speak to each other but rarely. And that only
when children return. Old people mumbling
low in the night of change and of ageing
when they think you asleep and not listening—
and we wide awake in the dark,
as when we were children.

The Butchers   MICHAEL LONGLEY

When he had made sure there were no survivors in his house
And that all the suitors were dead, heaped in blood and dust
Like fish that fishermen with fine-meshed nets have hauled
Up gasping for salt water, evaporating in the sunshine,
Odysseus, spattered with muck and like a lion dripping blood
From his chest and cheeks after devouring a farmer's bullock,
Ordered the disloyal housemaids to sponge down the armchairs
And tables, while Telemachos, the oxherd and the swineherd
Scraped the floor with shovels, and then between the portico
And the roundhouse stretched a hawser and hanged the women
So none touched the ground with her toes, like long-winged thrushes
Or doves trapped in a mist-net across the thicket where they roost,
Their heads bobbing in a row, their feet twitching but not for long,
And when they had dragged Melanthios's corpse into the haggard
And cut off his nose and ears and cock and balls, a dog's dinner,
Odysseus, seeing the need for whitewash and disinfectant,
Fumigated the house and the outhouses, so that Hermes
Like a clergyman might wave the supernatural baton
With which he resurrects or hypnotises those he chooses,
And waken and round up the suitors' souls, and the housemaids',
Like bats gibbering in the nooks of their mysterious cave
When out of the clusters that dangle from the rocky ceiling
One of them drops and squeaks, so their souls were bat-squeaks
As they flittered after Hermes, their deliverer, who led them
Along the clammy sheughs, then past the oceanic streams
And the white rock, the sun's gatepost in that dreamy region,
Until they came to a bog-meadow full of bog-asphodels
Where the residents are ghosts or images of the dead.

Wounds

MICHAEL LONGLEY

Here are two pictures from my father's head—
I have kept them like secrets until now:
First, the Ulster Division at the Somme
Going over the top with 'Fuck the Pope!'
'No Surrender!': a boy about to die,
Screaming 'Give 'em one for the Shankill!'
'Wilder than Gurkhas' were my father's words
Of admiration and bewilderment.
Next comes the London-Scottish padre
Resettling kilts with his swagger-stick,
With a stylish backhand and a prayer.
Over a landscape of dead buttocks
My father followed him for fifty years.
At last, a belated casualty,
He said—lead traces flaring till they hurt—
'I am dying for King and Country, slowly'.
I touched his hand, his thin head I touched.

Now, with military honours of a kind,
With his badges, his medals like rainbows,
His spinning compass, I bury beside him
Three teenage soldiers, bellies full of
Bullets and Irish beer, their flies undone.
A packet of Woodbines I throw in,
A lucifer, the Sacred Heart of Jesus
Paralysed as heavy guns put out
The night-light in a nursery for ever;
Also a bus-conductor's uniform—
He collapsed beside his carpet-slippers
Without a murmur, shot through the head
By a shivering boy who wandered in
Before they could turn the television down
Or tidy away the supper dishes.
To the children, to a bewildered wife,
I think 'Sorry Missus' was what he said.

13

She Pushed Her Secret Out

From: **The Bower**   VONA GROARKE

Arbor vitae—a *tree-like appearance seen when the human cerebellum is cut vertically.*
Chambers Concise Dictionary

When it does grow up one has no hesitation in calling it a tree but it is not so easy to define what is meant.
Ray Proctor, Trees of the World

POPLAR

He's a gossip and he brings it home to her
how big the world is, how small her doings are.
His statements have the ring of consequence,
so she listens and is sparing in response.
He could say anything to her, even her name, and still
sound like small leaves tossed in a summer squall.

WILLOW

We're told the day is promised poor,
but still the weather holds and not even the lake
is bothered by so much impending doom.
The one disturbing factor is the pike

which likes things sour, and so takes on the shore
and its neat symmetry, which he soon sets astir
as he smudges the surface, and ruffles the sand,
and lifts the moored rowboat a fraction higher.

One branch of a weeping-willow skims the surface
and is moved with the lightest of tremors
by the wave. Then the whole tree is suddenly at it,
twittering and jiggling like a nervous horse.

Someone looking from the window pulls her cardigan
tight around her chest and shivers slightly,
as though lifted too, then shrugs to say:
'Well, let it happen, it can do no harm to me'.

Rufus, standing on a flex so the light
dims for a second, offers added proof.
Someone setting down a bucket in the yard
is an echo of more thunder on the hoof.

One of the men decides to light a fire
which will warm them through the worst
of what's to come. 'Best be prepared',
he tells his woodpile, 'get in first'.

BOX

What I liked about him first off was his height—
five feet four—with a chest like Hercules and hands
like trowels. I'm four foot nine myself and I am tired
of being asked to sit on laps. I want a man
who can look me in the eye while standing up.

He says that I made a man of him with my busy hands,
that I put shape on him, egging him on towards
moves he'd not have made, left to himself. I don't know.
Sometimes I see him when he's perched at his desk.
He looks to me like a bigger man, trimmed back.

ELM

He says that he hardly notices, that I don't look all that different
and, now that the redness is gone and the stitches are out,
you'd think everything was the way it always was. I'm glad
to hear it, but I know it's crap. His tongue says it one way,

but his hands have it another. He hasn't touched me on that side
since the op. Oh, he'll work away at the other right enough,
but he turns his head (who'd blame him) towards the wall. I do
the rest myself, running my finger, for company, round the
   stump.

YEW

I misunderstood. He was talking about
what went on forever and was hard and dark
and never thought of death, and it so near.

I was seeing graveyards at dusk
with rooks and bats and a full but foggy moon,
while all the time he was talking about me.

COPPER-BEECH

He has taken to pottering and has planted a tree.
He takes long walks. He says no one listens to him
anyway. It's getting so I hate my days off work
and the way that he sours the house with his moods,
so I go into town with Grace, who never asks.

Last Monday, she held up a v-necked blouse
and said it would suit me—I should try it on.
She was looking me hard in the eye and I knew
what she was waiting for, and what it meant.
I came home to cry in my room. He did it again.

I might not need the scarf tomorrow. They're fading,
looking less like the liver-spots on my mother's wrists
and more like the leaves on the sapling
that I see him tending now with his gloves on,
to keep his hands and fingernails from harm.

. . . .

The Statue of the Virgin at Granard Speaks

PAULA MEEHAN

It can be bitter here at times like this,
November wind sweeping across the border.
Its seeds of ice would cut you to the quick.
The whole town tucked up safe and dreaming,
even wild things gone to earth, and I
stuck up here in this grotto, without as much as
star or planet to ease my vigil.

The howling won't let up. Trees
cavort in agony as if they would be free
and take off—ghost voyagers
on the wind that carries intimations
of garrison towns, walled cities, ghetto lanes
where men hunt each other and invoke
the various names of God as blessing
on their death tactics, their night manoeuvres.
Closer to home the wind sails over
dying lakes. I hear fish drowning.
I taste the stagnant water mingled
with turf smoke from outlying farms.

They call me Mary—Blessed, Holy, Virgin.
They fit me to a myth of a man crucified:
the scourging and the falling, and the falling again,
the thorny crown, the hammer blow of iron
into wrist and ankle, the sacred bleeding heart.

They name me Mother of all this grief
though mated to no mortal man.
They kneel before me and their prayers
fly up like sparks from a bonfire
that blaze a moment, then wink out.

It can be lovely here at times. Springtime,
early summer. Girls in Communion frocks
pale rivals to the riot in the hedgerows
of cow parsley and haw blossom, the perfume
from every rushy acre that's left for hay
when the light swings longer with the sun's push north.

Or the grace of a midsummer wedding
when the earth herself calls out for coupling
and I would break loose of my stony robes,
pure blue, pure white, as if they had robbed
a child's sky for their colour. My being
cries out to be incarnate, incarnate,
maculate and tousled in a honeyed bed.

Even an autumn burial can work its own pageantry.
The hedges heavy with the burden of fruiting
crab, sloe, berry, hip; clouds scud east
pear scented, windfalls secret in long
orchard grasses, and some old soul is lowered
to his kin. Death is just another harvest
scripted to the season's play.

But on this All Souls' Night there is
no respite from the keening of the wind.
I would not be amazed if every corpse came risen
from the graveyard to join in exaltation with the gale,
a cacophony of bone imploring sky for judgement
and release from being the conscience of the town.

On a night like this I remember the child
who came with fifteen summers to her name,
and she lay down alone at my feet
without midwife or doctor or friend to hold her hand
and she pushed her secret out into the night,
far from the town tucked up in little scandals,
bargains struck, words broken, prayers, promises,
and though she cried out to me in extremis
I did not move,
I didn't lift a finger to help her,
I didn't intercede with heaven,
nor whisper the charmed word in God's ear.

On a night like this I number the days to the solstice
and the turn back to the light.
       O sun,
centre of our foolish dance,
burning heart of stone,
molten mother of us all,
hear me and have pity.

If I Could Give You Now
CARMELITA MCGRATH

What I remember of you
is the very smallness of your wrists,
how the slightness of your body
made it dance like a stalk of grass in each small wind

and, oh, how we danced when the wind was wild and high,
blowing our traded secrets out over the bay!

You still believed
that a fat and magic man with twinkling eyes
and scads of gifts existed, loved you,
although there were compartments of your innocence
that had been invaded, then closed for (almost) ever.

And I never knew then I would break your heart,
telling you that Santa Claus was not what you thought
was a mother—not
a father, surely. For fathers
were the lords-a-leaping, drunk
for most of the twelve days of Christmas.

In return, you told me how women and men had sex,
making a circle and a kind of poker with your thin fingers:
'Nah, it'd crack off', I said,
and tried to draw it with a compass and protractor,
but none of the angles were persuasive. And how
did you know
such impossible things were possible?

Because someone had already tried
to show you how it worked
and wanted you to work it.

Age nine:

it seems so far away now; I never knew then
that when I said,
'Santa Claus is your mother',
I broke into the final place in your heart
that held out hope for magic
and belief
in a being
who, unlike Jesus and his vaporous angels,
knew how to make a kindly presence felt.

If I could give you now
what was taken away then,
I would—

would fill the meadows with angels bearing gifts
and populate the stars
with strange bright beings,
your name and love burning on their lips.

Adam and Eve on a Winter Afternoon

CARMELITA MCGRATH

Adam comes in from sawing wood
with a chip on his shoulder.
And grunts. And heaves the wood down,
a heavy drop filled with creeping, unsaid things,
to the woodbox.

And Eve is trying to imagine it not there,
that slow and trembling thing within his breath
that lives between inhale and exhale. This
must be just exertion, and yet it feels
like a weapon, not quite secret but concealed.

She has words for such days—*wood hyacinth,
aurora borealis, Harley-Davidson*—either
ethereal beauty or a fast-flying escape.
But the kitchen is a trap baited with supper cooking
and the imminent arrival of children.

And Adam says, 'Whas for supper?'
And Eve says, 'Soup'.
And he says, 'Any meat in it?
I hope you're not off meat again. Growing
children need their protein. And this
is no climate to be eating like rabbits'.

And then the old clock rescued from a house
where pouncing bargain hunters drove deals at a death sale
hammers four o'clock home.

And Eve thinks that four o'clocks are old-fashioned flowers,
and she stirs the soup and plunks down
in her bentwood rocker with her seed catalogues,
thinks *crocosmia*
thinks *branching tulip*
thinks *Apricot Beauty*
thinks *hemerocallis*

And the ragged thing between breath and breath
is there again, just for a second, a thing of air
with claws and teeth.

And Adam goes out for another load
before the early dark sinks in on him,
and while his saw buzzes
the language of massacre on wood
thinks *tomorrow's Friday*
thinks *pint of Guinness*
thinks *at least she dyed her hair*
thinks *I can hear the children*

Their footsteps saw over frozen grass, their voices
high, inadvertently calling everything back together,
one of them playing a blackbird's call on a recorder.

For the First Time in Months, She Feels Her Feet   CARMELITA MCGRATH

He was always going to look after them
until he went out one day
too far for his boat and the weather,
making all questions rhetorical,
whether he would change,
would go to the store for diapers
or cook meals, would keep loving
his wife's sister. Full fathom five
and it's all over, but wind whipping
on this icy slope; he tried to do too much,
then his boots got full and pulled him under.

She strokes her boy's hair;
absent fingers pull out strands
without even knowing, and the boy
must be grateful for the pain taking him out
of the trance state where his eyes stare
so hard that the hill divides
into pinpoints of light and colour
hard to put back together,
even that rose of blood on the snow
where the nail dug into his finger.

Later, she realizes that she can feel
the squish of water that tells her
her boots have soaked, and she feels
her feet for the first time in months,
and worries suddenly
that the boy will catch cold,
she pulls their eyes away from the hill,
their feet, towards town.
On the way down, she remembers the first time he hit her.

Breaking Ice   CARMELITA MCGRATH

A man is breaking ice outside his front door which faces east and somewhat north. That front door faces only the promise of the sun; the sun itself gone by morning half-time so that the ice builds and builds, pushing toward April.

She says, 'You need a pick to do that', but he only has a shovel, and so he pounds its blunt tip into the ice. Brilliant three-dimensional sparks fly out. She thinks mortar and pestle; thinks sorrow is what makes us work.

He pounds his sadness to dust, grinds her silence to powder, grinds woody ice-locked stems to *fines herbes* while the day fades to black.

They have talked already of when to tell the children.

But today they work like all work is waiting, and waiting is all work. Mortar and pestle. He grinds ice to shimmering dust, dreams of the grapefruit league and sees a white ball sailing through Florida's azure heaven. And she . . .

And she pries ice from thyme in the back garden. The sun warms her back and gives her hair red highlights that she can see when she bends over. Somewhere a ball slices the air, dividing the season into the dead winter / the new spring. There is less ice here out back. The garden faces southwest.

How She Had Her Nervous Breakdown   CARMELITA MCGRATH

She was standing by the dryer when the end-of-cycle timer went off. Rising, ears offended, she heard the call of church bells in the other ear or air, and a siren far away, faint as a kettle's first whistle, but heavy as damage, then all sounds blending into an alarm, a call. That

afternoon, walking in a mall in search of the world's warmest sweater and three pairs of children's sneakers, she dreamed of alone by a coddled fire, though her house had no fireplace, and she smoked a cigarette with such intensity, a man looking for a light had to say 'excuse me' three times before she pulled her eyes away from the merging greenness the leaves on the potted trees had become,
and saw his features
swing
into place,
like puzzle pieces shuffled.

Later, waiting in the yard in front of the elementary school, fleeting things moved at the outer edges of her vision, and she tried to place them, name them, but a buzzer rang, and children, including two of her own, swarmed toward her. In the car, the boy waved his small fingers in front of her face, 'Hullo, anybody home?' After

a weekend when sauces stuck to pots and silences grew monstrous, she sat in the doctor's office and said, 'I can't remember driving anywhere'.

Left with a prescription for dreamless sleep, a scrunched booklet, and another, slightly embarrassing appointment, then stood and looked at
the park,
the harbour,
the small shops,
saw how everything was made of waves that might at any moment
shift,
ripple
like stage curtains in a magic show,
and re-form
into a scene entirely unknowable and unfamiliar.

Touring the Manor Houses CARMELITA MCGRATH

Excuse me, but I'd rather not see
another broad room
where stippled light
released through leaves reveals
the desk where he wrote that famous tract on natural history,
or that table where he pinned his creatures
and, watching the sky,
ordered the harvest begun.

Not again—please—
her garden room
where her hat hangs
in replica, where she sighed for the apple blossoms,
not her parlour
where her ghost still sits on the green divan,
warming its ankles by the fire.

Show me instead the kitchen,
the distance from the pump,
the slop buckets, the vessels of disposal,
the flatirons,
show me that low stone room where the laundry was done,
the sheets boiled, the pots where hares were simmered,
the small white attic rooms
where the women whose features I bear
unpinned their hair with reddened hands
and dreamt of lovers
coming to them over fields
of August hay.

Baked in Chocolate

CARMELITA MCGRATH

Knowing that the ground horns of dead things
and nettles gathered in wildernesses had no power,
she took the moon instead and baked it in chocolate.

Knowing that three ancient words chanted
while a herb lay tied in ribbon under a pillow
had no power, she took a saxophone solo,
baked it in chocolate.

Knowing that after Christmas, there is only winter
for too long without relief or light, she took a June night,
baked it in chocolate.

Her lover praised the cake, dreamt off after supper
to walk under a moon on a night too strangely warm
for a jacket, only thought of returning home
when the saddest notes broke out of a third-floor window.

Summer Night Heat
CARMELITA MCGRATH

too bad you're not here.

Out in the garden, night-scented stock
breathes next to the deck
and the moon
is a suggestion three-quarters full
like me; the night is redolent
with scent . . . ideas . . . provocations:
too bad you're not here.

The air flexes masseur's fingers,
awakens tired skin; slit hem
of a sundress funnels the breeze
under;
I read poems with the tips of my fingers,
would massage you with their words,
make you feel their rhythms along your spine:

too bad you're out of town.

Here, for you, is a letter about the night,
composed on air and unsent:
The moon is three-quarters full,
and breezes run. I have Chardonnay and your absence
and other women's words
in the book you gave me.

too bad you're out of town

but no night's a waste;
I will write you the night, save it
for winter, the heat
of one
of our arguments.

Peirsifine

NUALA NÍ DHOMHNAILL

Ná bí buartha fúm, a mháthair,
is ná bí mallaithe,
cé go n'admhaím go rabhas dána
is nár dheineas rud ort,
gur thógas marcaíocht ón bhfear caol dorcha
ina Bh*MW*,
bhí sé chomh dathúil sin, is chomh mánla
ná féadfainn diúltú dhó.

Thug sé leis ar thuras thar sáile mé
thar raon m'aithne.
Bhí an gluaisteán chomh mear chomh síodúil sin
gur dhóigh leat go raibh sciatháin faoi.
Gheall sé sról is veilbhit dom
is thug sé dom iad leis.
Tá sé go maith dhom—ach aon rud amháin,
tá an tigh seo ana-dhorcha.

Deir sé go mbead i mo bhanríon
ar chríocha a chineáil,
go ndéanfaidh sé réalt dom chomh cáiliúil
le haon cheann acu i Hollywood.
Tugann sé diamaintí dom is seoda chun mo thola
ach tá an bia gann. Anois díreach
thugadar chugham úll gráinneach. Tá sé craorag
is lán de shíolta ar nós na mílte is na mílte

braonta fola.

Persephone Suffering from SAD
NUALA NÍ DHOMHNAILL

Now don't go ringing the cops,
Mum, and don't be losing the bap:
I admit I was out of line
and over the top
when I hitched a ride
with that sexy guy
in his wow of a BMW.
But he was such a super chat-up
I couldn't give him the push.

He booked us a foreign holiday
no travel agent runs—
his car so jet-propelled with revs
the engine soared on wings.
He said he would buy me velvet gowns
and satin underthings,
and his credit's fine. He leaves
me space, though I'd have to say
there's not much light in the place.

He's signing me the title deeds
to all his stately homes.
He's for putting my name in lights
as a star on the silver screen.
He has me flooded with rings
and pearls, but the menu's pretty thin—
I've just been served a pomegranate:
it's crimson, dripping with seeds—

a veritable *Céad Míle Fáilte* of drops of blood.

translated by Medbh McGuckian

An Snag Breac NUALA NÍ DHOMHNAILL

A mheaig, a shnaig bhric
is mór é do chreach
ar na héanlaithe beaga.

Chonac tú sa sceach
i mbun na gcaislín cloch
ag cur scaipeadh na mionéan orthu.

Chuais tríothu is tharstu
is fúthu is sa deireadh
níor fhág tú oiread is gearrcach acu.

I gclaí an mhóinéir
bhí nead ag an gcoinnleoir óir
is do chuiris an ruaig air,

mar a chuiris an teitheadh
ar an dá lasair choille
a neadaigh sa bhfiúise,

is níl an Diairmín Dreoilín
ina chodladh sa chlaí
soar ód' bhradaíocht bhorb

ná an Siobháinín Bhuí
ar a saoire i gCiarraí,
ar a n-imríonn tú cos ar bolg.

Ach rud is measa liom ná san
an chéirseach is an lon
curtha ó mhaith im' ghairdín cúil.

Is sé do ghágarlach fiain
ag bodhradh mo chinn
buile mhaise do mhasla,

a bhullaí mór éin;
báiléaraí, fear tréan,
an mheaig, an snag breac.

Ten Ways of Looking at a Magpie NUALA NÍ DHOMHNAILL

Magpie, your black and white
has put to flight
every bird smaller than yourself.

The hawthorn has caught you at
your work among the stonechats,
breaking up their meeting.

Beneath them you flew,
over and under and through,
till you left them not even a nestling.

In the meadow's edge
the linnet kept its eggs,
but you drove her from the bushes

as you have driven since
the pair of goldfinch
that had settled in the fuchsias.

Nor is the tiny goldcrest
safe in its nest
from you rudely pilfering the hedge;

and you come the heavy
with the yellowhammer
on its day out in Kerry.

But worse than all of them
the blackbird and his hen
you put out of action in my back garden.

And it's your infernal din
that really does my head in,
you bullyboy without pardon,

your crowning glory of abuse,
whether bailiff or terrorist,
foulmouthed, two-faced magpie.

translated by Medbh McGuckian

River of January   MEDBH MCGUCKIAN

I do not sing of arms and the man,
I have nothing to say which I can say.
People walk about as if they own
where they are, and they do.

But those separated by a forest
of error from the separated
call the deadly loneliness
by many other names.

How and why do we dream
of living in unity
with the island that has become
as the forest was, warming our hands

in her warm breast? Creating
a flower-rich shelter, or the heart
of a nest, in a wood left untouched
by the prospering suggestion of orchards?

It is just a promise and strong
but beautiful like every promise
in its pure mountain form
whose shadow was the forest cleared.

The old meanings of the forest
read the seasons in the seasonless,
treeless, herbless, overfished
sea bespread with eye-driven ships

and the fixed salts of plants
in the sand which paves the sea.
They fall into a light-bringing
language, till all the light

within the light, deceptive
as the leaf fall of the day
from a tree that has died in sleep,
satisfies, by its quality of chaliceness.

Slieve Gallion
MEDBH MCGUCKIAN
for Emily

That great central bone of mountain
belittling the apple-shaped earth,
or the unhandled marble of its head-bone,
warmed me to the very eyelids.

Find-spots of Judas-coloured blossom
wove bird-lure and man-burning furnaces
on its high quarried joy—
in a place not to be trodden

the neck-fetters of an asphalt smooth,
regrettably modern road paved the thread
of its voice—its breath-poem
into battle letters, its mouth music

into a pocketful of women-nation-
voters. I looked fifteen times
for that monosexual, banished river
smell, for its unnailing.

Hearing the Weather Fall

MEDBH MCGUCKIAN

The shutters folded back in their frames
with a pale movement,
a pacific repetition,
and only mirrors followed
to pierce where the day was stored,

each so enisled
and smiled at
by the sympathy of the tides,
looking less arrived
in a waveless bay,
and over, a bay of fields . . .

Now crowningly,
the droop of the sky
into my morning—
somebody would pay
for the night, a very soon
weekend—for the braking,
for the slowing-up,

for the uncharted pain
as then still forgiven.
A never-fighter,
running out a hand
to ask as from a death-bed
why this loves to happen,

I'd rather this fishing village
at the end of the world,
lying down and down a dull sea,
than the bound slope
of a suburban hill,
or everywhere that one visits
acquisitively,

than library voices
in the changed room.
The country's essence,
moored at the north
but with an air of being
washed out west,

could not forgo that kindling,
the arm which tightened
like a steady look from his
long eyes, knowing
the wrong wings are crossed up there.

Gábhar Thobac SEÁN Ó DUINNLÉ

Tráthnóna an tSathairn sea chonacsa an strapaire
A dhúid ar lasadh aige agus é 'na shuí,
Dhruideas in aice leis d'fhonn is go dtabharfadh sé
Blúire ar malairt dom nó gal den bpíp—

Siúd níor ceapadh dó ach gob amhail a chreachfainn é
Is nár dhóigh go mairfinn chun na fiacha a dhíol,
Is ní har mhaithe leis ná go dtabharfainn bearradh dhó,
Ach gur bhain fir mhaithe leis a chuaidh 'on chill!

Tobacco Shortage SEÁN Ó DUINNLÉ

Saturday of an evening I beheld my strapping fellow,
Sitting at his ease with his dooden nicely lit,
I ventured to approach him, hoping maybe for a mellow
Drag or, on account like, he might offer me a twist—

Such was far from his intention though, for fear I might
    denude him,
As it was not very likely I would live to see him paid;
And it is not from affection that I do not shave him shrewdly,
But respect for generations gone before him into clay!

translated by Máire Mhac an tSaoi

Bean an Fhir Rua   FILE GAN AINM

Tá siad á rá gur tú sáilín socair i mbróig,
Tá siad á rá gur tú béilín tana na bpóg,
Tá siad á rá, a mhíle grá, go dtug tú dom cúl—
Cé go bhfuil fear le fáil, gur leis an dtáilliúir Bean an Fhir Rua.

Do thugas naoi mí i bpríosún ceangailte cruaidh,
Boltaí ar mo chaolaibh agus míle glas as súd suas;
Thabharfainnse síog mar a thabharfadh an eala cois cuain
Le fonn a bheith sínte síos le Bean an Fhir Rua.

Shaoileas-sa, a chéadsearc, go mbeadh aointíos idir mé agus tú,
Agus shaoileas 'na dhéidh sin go mbréagfá mo leanbh ar do ghlúin;
Mallacht Rí Néimhe ar an té sin a bhain díom mo chlú,
Sin, agus uile go léir, lucht bréige idir mé agus tú.

Tá crann insa ghairdín ar a bhfásann duilliúr is bláth buí,
Is an uair a leagaim mo lámh air ritheann an fhuil óm' chroí;
Mo shólás go bás, is é 'fháil ó na flaithis anuas,
Aon phóigín amháin is é 'fháil ó bhean an Fhir Rua.

Ach go dtig lá an tsaoil 'na réabfar cnoic agus cuain,
Tiocfaidh smúit ar an ngréin 's beidh na néalta chomh dubh leis an ngual,
Beidh an fhairrge tirim is tiocfaidh na brónta 's an trua,
'S beidh an táilliúir ag scréachaigh i ngeall ar Bhean an Fhir Rua.

The Red-Haired Man Reproaches His Wife Who Has Left Him
POET UNKNOWN

They are saying your little heel fits snugly in the shoe,
They are saying your lips are thin, and saying they kiss well too;
You might have had many's the man, if what they are saying is true,
When you turned your back on your own, but only the tailor would do!

I'd have you know, nine months I was tethered in gaol,
Bolts on my ankles and wrists and a thousand locks on the chain,
And yet, my flight would be swift as the homeward flight of the swan
To spend but a single night with the Wife of the Red-Haired Man!

And I thought, 'One home we will share, Beloved, for you and for me',
And I thought, 'Tis you will sit there and coax my babe on your knee'.
Heaven's King's curse be on him who has taken away my good name!
So that lies, in the end of it all, separate us in shame.

A green tree grows in the garden, I lay my hand on the bark,
The flowers that it bears are yellow and the life-blood drains from my heart;
It would console me till death, like His grace from above that can,
If one small kiss I could get from the Wife of the Red-Haired Man!

There's a day in store for the world when harbour and hill will be riven,
When dust will smother the sun and coal-black clouds cover Heaven,
And pity and grief there will be in that day when the sea will run dry,
And remorse for the Wife of the Red-Haired Man will be loud in the tailor's cry!

translated by Máire Mhac an tSaoi

Taisigh Agad Féin Do Phóg

FILE GAN AINM

Taisigh agad féin do phóg,
  A inghean óg is geal déad;
Ar do phóig ní bhfaghaim blas,
  Congaibh uaim amach do bhéal!

Póg is romhillse ná mil
  Fuaras ó mhnaoi fhir tré ghrádh;
Blas ar phóig eile dá héis
  Ní bhfagha mé go dtí an brách.

Go bhfaicear an bhean-soin féin
  Do thoil éin Mhic Dé na ngrás,
Ní charabh bean tsean ná óg,
  Ós i a póg atá mar tá.

Keep To Yourself
Your Kisses

POET UNKNOWN

Keep to yourself your kisses,
   Bright teeth and parted lip,
Keep your mouth away from me,
   I have no mind for your kiss.

A kiss more sweet than honey
   From the wife of another man
Has left without taste all kisses
   That were since the world began.

Till, and please God I may—
   I see that woman again—
Her kiss being as it was—
   I ask no other till then.

translated by Máire Mhac an tSaoi

The Second Voyage

EILÉAN NÍ CHUILLEANÁIN

Odysseus rested on his oar, and saw
The ruffled foreheads of the waves
Crocodiling and mincing past; he rammed
The oar between their jaws, and looked down
In the simmering sea, where scribbles of weed defined
Uncertain depth, and the slim fishes progressed
In fatal formation, and thought

                    If there was a single
Streak of decency in those waves now, they'd be ridged,
Pocked and dented with the battering they've had
And we could name them as Adam named the beasts
Saluting a fresh one with dismay, or a notorious one
With admiration; they'd notice us passing
And rejoice at our destruction, but these
Have less character than sheep and need more patience.

I know what I'll do he said,
I'll park my ship in the crook of a long pier
(And I'll take you with me, he said to the oar)
I'll face the rising ground, and climb away
From tidal waters, up river-beds
Where herons parcel out the miles of stream,
Over the gaps in the hills, through warm
Silent valleys, and when I meet a farmer
Bold enough to look me in the eye
With 'where are you off to with that long
Winnowing fan over your shoulder?'
There I will stand still,
And I'll plant you as a gatepost or a hitching-post
And leave you for a tidemark. I can go back
And organise my house then.

                        But the profound
Unfenced valleys of the ocean still held him;
He had only the oar to make them keep their distance;
The sea was still frying under the ship's side.
He considered the water-lilies, and thought about fountains
Spraying as wide as willows in empty squares;
The sugarstick of water clattering into the kettle;
The flat lakes bisecting the rushes. He remembered spiders and
    frogs
Housekeeping at the wayside in brown trickles floored with
    mud,
Horsetroughs, the black canal with pale swans at dark;
His face grew damp with tears that tasted
Like his own sweat or the insults of the sea.

14

The Cost of a Good Canoe

The Cost of a Good Canoe

AL PITTMAN

Mike and I used to talk a lot
one time about flying
in to Red Indian Lake
and canoeing all the way out.

We'd live off the land
and shoot rapids no one
has ever seen and sleep
on the river banks and fry
rainbow trout at sun-up.

We figured it'd take two weeks
to come all the way out like that
and we'd spend whole afternoons
sitting in the Port Tavern
making plans for when we'd really do it.

This summer when I went home
Mike and I talked about it all again
and went over our plans again
sitting in the same old tavern
figuring on the cost of a good canoe
and what sort of supplies to take
and what would be the best time
of the year to go.

In the meantime fifteen years had gone by
but not once while we sat there
drinking beer and making plans
was there any mention of that sad fact.

Next summer when I go home
we'll talk about that trip again
and make more plans for when
we'll really do it
and someday if we are lucky enough
we'll be old men together—
two old men who've been friends
for more than a lifetime
sitting in a tavern agreeing perhaps
how nowadays they don't make canoes
the way they used to.

Gram Glover's Dream   AL PITTMAN
(from a picture of the same name by David Blackwood)

A long thin line
thinner and thinner as it goes
becomes a dot
disappears out where there is nothing

These are the islanders
leaving their island

huddled into the wind
they are going away

out where there is nothing
they have gone away to nothing

the long thin line winds away
in an endless swirl of snow

at the end of the line
turned to the wind
she stands looking back

if she had been farther up the line
she could have been spared this instant

but where she is
at the end of it
she is forced to confront
face to face
the final moment of their going

in a second
when this scene unfreezes
she will turn
become again the last of the line

will turn and walk away
will become nothing in the windy distance

in this instant however
she is frozen where she is

solidified against the wind
she faces the familiar house

on the window a flower pot
and in it a flower bloomed open
to the day's bright light

outside everything is frozen still
everything except the wind

and the wind's white howling

Shanadithit

AL PITTMAN

What I know of you is only
what my grade seven history book
told me.
That you were young when they caught you.
That your people lived in deerhide houses.
That they changed your name to Nancy.
That you died soon after.
That you were the last of the Beothuks.

You probably didn't know that
did you?
That you were the last of your people.
That when you went there was no one
to take your place.
I suppose you died thinking
there were uncles and cousins
with toothaches and babies
that there were hunters,
young men you'd like to be with,
coming home game-laden to campfires
on the shore of the lake
your executioners call Red Indian.

You didn't know
you'd end up in my grade seven history book
did you?

And when you died your lonely death,
when the white disease put an end to you,
you didn't know that all these years
beyond your decay I would long
to be with you, to tell you
I wouldn't forget. You didn't know
that I would have kissed you
and cried when you went.

Of course that has all to do
with my own images of you and they are
much too mixed up with technicolor movies
and my own boyish musings.

I see you as beautiful as Debra Paget
who played the role of an Indian girl
in a movie I barely remember.
I can't see you, no matter how hard
I try, mud-caked and offensive smelling.
I can't see you groaning and twisting
on the floor of your smokey mamateek
locked in any embrace with your rough
raw-boned cousins.

I see you
(and I know this is all wrong)
leaning over a blue pool. The sun
filters through the alders
and sends little shivers of light
bouncing off your golden thigh
where your beautifully embroidered dress
(like the one marked yours in the St. John's museum)
parts to let you bend.
Your reflection looks up to me
from the still water and your eyes
are two hollows deeper than any this brook
could fill. The eyes of a martyr,
of one who waits patiently for death
knowing that beyond all kindred deaths
yours will matter most.

Yet in all this there is a sadness
about you for you had not always
consented to your martyrdom. Before this,
before it had all been revealed to you
through witchcraft and religion,
you had wished rather that I would walk
buckskinned into your forest and take you
upstream to a place the shaman
and the gods had ordained for us.
And there, in an eternity of summers,
we would have loved each other gently
in the brook-cooled summer sun.

That dream, of course,
(though it pleases me that you had it)
was entirely impossible. For you had
to die as you did, you had to be the last
of your people before I could love you
at all.

I admit now
(putting this poem aside)
that my love for you has nothing
to do with you. Not as you were
or might have been in those few
of your own dead-end days.
For in those days surely my affection
would have been given over to some
Newfoundland lass with fair hair
and delicate English-pink skin.
There might have been times then when I
would have impressed her with stories
of how I raided your village, killed
your cousin, and laughed heartily
all the way home.

The workman who destroyed your grave
to build his portion of road
did not know what he was doing, did
not know that I would have knelt
in awe at that spot loving you
and condemning your death all in one prayer.
He did not know he ruined forever
my one chance to come close to you.
And therefore what is he guilty of
but depriving me of one singular
and pitiful indulgence? One moment
in my history when I could have knelt
over your fleshless remains and said
'Shanadithit, I love you'. What did he
do but save you the agony of one more lie?
Lie easy in your uneasy peace girl
and do not, do not, forgive those
who trespass against you.

Kelly At Graveside   AL PITTMAN
(for Rufus Guinchard)

In this wind-blown, wild-flowered
fenced-in meadow by the sea, this
bleak September day, we are the silent,
sombre witnesses to your burial
in the black earth.

The wind off the water is blowing the grass
as flat as a blanket, a green-grown shroud.
We lean into it, knowing this is as close
as we will ever get to you again.

A few feet (immeasurable miles)
north-north-east of your grave
(the hole in the ground you are
being put to bed in), your friend
and fellow fiddler, Kelly Russell,
stands upright in the wind, in stoic reverence.

I don't know what he's feeling.
I know only that he knows
you are going down, forever.

Later in the lounge down the road,
I think of the awful, wonderful burden
of his dual legacy.

His father was to this island with his words
what you have been to us with your music.
A glad burden, no doubt, to carry
beyond the grave. This, and that grave.

His father's words and your music, the language
that defines us, informs this silence, this rush
of wind, all our reasons for being here.
It all thrives alive in Kelly, standing there
at your graveside suffering his own grief,
commemorating his own infant history, as quiet
as a blank page, as silent as a stringless fiddle.

You are going down into the ground.
Close by, north-north-east of your grave, you are
alive and well. You are upright in the wind,
standing still in the gulf-battered grass
with all your music tingling in someone's
heart, his pocketful of fingers.
If there's anything at all to eternity, this is it.

This is how your life goes on.

This is how you live now as we turn away
from this raw wound in the earth, turn to go
down the road with our heart's consignment
of words, music, and everlasting silence.

The Pigeon on the Gate

AL PITTMAN

for Rufus Guinchard

Well hell!
Old friend.
Old fiddler.

Hawkes Bay was never like this
was it?

What with the lost women,
the porno shops,
the blue movies,
the concert violinist practising
down the hall.

Not much like the old logging camps
is it my friend?

Not much like your trapline country?

Not much like anything is it?

You and me
(you the 77 year old fiddler
come to sudden fame
me the 37 year old poet
come to nothing much)
here on the edge of a bed
in the Chelsea Inn wondering
how we might get the violinist
to join us.

Wondering if we can do
what we'd do at home. Go down
the hall, knock on the door and say
'Come on b'y, come on down for a drink'.

Wondering if that would be rude.
Wondering if he'd be rude in reply.

Just like home
isn't it old fiddler?

Sitting here twenty stories high
in the middle of the sin capital
of Canada afraid if we do the wrong thing
we will be accused of bad manners.

What odds about it sir.
You play your tunes for me
and I'll read my poems to you.

That way we'll do alright.

And not have to put our upbringing
on the line.

Living Alone

AL PITTMAN

Living alone becomes some people.
It is almost as though it were
normal, the way they come and go
into and out of their empty houses.
Their lawns are well kept, the hedges trimmed.
Or in winter the walkways and driveways
are level spaces enclosed within clean
snow-white walls. They don't live
among refuse, dirty dishes, unlaundered
linen, unread newspapers. Advertising flyers
don't grow mouldy in their mailboxes.
They don't forget to get margarine
or put out the garbage. They have salad
with their meals and set the table
before they eat. They have plants and/or cats
and nothing dies of neglect. There is
always toilet paper and dish detergent
and unstale bread. They answer their mail
and pay their bills. They sleep alone
and well at night. They are a strange breed
and much more numerous than you'd expect.
If you live alone you notice them
the way you'd notice all the cars similar
to the one you drive. I haven't learned yet
how to be similar. But then again, I've always
been a slow learner. I've never been
the recipient of sudden revelations.

As on the road to Damascus—Wham! Slam!
Saul is knocked to the ground
by a bolt of lightning fired by God.
He is momentarily stunned. He wakes up, shakes
his head, and mumbles 'Where am I?'
Then it hits him. The enlightenment.
He's a brand new man with a brand new name
and a brand new life; guaranteed for eternity.

I have no desire to be St. Paul
or any sort of saint. And I don't expect
any miraculous intervention to simplify
things. And though I intend to live
forever, I have no use whatsoever
for eternity or eternal bliss.

I want only to learn, however slowly, how
to live alone. How to get a good night's sleep
in an empty bed and know, without knowing
any more nightmares, that tomorrow
is garbage day and all my garbage
is ready to go.

The Dandelion Killers   AL PITTMAN
(for John Steffler)

They hate yellow blossoms
and stems whose winged seeds
can clock a lover's fate.

They prefer one shade
and shape of green, grave high,
as level as death.

They crouch in their houses
like soldiers at siege.
Stockpiled in the basement,
a lethal array of weapons.
All their purpose to kill
the colour yellow.

They dwell in panic
and must ever be alert.
The yellow enemy might return,
invade the lawn, thrive again,
spread into the kitchen,
the living room, the bedroom.
The bed.

Imagine having to make love
in a bed full of dandelions.
One hand on your lover's breast,
the other around the throat
of a flower. And not knowing,
night after night, which of you
will be first to touch the agony
of the other's golden death.

The Pink, White and Green

AL PITTMAN

(for Des Walsh)

The flag flat out.
The grass bent south-south-east.
The man mowing the meadow
is no gardener of gardens.
It just happens to be a good day
to take care of the country.

The waist-high hay falls away
in sea-green sheets with every swipe
of the stone-honed blade he swings
at the leaning field while cursing
this year's crop of resurrected rocks.

Without a wrinkle in the wind
the flag flies high overhead.

The man mowing the meadow
knows exactly who he used to be
when he took care of his land
without a care for anything
in the world outside those
four fortress fences, fading away now
to the colours of corruption and decay.

He knows the fence needs fixing and
the house uphill, a new coat of paint.
The latch on the garden gate ought to be
replaced, the clothesline pole secured.
But for now, today, there's the land
to be looked after, and the wind
is just right to slice the grass down hill
to the end of the overgrown slope
he's cared for always and only because
it was his and his alone. And theirs.

Back on to the house he's well aware
of his widow up there in the window
watching him sweep the summer's growth of grass
down to the ground, low below
the Pink, White and Green flag
flying high above the only nation
he and she have ever known.

St. Leonard's Revisited

AL PITTMAN

We came ashore
where wildflower hills
tilted to the tide
and walked
sad and gay
among the turnip cellars
tripping over the cremated
foundations
of long-ago homes
half buried
in the long years' grass

Almost reverently
we walked among the rocks
of the holy church
and worshipped roses
in the dead yard
and came again to the cove
as they did after rosary
in the green and salty days

And men offshore
hauling traps
wondered what ghosts
we were
walking with the forgotten sheep
over the thigh-high grass paths
that led
like trap doors
to a past
they could hardly recall

The Fish

MICHEL SAVARD

To Jack

Will went first
overboard overnight
He was out there whittling
I saw a silver blade
gannet or sudden tern
slice his head off
He slid along the stern
silent in the wet gloom
The fish watched him
in nervous schools
as he sank toward them
to the ocean floor

★ ★ ★

Then Peter the skipper
went missing
After the fish failed to show
on the familiar charts
he tried to charm our bearings
between a barrel of rum
and the gray depths of silence
One evening after a fog
he failed to emerge from below
Alex the mechanic Ted and I
ventured past the door but
he had vanished and his dog
kept howling at a star
that wasn't there before

★ ★ ★

Alex was next to go
on a night like this one
The waves were lame
their fiddles lapsing in old waltzes
barely a fickle breeze to lean upon
The ocean looked old
exhausted from too much heat
Alex was down carving the machines
when a rumble shook the boat
There was smoke in the hold
We were numbed
He lay against the greasy planks
just where the blast shoved
his two-hundred pound frame
a cotton doll in a toy box
his eyes bulging they wouldn't close
Drop drop drop water drops
Stench of old oils overheated
The moon above the porthole hung
like a hoop he wouldn't pass

★ ★ ★

Then Ted's turn came
He choked on a ballad
he had almost finished
Radio Tokyo was sizzling
on the short wave
Moths by the hundreds
slipped out of his lips
I saw them fluttering
crazily in the glow
of the kerosene lamp
Soon his never-ending body
was entirely vacant
lead-heavy
a heap of meat
I covered with salt

★ ★ ★

I alone made it ashore
with a boatful of fish
Became the prime suspect
And though the room
where I am kept to moan
is white and deep and dark
I know
they have started to dig
a deeper hole for me

La pêche

MICHEL SAVARD

à Jack

Jean le premier partit
une nuit par-dessus le bordage
Il picossait tranquille sur le pont
quand la lame d'argent d'un fou
peut-être ou d'une sterne
lui a ouvert la gorge net
Dans l'eau glauque il a glissé
sans bruit contre la coque
Les poissons en bancs
l'ont regardé nerveux
lentement planer sur fond d'étoiles
jusqu'à eux

★ ★ ★

Puis vint le tour de Pierre
capitaine en allé de sa tête
qui ne faisait plus le point
qu'au clair de son whisky
et voulait charmer le sort
du plus gris des silences
Un soir après la brume
il ne remontait pas
Alex le mécano Fred et moi
avons passé la porte mais
il n'était plus là son chien seul
au hublot hurlait à une étoile
qu'on n'a pas reconnue

★ ★ ★

Alex fut le suivant
à l'aube mélancolique
La houle était sage
écoulant de vieux airs de valse
au souk des brises rares
L'océan paraissait usé jusqu'à la corde
épuisé par la canicule
Alex fricotait au pays des machines
quand le bateau fut secoué
Dans la cale enfumée
on est restés saisis
Sur les planches graisseuses
où l'explosion avait jeté ses cent kilos
il était écrasé comme poupée de son
Ses yeux saillaient
qu'on n'a pas pu fermer
Floc floc floc faisait la flaque
Miasmes de vieille huile chauffée
La lune accrochée au hubot
était ce cerceau de papier
qu'il ne crèverait pas

        ★ ★ ★

Et puis Fred a suivi
étranglé par la ballade
qu'il allait achever
Radio Tokyo grésillait
sur ondes courtes
J'ai vu des mites par milliers
s'envoler de sa bouche béante
pour aller tournoyer
dans l'orbe jaune du fanal
Son corps interminable s'est lentement vidé
n'est resté que le plomb d'un tas de viande
que j'ai couvert de sel

        ★ ★ ★

Je fus le seul à toucher terre
dans un bateau plein de poisson
seul témoin seul suspect
Et si la pièce où l'on me garde
est blanche et sombre et profonde
dans mon délire je sais bien
qu'ils me creusent quelque part
en ce moment même
un trou plus profond

The Second Coming

KYRAN PITTMAN

'Four Horsemen of the Apocolypse
Photographed in Arizona
Just Days Ago!'
—*World Weekly News*

Just days ago
we seen them riding
east of Hayden
twenty feet high
in snakeskin boots
and Levis.
Thought they was
a Marlboro billboard
come to life.

Reckon they rode north
from Nogales
same route el Chupacabras
the goatsucker
came up last year.
The Mexicans hereabouts
stringing garlic bulbs
like they was Christmas lights
ever since.

Folks say
it's a sign
that the end times are near.
It's a sign, I say
that nothing good ever
came out of Nogales
and you've got to wonder
just what the hell
is going to slouch
out of there next.

Snipers in
Derelict Houses
ALAN GARVEY

Now clouds creep away; hushed wind
warning footpath and kerb, the trampled
grass and busy doorway where winos camp

in ammoniac stink of vomit and urine
dirt-cheap drink. Newspapers barrack
themselves into blocks and damp black

slogans crawl along a crumbling hall
while I search for a knothole or two
in boarded windows too mean to

let in more than slivers of sunshine.
Still, work must be done. Long Kesh
has my brother, his grilled fingers, mesh,

barbed wire and pigeons' feet, hard rain he sees
but cannot see glistening his native streets.
A neighbouring bell-tower levies a toll, rings its

hymns for a *brick* framed by a tattooed wall.
It's heads or harps, the fairest of bets,
but the coin is mine and I haven't called yet.

His head and shoulders are caught in the nook
of a crosshairs' quadrant, a gallows tree crook.
Go ahead—rub your neck, maybe it's bruised?

Maybe some sweetheart took a chunk out of you.
My rifle's butt brushes my hip as I roll to get
a better view, a lover in discovery's delight

at something new, like a barrel smooth, snug
as a cigarette between lipstick teeth;
impatient for a spark, for the shark to rise

from beneath. This pleasure's momentary, pos-
ition absurd, a few column inches, an arch
of gunshots' pious words, the draped flag's

parsimony of tears wrung from stiff upper lips. O
sword which summons our blood and controls
the image onscreen, the printed word, little

things like when and where we walk, with whom
we speak; the meekest of cheeks will turn.
You know for what we yearn

for, ravenous graves, whose earth's heaped high
and your blood bleaching the rods in our eyes
as the rising sun reveals an open sky.

brick—slang for a British infantryman

15
That you Might Reach Out

Incantata
In memory of Mary Farl Powers

PAUL MULDOON

I thought of you tonight, *a leanbh*, lying there in your long
    barrow
colder and dumber than a fish by Francisco de Herrera,
as I X-Actoed from a spud the Inca
glyph for a mouth: thought of that first time I saw your pink
spotted torso, distant-near as a nautilus,
when you undid your portfolio, yes indeedy,
and held the print of what looked like a cankered potato
at arm's length—your arms being longer, it seemed, than Lugh's.

Even Lugh of the Long (sometimes the Silver) Arm
would have wanted some distance between himself and the
    army-worms
that so clouded the sky over St. Cloud you'd have to seal
the doors and windows and steel
yourself against their nightmarish *déjeuner sur l'herbe*:
try as you might to run a foil
across their tracks, it was to no avail;
the army-worms shinnied down the stove-pipe on an army-
    worm rope.

I can hardly believe that, when we met, my idea of 'R and R'
was to get smashed, almost every night, on sickly-sweet
　Demarara
rum and Coke: as well as leaving you a grass widow
(remember how Krapp looks up 'viduity'?),
after eight or ten or twelve of those dark rums
it might be eight or ten or twelve o'clock before I'd land
back home in Landseer Street, deaf and blind
to the fact that not only was I all at sea, but in the doldrums.

Again and again you'd hold forth on your own version of
　Thomism, your own *Summa*
Theologiae that in everything there is an order,
that the things of the world sing out in a great oratorio:
it was Thomism, though, tempered by *La Nausée*,
by His Nibs Sam Bethicket,
and by that Dublin thing, that an artist must walk down Baggott
Street wearing a hair-shirt under the shirt of Nessus.

'D'éirigh mé ar maidin', I sang, *'a tharraingt chun aoinigh mhóir'*:
our first night, you just had to let slip that your secret amour
for a friend of mine was such
that you'd ended up lying with him in a ditch
under a bit of whin, or gorse, or furze,
somewhere on the border of Leitrim, perhaps, or Roscommon:
'gamine', I wanted to say, 'kimono';
even then it was clear I'd never be at the centre of your universe.

Nor should I have been, since you were there already, your own
　Ding
an sich, no less likely to take wing
than the Christ you drew for a Christmas card as a pupa
in swaddling clothes: and how resolutely you would pooh pooh
the idea I shared with Vladimir and Estragon,
with whom I'd been having a couple of jars,
that this image of the Christ-child swaddled and laid in the
　manger
could be traced directly to those army-worm dragoons.

I thought of the night Vladimir was explaining to all and sundry
the difference between *geantrai* and *suantrai*
and you remarked on how you used to have a crush
on Burt Lancaster as Elmer Gantry, and Vladimir went to brush
the ash off his sleeve with a legerdemain
that meant only one thing—'Why does he put up with this crap?'—
and you weighed in with 'To live in a dustbin, eating scrap,
seemed to Nagg and Nell a most eminent domain'.

How little you were exercised by those tiresome literary intrigues,
how you urged me to have no more truck
than the Thane of Calder
with a fourth estate that professes itself to be *'égalitaire'*
but wants only blood on the sand: yet, irony of ironies,
you were the one who, in the end,
got yourself up as *a retiarius* and, armed with net and trident,
marched from Mount Street to the Merrion Square arena.

In the end, you were the one who went forth to beard the lion,
you who took the DART line
every day from Jane's flat in Dun Laoghaire, or Dalkey,
dreaming your dream that the subterranean Dodder and Tolka
might again be heard above the *hoi polloi*
for whom Irish 'art' means a High Cross at Carndonagh or Corofin
and *The Book of Kells*: not until the lion cried craven
would the poor Tolka and the poor Dodder again sing out for joy.

I saw you again tonight, in your jump-suit, thin as a rake,
your hand moving in such a deliberate arc
as you ground a lithographic stone
that your hand and the stone blurred to one
and your face blurred into the face of your mother, Betty Wahl,
who took your failing, ink-stained hand
in her failing, ink-stained hand
and together you ground down that stone by sheer force of will.

I remember your pooh poohing, as we sat there on the
   'Enterprise',
my theory that if your name is Powers
you grow into it or, at least,
are less inclined to tremble before the likes of this bomb-blast
further up the track: I myself was shaking like a leaf
as we wondered whether the IRA or the Red
Hand Commandos or even the Red
Brigades had brought us to a standstill worthy of Hamm and
   Clov.

Hamm and Clov; Nagg and Nell; Watt and Knott;
the fact is that we'd been at a standstill long before the night
things came to a head,
long before we'd sat for half the day in the sweltering heat
somewhere just south of Killnasaggart
and I let slip a name—her name—off my tongue
and you turned away (I see it now) the better to deliver the sting
in your own tail, to let slip your own little secret.

I thought of you again tonight, thin as a rake, as you bent
over the copper plate of 'Emblements',
its tidal wave of army-worms into which you all but disappeared:
I wanted to catch something of its spirit
and yours, to body out your disembodied *vox
clamantis in deserto*, to let this all-too-cumbersome device
of a potato-mouth in a potato-face
speak out, unencumbered, from its long, low, mould-filled box.

I wanted it to speak to what seems always true of the truly great,
that you had a winningly inaccurate
sense of your own worth, that you would second-guess
yourself too readily by far, that you would rally to any cause
before your own, mine even,
though you detected in me a tendency to put
on too much artificiality, both as man and poet,
which is why you called me 'Polyester' or 'Polyurethane'.

That last time in Dublin, I copied with a quill dipped in oak-gall
onto a sheet of vellum, or maybe a human caul,
a poem for *The Great Book of Ireland*: as I watched the low
swoop over the lawn today of a swallow
I thought of your animated talk of Camille Pissarro
and André Derain's *The Turning Road, L'Estaque*:
when I saw in that swallow's nest a face in a mud-pack
from that muddy road I was filled again with a profound sorrow.

You must have known already, as we moved from the 'Hurly
    Burly' to McDaid's or Riley's,
that something was amiss: I think you even mentioned a
    homeopath
as you showed off the great new acid-bath
in the Graphic Studio, and again undid your portfolio
to lay out your latest works; I try to imagine the strain
you must have been under, pretending to be as right as rain
while hearing the bells of a church from some long-flooded
    valley.

From the Quabbin reservoir, maybe, where the banks and
    bakeries
of a dozen little submerged Pompeii reliquaries
still do a roaring trade: as clearly as I saw your death-mask
in that swallow's nest, you must have heard the music
rise from the muddy ground between
your breasts as a nocturne, maybe, by John Field;
to think that you thought yourself so invulnerable, so inviolate,
that a little cancer could be beaten.

You must have known, as we walked through the ankle-deep
    clabber
with Katherine and Jean and the long-winded Quintus Calaber,
that cancer had already made such a breach
that you would almost surely perish:
you must have thought, as we walked through the woods
along the edge of the Quabbin,
that rather than let some doctor cut you open
you'd rely on infusions of hardock, hemlock, all the idle weeds.

I thought again of how art may be made, as it was by André
   Derain,
of nothing more than a turn
in the road where a swallow dips into the mire
or plucks a strand of bloody wool from a strand of barbed wire
in the aftermath of Chickamauga or Culloden
and builds from pain, from misery, from a deep-seated hurt,
a monument to the human heart
that shines like a golden dome among roofs rain-glazed and
   leaden.

I wanted the mouth in this potato-cut
to be heard far beyond the leaden, rain-glazed roofs of Quito,
to be heard all the way from the southern hemisphere
to Clontarf or Clondalkin, to wherever your sweet-severe
spirit might still find a toe-hold
in this world: it struck me then how you would be aghast
at the thought of my thinking you were some kind of ghost
who might still roam the earth in search of an earthly delight.

You'd be aghast at the idea of your spirit hanging over this vale
of tears like a jump-suited jump-jet whose vapour-trail
unravels a sky: for there's nothing, you'd say, nothing over
and above the sky itself, nothing but cloud-cover
reflected in a thousand lakes; it seems that Minne-
sota itself means 'sky-tinted water', that the sky is a great slab
of granite or iron ore that might at any moment slip
back into the worked-out sky-quarry, into the worked-out sky-
   mines.

To use the word 'might' is to betray you once too often, to betray
your notion that nothing's random, nothing arbitrary:
the gelignite weeps, the hands fly by on the alarm clock,
the 'Enterprise' goes clackety-clack
as they all must; even the car hijacked that morning in the Cross,
that was preordained, its owner spread on the bonnet
before being gagged and bound or bound
and gagged, that was fixed like the stars in the Southern Cross.

That fact that you were determined to cut yourself off in your
    prime
because it was *pre*-determined has my eyes abrim:
I crouch with Belacqua
and Lucky and Pozzo in the Acacacac-
ademy of Anthropopopometry, trying to make sense of the
    '*quaquaqua*'
of that potato-mouth; that mouth as prim
and proper as it's full or self-opprobrium,
with its '*quaquaqua*', with its 'Quoiquoiquoiquoiquoiquoiq'.

That's all that's left of the voice of Enrico Caruso
from all that's left of an opera-house somewhere in Matto
    Grosso,
all that's left of the hogweed and horehound and cuckoo-pint,
of the eighteen soldiers dead at Warrenpoint,
of the Black Church clique and the Graphic Studio claque,
of the many moons of glasses on a tray,
of the brewery-carts drawn by moon-booted drays,
of those jump-suits worn under your bottle-green worsted cloak.

Of the great big dishes of chicken lo mein and beef chow mein,
of what's mine is yours and what's yours mine,
of the oxlips and cowslips
on the banks of the Liffey at Leixlip
where the salmon breaks through the either/or neither/nor nether
reaches despite the temple-veil
of itself being rent and the penny left out overnight on the rail
is a sheet of copper when the mail-train has passed over.

Of the bride carried over the threshold, hey, only to alight
on the limestone slab of another threshold,
of the swarm, the cast,
the colt, the spew of bees hanging like a bottle of Lucozade
from a branch the groom must sever,
of Emily Post's ruling, in *Etiquette*,
on how best to deal with the butler being in cahoots
with the cook when they're both in cahoots with the chauffeur.

Of that poplar-flanked stretch of road between Leiden
and The Hague, of the road between Rathmullen and Ramelton,
where we looked so long and hard
for some trace of Spinoza or Amelia Earhart,
both of them going down with their engines on fire:
of the stretch of road somewhere near Urney
where Orpheus was again overwhelmed by that urge to turn
back and lost not only Eurydice but his steel-strung lyre.

Of the sparrows and finches in their bell of suet,
of the bitter-sweet
bottle of Calvados we felt obliged to open
somewhere near Falaise, so as to toast our new-found *copains*,
of the priest of the parish
who came enquiring about our 'status', of the hedge-clippers
I somehow had to hand, of him running like the clappers
up Landseer Street, of my subsequent self-reproach.

Of the remnants of Airey Neave, of the remnants of
    Mountbatten,
of the famous *andouilles*, of the famous *boudins
noirs et blancs*, of the barrel-vault
of the Cathedral at Rouen, of the flashlight, fat and roll of felt
on each of their sledges, of the music
of Joseph Beuys's pack of huskies, of that baldy little bugger
mushing them all the way from Berncastel through Bacarrat
to Belfast, his head stuck with honey and gold-leaf like a mosque.

Of Benjamin Britten's *Lachrymae*, with its gut-wrenching viola,
of Vivaldi's *Four Seasons*, of Frankie Valli's,
of Braque's great painting *The Shower of Rain*,
of the fizzy, lemon or sherbet-green *Ranus ranus*
plonked down in Trinity like a little Naugahyde pouffe,
of eighteen soldiers dead in Oriel,
of the weakness for a little fol-de-rol-de-rolly
suggested by the gap between the front teeth of the Wife of Bath.

Of *A Sunday Afternoon on the Island of La Grande Jatte*, of
    Seurat's
piling of tesserae upon tesserae
to give us a monkey arching its back
and the smoke arching out from a smoke-stack,
of Sunday afternoons in the Botanic Gardens, going with the
    flow
of the burghers of Sandy Row and Donegal
Pass and Andersonstown and Rathcoole,
of the army Landrover flaunt-flouncing by with its heavy
    furbelow.

Of Marlborough Park, of Notting Hill, of the Fitzroy Avenue
immortalized by Van 'His real name's Ivan'
Morrison, 'and him the dead spit
of Padraic Fiacc', of John Hewitt, the famous expat,
in whose memory they offer every year six of their best milch
    cows,
of the Bard of Ballymacarrett,
of every ungodly poet in his or her godly garret,
of Medhbh and Michael and Frank and Ciaran and 'wee' John
    Qughes.

Of the Belfast school, so called, of the school of hard knocks,
of your fervent eschewal of stockings and socks
as you set out to hunt down your foes
as implacably as the *tóraidheacht* through the Fews
of Redmond O'Hanlon, of how that 'd' and that 'c' aspirate
in *tóraidheacht* make it sound like a last gasp in an oxygen-tent,
of your refusal to open a vent
but to breathe in spirit of salt, the mordant salt-spirit.

Of how mordantly hydrochloric acid must have scored and
    scarred,
of the claim that boiled skirrets
can cure the spitting of blood, of that dank
flat somewhere off Morehampton Road, of the unbelievable
    stink

of valerian or feverfew simmering over a low heat,
of your sitting there, pale and gaunt,
with that great prescriber of boiled skirrets, Dr John Arbuthnot,
your face in a bowl of feverfew, a towel over your head.

Of the great roll of paper like a bolt of cloth
running out again and again like a road at the edge of a cliff,
of how you called a Red Admiral a Red
Admirable, of how you were never in the red
on either the first or the last
of the month, of your habit of loosing the drawstring of your purse
and finding one scrunched-up, obstreperous
note and smoothing it out and holding it up, pristine and pellucid.

Of how you spent your whole life with your back to the wall,
of your generosity when all the while
you yourself lived from hand
to mouth, of Joseph Beuys's pack of hounds
crying out from their felt and fat 'Atone, atone, atone',
of Watt remembering the *'Krak! Krek! Krik!'*
of those three frogs' karaoke
like the still, sad, *basso continuo* of the great quotidian.

Of a ground bass of sadness, yes, but also a sennet of hautboys
as the fat and felt hounds of Beuys O'Beuys
bayed at the moon over a caravan
in Dunmore East, I'm pretty sure it was, or Dungarvan:
of my guest appearance in your self-portrait not as a hidalgo
from a long line
of hidalgos but a hound-dog, a *leanbh*,
a dog that skulks in the background, a dog that skulks and stalks.

Of that self-portrait, of the self-portraits by Rembrandt van Rijn,
of all that's revelation, all that's rune,
of all that's composed, all composed of odds and ends,
of that daft urge to make amends
when it's far too late, too late even to make sense of the clutter
of false trails and reversed horseshoe tracks
and the aniseed we took it in turn to drag
across each other's scents, when only a fish is dumber and colder.

Of your avoidance of canned goods, in the main,
on account of the exceeeeeeeeeeeeeeeeedingly high risk of ptomaine,
of corned beef in particular being full of crap,
of your delight, so, in eating a banana as ceremoniously as Krapp
but flinging the skin over your shoulder like a thrush
flinging off a shell from which it's only just managed to disinter
a snail, like a stone-faced, twelfth-century
FitzKrapp eating his banana by the mellow, yellow light of a rush.

Of the 'Yes, let's go' spoken by Monsieur Tarragon,
of the early-ripening jardonelle, the tumorous jardon, the jargon
of jays, the jars
of tomato relish and the jars
of Victoria plums, absolutely *de rigueur* for a passable plum baba,
of the drawers full of balls of twine and butcher's string,
of Dire Straits playing 'The Sultans of Swing',
of the horse's hock suddenly erupting in those boils and buboes.

Of the Greek figurine of a pig, of the pig on a terracotta frieze,
of the sow dropping dead from some mysterious virus,
of your predilection for gammon
served with a sauce of coriander or cumin,
of the slippery elm, of the hornbeam or witch-, or even wych-,
hazel that's good for stopping a haemor-
rhage in mid-flow, of the merest of mere
hints of elderberry curing everything from sciatica to a stitch.

Of the decree *condemnator*, the decree *absolvitor*, the decree *nisi*,
of *Aosdána*, of *an chraobh cnuais*,
of the fields of buckwheat
taken over by garget, inkberry, scoke—all names for pokeweed—
of *Mother Courage*, of *Arturo Ui*,
of those Sunday mornings spent picking at sesame
noodles and all sorts and conditions of dim sum,
of tea and ham sandwiches in the Nesbitt Arms hotel in Ardara.

Of the day your father came to call, of your leaving your sick-
  room
in what can only have been a state of delirium,
of how you simply wouldn't relent
from your vision of a blind
watch-maker, of your fatal belief that fate
governs everything from the honey-rust of your father's terrier's
eyebrows to the horse that rusts and rears
in the furrow, of the furrows from which we can no more deviate

than they can from themselves, no more than the map of Europe
can be redrawn, than that Hermes might make a harp from his
  harpe,
than that we must live in a vale
of tears on the banks of the Lagan or the Foyle,
than that what we have is a done deal,
than that the Irish Hermes,
Lugh, might have leafed through his vast herbarium
for the leaf that had it within it, Mary, to anoint and anneal,

than that Lugh of the Long Arm might have found in the midst of
lus na leac or *lus na treatha* or *Frannc-lus*,
in the midst of eyebright, or speedwell, or tansy, an antidote,
than that this *Incantata*
might have you look up from your plate of copper or zinc
on which you've etched the row upon row
of army-worms, than that you might reach out, arrah,
and take in your ink-stained hands my own hands stained with ink.

Early Christian Ireland Wedding Cry   PAUL DURCAN

I

And now that these two earthlings have been by the poet-priest blessed
I will be able to telephone Sarah and burst out
'May I speak to your *husband?*'
Or to telephone Mark and burst out
'May I speak to your *wife?*'
How knees-on-the-full-moon I will feel to bawl
Such interstellar language: 'Husband', 'wife'—
Vocabulary as prehistoric as a tree.
Children—to see the world—climb the treetops of matrimony.
It was for matrimony that we earthlings espoused language;
'Husband', 'wife'. Eureka!
The waters of reality are spousal—Gerard Manley Archimedes.
Be it manmade canal or iceage mountain stream,
Water is hand-over-hand, pooled magnanimity.

II

Mark Joyce, Sarah Durcan, we thank you
For shepherding us all to this far, secret, idyllic niche;
Nephin, Lough Conn, Rake Street, Enniscoe.

By marrying each other, you are marrying us
To the marriage place—to the mountain
And to the lake; to the street and to the house.

Long after this afternoon is mustard ashes,
Our eyes will remain upon the mountain,
Sipping insights from our primary sources:

All our childhoods—all those eras:
All those epochs of contemplation when it was nothing
To spend all day on the lakeshore gazing upon the waters;

The unfathomable ticking of one's own heart;
The inscrutable parades of waves;
The unimaginable bottom of the lake.

All those rain curtains of Sunday afternoons
Driving up to Enniscoe House to see what it looked like
And to glean what could be gleaned from the prospect.

All those six-month summers gazing upon the mountain,
Robed in her grey blueness over Conn;
Taliswoman of our fortune and our fate;

Deferring to her for our stimulation and our aim.
Waiting for her to wash herself in a dawn sky
Her man assembles their abode of grass and rain.

III

Marriage is the sunrise of contemplation
In which two creatures compose themselves
Inside the catastrophe of war.
Each is the other's cloak and asylum.
In the last of the light they cleave to one another
On the barbed-wire shore.

Back to back in the weeping and warring night
One sleeps while the other tracks
The cracks upon the moon-stacked windowpane;
The other sleeps and the one awakes
To track a snail shadowing the moon
On that polar hike across the cracked glass.
You are the meaning of my life
And I of yours—the piscina in the niche.

IV

On Midsummer's Day when this chapel was being built,
A housepainter from Lahardaun cried from his ladder:
'Raise high the roofbeams, carpenter!
On Midsummer's Day a hundred years from now
A Durcan will step into this chapel to marry a Joyce!
The tabernacle will needs be inserted in the wall!
Needs be rakes of candlestick racks!
These Joyces and these Durcans—in their communions,
They are fierce people for the lighting of candles!
Needs be also the outside freshly whitewashed
For these two will also be painters!
Members of the craft as well as of the wedding!
We will need burial grounds around the chapel
Because these two will also be philosophers
Who ponder mortality—
How mortality is the mother of integrity'.

V

All things come in twos—which is why
Marriage is the paradigm of science.
The code of all physics and all chemistry is marriage;
The figure of all energy is two.
Caspar the Cat, I dive round the villages of Mayo—
Hollymount, Roundfort, Turlough, Straide—
Doff my Castlebar hat with its white cockade,
Lean upon my Westport stick with its brass ferrule,
And twinkling at the gate of the scythed hayfield
At the top of Rake Street
I wait for thee, my love, to take my arm
And be my spouse for now and evermore.
One by one we enter the aisle of Rake Street
In order to exit it as two.

VI

By the waters of Conn, under the eye of Nephin,
We sit down and kneel and laugh and pray.
Cloud systems that began their lives in Labrador
Empty their waters on Nephin's peaks;
Mountain streams charge down the mountainside
Past the two-light east window, the lake
Brims, turns over on its sleeping side,
Yawns, smiles, frowns, goes on
Dreaming its 600 million-year-old dream—
This is where the Durcans and the Joyces hail from:
Our dreamspace, the County of Mayo!
We—the wedding guests—die out of the frame
Leaving Mark and Sarah alone in the storm,
Secure in the fleece of the sheep of the yew tree,
Their foreheads thumbed by the asylum-seeker Christ
Who stowed away into earthlingland to secrete compassion;
Leaving them in peace – together, each to each—
Let us now praise these waters and the mountain:
The sleeping woman with her waking man.

21 June 2000

Apoqnmuinen (Thank you Great Spirit)

MORLEY LOON AND
DONNA AUGUSTINE
(THUNDERBIRD TURTLE WOMAN)

Apoqnmuinen ta'n teli l'nu-ktapekia'tiek
Apoqnmuinen ta'n teli l'nu-amalkaltultiek
Apoqnmuinenta'n tali l'nui-alasutma'tiek
Apoqnmuinen Niskaminu mut awan'ta'sualinen

Yo' ya' hi ei ya hio' ya hie
Yo' ya' hi ei ya hio' ya hie
Yo' ya' hi ei ya hio' ya hie
Yo' ya' hi ei ya hio'

Thank you Great Spirit for thunder in the sky
Thanks for the seasons that are a part of life
Thanks for the day time and for the night
Thanks for the ways of our lives

(Repeat Chant)

Apoqnmuinen ta'n teli l'nu-ktapekia'tiek
Apoqnmuinen ta'n teli l'nu-amalkaltultiek
Apoqnmuinenta'n tali l'nui-alasutma'tiek
Apoqnmuinen Niskaminu mut awan'ta'sualinen

(Repeat Chant)

Notes on Contributors
(Newfoundland & Labrador)

Augustine, Donna (Thunderbird Turtle Woman) (1952 -):
Donna Augustine / Thunderbird Turtle Woman is a traditionalist of the Mi'kmaq Nation. She conducts native ceremonies and is an educator of cultural and spiritual ways. She is a singer, songwriter, and storyteller and has travelled throughout North America and, recently, central South America and Europe sharing Native teachings and prophecies. Her main work involves the repatriation and guardianship of sacred ancestral remains of her people.

Avis, Nick (1957 -):
Nick Avis lives in St. John's, Newfoundland, where he practices law. His poetry, literary criticism and book reviews have been published nationally and internationally. He is currently President of Haiku Canada and poetry editor for a small press publication in Québec. His collection *footprints* won a Haiku Society of America Book Award in 1994. Avis is working on a new manuscript and will have works included this year in several international anthologies.

Babstock, Ken (1970 -):
Ken Babstock was born in Newfoundland and grew up in the Ottawa Valley. His work has won Gold in Canada's National Magazine Awards and earned him a visit to the International Poetry Festival in Rotterdam, Holland, in 2002. *Mean*, his first collection, won the Atlantic Poetry Prize and the Milton Acorn Award. *Days into Flatspin* won a K. M. Hunter Award and was shortlisted for the Winterset Award. He is currently serving as poetry editor for House of Anansi Press.

Burke, Johnny (1851 - 1930):
'The Bard of Prescott Street' is a colourful character in Newfoundland's history. Burke printed his ballads on his own press and sold them on the city streets for a few cents a copy. His experience as an auctioneer clerk and theatre manager, as well as the experience he gained from various other jobs which demanded the skills of a person comfortable with the public's attention, served him and his literature well. He bolstered the distribution of his own writing by using a gramophone to attract customers. He helped to produce variety shows, and he wrote musical comedies which were popular with the public. A true balladeer and people's poet, Johnny Burke wrote for the masses and immortalized in satire and humour those local details and people that surrounded him in St. John's, the city he was born in and died in.[1]

Butt, Len: Not much information exists about Mr. Butt. John Ashton, professor of folklore at Sir Wilfred Grenfell College in Corner Brook, explains that Len Butt worked at the lumber camp in Bishop's Falls in the 1940s where it is said he wrote the song 'Jerry Ryan'.

---

[1] 'Burke, John', *Dictionary of Newfoundland and Labrador Biography* (St. Johns: Harry Cuff, 1990) 38; 'Burke, Johnny', *Encyclopedia of Newfoundland and Labrador* vol. 1 (St. John's: Newfoundland Book Publishers, 1981) 295.

Byrne, Pat (1943 -):
Pat Byrne is a professor in the Department of English Language and Literature and the Department of Folklore at Memorial University of Newfoundland. His academic interests include short fiction, Newfoundland literature and folklore, Shakespeare, and modern American and Canadian fiction. He has published on the influence of the McNulty family on Newfoundland music, on the manifestations of the tall tale in Newfoundland literature, on invented traditions in Newfoundland popular culture, on the influence of folklore and literature on the image of Newfoundland within the Canadian context, and on the interrelationships between folklore and literature. He is also a published poet and songwriter and has performed at numerous folk festivals, as well as on radio and television. Active in amateur theatre, he had starring roles in the original productions of Al Pittman's *A Rope Against the Sun* and *West Moon*. He also collaborated with Pittman in the writing of several songs.

Crummey, Michael (1965 -):
Michael Crummey has published three books of poetry, most recently *Salvage* (McClelland and Stewart, 2002). He has also published a collection of short stories (*Flesh and Blood*, Beach Holme, 1998) and a novel (*River Thieves*, Doubleday 2001). *River Thieves* was nominated for the Giller Prize, the Commonwealth Writers' Prize and the Books in Canada First Novel Award. It was given the Atlantic Fiction Award and the Winterset Award. Michael was born and raised in Newfoundland and lives in St. John's where he is at work on a new novel.

Dalton, Mary (1950 -):
Mary Dalton lives in St. John's, where she teaches in the Department of English at Memorial University of Newfoundland. She is the author of *The Time of Icicles* and *Allowing the Light*, both published by Breakwater. Her latest collection of poems, *Merrybegot*, was published by Véhicule Press of Montreal in 2003.

Dawe, Tom (1940 -):
Born in Long Pond, Manuels, Conception Bay, Tom Dawe has been a professor of English at Memorial University, a visual artist, editor, folklorist and writer for both children and adults. His last book of poetry, *In Hardy Country*, was published by Breakwater Books, St. John's, in 1993. A book-length critical analysis of his work, *Rewriting Newfoundland Mythology*, by Martina Seifert, was published by Garda+Wilch Verlag, Berlin and Massachusetts, in 2002.

Devine, John Martin (1876 - 1959):
John Martin Devine was a businessman and poet. He was born in King's Cove on the east coast of Newfoundland. As a young boy, he mowed Pat Murphy's meadow, and, at the age of fourteen when his father died, he left school and took over his father's job of delivering His Majesty's mail. He thus became the sole support for his mother and three younger brothers. He married in 1902

and had nine children, five of whom survived. He became a businessman on Water Street, St. John's, working in wholesale dry goods. A supporter of confederation with Canada, he was good friends with Joey Smallwood, and they often walked together around Windsor Lake. In April 1921, under the government of Sir Richard Squires, J. M. was appointed Trade Commissioner to the United States and, with his family, settled in Ridgefield Park, New Jersey. It was his responsibility to promote the Newfoundland fish trade and other products in the import/export business. During his ten-year span in the New York area, J. M. penned several poems expressing his longing and fondness for Newfoundland. When that job was terminated due to political changes in Newfoundland, he formed the Anglo-American export company through which he continued to do business with various Newfoundland companies. He returned to Newfoundland in 1931 and started a family clothing store called The Big 6. A self-educated man, he enjoyed debating and writing poetry. He had a fondness for the Irish heritage of Newfoundland culture and promoted its music through The Big 6 radio program.

Dicker, Sid (1925 - 2000):
Sid was a long-time resident of Nain. He was a Kivgat (Church Elder) and a well-respected man in Nain, the most northerly community in Labrador. When Sid was a young man, Nain had no radio station and no access to radio except through two way radio or short wave. However, beginning in 1949 and up until the early 1950s, the Moravian Mission (under Reverend Peacock) in Nain had a radio station that broadcast church services. They also invited local people to sing, and one of these people was Sid Dicker. He and several of his friends, including Jerry Sillett (who later became chief elder), taught themselves to play guitar by following a book of chords. They also had access to a book of 'cowboy' songs, including Hank Snow and Doc Williams tunes—tunes they had never heard but which they learned to like because of the harmonies and lyrics. This Moravian broadcast, which was not officially a radio station, was heard as far south as Nova Scotia and as far east as Greenland. Sid started writing in the 1980s, and he wrote all of his songs in Inuktitut first except for his best-known song, which is often sung bilingually—*'Inniugiamik Labadurimi'* / 'Sons of Labrador'. This is the theme song for the Okalakatiget Society's Television programming which airs nationally once a week. (note by Tim Borlase)

Doyle, Gerald S. (1892 - 1956):
Gerald S. Doyle was a Bonavista Bay man who was born in King's Cove and whose early work experience with the Chase Medicine Company in St. John's inspired him to open his own business and distribute products, most notably patent medicines. Doyle had a keen interest in folklore, and he collected and published verse and songs in various editions of his *Old-Time Songs and Poetry of Newfoundland*. Doyle is also known for a radio news bulletin which bore his name and which, beginning in 1932, began to air local-interest stories across Newfoundland.[2]

[2] 'Doyle, Gerald S.', *Dictionary of Newfoundland and Labrador Biography* (St. John's: Harry Cuff, 1990) 87; 'Doyle, Gerald S.', *Encyclopedia of Newfoundland and Labrador* vol. 1 (St. John's: Newfoundland Book Publishers, 1981) 641.

Elliott, David (1923 - 1999):
Born in Garnish, on the Burin Peninsula, 'Smokey' spent his life in a series of Newfoundland outport communities. At fifteen, he left school to become a telegraph operator. At twenty-five, he entered Memorial University of Newfoundland where he became the first honours graduate in English. He was a civil servant, soldier, clinical psychologist, and he worked as an editor with the Queen's Printer in Ottawa. He lectured in the English Department at Sir Wilfred Grenfell College from 1975 to 1989.

Francis, Bernie (1948 -):
Bernie Francis grew up on the Membertou reserve in Sydney, Nova Scotia. From 1984 until April 2003, he was an Assistant Professor at the University College of Cape Breton in Sydney. At the moment, he is teaching a martial arts course in Halifax and is preparing to go to Hawaii for three months where he will take a look at South Pacific languages. The most exciting part of Bernie's life was to develop, with his working partner, Doug Smith, an orthography for the Mi'kmaw language to be used by schools and former students who, now teachers, will instruct their students in Mi'kmaw. When Bernie sees that his own people are beginning to read and write in their own language, it is the greatest satisfaction of all. Now, Bernie has embarked upon a study of Québecois French in Trois Rivières.

Grace, John:
The editors have been able to find only the following information about John Grace: '["The Petty Harbour Bait Skiff"] is attributed to the writing of John Grace, a St. John's sailor who later died in Brazil' (*Come and I Will Sing You*, 154).

Hutchings, Eugene (1932 -):
Eugene has been a carpenter for most of his life. He plays the violin, mandolin and guitar, and he has been writing songs for years.

Kelland, Otto (1904 -):
Otto Kelland was born on August 31, 1904 in Lamaline on the Burin Peninsula. He served in the public service for 52 years, first as a policeman, then as Superintendent of the Penitentiary and, later, as a model ship builder with the then Fisheries College. He has never really retired as he still builds model dories. 'Let Me Fish Off Cape St. Mary's' was written in 1945 and was based on a conversation he had with a young man he met on the waterfront. It is now known as the unofficial anthem of Newfoundland.

LeMessurier, H. W. (1848 - 1931):
A civil servant for most of his life, LeMessurier attempted several times to work his way into the arena of professional governmental politics. He was an avid curler and is best known for his song 'The Ryans and the Pittmans'.[3]

---

[3] 'LeMessurier, Henry W.', *Dictionary of Newfoundland and Labrador Biography* (St. John's: Harry Cuff, 1990) 197.

MacKenzie, Marguerite (1946 -):
Marguerite MacKenzie teaches Linguistics at Memorial University, Newfoundland and works with speakers of Cree, Innu (Montagnais) and Naskapi on dictionaries, grammars and language training materials. She is co-editor of the *East Cree Lexicon: Eastern James Bay Dialects* (1987) and the *Naskapi Lexicon* (1994). She works with the Innu of Labrador to produce language reference materials to be used in the schools, with the aim of teaching the primary grades only in Innu-aimun.

McGrath, Carmelita (1960 -):
Poet and fiction writer Carmelita McGrath is the author of seven books. Her poetry collections are *Poems on Land and on Water* (Killick Press, 1992), *To the New World* (Killick, 1997, winner of the Atlantic Poetry Prize) and *Ghost Poems* (Running the Goat Books & Broadsides, 2001).

Payne, Daniel (1977 -):
Daniel grew up in Cow Head and still spends most of his summers there. His work as an actor and musician has taken him from Newfoundland to Ireland several times. In both places he has made a point of recording and learning the traditional music he finds. 'The Wave that Hit St. Brides' was written for Rising Tide Theatre's Revue '98.

Payne, Stephanie (1979 -):
Stephanie Payne grew up in the town of Cow Head on the Great Northern Peninsula. She wrote the song 'Home Free' in 1995 for the fishermen (and women) of Newfoundland and Labrador. During his visit to Corner Brook in 2003, Paul Durcan heard Stephanie Payne sing, and he said she was 'as mesmerizing a young singer as a young Joan Baez' *(Paul Durcan's diary)*.

Pittman, Al (1940 - 2001):
Born in St. Leonard's, Placentia Bay, Al Pittman, 'the Patrick Kavanagh of modern Newfoundland', as Paul Durcan puts it *(Paul Durcan's diary)*, was also a dramatist, short-story writer and author of children's stories. In August 2001, his acclaimed play, *West Moon*, and a Newfoundland cast toured Dublin, Listowel, Inishbofin, Kilmallock and Waterford. In 2003, Breakwater published a major selection of his poems, *An Island in the Sky*. This work was well under way before his death and is edited by Martin Ware, who provides an important introduction to and critical examination of Al's poetry, and Stephanie McKenzie. Al met Paul Durcan, his favourite contemporary Irish poet, in November 2000 in Jury's Hotel in Ballsbridge.

Pittman, Kyran (1969 -):
Kyran Pittman has lived in Little Rock since emigrating from Newfoundland in 1996. She has published poems internationally in a number of anthologies, as well as in a limited edition chapbook. In 2003, she participated in the Irish launch of *The Backyards of Heaven*, with readings in Waterford, Cork, Galway and Dublin.

Power, Gregory (1909 - 1997):
A remarkable man, Gregory Power was an athlete, farmer, poet, union activist and politician. A hurdler and member of the Newfoundland team that competed in the 1930 British Empire Games, he was elected to the Newfoundland Sports Hall of Fame in 1983. In his political career, he was elected to government in 1951 and became Finance Minister under Joe Smallwood until he fell out with the Premier over his economic policies. He was a brilliant political satirist, as well as a poet, and he published two books, *Gems of Newfoundland Poetry*, in 1967, and *The Power of the Pen* (edited by Harold Horwood and published by Harry Cuff) in 1989.

Pratt, E. J. (1882 - 1964):
Edwin John Pratt is one of Newfoundland's and Canada's foremost poets. Born in Western Bay, he spent the first twenty years of his life mainly in the outports of Newfoundland. The grandson of a sea captain and son of a Methodist minister who was often called upon to help deal with the many tragedies of his parishioners, Pratt saw too clearly the hard and dangerous lives of those who made their living on the sea. Following his father into the ministry at first, he preached and taught in Moreton's Harbour, Clarke's Beach, Bell Island, and Portugal Cove. At the University of Toronto's Victoria College, Pratt began his studies in theology, psychology and literature in 1907, eventually taking a position at the College teaching literature, a position that he held from 1919 until 1953. Although he lived most of his life in Toronto, the memorable experiences of his early years mark his work from beginning to end. His first book of poetry, *Newfoundland Verse*, was published in 1923 at the age of 40. He was to publish 13 more volumes of poetry, as well as several other selected and collected works. Pratt was a founding member of the Canadian Authors Association and the first editor of *Canadian Poetry Magazine*. In his lifetime, he received a great deal of recognition for his writing. He won the Governor General's Award for Poetry in 1937, 1940 and 1952. In addition to many other honours and honorary degrees, he was elected to the Royal Society of Canada.

Savard, Michel (1953 -):
Born in 1953 in Rivière-du-Loup, Québec, Michel Savard has published three books of poems at the Éditions du Noroît: *Forages* in 1982 (winner of the Governor General's Award for Poetry in French), *Cahiers d'anatomie* in 1985, and *Le sourire des chefs* in 1987. He has lived since 1987 in St. John's, Newfoundland, where he works as a translator and father. He is presently working on a new book.

Scammell, Arthur (1913 - 1995):
Born in Change Islands, Notre Dame Bay, Arthur Scammell would become a notable Newfoundland voice. He laid the foundation for a solid reputation when he wrote 'Squid-jiggin' Ground' at the age of fifteen, long before his education at Memorial University College, his experience as a school teacher in small towns in Newfoundland and his undergraduate studies at McGill University led him to embark upon a lengthy teaching career at Royal High

School in Montreal. Scammell co-founded the *Atlantic Guardian*, a Montreal magazine which boasted of Newfoundland from away, and it is not difficult to see why he inevitably returned home for retirement. Amongst other accomplishments, he published *My Newfoundland* and was given an honorary doctorate by Memorial University.[4]

Steffler, John (1947 -):
John Steffler is the author of one novel, *The Afterlife of George Cartwright*, and five collections of poems: *An Explanation of Yellow*, *The Wreckage of Play*, *The Grey Islands*, *That Night We Were Ravenous* and *Helix*. He lives in Corner Brook, Newfoundland and is presently working on his second novel.

Tuglavina, Joe K. (1945 - 1996):
Joseph Kefas Andreas Tuglavina was born in Hebron, Labrador on May 11, 1945. His family was dislocated to Hopedale in 1959. They then moved to Makkovik in 1960 and then to Nain in 1961. He married Ernestina Jararuse on November 24, 1968 and they had seven children.

Wadham:
Wadham is said to have been a naval officer who, in 1756, wrote 'Wadham's Song'. It is thought that the Wadham Islands, or Wadhams, a group of islands at the eastern entrance to Sir Charles Hamilton sound, southeast of Fogo Island, might have been named after him.[5]

Walker, Mark (1846 - 1924):
Mark Walker is one of Newfoundland's best examples of a writer of 'hedge school master poetry'. His peak of composition seems to have been in the 1870s. He left Newfoundland in 1904 and emigrated to Boston, Massachusetts, where he died in 1924. (note by Philip Hiscock)

Walsh, Des (1954 -):
Des Walsh was born in St. John's. His books of poetry include *Seasonal Bravery*, *Love and Savagery* and *The Singer's Broken Throat*. He co-wrote the T.V. drama *The Boys of St. Vincent* and wrote the script for the eight-hour T.V. adaptation of Bernice Morgan's novel *Random Passage*. In 2002, Breakwater also published his play *The Moon Shone Bright*.

Wareham, Baxter (1944 -):
Baxter Wareham is a retired high-school teacher. He has attended numerous folk festivals in America and Europe. He has several readings to his credit and is presently captain of a pilot boat out of Arnold's Cove, Newfoundland.

---

4 'Obituary: Arthur Scammell', *Gazette* (Memorial University of Newfoundland) 7 Sept. 1995: 2 ; 'Scammell, Arthur Reginald', *Dictionary of Newfoundland and Labrador Biography* (St. John's: Harry Cuff, 1990) 305; 'Scammell, Arthur Reginald', *Encyclopedia of Newfoundland and Labrador* vol. 5 (St. John's: Harry Cuff, 1994) 97.

5 'Wadham Islands', *Encyclopedia of Newfoundland and Labrador* vol. 5 (St. John's: Harry Cuff, 1994) 495.

Watts, Enos (1930 -):
Born in Long Pond, Manuels (now Conception Bay South), Enos Watts is one of Newfoundland's most respected poets. He has published two collections of poetry, *After the Locusts* (Breakwater, St. John's, 1974) and *Autumn Vengeance* (Breakwater, St. John's, 1986) and is presently working on a new manuscript. Enos was a school teacher and administrator for over 20 years in Stephenville and in the 1970s wrote a weekly column for *The Georgian*. He worked with the Canada Studies Foundation on curriculum development for many years and co-authored a number of pilot publications.

Withers, Jack (1899 - 1964):
Born in Canso, Nova Scotia, John Edward Withers was an electrician, musician and writer. He is perhaps best known for the radio scripts he wrote for 'The Irene B. Mellon', a weekly radio serial. A man of diverse talents and abilities, he also directed, produced and performed for the same popular program.[6]

---

6 'Withers, Edward John', *Encyclopedia of Newfoundland and Labrador*, vol. 5 (St. John's: Harry Cuff, 1994) 602.

Acknowledgements (Newfoundland & Labrador)

Thanks are due to the copyright holders of the following poems for permission to reprint them in this anthology. Poems are printed or reprinted by permission of the authors, or representatives, and publishers, as appropriate.

'A Great Big Sea Hove in Long Beach': from *Old-Time Songs and Poetry of Newfoundland*, 2nd ed. (St. John's: Gerald S. Doyle, 1940). Reprinted by permission of the Doyle family.

'Anti-Confederation Song': from *Old-Time Songs and Poetry of Newfoundland*, 2nd ed. (St. John's: Gerald S. Doyle, 1940). Reprinted by permission of the Doyle family.

Avis, Nick: 'after making love . . .', 'we return . . .', 'snowdrifts at my door . . .', 'the village graveyard . . .', 'the young plum pickers . . .', and 'a wedge of geese . . .' (a sequence of haiku in 'descending the mountain' from *Bending with the Wind* (1993). Reprinted by permission of Breakwater Books.

Babstock, Ken: 'Drawing Skeletons' and 'Bonavista' from *Mean* (1999). 'Bottled Rabbit' from *Days into Flatspin* (2001). Reprinted by permission of House of Anansi Press.

Burke, Johnny: 'The Kelligrews Soiree' from *Old-Time Songs of Newfoundland*, 3rd ed. (St. John's: Gerald S. Doyle, 1955). 'Betsy Brennan's Blue Hen' from *Old Time Songs and Poetry of Newfoundland*, 4th ed. (St. John's: Gerald S. Doyle, 1966). Reprinted by permission of the Doyle family.

Butt, Len: 'Jerry Ryan' from *Come and I Will Sing You* (ed. Genevieve Lehr, collected by Genevieve Lehr and Anita Best, 1985). Reprinted by permission of University of Toronto Press.

Byrne, Pat and Al Pittman: 'The Government Game'. Printed by permission of Pat Byrne and the Pittman estate.

'Chrissey's Dick': from *Come and I Will Sing You* (ed. Genevieve Lehr, collected by Genevieve Lehr and Anita Best, 1985). Reprinted by permission of University of Toronto Press.

Crummey, Michael: ' " Magic lantern". (April, 1889)', ' " The price of fish". (September, 1887)', ' " Now in Africa among the Natives". (1891)', ' " A narrow escape almost but saved". (1892)', ' " Distance from Newfoundland.

Northernmost grave in the world". (1913)'. '"At home on a cold winter's night. The changing scenes of Life". (1928)', '"An old sailor's portion". (1932)', 'Stones', 'Flame', 'Naming the Islands', from *Hard Light* (1998). Reprinted by permission of Brick Books. 'Fog City' from *Salvage* (2002). Reprinted by permission of McClelland and Stewart.

Dalton, Mary: 'dead Indians' from *Allowing the Light* (1993). Reprinted by permission of Breakwater Books. 'Rosella and Bride', 'Bachelor Brothers', 'Brin', 'Mad Moll and Crazy Betty', 'Old Holly', and 'Old Roman Candle' from *Merrybegot* (2003). Reprinted by permission of Signal Editions, Véhicule Press. An earlier version of 'Bachelor Brothers' appeared in *Allowing the Light*.

'The Dark-eyed Sailor': from *Come and I Will Sing You* (ed. Genevieve Lehr, collected by Genevieve Lehr and Anita Best, 1985). Reprinted by permission of University of Toronto Press.

Dawe, Tom: 'Edwardians (Old Photograph)', 'Daedalus', 'The French Shore Man', 'The Mummer', 'In Picasso's "Madman"' and 'The Veteran (1)' from *In Hardy Country* (1993). Earlier versions of the latter three appeared in *Island Spell* (Harry Cuff, 1981). Reprinted by permission of Breakwater Books.

Devine, John: 'Pat Murphy's Meadow' from *Catch ahold this one . . . Songs of Newfoundland & Labrador*, vol. 1 (ed. Eric West, St. John's: Vinland Music, 1991). Reprinted by permission of Anne Devine.

Dicker, Sid: 'Surutsiutluta' / '*When We Were Children*' from *Songs of Labrador* (ed. and comp. Tim Borlase, Fredericton: Goose Lane and Labrador East Integrated School Board, 1993). Reprinted by permission of Mary Dicker.

Elliott, David: 'Lighthouse', 'Frank', 'Mattie', Resonance', 'Talking to Trees', and 'Magdalen at the Tomb' from *The Edge of Beulah* (1988). Reprinted by permission of Breakwater Books. 'Othello's Own Brother'. Printed by permission of Rosalie Elliott.

Francis, Bernie: transliteration of 'The Lord's Prayer' from the old Mi'kmaw system into the new Mi'kmaw orthography. Printed by permission of Bernie Francis.

Grace, John: 'Petty Harbour Bait Skiff' from *Come and I Will Sing You* (ed. Genevieve Lehr, collected by Genevieve Lehr and Anita Best, 1985). Reprinted by permission of University of Toronto Press.

ACKNOWLEDGEMENTS 563

Hutchings, Eugene: 'Bucksaw Blues'. Printed by permission of the author.

Kelland, Otto: 'Let Me Fish Off Cape St. Mary's' from *Bow Wave: Poems and Songs* (Otto Kelland, 1988). Reprinted by permission of the author. This song first appeared in a different version in *Old Time Songs of Newfoundland*, 3rd ed. (St. John's: Gerald S. Doyle, 1955). Reprinted by permission of the Doyle family.

LeMessurier, H. W.: 'The Ryans and the Pittmans' from *Old-Time Songs and Poetry of Newfoundland*, 2nd ed. (St. John's: Gerald S. Doyle, 1940). Reprinted by permission of the Doyle family.

Loon, Morley and Donna Augustine (Thunderbird Turtle Woman): 'Apoqnmuinen / *Thank You Great Spirit*'. Printed by permission of Donna Augustine.

'Lukey's Boat': from *Old-Time Songs of Newfoundland*, 3rd ed. (St. John's: Gerald S. Doyle, 1955). Reprinted by permission of the Doyle family.

McGrath, Carmelita: 'If I Could Give You Now', 'Adam and Eve on a Winter Afternoon', 'For the First Time in Months, She Feels Her Feet', 'Breaking Ice', 'How She Had Her Nervous Breakdown', 'Touring the Manor Houses', 'Baked in Chocolate' (published as part of the sequence 'Aphrodisiacs for a Newfoundland Winter') and 'Summer Night Heat' (published as part of the sequence 'Sextet') from *To The New World* (Killick, 1997). Reprinted by permission of the author.

MacKenzie, Marguerite: translation of 'Meshapush', 'Giant Hare'. Printed by permission of the translator.

'Meshapush': from *Myths and Tales from Sheshatshit*, Booklet 1 (narrated by Edward Rich and collected by Madeleine Lefebvre and Robert Lanari in 1967; edited by José Mailhot and collaborators, St. John's: Labrador Innu Text Project, 1999). Reprinted by permission of José Mailhot and Marguerite MacKenzie.

'North Twin Lakes': collected from Obediah Payne who learned the song from his father who got it from the lumbering camps in Deer Lake, Newfoundland.

Payne, Daniel: 'The Wave that Hit St. Bride's'. Printed by permission of the author.

Payne, Stephanie: 'Home Free'. Printed by permission of the author.

Pittman, Al: 'The Cost of a Good Canoe', 'St. Leonard's Revisited', 'The Pigeon on the Gate', 'Shanadithit', and 'Gram Glover's Dream' from *Once when I was drowning* (1978). The first two originally appeared in different versions in *Seaweed and Rosaries* (Montreal: Poverty Press, 1968) and the latter two in *Through One More Window* (Breakwater, 1974). 'Kelly at Graveside', 'Living Alone', and 'The Dandelion Killers' from *Dancing in Limbo* (1993). 'Cradle Hill' and excerpt from *West Moon* from *West Moon* (1995). 'The Pink, White and Green' from *Thirty-for-Sixty* (1999). Printed by/reprinted by permission of Breakwater Books.

Pittman, Kyran: 'The Second Coming'. Printed by permission of the author.

Power, Gregory: 'Bogwood' from *Banked Fires: An Anthology of Newfoundland Poetry* (St.John's: Harry Cuff, 1989). Reprinted by permission of Gregory Power Jr. This poem first appeared in a collection of O'Leary Prize winners, *Poems of Newfoundland* (ed. Michael Harrington, St. John's: F. M. O'Leary, 1953).

Pratt, E. J.: 'The Ice-Floes', 'The Fog', 'The Ground Swell', and 'Come Not the Seasons Here' (first published in *Newfoundland Verse*, Toronto: Ryerson, 1923), the excerpt from *The Roosevelt and the Antinoe* (first published in *The Roosevelt and the Antinoe*, New York: Macmillan 1930), 'Erosion' (first published in *Many Moods*, Toronto: Macmillan 1932), 'Come Away, Death' (first published in *Still Life* and *Other Verse*, Toronto: Macmillan, 1943) from *The Collected Poems of E. J. Pratt*, 2nd ed. (Toronto: MacMillan, 1958). Reprinted by permission of the University of Toronto Press.

'The Prison of Newfoundland': from *Come and I Will Sing You* (ed. Genevieve Lehr, collected by Genevieve Lehr and Anita Best, 1985). Reprinted by permission of the University of Toronto Press.

Savard, Michel: 'The Fish' / '*La pêche*'. Printed by permission of the author.

Scammell, Arthur: 'Squid-jiggin' Ground' from *Old-Time Songs of Newfoundland*, 3rd ed. (St. John's: Gerald S. Doyle, 1955). Reprinted by permission of Star Quality Music, courtesy of Unidisc Music Inc.

Steffler, John: 'The Horses' from *An Explanation of Yellow* (Ottawa: Borealis, 1980); 'Saint Laurence's Tears', 'Boiler Room Men', and 'The New Sled' from *The Wreckage of Play* (Toronto: McClelland and Stewart, 1988). Reprinted by permission of the author. 'Cedar Cove' and 'That Night We Were Ravenous' from *That Night We Were Ravenous* (1998). Reprinted by permission of McClelland and Stewart. 'he's out there . . .', 'Nels and his wife . . .', 'they all save . . .', 'I thought I was headed . . .', 'when the rain comes . . .', 'on the bunk . . .', 'ducks swoop low . . .', *Nels*: 'There was my great-uncle . . .', *Nels*: 'From the month of June . . .' and *Nels*: 'This one spring . . .' from *The Grey Islands* (2000). Reprinted by permission of Brick Books. 'he's out there . . .' and 'ducks swoop low . . .' originally appeared in different versions when *The Grey Islands* was first published by McClelland & Stewart in 1985. 'Sour Fire', 'Smoke', and 'Arriving in Russell' from *Helix: New and Selected Poems* (2003). Reprinted by permission of Signal Editions, Véhicule Press.

Tuglavina, Joe K.: 'RosiaKKulak' / *'Beautiful Rose'* from *Songs of Labrador* (ed. and comp. Tim Borlase, Fredericton: Goose Lane and Labrador East Integrated School Board 1993). Reprinted by permission of Ernestina Tuglavina.

'Uvanga, Uvanga': from *Songs of Labrador* (ed. and comp. Tim Borlase, Fredericton: Goose Lane and Labrador East Integrated School Board 1993).

'Wadhams Song': from *Songs Sung by Old Time Sealers of Many Years Ago* (St. John's: James Murphy, 1925).

Walker, Mark: 'Tickle Cove Pond' from *Old-Time Songs of Newfoundland*, 3rd ed. (St. John's: Gerald S. Doyle, 1955). Reprinted by permission of the Doyle family. For 'Fanny's Harbour Bawn' from Anita Best (personal collection).

Walsh, Des: 'March 3, 1999—Notes on an upcoming anniversary', 'On a train heading northeast', 'The triangle of the heart', 'Wednesday', 'My friend's death', 'The Launch, Trinity Shipbuilders, Trinity, June 24, 1995', 'On being Catholic and loving the treachery of winter', and 'I love you more than any God, not falsely' from *The Singer's Broken Throat* (2003). Reprinted by permission of Talonbooks.

Wareham, Baxter: 'Rubber Boots'. Printed by permission of the author.

'The *Water Witch*': from *Come and I Will Sing You* (ed. Genevieve Lehr, collected by Genevieve Lehr and Anita Best, 1985). Reprinted by permission of University of Toronto Press.

Watts, Enos: 'Cain', 'Yo-yo', 'Longliner at Sunset', 'Confrontation' and 'Roses and Attic Throats' from *Autumn Vengeance* (1986). Earlier versions of the latter three appeared in *After the Locusts* (1974). Reprinted by permission of Breakwater Books. 'The Red-Throated Loon', 'Window', 'The Balcony Door', 'Waiting for Sunrise: Early December' and 'Summer Solstice'. Printed by permission of the author.

Withers, Jack: 'The Cliffs of Baccalieu' from *Sing around this one . . . Songs of Newfoundland & Labrador* vol. 2 (ed. Eric West, Ladle Cove, NL: Vinland

Music, 1997). Reprinted by permission of Morning Music Limited.

'The Wreck of the Steamship *Ethie*': from *Ballads and Sea Songs of Newfoundland* (ed. and comp. Elisabeth Bristol Greenleaf, Cambridge: Harvard UP: 1933). Elisabeth Greenleaf attributes this song to Miss Burney Eason of Port Saunders.

Notes on the Text
(Newfoundland & Labrador)

'A Great Big Sea Hove in Long Beach': Philip Hiscock recalls that this song came out of Bonavista in the 1920s.

'Anti-Confederation Song': In *Sing around this one . . . Songs of Newfoundland & Labrador*, vol. 2, Philip Hiscock provides the following notes on this song: 'Often said to have been written by politician and businessman Charles Fox Bennett (1793-1883), this is just one of several songs that have survived from the political battles of the 1860s. Bennett certainly did use it in his 1869 campaign against Confederation with Canada. He carried the song around the island of Newfoundland by boat during the campaign, and had it sung at rallies. Its conservative economic message was not as powerful as its slogan, "Come near at your peril, Canadian wolf" which has been emblematic for Newfoundland nationalists for over a century'.[1]

'The Cliffs of Baccalieu': Philip Hiscock notes the following: '[t]his song was first sung in April 1934 on *The Adventures of the Irene B. Mellon*, a popular radio serial in St. John's. Jack Withers (1899-1964) wrote and directed the show, including his song 'The Cliffs of Baccalieu'. Entirely from his imagination, it nonetheless represents the dangerous trips that Newfoundland schooners really made every fall returning from the Labrador fishery. The song came to be associated with the clear tenor voice of the Bosun on the Mellon, Patty DeBourke (1911-1997). It has been a perennial favourite, revived in the 1980s by Ryan's Fancy and Stan Rogers and in 1997 by Bristol's Hope. This version uses the original words written by Jack Withers'. *(Sing around this one)*

'Fanny's Harbour Bawn': Philip Hiscock explains that no full version of this song was published before 1900 but that it was probably in oral circulation for two or three decades before that. Hiscock also notes that the song was published many times in the first 25 or 30 years of the 20th century and that one writer in that period spoke of the song's great popularity, so great that he needn't even give the words. Gerald Doyle published 'Fanny's Harbour Bawn' in 1927 and 1940. Hiscock notes that Anita Best's version includes more of the florid language the song is known for than some other versions do and that his suspicion is that the floridity is original. (personal correspondence)

'For to Fit You Out for Sea': The title of the book's first section is taken from a Newfoundland song, 'Peter Street', a work not included in this anthology.

'The Government Game': The lyrics were mainly written by Al Pittman, though Pat Byrne contributed to it and adapted it to fit the melody of Dominic Behan's 'The Patriot Game'.

---

[1] Philip Hiscock, notes, *Sing around this one . . . Songs of Newfoundland & Labrador*, vol. 2, ed. and arr. Eric West (Ladle Cove, NL: Vinland Music, 1997).

From *The Grey Islands:* John Steffler wrote this book on the Grey Islands, which are found just off the far-north coast of Newfoundland. The selections represented here are separate works and are not to be considered extracts from the same poem.

'The Ice-Floes': For many years, Newfoundland fishermen lived and worked in what was essentially a cashless society. Under the 'truck system', their annual catch was turned over to merchants based mainly in St. John's in exchange for supplies to get them through the winter and to outfit them for the next season's fishing. The annual seal hunt provided them with one of their few opportunities to earn cash. However, it has also been responsible for some of their greatest disasters. In the Greenland disaster of 1898, 48 men were lost, and, in the *Newfoundland* disaster in 1914, 50 were lost. The *Eagle* was a sealing ship that Pratt would have known from his youth, but, as is mentioned in the annotations to *E. J. Pratt: Complete Poems* (ed. Sandra Djwa and R. G. Moyles, Toronto: University of Toronto Press, 1989), the ship was never involved in a disaster of the sort dealt with in 'The Ice-Floes'.

In a commentary on the poem, Pratt mentions that the sealers 'try to get into the herd by the middle of March, because when the young seals are about a month old they "dip" or take to the water, being shoved off the ice by their mothers . . . . If the seals manage to get to the water before the ships arrive they are safe . . . . As soon as a ship gets into a patch of seals, and into very thick ice where further progress is impossible, she is said to "burn down," and the crew are ordered over the rails for the kill . . . . In the course of a day's pursuit, the men may be separated from their ship by miles, necessitating hours to reach her position after the scream of the siren or the flag-signal had indicated a fall in the barometer. . . . Sometimes, especially when the wind is off-shore, the pack gets broken up into fragments or pans and numbers of the crew may be borne out to sea' (from *E. J. Pratt: E. J. Pratt on His Life and Poetry,* ed. Susan Gingell, U. of T. Press, 1983).

'The Kelligrews Soiree': Though Gerald S. Doyle represented this song as 'The Kelligrew's Soiree', the editors have modified the punctuation. Kelligrews is a town twenty miles outside St. John's on Conception Bay and is part of the modern-day community Conception Bay South.

'The Lord's Prayer': This is Bernie Francis' transliteration of The Lord's Prayer from the old Mi'kmaw writing system into the new Mi'kmaw writing system which Francis and his working partner, Doug Smith, created.[2] The Smith/Francis orthography was a pragmatic response to and consequence of a mandate in Nova Scotia's Mi'kmaw communities in the 1970s. Various missionaries in Mi'kmaw communities had controlled and distorted the written Mi'kmaw language for a long while. From the early to mid-eighteenth century, a missionary by the name of Abbé Maillard had used the Roman alphabet to

---

[2] The word Mi'kmaw is used when it is in an adjectival position or when it is used to represent the singular (e.g. mi'kmaw person, mi'kmaw people, mi'kmaw nation, a mi'kmaw). Mi'kmaq represents the plural (many mi'kmaq; the mi'kmaq; the land of the mi'kmaq). (Bernie Francis, personal correspondence)

represent the Mi'kmaw language. However, he did not teach it to the Mi'kmaw people, because, representative of the Catholic Church, he did not want them to use anything else but the hieroglyphic system which had been used to represent the Catholic doctrine. Silas T. Rand began working on the Mi'kmaw language around the 1830s, and he published a dictionary near the latter end of the nineteenth century and also documented Mi'kmaw legends using the Roman alphabet. However, there were two problems with Rand's system and work: 1) Rand was a Baptist, whereas, by that time, Mi'kmaw people had been indoctrinated to be Catholics and 2) Rand over-differentiated the Mi'kmaw sound system in that he used too many letters of the Roman alphabet to represent Mi'kmaw sounds. The next missionary to be considered here is Father Pacifique, a Capucin missionary from France who, in the late nineteenth century and after studying the attempt at devising a writing system for Mi'kmaw, set to work on a new orthography which better represented the Mi'kmaw language. He developed a new orthography consisting of thirteen letters of the Roman alphabet and published *The Micmac Grammar of Father Pacifique*. However, there was also a problem with his writing system in that he under-differentiated the sound system, leaving too much guesswork when reading it. The Smith/Francis orthography, a response to a serious need, employs a phonemic principle, meaning that one letter represents one sound, one sound one letter. (Bernie Francis, personal interview)

'Lukey's Boat': Philip Hiscock says that Virtue Kean is often said to be the author. (personal correspondence)

' "Magic lantern". (April, 1889)', ' "The price of fish". (September, 1887)', ' "Now in Africa among the Natives". (1891)', ' "A narrow escape almost but saved". (1892)', ' "Distance from Newfoundland. Northernmost grave in the world". (1913)'. ' "At home on a cold winter's night. The changing scenes of Life". (1928)' and ' "An old sailor's portion" (1932)'. These poems by Michael Crummey appear in a section of *Hard Light* entitled 'Discovering Darkness'. In this text, Crummey provides the following explanation of the sequence: 'Discovering Darkness was inspired by *On the High Seas*, the diary of Captain John Froude (1863-1939), published in 1983 by Jesperson Press. Born in Twillingate, Newfoundland, he worked as a fisher, sealer and miner before spending a number of years travelling around the globe as a seaman on tall ships and steamers. The titles of all the poems are taken directly from the diary. Most of the experiences related, the references to history, mythology, science and religion, along with many of the sentiments expressed, can be found in some form or other in *On the High Seas* as well. In several pieces, I have acted as much as editor as writer. But the sequence is not meant to be biography. Throughout I've been free with names, dates, places and anything else I felt the poems required'.

Meshapush **/ Giant Hare**: a traditional Innu tale of how fire was brought to people.

Innu myths and legends are traditional narratives which form the *atanukan* genre: tales set in an earlier time, before the world of today, in a time when animals spoke as men, intermarried with women, and moved easily between their animal and human forms. This tale of how *Meshapush*, or Giant Hare, brought fire to humans would be told in various versions with details differing according to the storyteller. Traditionally, *atanukana* are recited in the context of small family units in winter camps, where the Innu have traveled hundreds of miles during the summer gathering places to find caribou. Semi-nomadic hunters, the Innu have depended on caribou for meat and material for making the clothing and snowshoes so necessary for winter travel over vast areas.

The late Edward Rich was a master storyteller whose extensive repertoire included not only *atanukan* but also *tipatshimun*, the more recent tales of oral history. When recorded in 1967, he resided in Sheshatshiu (formerly known as North-West River), Labrador where he had emigrated from the more northerly community of Davis Inlet (recently relocated to Natuashish). These two Labrador Innu communities of about 3,000 people form part of the Innu Nation which extends over south-eastern Québec, where an additional 10,000 people live in 9 communities.

This version of *Meshapush* was collected by students from the Laboratoire d'anthropologie amérindienne in 1967 and transcribed and edited in Innu through a project directed by Marguerite MacKenzie of the Department of Linguistics at Memorial University. Funding was provided by the Institute of Social and Economic Research and the J. R. Smallwood Centre for Newfoundland Studies of Memorial University, by the Canada Council for the Arts (First Peoples Words: Printed and Spoken) to the St. John's Native Friendship Centre Association and by the Social Sciences and Humanities Research Council. Initial transcription of the Innu tape was provided by Matiu Rich and Etienne Andrew, with final transcriptions by Josephine Bacon and José Mailhot and final editing by Desneiges Mollen, Céline Bellefleur and José Mailhot. The original Innu version was published in *Myths and Tales from Sheshatshit*, Booklet 1 (collected by Madeleine Lefebvre and Robert Lanari in 1967; edited by José Mailhot and collaborators, St John's, Newfoundland: Labrador Innu Text Project, 1999). The translation, by Marguerite MacKenzie, with thanks to Julie Brittain and Simon Fortin, appears here for the first time. An analysis of selected linguistic features of the myth appears in Laurel-Anne Hasler's MA thesis *Obviation in two Innu-aimun atanukana* (Memorial University 2002).

A feature of this story is the inclusion of a song which Meshapush sings to control the whales. Singing to the accompaniment of a drum is a primary method of Innu communication with the world of animals and spirits, the other being through dreaming. Songs are normally specific to a particular hunter, often coming to him in dream; they are not sung by others unless overtly handed on by the singer. They tend to be short and repetitive, sometimes containing archaic language, and can be difficult for anyone other than the singer to interpret.

The myth includes a number of cultural references to traditional Innu life in the bush. The term for a net is also used for a spider web; in the neighbouring dialect of East Cree, the spider is referred to as 'net-maker'. The term 'harewood', in which Hare hides is obscure, seems to refer to phosphorescent rotted wood used to smoke-tan hides for mittens and moccasins. 'Babiche' is a Canadian word referring to the thong cut from untanned hide and woven as the webbing of snowshoes. In the story, babiche is used for weaving a net, a quick alternative to using fine tree roots. Putting the net in an armpit to dry out reflects the common practice of warming frozen hands in the same place. The use of metal for a knife is a modern reference, as bone or caribou antler would have been used in pre-European contact times. Nowadays, a piece of metal, such as a file, is heated, shaped and tempered into a knife, spear or ice chisel.

'The Roosevelt and the Antinoe': Pratt's subject is a stirring rescue at sea made in the midst of a winter storm in 1926, one of the greatest Atlantic storms on record. In this dramatic celebration of the heroism and resourcefulness of Captain Fried and his crew in coming to the aid of the sailors on the sinking Antinoe, a small British grain-freighter, readers can see Pratt's work in the light of the Anglo-Saxon scop and the Newfoundland outport singer and storyteller. Following in this tradition, he is the entertainer and the celebrator of what he perceived to be the values of Newfoundland, a set of values he refers to in the poem as 'the old way / Of the sea'. But Pratt has his modern side as well, and that can be seen especially in passages like the one in this excerpt focussing on the use of the direction-finder to locate the disabled *Antinoe*. In 1902, he had been fortunate enough to meet Marconi in St John's the day before the historic message was sent from Signal Hill in St. John's to Lizard Point in Cornwall. Profoundly inspired by the experience and what it seemed to signify for the human race, he wrote as clearly about technology and both its promise and danger for modern man as any poet has done.

'Rubber Boots': This song is based on the Irish song 'Navvy Boots' to which Baxter Wareham added a first and last verse.

Notes on Contributors (Ireland)

Campbell, Joseph (1879 – 1944):
For Joseph Campbell, poet and doer, 'Vision, Energy, Bleakness' ('The Key' 1919) were the three essential qualities of Irish poetry, and these he sought to emulate in his own work. He was editor of *Uladh*, the journal of Ulster Literary Theatre. He contributed to Griffith's *United Irishmen* and to O'Grady's *All-Ireland Review*. Later a member of the Irish Volunteers, he was a rescue worker during the Easter Rising. An anti-Treaty republican, he was interned at the Curragh for eighteen months. In 1925 in the United States he founded the School for Irish Studies. Austin Clarke edited *The Poems of Joseph Campbell* in 1963 (Allen Figgis). Campbell remains an important voice in Irish lyric poetry.

Casey, John Keegan (1846 – 1870):
John Keegan Casey is remembered today for his popular ballad 'The Rising of the Moon'. As a midland poet, he celebrated his childhood near the river Inny, but his themes are mostly in the domains of heroic patriotism and romantic, if often, blighted love. He died young, weakened in health after a prison sentence for Fenian sympathies. His Dublin funeral, drawing a crowd of some fifty-thousand people, became one of the largest demonstrations of nationalist feeling of the period.

Clarke, Austin (1896 – 1974):
Austin Clarke was a versatile writer: poet, playwright, literary journalist, novelist and broadcaster on radio. His early epic poetry won him justified comparison with Yeats; he is considered the finest talent of the generation after Yeats. In drama, alone, his twenty-one plays constitute a significant achievement. His *Mnemosyne Lay in Dust* (1966) is one of the great long poems of the twentieth century. He is remembered for his political and social satires, his powerful autobiographical poems, his linguistic experimentation and comic imagination and, perhaps most significantly, for the cheerful sensuality of his novels and his exuberant non-judgemental celebration of love and sensuality in a repressed Ireland.

Coady, Michael (1939 –):
Michael Coady was born in Carrick-on-Suir, Co. Tipperary, where he still lives. He is the author of five collections of poetry. In 1989 he travelled to Newfoundland with the support of the Arts Council of Ireland. His latest collection, *One Another* (2003), was published by The Gallery Press. He is a member of *Aosdána*.

Coffey, Brian (1905 – 1995):
Brian Coffey was the son of the first president of University College Dublin and a friend of Denis Devlin with whom he published *Poems* in 1930. He lived in Paris where he became a lifelong friend of Samuel Beckett. He translated and was heavily influenced by French modernist poetry. In his later work, such as

Advent (1971) and *Death of Hector* (1979), he experimented with visual effects. The Dedalus Press published his *Poems and Versions*, 1929 – 1990 (1991).

Cronin, Anthony (1928 –):
Anthony Cronin is the originator of *Aosdána* and a poet, novelist, critic, editor and biographer. He was born in Wexford and educated at University College Dublin. His articles written for *The Irish Times* were published as *An Irish Eye* in 1985, and his literary works include *R. M. S. Titanic* (1967) and *Relationships* (1992). *The End of the Modern World* (1989), in particular, exemplifies his characteristic toughness, intelligence and inventiveness. His biographies of Flann O'Brian and Samuel Beckett have been widely acclaimed and add to a reputation already well established by his wide-ranging scholarship and cultural criticism. His *Collected Poems* will be published by New Island Books in 2004.

Curran, John Philpot (J. P.) (1750 – 1817):
A distinguished orator, wit and lawyer, J. P. Curran defended many of the United Irishmen in the 1790s. He opposed the Act of Union (1800) but later accepted judicial office as Irish Master of the Rolls (1806). An associate of Moore and Byron, his later years were clouded by depression. His verse remains uncollected. The original of John F. Kennedy's saying about eternal vigilance being the price of freedom is attributed to John Philpot Curran.

Devlin, Denis (1908 – 1959):
Denis Devlin was a poet and diplomat. He was born in Scotland of Irish parents. He was educated by the Christian brothers and the Jesuits at Belvedere College and spent one year preparing for the priesthood. He then transferred to University College Dublin. His poems reflect a religious fervour and a deep attachment to places he visited. His works include *Intercessions* (1937) and *Lough Derg and Other Poems* (1946). The Dedalus Press published the *Collected Poems of Denis Devlin*, edited by J.C.C. Mays (1989).

Durcan, Paul (1944 –):
Paul Durcan's first book, *Endsville* (with Brian Lynch), appeared in 1967 and has been followed by 17 others, including *Daddy, Daddy* (Winner of the Whitbread Award for Poetry, 1990), *A Snail in My Prime: New and Selected Poems* (1993), *Christmas Day* (1996) and *Greetings to Our Friends in Brazil* (1999). Paul has read his poetry in over twenty-one countries, including Newfoundland (The March Hare Festival 2003). In 2001, he received a Cholmondeley Award for poetry. He is a member of *Aosdána* and lives in Dublin. *Paul Durcan's diary* was published by New Island in 2003 and contains two chapters on his visit to Newfoundland.

Garvey, Alan (1975 –):
Arts Administrator, Alan Garvey has published in magazines such as *THE SHop*, *Southword* and *The Stinging Fly* and has two Chapbooks, *Dear Whoever* (2001) and *Herself in air* (2003). He is the Administrator of The Seán Dunne Festival.

Groarke, Vona (1964 –):
Vona Groarke's first collection of poetry, *Shale* (The Gallery Press, 1994), won the Brendan Behan Memorial Award in 1995. Her second collection of poems, *Other People's Houses*, was published in 1999 by The Gallery Press. Recent prizes won include the Strokestown International Poetry Competition (1999), the Stand International Poetry Competition (2000) and the Davoren Hanna Prize (2001). Her third collection, *Flight*, published in Spring, 2002, was shortlisted for the Forward Prize for Best Collection in the UK.

Healy, James N. (1916 – 1993):
In his important *Irish Songs of the Sea*, James N. Healy gathered fifty-four complete songs with accompanying music in a neglected genre of Irish Tradition. Healy was both actor and theatrical producer. He specialised, also, in collecting songs and ballads that are centuries old.

Heaney, Seamus (1939 –):
Awarded the Nobel Prize for Literature in 1995, Seamus Heaney is one of the foremost poets of his generation. A leading critic, essayist, editor and translator, he has twice won the Whitbread Book of the Year for *The Spirit Level* (1996) and *Beowulf* (1999). His latest collection is *Electric Light*, from Faber & Faber (2001). Unique in Ireland, he is critically acclaimed and popular.

Hewitt, John (1907 – 1987):
John Hewitt is regarded as the father figure of modern Ulster poetry. His published work comprises fourteen volumes of poetry as well as literary criticism and studies of painters. An enduring pre-occupation of Hewitt's is the complex and fraught relationship between planters and Gael in north-east Ulster. His poetry is prized for its innate strength, integrity of purpose, lucidity, precision and compassionate nature. *The Collected Poems of John Hewitt* was published by Blackstaff Press (1991).

Hyde, Douglas (1860 – 1949):
First President of Ireland (1938 – 1945), Douglas Hyde had a distinguished career: a brilliant linguist, folklorist, scholar of Irish Literature, translator, a founder Member of the Gaelic League, Professor of Modern Irish in UCD (1909 – 1932) and Senator (1925 – 1926). He was the author of many books and articles, including the famous *Love Songs of Connacht* (1893). His play *Casadh an tSúgáin* (1901) was the first play in Irish to appear professionally on stage. There are accounts of Hyde in W. B. Yeats's *Autobiographies* and George Moore's *Hail and Farewell*.

Kavanagh, Patrick (1904 – 1967):
Patrick Kavanagh was born in Inniskeen, Co. Monaghan and died in Dublin. He was a poet whose celebration of Ireland encompassed both the harshness and the spirituality of Irish life and landscape. His poetry ranges over his experiences from childhood innocence, as in 'A Christmas Childhood', to the bitterness of 'Stoney Grey Soil' and the humbling spirituality of the Dublin-

inspired Canal Bank poems. He also wrote two novels: *Tarry Flynn* (1948), which was made into a play and performed by the Abbey Theatre, and an early work entitled *The Green Fool* (1938). When his *The Great Hunger* was published in 1942, all copies were seized by order of the then Minister for Justice.

Kinsella, Thomas (1929 –):
Poet, translator from old and modern Irish, professor of poetry in Southern Illinois University and Temple University, Philadelphia, founder and director of Temple University Irish Tradition Programme in Dublin, Thomas Kinsella retired in 1990 and lives in Wicklow and Philadelphia. A Writer-in-Residence post is scheduled for UCD in 2004. Publications with Dolmen Press, Oxford University Press and Carcanet Press include *Collected Poems* (1996), *The Táin* (1969), *An Duanaire: Poems of the Dispossessed* (1986), and *The Dual Tradition: An Essay on Poetry and Politics in Ireland* (1995). His version of *The Táin* (1969), with illustrations by Louis Le Brocquy, was a landmark publication in Ireland.

Longley, Michael (1939 –):
Michael Longley was born in Belfast and educated at Royal Belfast Academical Institution and TCD where he read Classics: the classics, especially Homer, exercise an important influence on his work. His collection *The Weather in Japan* (2000) won *The Irish Times* Prize for poetry, The Hawthorndon Prize and the T. S. Eliot Prize. He worked for The Arts Council of Northern Ireland from 1970 until 1991. He was awarded the Queen's Medal for Poetry in 2001. His *Selected Poems* was published in 1998.

MacColl, Ewan (1915 - 1989):
Born Jimmie Miller in working class Lancashire, Ewan MacColl changed his name in sympathy with the Lallans' Movement in Scotland. For some sixty years in the vanguard of political struggle, writing and producing plays, composing songs and scripts on apartheid, fascism, workers' and human rights, Ewan MacColl, in his creative work, attempted to bridge the chasm between the literary and the oral in our traditions. With Seamus Ennis, Alan Loman and others, he founded the Ballads and Blues Club, later to become the famed Signers Club (1953 - 1991). His partner, Peggy Seeger, gathered 200 of his songs into the *Essential Ewan MacColl Songbook* (2001).

MacConmara, Donnchad Rua (1715 – 1810):
Donnchad Rua MacConmara's most famous poem is 'Eachtra Ghiolla an Amaráin', which humourously describes a sailing-ship journey over the Atlantic; sections of the poem (in addition to those reproduced in this book) describe an Aisling vision the poet had and a dramatic escape from an attacking French frigate. While probably at his best as a comical writer, he also composed 'Aoir do na Sagartaibh', a satire on the Catholic clergy of his times, the popular 'Bán Chnuic Éireann Óighe', a famous repentance song, 'An Aithrighe', and a Latin elegy for his poet friend Tadhg Gaedhealach Ó Súilleabháin. Born in Clare, Donnchad Rua worked as a teacher in the Sliabh

gCua area in Waterford. He is buried in Newtown, Kilmacthomas, which hosts an August Festival in his honour.

Mac Lochlainn, Gearóid (1966 -):
Gearóid Mac Lochlainn is a bi-lingual poet and musician from Belfast. His latest collection—*Stream Of Tongues / Sruth Teangacha*, (published by Cló Iar Chonnachta), which includes a CD recording of the poet's performance, received The Michael Hartnett Poetry Award 2002, The Irish American Cultural Institute Butler Award 2002, The Open House Literature Award for Poetry 2002 and the Eithne and Rupert Strong Award 2003. He is Writer-in-Residence at the University of Ulster at Coleraine and has received an award from the President of Ireland, Mary McAleese, in recognition of his work.

McBurney, William B. (d.c. 1919):
William B. McBurney, whose fame rests on 'The Croppy Boy', was a contributor to *The Nation*, founded by Thomas Davis. McBurney also wrote under the pseudonym Carroll Malone.

McCall, P. J. (1861 – 1919):
P. J. McCall's books include *The Shadow of St. Patrick* (1894) and *The Fenian Nights' Entertainment* (1897). 'Boolavogue' was written to coincide with the centenary of the 1798 Rebellion. The song commemorates the opening hostilities near Enniscorthy and the famous '98 rebel priest who acted in defiance of his bishop.

McGuckian, Medbh (1950 –):
Belfast poet, her latest collection of eight volumes is *Had I A Thousand Lives* (2003), published by The Gallery Press. She teaches creative writing at Queen's University and has been visiting fellow at the University of California, Berkeley. She specialises in richly associative, dislocating imagery to explore gender issues.

Mahon, Derek (1941 –):
Derek Mahon, born in Belfast in 1991, studied at TCD, Dublin and the Sorbonne. He has worked as journalist and screenwriter in London and New York where he also taught at Barnard and NYU. His *Selected Poems* appeared in 1990 from The Gallery Press. He has received many awards for his work, including Lannan and Guggenheim Fellowships. The Gallery Press published *The Hudson Letter* (1995), Racine's *Phaedra* and *Journalism, selected prose* (both 1996).

Mangan, James Clarence (1803 – 1849):
Born into an impoverished Dublin family, Mangan spent ten tedious years as an office clerk (1817-1827) before becoming a freelance writer. The years 1832 to 1839, during which he worked on the Ordnance Topographical Survey, were pivotal to his career, for he met and was influenced by Petrie, O'Donovan and O'Curry. They inspired his adaptation and absorption of Irish

poetry and folklore, and these are the principal features of his work on which his reputation as an outstanding Irish poet rests. Among his most famous poems are 'Dark Rosaleen' and 'O'Hussey's Ode to the Maguire', which replicate the complicated rhyme schemes and long lines of Old Irish poetry. Mangan wrote initially for *The Nation* and contributed to leading Dublin literary journals of the time, including *The Dublin University Magazine*. He is often compared to Edgar Allan Poe because of his commitment to experimentation in verse techniques and fascination with psychological trauma. An addict at the end of his life, starved and exhausted, he died of cholera. The Gallery Press has published his work in *Poems* (2003).

Meehan, Paula (1955 –):
Paul Meehan lives in Dublin. She has published five collections of poetry, the most recent being *DHARMAKAYA* (Carcanet Press/Wake Forest University Press). She has also written for the theatre, for contemporary dance companies, and in collaboration with visual artists and musicians.

Merriman, Brian (1750 – 1805):
Gaelic scholar, keeper of a successful school of mathematics, musician, married man with two daughters, and a progressive small farmer winning prizes for his flax, Brian Merriman reputedly wrote his *tour de force, Cúirt an Mhéan Oíche*, around 1780 while he was laid up with an injured foot. His one major subversive poem displays a comic eloquence and burlesque energy, subverting literary conventions stretching back to medieval song and Courts of Love. It is a sustained invective on marriage, matchmaking and the sexual politics of male and female in the Ireland of his day.

Mhac an tSaoi, Máire (1922 –):
Máire Mhac an tSaoi has published four books of poems, including *An Cion Go Dtí Seo* (Sairséal, 1987). Awards include an honorary degree from the National University of Ireland and the 1988 O'Shaughnessy Award for Poetry. She has held academic appointments at Queen's College, New York and the University of Pennsylvania. She has been editor of *Poetry Ireland Review* and an Associate Fellow at the National Humanities Center in Virginia. She lives on Howth in Dublin.

Milliken (or Millikin), Richard Alfred (Dick Millikin) (1707 – 1815):
A master of the burlesque, Dick Millikin is the author of 'De groves of de Pool'. He co-edited a magazine, *The Casket*, which closed down at the outbreak of the United Irishmen's Rebellion, when he joined the Cork Royal Volunteers. He later published poetry, fiction and drama.

Montague, John (1929 –):
John Montague was born in 1929 in Brooklyn and was raised in Co. Tyrone. He is the author of over a dozen collections of poetry, including *Collected Poems* (Wake Forest, 1995). He has alternated between Albany, as Poet-in-Residence at the New York State Writers' Institute, and West Cork. The Gallery Press re-

printed his *Collected Poems* in 1998. He edited The *Faber Book of Irish Verse* (1974) and published a volume of autobiographical reminiscences and literary essays *The Figure in the Cave* (1990). His *Death of a Chieftain* (1964) is a celebrated collection of short stories. In 1998, he was appointed first holder of the Ireland Chair of Poetry.

Moore, Thomas (1779 – 1852):
Thomas Moore's reputation rests in the main on his famous *Irish Melodies* which are based on airs recorded by Edward Bunting. A critic described the 1810 collection as having 'more politics than harmony'. Moore advocated the Catholic Nationalist tradition in the politics of the 1820s. His later years were suffused with distress and illness: he witnessed the death of his five children. Essentially a lyric poet, his sensitivity to the spirit of Irish Music and its rhythms had a hypnotic influence on Irish writing in English.

Muldoon, Paul (1951 –):
Professor in the Humanities at Princeton University. In 1999, Paul Muldoon was elected Professor of Poetry at the University of Oxford. His collections of poetry include N*ew Weather* (1973), *Meeting The British* (1987), *Madoc: A Mystery* (1990), *Hay* (1998), *Poems 1968-1998* (2001) and *Moy Sand and Gravel* (2002). A Fellow of the Royal Society of Literature and the American Academy of Arts and Sciences, he was given an American Academy of Arts and Letters award in literature in 1996. Other recent awards are the 1994 T. S. Eliot Prize, the 1997 *Irish Times* Poetry Prize and the Pulitzer Prize for Poetry in 2003. He has been described by *The Times Literary Supplement* as 'the most significant English-language poet born since the Second World War'.

Murphy, Richard (1927 –):
Richard Murphy was born in the west of Ireland in 1927. Major works as a poet include *The Battle of Aughrim* (1968), Faber, *High Island* (1974), Faber, and *The Price of Stone* (1985), Faber. Gallery Press published his *Collected Poems* in 2000. Richard published a memoir, *The Kick* (Granta), in 2002.

Ní Chonaill, Eibhlín Dubh (fl. 1770):
Eibhlín Dubh Ní Chonaill is famed for one of the great laments and memorable love poems in the Irish language. Educated, a member of the well-to-do O'Connell family in Derrynane, Co. Kerry, she eloped with Art Ó Laoghaire, a spirited young captain of the Hungarian Hussars back in Ireland from service in Europe. Both settled on the Ó Laoghaire lands near Macroom, Co. Cork. Outlawed by the High Sheriff of the district, Art Ó Laoghaire was shot dead on 4th May, 1773. Eibhlín Dubh's studied lament for him, *Caoineadh Airt Uí Laoghaire*, is in the folk tradition. She successfully prosecuted his killer.

Ní Chuilleanáin, Eiléan (1942 –):
Born in Cork 1942, now a Fellow of Trinity College, Dublin, Associate Professor of English, and Dean of the Faculty of Arts (Letters), Eiléan Ní Chuilleanáin's books of poetry include *Acts and Monuments* (1973), *Site of*

Ambush (1975), *The Second Voyage* (1977), *The Magdalene Sermon* (1989), *The Brazen Serpent* (1994) and *The Girl Who Married the Reindeer* (2001). In 1992, she received the O'Shaughnessy Award for Poetry from the Irish American Cultural Institute. In 1996, she was elected to *Aosdána*.

Ní Dhomhnaill, Nuala (1952 –):
Nuala Ní Dhomhnaill, born in Lancashire, England, in 1952 of Irish-speaking parents, grew up in the Dingle Gaeltacht and in Co. Tipperary. She attended University College, Cork, where she became involved with the *Innti* school of poets. The author of many volumes of poetry, including *The Astrakhan Cloak* (Gallery, 1992), she is a member of *Aosdána* and the recipient of the 1988 O'Shaughnessy Award for poetry and the 1991 American Ireland Fund Literary Award. *The Water Horse* (1999), with translations by Medbh McGuckian and Eiléan Ní Chuilleanáin, was published by The Gallery Press.

Ní Uallacháin, Pádraigín (1950 –):
Pádraigín Ní Uallacháin is a native Irish speaker from Oriel, a region that takes in part of counties Armagh, Monaghan and Louth. She has recorded six albums of traditional songs. Her father, Pádraig, was a collector of Gaelic folklore, and she is married to Len Graham, one of Ireland's most distinguished traditional singers. Pádraigín has worked as producer and presenter with RTÉ. Working as a full-time musician since 1999, she is the recipient of many cultural and academic awards and is the author of *A Hidden Ulster: People, Songs and Traditions of Oriel* (Four Courts Press). She tours extensively as singer and lecturer.

O'Callaghan, Julie (1954 –):
Julie O'Callaghan was born in Chicago and has lived in Ireland since 1974. She has published three collections of poetry for adults and two for children. She won the Michael Hartnett Award for Poetry in 2001. She works in the library of Trinity College Dublin. Her Collection *No Can Do* (2000) was a Poetry Book Society Recommendation.

O'Donoghue, Bernard (1945 –):
Bernard O'Donoghue lectures in medieval English at the University of Oxford. He was born in Cork, and his poetry often recalls his place of origin. His collection *Gunpowder* (1995) won the Whitbread Book of the Year Award. *Outliving* was published in 2003.

Ó Direáin, Máirtín (1910 – 1988):
Short-story writer, essayist and playwright, Máirtín Ó Direáin firmly established his reputation as a poet with *Rogha Danta* (1949). As with Ó Riordáin, there is a desolate aura about his poetry, suffused as it is with a wasting of personal, social and humane values in an environment that is hostile and impoverished in spirit and culture. Even in his darkest poems, however, Ó Direáin sounds out universals in a search for the authentic and the abiding. He was the recipient of many awards for his poetry. He worked as a civil servant with the Department of Education.

Ó Duinnlé, Seán (1812 - 1889):
Seán Ó Duinnlé was a poet from the Blasket Islands. He belonged to the landless class of labourers in the nineteenth century. His island community spoke his poetry and admired him greatly for the eloquence, beauty and strength of his poems.

Ó Flannghaile, Tomás (1846 – 1916):
Poet, teacher and editor, Tomás O'Flannghaile held teaching posts in England and learned to write Irish in his youth. He was one of the poets of the language revival movement and taught Irish classes in the Southwark Literary Society. He edited Mícheál Ó Coimín's *Laoi Oisín i dTír na nÓg* (1896) and Donnchad Rua MacConmara's *Eachtra Ghiolla an Amaráin* (1897). Donncha Ó Liatháin edited his poems and essays in *Tomás Ó Flannghaile, Scoláire agus File* (1940).

O'Grady, Desmond (1935 –):
Educated at UCD and Harvard, where he was awarded a doctorate in Celtic and Comparative Studies, Desmond O'Grady's prolific and underrated output of twenty-nine books of poetry and translation includes *The Dying Gaul* (1968), *Alexandra Notebook* (1989) and *Trawling Traditions: Translations, 1954 – 1994* (1994) with its versions of classical, Arabic and European poetry in the Poundian mode. A friend of Beckett in Paris and a befriender of Ezra Pound in Rome, where O'Grady taught for some time, he lives today at Kinsale, Co. Cork.

O'Hagan, John (1822 – 1890):
John O'Hagan in his time was political activist, Young Irelander, poet, translator and judge. Called to the bar in 1845, he became Queen's Counsel in 1865. Prime Minister Gladstone appointed him first Judicial Commissioner of the Irish Land Commission in 1881. He published a translation of *Le Chanson de Roland* before his death. His best-known poems were printed in *The Spirit of the Nation*.

Ó hÓgáin, Dáithí (1949 –):
Writer in Irish and English. Born Bruff, Co. Limerick, 1949. Author of seven books of poetry, three collections of short stories, and over twenty books on literary, folkloric and historical topics. His collected poems in English, *Footsteps from Another World*, was published in 2002. A well-known radio and TV broadcaster, he has lectured and read poetry throughout Ireland and in many other countries. Associate Professor of Irish Folklore at University College Dublin.

Ó Mileadha, Pádraig (1877 – 1947):
Pádraig Ó Mileadha came from Sliabh gCua, Co. Waterford which lies midway between Clonmel and Dungarvan. Sliabh gCua is famed for its Irish Gaelic heritage of song, learning, folklore and hospitality. According to Donnchad Rua MacConmara, who taught there, 'Shliabh Geal g-Cua rug buaidh na féile'/ 'bright Slieve gCua won the palm for hospitality' (*Eachtra Ghiolla an Amaráin*).

In 1903, Pádraig emigrated to Swansea in search of work. He became a trade union activist and got involved in local politics. 'Sliabh Geal gCua na Féile' is an exile's lament. Pádraig Ó Mileadha returned to Waterford in 1922, devoting the rest of his life to teaching and promoting the Irish Language in West Waterford around Dungarvan.

Ó Muiríosa, Seán (fl. 1890):

Seán Ó Muiríosa was a farmer from Tuar an Fhíona (Tooraneena) in the Sliabh gCua area of Waterford. He is remembered for composing a keen on the death of his daughter. In Ireland, elegies or keens/caoineadh constituted the most successful poetry of the nineteenth century.

Ó Reachtabhra, Antoine (Raifteirí) (1779 – 1835):

Raifteirí was born in Co. Mayo. Though blinded by smallpox as a boy and illiterate, he became one of Ireland's most famous wandering minstrels, his poems and songs responding to contemporary events, such as agrarian unrest and the campaigns of O'Connell for Catholic empowerment. Raifteirí wrote poems in the Irish love-song tradition, contentious verse with fellow poets, humorous poems and poems on historical themes. One of his most memorable songs is 'Eanach Dhúin', a sustained lament for people drowned in a boating accident at Annaghdown in Lough Corrib in 1828. Ciarán Ó Coigligh has edited *Raiftearaí: Amhráin agus Danta* (1987).

Ó Ríordáin, Seán (1916 – 1977):

Already isolated in the family home because of persistent tuberculosis, Seán Ó Ríordáin plunged even deeper into a dark interior 'mindspace' on the death of his mother, which left him living alone. His poetry bravely confronts essential questions about the nature of human existence and the individual's place in a universe with scant meaning. Working first as a clerk with Cork City Council, Seán Ó Ríordáin lectured later in Irish at University College, Cork where he profoundly influenced the young *Innti* generation of Irish Language poets. A celebrated work of his is *Eireaball Spideoige* (1952).

Ó Searcaigh, Cathal (1956 –):

Cathal Ó Searcaigh was born in the Donegal Gaeltacht in 1956. He studied French, Russian and Irish at the National Institute of Higher Education in Limerick and Celtic Studies at Maynooth College. He is author of many collections of poems, including *An Bealach 'na Bhaile/Homecoming: Selected Poems* (Clo Iar-Chonnachta, 1993). He was Writer-in-Residence at the University of Ulster and Queen's University, Belfast. Arlen House have published *On the Side of Light* (2002), a book of critical essays on Cathal Ó Searcaigh's work.

Ó Súilleabháin Amhlaoibh (1780 – 1858):

Amhlaoibh Ó Súilleabháin taught school in Callan, Co Kilkenny and ran a shop there. He is remembered for a remarkable diary which, while written in prose, clearly exhibits the rhythms of poetry.

Ó Tuama, Seán (1926 –):
Seán Ó Tuama was born in Cork. Retired Professor of Irish Language and Culture at University College Cork, he has lectured extensively in American, English and French Universities. Poet, playwright and editor, his anthology *An Duanaire 1600-1900: Poems of the Dispossessed* (1981) with Thomas Kinsella introduced the poetry in Irish of that period to a new and wider audience. His *Repossessions* (1995), selected essays on Irish Literary Heritage, examines in depth the poetry of Seán Ó Riordáin, Nuala Ní Dhomhnaill, Brian Merriman, Eibhlín Dubh Ní Chonaill (*Caoineadh Airt Uí Laoghaire*) and Aogán Ó Rathaille, among others.

Paulin, Tom (1949 –):
Poet, essayist, critic, university lecturer, T. V. panelist, dramatist and Faber editor, Tom Paulin has written eight books of poetry which include *Selected Poems 1972 – 1990, The Wind Dog* (1999) and *The Invasion Handbook* (2002). He has been influenced by the republican principles of the United Irishmen. Often lyrical and political in tone, his poetry is distinguished by a keen acerbic wit and a moral earnestness. He is a former director of Field Day and has adapted plays by Sophocles.

Sullivan, Timothy Daniel (1827 – 1914):
Brother to Alexander Martin Sullivan, editor of *The Nation* (1855 – 1877) and founder member of The Irish Party, Timothy Daniel Sullivan, nationalist, journalist and politician was MP for Westmeath (1880 – 1885), for Dublin (1885 – 1892), for Donegal (1892 – 1900) and Lord Mayor of Dublin (1886 – 1887). He is best known as the author of 'God Save Ireland', the unofficial national anthem of old nationalist Ireland. This was published in *The Nation* in 1867 to honour the Manchester Martyrs. His ballad with the opening line 'Deep in Canadian Woods' probably commemorates the Fenian Brotherhood Raids into Canada (1866 – 1870) contemporaneous with the abortive Irish Rising of 1867.

Waller, John Francis (1809 – 1894):
Poet and editor, John Francis Waller was a lawyer and became Registrar of Rolls in 1867. He was a founder member of the *Dublin University Magazine*. His verse and prose were collected as *The Slingsby Papers* (1852). 'The Spinning Wheel', popularised by Delia Murphy in the 1940s, is his most memorable song.

Wolfe, Rev Charles (1791 – 1823):
Clergyman and poet, Charles Wolfe is primarily remembered for 'The Burial of Sir John Moore'. The original copy, in Wolfe's own ms, is in the Royal Irish Academy, Dublin. Wolfe's poems were collected in 1825 and reprinted in 1903 by Caesar Litton Falkiner.

Yeats, W. B. (1865 – 1939):
W. B. Yeats was born in Dublin and won the Nobel Prize for literature in 1923. He is one of the great modernist figures of the twentieth century. He was poet,

playwright, essayist, critic, senator of the Irish Free State, founder of the Abbey Theatre and the most influential figure in the Irish Literary Revival at the turn of the twentieth century. Among his closest associates were the playwright John Millington Synge and the formidable Lady Gregory, while much of his poetry is haunted by the image of Maud Gonne. Yeats's work reflects a desire to transform the half-forgotten mythologies and folklore of Ireland into great literature and gives both name and impetus to the romantic idea of Ireland we have come to associate with the Celtic Twilight. Yeats was in part influenced in his poetic plays by the Japanese Noh drama. Among his many seminal poetic works are *Responsibilities* (1914) and *The Tower* (1928).

Acknowledgements (Ireland)

Thanks are due to the copyright holders of the following poems for permission to reprint them in this anthology. Poems are printed or reprinted by permission of the authors, or representatives, and publishers, as appropriate.

Campbell, Joseph: 'I Will Go With My Father A-Ploughing' from *The Poems of Joseph Campbell* (1963), edited by Austin Clarke, Allen Figgis.

Casey, John Keegan: 'The Rising of the Moon' from *Irish Minstrelsy Being a Selection of Irish Songs, Lyrics and Ballads*, edited with notes and introduction by H. Halliday Sparling, London: Walter Scott Ltd.

Clarke, Austin: 'Forget Me Not' from *Collected Poems*, Dolmen Press (1974). Reprinted by permission of R. Dardis Clarke, 17, Oscar Square, Dublin 8.

Coady, Michael: 'The Carrick Nine' from *One Another* (2003). Reprinted by permission of The Gallery Press.

Coffey, Brian: an excerpt from *Missouri Sequence* from *Poems and Versions 1929 – 1990* (1991). Reprinted by permission of The Dedalus Press.

Cronin, Anthony: *R.M.S. Titanic*. Reprinted by permission of the author. The poem was included in *Longer Contemporary Poems* (1966), Penguin.

Curran, J. P.: 'The Night Before Larry was Stretched' from *The Dublin Comic Songster: Containing a Choice Collection of Irish, English and Scottish Comic Songs* (1845), James Duffy: Angelsea Street.

Devlin, Denis: 'The Tomb of Michael Collins' from *Collected Poems of Denis Devlin* (1989), edited by J.C.C. Mays. Reprinted by permission of The Dedalus Press.

Durcan, Paul: 'Early Christian Ireland Wedding Cry' from *Cries of an Irish Caveman* (2001), published by Harvill Press. Reprinted by permission of The Random House Group.

Garvey, Alan: 'Snipers in Derelict Houses'. Printed by permission of the author.

Groarke, Vona: an excerpt from 'The Bower' from *Flight* (2002). Reprinted by permission of The Gallery Press.

Healy, James N.: 'A Sweet Little Song' from *Irish Songs of the Sea*, Ossian, published in association with Mercier Press. Reprinted by permission of John Loesberg, Ossian Publications.

Heaney, Seamus: 'Clearances' and excerpt from *Sweeney Astray* from *Opened Ground* (1998). Reprinted by permission of Faber and Faber.

Hewitt, John: 'The Green Shoot', 'The Scar', 'A Belfastman Abroad Argues with Himself', 'Calling on Peadar O'Donnell at Dungloe', 'In recollection of Drumcliffe, September 1948' and 'Eager Journey' from *The Collected Poems of John Hewitt* (1991). Reprinted by permission of Blackstaff Press on behalf of the estate of John Hewitt.

Hyde, Douglas: the translations *'The Coolun'* / 'An Chúilfionn', *'Breed Astore'* / 'Brighid A Stóir, *'Oh, Youth Whom I Have Kissed'* / 'Cailín Beag an Ghleanna' from *Abhráin Ghradha Chuige Chonnacht, Love Songs of Chonnacht being the fourth chapter of the Songs of Chonnacht* (1895), 2nd edition, Gill and Sons, Dublin.

Kavanagh, Patrick: 'Epic', 'The One', 'On Raglan Road' and excerpt from *The Great Hunger* from *Selected Poems* (2000). Reprinted by permission of the Trustees of the Estate of the late Katherine B. Kavanagh, through the Jonathan Williams Literary Agency.

Kinsella, Thomas: 'Butcher's Dozen (1972)', 'Dick King', 'The Poet Egan O'Rahilly, Homesick in Old Age', 'The Route of *The Tain'* from *Collected Poems* (2001) Carcanet. For his translations as follows: excerpt from *The Lament for Art Ó Laoghaire*, excerpt from The Midnight Court, 'Eanach Dhúin', 'A Father's Lament', 'A Widow's Lament', 'The Jail of Clonmel', 'Remember that Night', 'Deirín Dé', 'Blessed Mary', 'To Christ the Seed'. All reprinted by permission of the author. Original texts in Irish from *An Duanaire* by permission of Bord na Gaeilge.

Longley, Michael: 'The Butchers' and 'Wounds' from *Selected Poems* by Michael Longley, published by Jonathan Cape. Reprinted by permission of The Random House Group.

MacConmara, Donnchad Rua: excerpt from 'Eachtra Ghiolla an Amaráin' / *'Adventures of a Luckless Fellow'* from *Eachtra Ghiolla an Amaráin and other poems* (1897) edited by Tomás Ó Flannghaile, Sealy, Bryers and Walker; for 'Donnchad Rua i dTàlamh-an-Éisc' / *'Donnchad Rua in Newfoundland'* from *Dánta agus Beatha Donnchadha Ruaidh Mhic Chonmara* (1907) by Seaghán Pléimionn, Comhlucht Oideachais na hÉireann, Teor.

Mac Lochlainn, Gearóid: 'Ciréib' / *'Riot'*, 'Paddy' / *'Paddy'* from *Sruth Teangacha / Stream of Tongues* (2003). Reprinted by permission of Cló Iar-Chonnachta.

Mhac an tSaoi, Máire: the translations *'The Red-Haired Man Reproaches His Wife'* / 'Bean An Fhir Rua'; *'Tobacco Shortage'* / 'Gábhar Thobac' and *'Keep to Yourself Your Kisses'* / 'Taisigh Agad Féin Do Phóg' from *Trasládáil*

(1997), published by Lagan Press. Reprinted by permission of Máire Mhac an tSaoi.

McGuckian, Medbh: 'River of January', 'Slieve Gallion' and 'Hearing the Weather Fall' from *Had I A Thousand Lives* (2003). Reprinted by permission of The Gallery Press.

Mahon, Derek: 'The Snow Party' from *Collected Poems* (1999). Reprinted by permission of The Gallery Press.

Mangan, James Clarence: 'Siberia' from *Poems* (2003), edited and introduced by David Wheatley. *Poems* (2003) is published by The Gallery Press.

Meehan, Paula: 'The Statue of the Virgin at Granard Speaks' from *The Man Who Was Marked by Winter* (1991). Reprinted by permission of The Gallery Press.

Millikin, Dick: 'De groves of de Pool' from *The Popular Songs of Ireland* by Thomas Crofton Croker (m.dcc.xxxix), Henry Colburn.

Montague, John: 'Hymn to the New Omagh Road' from *The Rough Field* (1989). Reprinted by permission of The Gallery Press and Wake Forest University Press.

Moore, Thomas: 'A Pastoral Ballad by John Bull' from *The Faber Book of Irish Verse* (1974), edited by John Montague.

Muldoon, Paul: 'Incantata' from *The Annals of Chile* (1994). Reprinted by permission of Farrar, Straus and Giroux and Faber and Faber.

Murphy, Richard: 'The Cleggan Disaster' and an excerpt from *The Battle of Aughrim* from *Collected Poems* (2000). Reprinted by permission of The Gallery Press and Wake Forest University Press.

Ní Chuilleanáin, Eiléan: 'The Second Voyage' from *The Second Voyage* (1986). Reprinted by permission of The Gallery Press and Wake Forest University Press.

Ní Dhomhnaill, Nuala: 'Peirsifine' / '*Persephone Suffering from SAD*' and 'An Snag Breac' with translations by Medbh McGuckian from *The Water Horse* (1999). Reprinted by permission of The Gallery Press.

Ní Uallacháin, Pádraigín: the translations '*Rise Up My Darling*' / 'Éirigh Suas, a Stóirín', '*We Brought the Summer With Us*' / 'Thugamar Féin an Samhradh Linn', '*The White Calves*' / 'Na Gamhna Geala' and '*A Lass from County Louth*' / 'Cailín as Contae Lú' from *A Hidden Ulster: People, Songs and*

Traditions of Oriel (2003), published by Four Courts Press. Reprinted by permission of Pádraigín Ní Uallacháin.

O'Callaghan, Julie: excerpts from 'Sketches for an Elegy' from *No Can Do* (2000). Reprinted by permission of Bloodaxe Books.

Ó Direáin, Máirtín: 'Dínit an Bhróin' / *'Grief's Dignity'*, 'Cranna Foirtil' / *'Stout Oars'* and 'Berkeley' / *'Berkeley'* from Máirtín Ó Direáin, *Tacar Dánta / Selected Poems* (1984), edited by Tomás Mac Síomóin and Douglas Sealy, Goldsmith.

O'Donoghue, Bernard: 'Telegrams' and 'The Twisting of the Rope' from *Outliving* (2003), published by Chatto & Windus. Reprinted by permission of The Random House Group.

Ó Flannghaile, Tomás: excerpt from 'Eachtra Ghiolla an Amaráin' / *The Adventures of a Luckless Fellow* from *Eachtra Ghiolla an Amaráin and other poems*, Sealy, Bryers and Walker, Dublin, 1897.

O'Grady, Desmond: 'Homecoming' from *The Road Taken: Poems 1956–1996*, (1996) Salzburg University Press. Reprinted by permission of the author.

O'Hagan, John: 'Famine and Exportation' from *Songs and Ballads of Young Ireland* (1869), edited by Martin MacDermott, Downey and Sons, London.

Ó Mileadha, Pádraig: 'Sliabh Geal gCua na Féile' / *'Bright and Welcoming Mountain'*. Reprinted by permission of David & Maurice O'Hallahan.

Ó Ríordáin, Seán: 'Adhlacadh Mo Mháthar' / *'My Mother's Burial'* from *Eireaball Spideoige* (1952); 'Claustrophobia' / *'Claustrophobia'*, 'Reo' / *'Freeze'*, 'Fiabhras' / *'Fever'* and 'Na Leamhain' / *'The Moths'* from *Brosna* (1964). Reprinted by permission of Sáirséal Ó Marcaigh.

Ó Searcaigh, Cathal: 'Do Jack Kerouac' / *'To Jack Kerouac'*, 'Transubstaintiú'/ *'Transubstantiation'*, 'Dia: Nótaí Anailísí' / *'God: Analyst's Notes'*, 'Haikú' / *'Haiku'* and 'I gCeann mo Thrí Bliana a Bhí Mé' / *When I Was Three* from *An Bealach 'na Bhaile / Homecoming* (2000). Reprinted by permission of Cló Iar-Chonnachta.

Paulin, Tom: 'Purity' from *The Strange Museum* (1980), for 'A Nation, Yet Again', 'Desertmartin' and 'Of Difference Does It Make' from *Liberty Tree* (1983). Reprinted by permission of Faber and Faber.

Waller, John Francis: 'The Spinning Wheel' from *The Slingsby Papers* (1852) and featured in James N. Healy's *Love Songs of the Irish* (1977).

Wolfe, Rev. Charles: 'The Burial of Sir John Moore' from *The Ballad Poetry of Ireland,* edited by Sir Charles Gavin Duffy. A facsimile reproduction of the fourth edition (1869), with an introduction by Leonard R. N. Ashley, Scholar's Facsimile and Reprints, Dillmar, New York, 1973.

Yeats, W. B.: 'The Song of Wandering Aengus', excerpt from 'The Wanderings of Oisin', 'Down By the Salley Gardens', 'In Memory of Eva Gore-Booth and Con Markiewicz', 'Easter 1916', excerpt from 'Meditations in Time of Civil War', 'The Wild Swans at Coole' and 'Sailing to Byzantium' by permission of A. P. Watt on behalf of Michael B. Yeats from *W. B. Yeats Selected Poems* (2000), Penguin Classics.

Notes on the Ballads and Songs of Ireland

According to Colm O Lochlainn[1], the ballad is an 'authentic reflex of the Irish spirit in Gaelic or in English'. Ballads and songs are part of the poetic tradition, being indissolubly linked with it. They speak for the people, and comment on life by telling some story or other in a popular style. Disdaining the high-brow or pretentious, the anonymous ballad has always been a significant medium of the people for heightened remembrance of local events in good times and in bad. The speaker, or singer, represents a local viewpoint, albeit personalised, and disappears for safety reasons and sometimes with good cause, apparently satisfied, anonymously back into the crowd. One remembers the brutal treatment meted out to the young ballad maker John Keegan Casey in prison.

'Priosún Chluain Meala' /' *The Jail of Clonmel*' and 'Na Connerys' / '*The Connerys*' highlight the legal injustices and draconian law enforcement policies of their periods. 'Henry Joy McCracken' and 'Rody McCorley', along with 'The Croppy Boy' and 'Boolavogue', celebrate executed heroes of the 1798 Rebellion. 'Dublin After the Union' satirises the nefarious politics associated with the 1800 Act of Union between Great Britain and Ireland. 'Annie Moore' recounts the killing of seventeen-year-old Ann Moore on the way to visit a friend during an Orange versus Green riot in Belfast in 1835. 'Carrickfergus', 'The Streams of Bunclody', and 'The Belfast Mountains' speak of personal dislocation and loss of love for reasons stated or unstated. The sequence 'An Chúilfhionn' to 'An cuimhin leat an óiche úd' treats of the varied constancy, or inconstancies, of love.

'The Tramway Line' sings of the extension of the Belfast tramway system to Balmoral in the early 1890s. It is in the music hall idiom with a sing-along chorus. 'The *Montague*', with its chorus, is a Wexford sea song. The chorus, uniting the singer with his or her audience, is a feature of many of the pieces chosen.

Songs of labour and toil, songs of partying sometimes linked with the macabre, reflect the actual nature of existence as people saw it and experienced it themselves.

The authors are indebted as follows:

'The Banks of Newfoundland', **'The Montague'**, from *Songs of the Wexford Coast 1948,* collected by Joseph Ransom, C.C., John English & Co. Limited, Wexford.

'Dublin after the Union' from *Popular Songs of Ireland* 1886, collected by Thomas Crofton Croker with an introduction by Henry Morley. London:

---

[1] Colm O' Lochlainn's comprehensive collections of Irish ballads include his *Irish Street Ballads* (first and second collections).

George Routledge and Sons Ludgate Hill, New York: 9 Lafette Place, Broadway. It is believed that this song was penned by Edward Lysaght (1763 - 1810). Born in Clare, Edward entered T.C.D. in 1779. He was called to the bar in 1788 and settled in Dublin. His reputation as poet and wit was very great. His poems and songs were published posthumously as *Poems* in 1811.

'The Pope' and **'Finnegan's Wake'** from *The Dublin Comic Songster; Containing a Choice Collection of Irish, English and Scottish Comic Songs*, Dublin (1845): published by James Duffy, Anglesea Street.

'The Belfast Mountains', **'The Tramway Line'**, **'Henry Joy McCracken'**, and **'Annie Moore'** from *Belfast City of Song* (1989), edited by Maurice Leyden, with a foreword by David Hammond, Brandon/Mount Eagle Publications.

'Carrickfergus', a song of uncertain origin, and in its various forms, incomplete; from *Songs of the Irish* (1977), selected and edited by James N. Healy, The Mercier Press.

'The Streams of Bunclody', a lilting triste melody from Co. Wexford: Bunclody lies beneath Mount Leinster's shadow; from *Love Songs of the Irish* (1977), selected and edited by James N. Healy, The Mercier Press.

'The Shoals of Herring'. The text of the original ballad by Ewan MacColl is given here. It was written for the BBC Radio documentary 'Singing the Fishing' in the Radio Ballad Session (1959). The Irish folk group, The Clancy Brothers, appropriated MacColl's song for an Irish consciousness and a new version emerged, telling of a skirmish between the Kilkeel and Passage East fishermen:
Territorial waters meant naught to us
Sure and hadn't we an Irish rearin'
And on top of that we'd the Dail's permission
To go sailing after shoals of herrin'....
The original text, however, remained the favourite for Irish audiences and is found in Pete Seeger's book *The Incompleat Folksinger*.
Copyright 1962 by STORM KING MUSIC. INC.

'Na Connerys / *The Connerys'*, 'Dónall Óg / *Young Donal*' and **'An Droighneán Donn /** *The Dark Thorn* **Tree**' from *Binneas Thar Meon* (1994). Iml. 1. Cnuasach d'amhráin agus de cheolta a dhein Liam de Noraidh in oirthear Mumhan / *A collection of songs and airs made by Liam de Noraidh in east Munster,* edited by Dáithí Ó hÓgáin in collaboration with Marion Deasy

NOTES 593

and Ríonach uí Ógáin, Comhairle Bhéaloideas Éireann, An Coláiste Ollscoile, Baile Átha Cliath.

'The Croppy Boy' and **'The Spinning Wheel'** from *A Treasury of Irish Poetry* (1990), edited by Stopford A. Brook, T. W. Rolleston, Smith, Elder & Co. London.

'Boolavogue', ballad published in sheet music (1951), Walton Manuscripts Ltd. Dublin. There are different versions of this ballad from different sources. The original was written by P. J. McCall.

'Deep in the Canadian Woods' written by Timothy Daniel Sullivan and published in *Ireland The Songs* (1993) vol. 2, Walton Manuscripts Ltd. Dublin.

'Na Gamhna Geala' is thought to be a veiled reference to the times of the Wild Geese. Another version of the song is 'Na Géadhna Geala' / *'The White Geese'*.

Additional contextual commentary is provided in the relevant biographical notes.

Index of poets

A
Avis, Nick 272
Augustine, Donna (Thunderbird Turtle Woman) 551

B
Babstock, Ken 427, 429, 430
Burke, Johnny 103, 105
Butt, Len 59
Byrne, Pat 97

C
Campbell, Joseph 54
Casey, John Keegan 72
Clarke, Austin 264
Coady, Michael 117
Coffey, Brian 258
Cronin, Anthony 189
Crummey, Michael 389, 391, 392, 393, 394, 396, 398, 399, 400, 402, 403
Curran, J. P. 111

D
Dalton, Mary 306, 307, 308, 309, 310
Dawe, Tom 289, 290, 292, 294, 295
Devine, John 57
Devlin, Denis 255
Dicker, Sid 181
Durcan, Paul 547

E
Elliott, David 334, 337, 338, 339, 340, 342, 343

F
Francis, Bernie (Translator) 183

G
Garvey, Alan 532
Grace, John 12
Groarke, Vona 471

H
Healy, James N. 153
Heaney, Seamus 367, 372
Hewitt, John 453, 454, 455, 456, 457, 458
Hutchings, Eugene 61

K
Kavanagh, Patrick 273, 274, 275, 279
Kelland, Otto 27
Kinsella, Thomas 65, 280, 345, 356

L
LeMessurier, H. W. 21
Longley, Michael 468, 469
Loon, Morley 551
Lysaght, Edward 82

M
McBurney, William B. 77
McCall, P. J. 73
MacColl, Ewan 26
MacConmara, Donnchad Rua 32, 45
McGrath, Carmelita 478, 480, 482, 483, 484, 486, 487, 488
McGuckian, Medbh 494, 496, 497
MacKenzie, Marguerite (Translator) 5
Mac Lochlainn, Gearóid 444, 446
Mahon, Derek 271
Mangan, James Clarence 94
Meehan, Paula 475
Merriman, Brian 138
Mhac an tSaoi, Máire 499, 501, 504
Millikin, Dick 79
Montague, John 362
Moore, Thomas 85
Muldoon, Paul 535
Murphy, Richard 219, 348

N
Ní Chonaill, Eibhlín Dubh 125
Ní Chuilleanáin, Eiléan 505
Ní Dhomhnaill, Nuala 489, 491

O
O'Callaghan, Julie   377
Ó Direáin, Máirtín   282, 284, 286
O'Donoghue, Bernard   463, 465
Ó Duinnlé, Seán   499
O'Grady, Desmond   466
O'Hagan, John   92
Ó Mileadha, Pádraig   62
Ó Muiríosa, Seán   43
Ó Reachtabhra / Raifteirí, Antoine   38
Ó Ríordáin, Seán   324, 328, 329, 330, 332
Ó Searcaigh, Cathal   433, 438, 439, 440, 442
Ó Súilleabháin, Amhlaoibh   87

P
Paulin, Tom   459, 460, 461, 462
Payne, Daniel   24
Payne, Stephanie   58
Pittman, Al   97, 177, 178, 507, 509, 511, 515, 517, 519, 521, 522, 524
Pittman, Kyran   531
Power, Gregory   288
Pratt, E. J.   200, 204, 229, 231, 232, 233

R
Rich, Edward (Narrator)   1

S
Savard, Michel   525
Scammell, Arthur   113
Steffler, John   405, 406, 407, 408, 409, 410, 411, 412, 414, 415, 416, 417, 418, 420, 422, 423, 424
Sullivan, Timothy Daniel   52

T
Tuglavina, Joe K.   234

W
Wadham   9
Walker, Mark   55, 147

Waller, John Francis   157
Walsh, Des   298, 299, 300, 301, 302, 303, 304, 305
Wareham, Baxter   109
Watts, Enos   311, 313, 314, 315, 317, 319, 320, 321, 322, 323
Withers, Jack   11
Wolfe, Rev. Charles   83

Y
Yeats, W. B.   236, 237, 242, 243, 244, 247, 252, 253

Index of titles

A Belfastman Abroad Argues with Himself	John Hewitt	455
A Great Big Sea Hove in Long Beach	Trad	23
A Mhuire na nGrás / *Blessed Mary*	Trad	184
'A narrow escape almost but saved'. (1892)	Michael Crummey	393
A Nation, Yet Again	Tom Paulin	462
A Pastoral Ballad by John Bull	Thomas Moore	85
A Sweet Little Song	James N. Healy	153
'a wedge of geese . . .'	Nick Avis	272
Adam and Eve on a Winter Afternoon	Carmelita McGrath	480
Adhlacadh Mo Mháthar / *My Mother's Burial*	Seán Ó Ríordáin	324
Ag Críost An Síol / *To Christ The Seed*	Trad	187
'after making love . . .'	Nick Avis	272
An Chúilfhionn / *The Cooleen,* or *Coolun*	Trad	151
An cuimhin leat an oíche úd / *Remember that Night*	Trad	175
An Draighneán Donn / *The Dark Thorn Tree*	Trad	173
'An old sailor's portion'. (1932)	Michael Crummey	398
An Snag Breac /		
Ten Ways of Looking at a Magpie	Nuala Ní Dhomhnaill	491
Annie Moore	Trad	91
Anti-Confederation Song	Trad	96
Apoqnmuinen / *Thank You Great Spirit*	Morley Loon, Donna Augustine	551
Arriving in Russell	John Steffler	423
'At home on a cold winter's night. The changing scenes of Life'. (1928)	Michael Crummey	396
Bachelor Brothers	Mary Dalton	306
Baked in Chocolate	Carmelita McGrath	487
Bean an Fhir Rua / *The Red-Haired Man Reproaches*		
His Wife Who Has Left Him	File Gan Ainm	500
Berkeley / *Berkeley*	Máirtín Ó Direáin	286
Betsy Brennan's Blue Hen	Johnny Burke	105
Bogwood	Gregory Power	288
Boiler Room Men	John Steffler	407
Bonavista	Ken Babstock	430
Boolavogue	P. J. McCall	73
Bottled Rabbit	Ken Babstock	427
Breaking Ice	Carmelita McGrath	483
Brighid a Stóir / *Breed Astore*	Trad	159
Brin	Mary Dalton	307
Bucksaw Blues	Eugene Hutchings	61
Butcher's Dozen (1972)	Thomas Kinsella	356
Cailín as Contae Lú / *A Lass From County Louth*	Trad	169

Cailín Beag an Ghleanna /		
Oh, Youth Whom I Have Kissed	Trad	161
Cain	Enos Watts	317
Calling on Peadar O'Donnell at Dungloe	John Hewitt	456
As: Caoineadh Airt Uí Laoghaire /		
From: *The Lament for Art Ó Laoghaire*	Eibhlín Dubh Ní Chonaill	125
Caoineadh Athar / *A Father's Lament*	Seán Ó Muiríosa	43
Caoineadh Baintrí / *A Widow's Lament*	Amhlaoibh Ó Súilleabháin	87
Carrickfergus	Trad	49
Cedar Cove	John Steffler	418
Chrissey's Dick	Trad	108
Círéib / *Riot*	Gearóid Mac Lochlainn	444
Claustrophobia / *Claustrophobia*	Seán Ó Ríordáin	328
Clearances	Seamus Heaney	367
Come Away, Death	E. J. Pratt	229
Come Not the Seasons Here	E. J. Pratt	233
Confrontation	Enos Watts	319
Cradle Hill	Al Pittman	178
Cranna Foirtil / *Stout Oars*	Máirtín Ó Direáin	284
As: Cúirt an Mheán Oíche /		
From: *The Midnight Court*	Brian Merriman	138
Daedalus	Tom Dawe	295
De groves of de Pool	Dick Millikin	79
dead Indians	Mary Dalton	310
Deep in the Canadian Woods	Timothy Daniel Sullivan	52
Deirín Dé / *Deirín Dé*	Trad	179
Desertmartin	Tom Paulin	460
Dia: Nótaí Anailísé / *God: Analyst's Notes*	Cathal Ó Searcaigh	439
Dick King	Thomas Kinsella	280
Dínit an Bhróin / *Grief's Dignity*	Máirtín Ó Direáin	282
'Distance from Newfoundland.		
Northernmost grave in the world'. (1913)	Michael Crummey	394
Do Jack Kerouac / *To Jack Kerouac*	Cathal Ó Searcaigh	433
Dónall Óg / *Young Donal*	Trad	171
Donnchad Ruadh i dTalamh-an-Éisc /		
Donnchad Ruadh in Newfoundland	Donnchad Rua MacConmara	45
Down by the Salley Gardens	W. B. Yeats	242
Drawing Skeletons	Ken Babstock	429
'Dritheog nó dhó fágtha . . .', /		
'*An ember or two glow . . .*'	Cathal Ó Searcaigh	440
Dublin After the Union	Edward Lysaght	82
'ducks swoop low . . .'	John Steffler	415
As: Eachtra Ghiolla an Amaráin / From: *The Adventures*		
of a Luckless Fellow	Donnchad Rua MacConmara	32
Eanach Dhúin / *Eanach Dhúin*	Antoine Ó Reachtabhra / Raifteirí	38

Index of Titles

Eager Journey	John Hewitt	458
Early Christian Ireland Wedding Cry	Paul Durcan	547
Easter 1916	W. B. Yeats	244
Edwardians (Old Photograph)	Tom Dawe	294
Éirigh Suas, a Stóirín / Rise Up, My Darling	Trad	163
Epic	Patrick Kavanagh	273
Erosion	E. J. Pratt	232
Famine and Exportation	John O'Hagan	92
Fanny's Harbour Bawn	Mark Walker	147
Fiabhras / Fever	Seán Ó Ríordáin	330
Finnegan's Wake	Trad	99
Flame	Michael Crummey	400
Fog City	Michael Crummey	402
For the First Time in Months, She Feels Her Feet	Carmelita McGrath	482
Forget Me Not (1962)	Austin Clarke	264
Frank	David Elliott	338
Gábhar Thobac / Tobacco Shortage	Seán Ó Duinnlé	499
'Gealach na gcoinleach' / 'Harvest moon'	Cathal Ó Searcaigh	440
Giant Hare	Marguerite MacKenzie (Translator)	5
Gram Glover's Dream	Al Pittman	509
Haikú / Haiku	Cathal Ó Searcaigh	440
'he's out there . . .'	John Steffler	409
Hearing the Weather Fall	Medbh McGuckian	497
Henry Joy McCracken	Trad	74
Home Free	Stephanie Payne	58
Homecoming	Desmond O'Grady	466
How She Had Her Nervous Breakdown	Carmelita McGrath	484
Hymn to the New Omagh Road	John Montague	362
I gCeann mo Thrí Bliana, a Bhí Mé / When I Was Three	Cathal Ó Searcaigh	442
I love you more than any God, not falsely	Des Walsh	305
'I thought I was headed . . .'	John Steffler	412
I Will Go With My Father A-Ploughing	Joseph Campbell	54
If I Could Give You Now	Carmelita McGrath	478
In Memory of Eva Gore-Booth and Con Markiewicz	W. B. Yeats	243
In Picasso's 'Madman'	Tom Dawe	292
In recollection of Drumcliffe, September 1948	John Hewitt	457
Incantata	Paul Muldoon	535
Jerry Ryan	Len Butt	59

Kelly at Graveside	Al Pittman	515
Let Me Fish Off Cape St. Mary's	Otto Kelland	27
Lighthouse	David Elliott	337
Living Alone	Al Pittman	519
Longliner at Sunset	Enos Watts	321
Lukey's Boat	Trad	18
Mad Moll and Crazy Betty	Mary Dalton	308
Magdalen at the Tomb	David Elliott	343
'Magic lantern'. (April 1889)	Michael Crummey	389
March 3, 1999—Notes on an upcoming anniversary	Des Walsh	298
Mattie	David Elliott	339
From: Meditations in Time of Civil War	W. B. Yeats	247
Meshapush	Edward Rich (Narrator)	1
From: *Missouri Sequence*:		
Nightfall, Midwinter, Missouri	Brian Coffey	258
Mo bhrón ar an bhfarraige / *My grief on the ocean*	Trad	155
My friend's death	Des Walsh	302
Na Connerys / *The Connerys*	Trad	70
Na Gamhna Geala / *The White Calves*	Trad	167
Na Leamhain / *The Moths*	Seán Ó Ríordáin	332
Naming the Islands	Michael Crummey	403
'Nels and his wife . . .'	John Steffler	410
Nels: 'From the month of June . . .'	John Steffler	416
Nels: 'There was my great-uncle . . .'	John Steffler	415
Nels: 'This one spring . . .'	John Steffler	417
North Twin Lakes	Trad	101
'Now in Africa among the Natives'. (1891)	Michael Crummey	392
Of Difference Does it Make	Tom Paulin	459
'Oíche fhada gheimhridh—' /		
'*Long Winter's night*—'	Cathal Ó Searcaigh	440
Old Holly	Mary Dalton	308
Old Roman Candle	Mary Dalton	309
On a train heading northeast	Des Walsh	299
On being Catholic and loving the treachery of winter	Des Walsh	304
On Raglan Road	Patrick Kavanagh	279
'on the bunk . . .'	John Steffler	414
Othello's Own Brother	David Elliott	334
Paddy / *Paddy*	Gearóid Mac Lochlainn	448
Pat Murphy's Meadow	John Devine	57
Peirsifine / *Persephone Suffering from SAD*	Nuala Ní Dhomhnaill	489
Priosún Chluain Meala / *The Jail of Clonmel*	Trad	67
Purity	Tom Paulin	461

R.M.S. Titanic	Anthony Cronin	189
Reo / *Freeze*	Seán Ó Ríordáin	329
Resonance	David Elliott	340
River of January	Medbh McGuckian	494
Rody McCorley	Trad	75
Rosella and Bride	Mary Dalton	306
Roses and Attic Throats	Enos Watts	322
RosiaKKulak / *Beautiful Rose*	Joe K. Tuglavina	234
Rubber Boots	Baxter Wareham	109
Sailing to Byzantium	W. B. Yeats	253
Saint Laurence's Tears	John Steffler	406
Shanadithit	Al Pittman	511
Siberia	James Clarence Mangan	94
From: Sketches for an Elegy	Julie O'Callaghan	377
Sliabh Geal gCua na Féile / *Bright and Welcoming Mountain*	Pádraig Ó Mileadha	62
Slieve Gallion	Medbh McGuckian	496
Smoke	John Steffler	422
Snipers in Derelict Houses	Alan Garvey	532
'snowdrifts at my door . . .'	Nick Avis	272
Sour Fire	John Steffler	420
'Speal mo sheanathar . . .', / *'My grandfather's scythe . . .'*	Cathal Ó Searcaigh	440
Squid-jiggin' Ground	Arthur Scammell	113
St. Leonard's Revisited	Al Pittman	524
Stones	Michael Crummey	399
Summer Night Heat	Carmelita McGrath	488
Summer Solstice	Enos Watts	311
Surutsiutluta / *When We Were Children*	Sid Dicker	181
From: *Sweeney Astray*	Seamus Heaney	372
Taisigh Agad Féin Do Phóg / *Keep to Yourself Your Kisses*	Máire Mhac an tSaoi (Translator)	503
Talking to Trees	David Elliott	342
Telegrams	Bernard O'Donoghue	463
That Night We Were Ravenous	John Steffler	424
The Adventures of a Luckless Fellow	Donnchad Rua MacConmara	35
The Balcony Door	Enos Watts	315
The Banks of Newfoundland	Trad	28
From: *The Battle of Aughrim*	Richard Murphy	348
The Belfast Mountains	Trad	150
From: 'The Bower'	Vona Groarke	471
The Burial of Sir John Moore	Rev. Charles Wolfe	83
The Butchers	Michael Longley	468
The Carrick Nine	Michael Coady	117
The Cleggan Disaster	Richard Murphy	219

The Cliffs of Baccalieu	Jack Withers	11
The Cost of a Good Canoe	Al Pittman	507
The Croppy Boy	William B. McBurney	77
The Dandelion Killers	Al Pittman	521
The Dark-eyed Sailor	Trad	144
The Fish / *La pêche*	Michel Savard	525
The Fog	E. J. Pratt	231
The French Shore Man	Tom Dawe	290
The Government Game	Pat Byrne, Al Pittman	97
From: *The Great Hunger*	Patrick Kavanagh	275
The Green Shoot	John Hewitt	453
The Ground Swell	E. J. Pratt	232
The Horses	John Steffler	405
The Ice-Floes	E. J. Pratt	200
The Kelligrews Soiree	Johnny Burke	103
The Launch, Trinity Shipbuilders, Trinity, June 24, 1995	Des Walsh	303
The Lord's Prayer	Bernie Francis	183
The *Montague*	Trad	20
The Mummer	Tom Dawe	289
The New Sled	John Steffler	408
The Night Before Larry Was Stretched	J. P. Curran	111
The One	Patrick Kavanagh	274
The Petty Harbour Bait Skiff	John Grace	12
The Pigeon on the Gate	Al Pittman	517
The Pink, White and Green	Al Pittman	522
The Poet Egan O'Rahilly, Homesick in Old Age	Thomas Kinsella	65
The Pope	Trad	115
'The price of fish'. (September, 1887)	Michael Crummey	391
The Prison of Newfoundland	Trad	51
The Red-Throated Loon	Enos Watts	313
The Rising of the Moon	John Keegan Casey	72
From: *The Roosevelt and the Antinoe*	E. J. Pratt	204
The Route of *The Táin*	Thomas Kinsella	345
The Ryans and the Pittmans	H. W. LeMessurier	21
The Scar	John Hewitt	454
The Second Coming	Kyran Pittman	531
The Second Voyage	Eiléan Ní Chuilleanáin	505
The Shoals of Herring	Ewan MacColl	26
The Snow Party	Derek Mahon	271
The Song of Wandering Aengus	W. B. Yeats	236
The Spinning Wheel	John Francis Waller	157
The Statue of the Virgin at Granard Speaks	Paula Meehan	475
The Streams of Bunclody	Trad	50
The Tomb of Michael Collins	Denis Devlin	255
The Tramway Line	Trad	146
The triangle of the heart	Des Walsh	300
The Twisting of the Rope	Bernard O'Donoghue	465

The Veteran (1)	Tom Dawe	295
'the village graveyard . . .'	Nick Avis	272
From: The Wanderings of Oisin	W. B. Yeats	237
The *Water Witch*	Trad	15
The Wave that Hit St. Brides	Daniel Payne	24
The Wild Swans at Coole	W. B. Yeats	252
The Wreck of the Steamship *Ethie*	Trad	30
'the young plum pickers . . .'	Nick Avis	272
'they all save . . .'	John Steffler	411
Thugamar Féin an Samhradh Linn / *We Brought the Summer With Us*	Trad	165
Tickle Cove Pond	Mark Walker	55
Touring the Manor Houses	Carmelita McGrath	486
Transubstaintiú / *Transubstantiation*	Cathal Ó Searcaigh	438
Uvanga, Uvanga	Trad (Inuktitut)	186
Wadhams Song	Wadham	9
Waiting for Sunrise: Early December	Enos Watts	323
'we return . . .'	Nick Avis	272
Wednesday	Des Walsh	301
'when the rain comes . . .'	John Steffler	412
Window	Enos Watts	314
Wounds	Michael Longley	469
Yo-yo	Enos Watts	320

Index of First Lines

A

A Bhríghid a stóir ná pós an sean duine	159
A cairn of stones tells the story	394
A cobble thrown a hundred years ago	367
A dream: of a stand of pole birch straight ahead	427
A great big sea hove in Long Beach	23
A honey mist on a day of frost, in a dark oak wood	152
A hundred men think that I belong to them when I drink ale. I	174
A long thin line	509
A lot of it was learning to live with cruelty. To live cruelly	399
A man is breaking ice outside his front door which faces east and	483
A man lived down by the castle	465
A mheaig, a shnaig bhric	491
A Mhuire na ngrás	184
A ógánaigh óig mar reultan tríd an g-ceó	161
A Shliabh gheal gCua na féile, is fada uait i gcéin mé	62
A short jacket is being made since morning for us, and a trousers	71
'a wedge of geese . . .	272
A white wind tore	315
Aboard a Scotch boat shipping a cargo of	393
Adam comes in from sawing wood	480
Admit the fact, you might have stood your ground	455
'after making love . . .	272
Ag Críost an síol, ag Críost an fómhar	187
Ag sioscadh trí do shaothar anocht tháinig leoithne na cuimhne chugham ó gach leathanach	433
Alone on the beach this morning	295
Among the plovers and the stonechats	459
An ancient bridge, and a more ancient tower	247
An cuimhin leat an oíche úd	175
An ember or two glow	441
And now that these two earthlings have been by the poet-priest blessed	547
And then I mounted and she bound me	237
Apoqnmuinen ta'n teli l'nu-ktapekia'tiek	551
Ar charraig, a Easpaig Chluana	286
. . . As I had gone out by way of the Abha Bheag I decided to	89
As I roamed out one evening	147
As I roved out one evening in the month of sweet July	91
As I was walking one evening fair	45, 47
As the bull-dozer bites into the tree ringed hillfort	362
At Boolavogue as the sun was setting o'er the bright May meadows of Shelmalier	73
At noon, in the dead centre of a faith	460

B

Backing a *Bass Ireland* lorry across the road	446
Ba ghnáth mé ag siúl le ciumhais na habhann	138
BASHÓ, coming	271
Beautiful Rose, beautiful Rose	235
Being on the banks of Clady, I heard a maid complain	150
Beside the wine there's a candle and terror, the statue of my Lord	328
Between the thought and the word	438
Bhí mé lá breá aerach ag dul bóthar a' Mhaighre	169
Blessed Mary	185
Boiler room men in their nests	407
Bound for Great Britain and	389
Brin for a sack of coal	307
By the brink of the river I'd often walk	141

C

Call it the solstice, call it	311
Ceó meala lá seaca, ar choilltibh dubha daraighe	151
Coinnigh do thalamh, a anam liom	284
Come all ye true-born fishermen and listen to my song	15
Come all ye young fellows, don't be in a hurry	61
Come all you true countrymen, come listen to me	30
Come all you young fellows and list while I tell	97
Come tender hearted Christians all, pay attention to me	75
Comes not the springtime here	233
Cúlaíonn beirt dhéagóirí, scairfeanna thar a mbéal	444

D

Dawn from the Foretop! Dawn from the Barrel!	200
dead Indians are safer	310
Deep in Canadian woods we've met	52
Deirín dé, deirín dé	179, 180
D'éis imeacht ann cois na hAbha Bige, shíleas teacht abhaile	87
'Did ya hear about Donal's wee brother	448
Do chuir mé slán lém' cháirdibh in aenfheacht	32
Down by the salley gardens my love and I did meet	242
'Dritheog nó dhó fágtha...	440
Driving from Stephenville in the late October	424
ducks swoop low over the	415

E

End of a day in the wet trench	463
Eukuan tshe atanutsheian	1
Everyone in the cove is sorry for me	337
Excuse me, but I'd rather not see	486
Exiled from the sun	317

F

Farewell I bid to my friends ere leaving	35
Five boats were shooting their nets in the bay	219
For them it is always Sunday afternoon	294
From Bonavista Cape to the Cabot Isles	9
From early hours to late	439
From the month of June to the month of October, Aaron Shale	416
From the widow McKenny	105
Fuaim ag leamhan leochaileach, iompó leathanaigh	332

G

'Gealach na gcoinleach	440
Gene sat on a rock, dangling our map	345
Golden summer, lying in the meadows	166
'Good men and true! In this house who dwell	77
Green, blue, yellow and red	274
Grian an Mheithimh in úllghort	324

H

Harvest moon	441
He climbed to his feet in the cold light, and began	65
He was always going to look after them	482
He'd seen it before	322
Her high freeboard towering above the pier	204
Here are two pictures from my father's head	469
He's a gossip and he brings it home to her	471
he's out there the kids say pointing	409
How justly alarmed is each Dublin cit	82
Hurrah for our own native isle, Newfoundland	96

I

I am an old man now	398
I can tell you, now that you're dead	302
I do not sing of arms and the man	494
I dtráth agus in antráth	439
I fished with my father when I was young	58
I have found out a gift for my Erin	85
I have had a fair trial on the fishing line now	391
I have lived in important places, times	273
I have many stories to tell about our childhood	182
I have met them at close of day	244
I like talking to trees	342
I love you more than any God, not falsely	305
I once had a glimpse	283
I remember striding through the August twilight	456
I shall be a footnote and a reference	334
I thought I was headed for silence	412

I thought of you tonight, *a leanbh*, lying there in your long barrow	535
I was just thinking of Mattie	339
I was once the best mummer	289
I was with men, women and children	303
I went out to the hazel wood	236
I went with Anger at my heel	356
I will go out tomorrow to Newry fair	164
I will go with my father a-ploughing	54
I will monitor the movement of tides	300
I wish I was in Carrickfergus	49
I'd watch her each evening	321
I'll not forget that foreign scene	295
I'm a hardy old sailor from Newfoundland's shore	109
I'm up early to catch	323
Idir an smaoineamh agus an briathar	438
If you go tomorrow to Tuar an Fhíona	44
If your wharf is washed away	418
Iles des Esquimaux. Indian Island, Indian Bay, Indian Tickle	403
In aice an fhíona	328
In cuttin' and haulin' in frost and in snow	55
In my harsh city, when a Catholic priest	453
In Siberia's wastes	94
In this wind-blown, wild-flowered	515
In your ghost, Dick King, in your phantom vowels I read	280
It can be bitter here at times like this	475
It stole in on us like a foot-pad	231
It took the sea a thousand years	232
It was on the Belfast Mountains I heard a maid complain	74
It's about a maiden was young and fair	144

J

Jack and I are resting	377
Jean le premier partit	528
June sun in an orchard, a rustle in the silk of evening, an ill	326
Just days ago	531

K

Keep to yourself your kisses	504
Kind gents list with polite attention	146
Knowing that the ground horns of dead things	487

L

Living alone becomes some people	519
Living in Cow Head, Newfoundland, you'd draw	429
Long Winter's night	441

M

Má fhaighimse sláinte beidh caint is tráchtadh	38
Má théann tú amárach go dtí Tuar an Fhíona	43
Magpie, your black and white	492
Maidin sheaca ghabhas amach	329
Mellow the moonlight to shine is beginning	157
Mike and I used to talk a lot	507
Mo bhrón ar an bhfarraige	155
Mo ghrá go daingean tu	125
Much I remember of the death of men	255
My calves are the white calves	168
My grandfather's scythe	441
My grief on the ocean	156
My mother's father, when he came to die	458
My steadfast love	132

N

Ná bí buartha fúm, a mháthair	489
Nels and his wife and half a dozen or so of their kids are	410
No questions of falling then	406
Nochtaíodh domsa tráth	282
Not a drum was heard, not a funeral-note	83
November bluster	396
November winds move these leaves toward	304
Now all you young men who go chopping	59
now and then	405
Now clouds creep away; hushed wind	532
Now de war, dearest Nancy, is ended	79
Now don't go ringing the cops	490
Now I will tell a legend	5
Now you may bless your happy lot that live secure on shore	28

O

Ó, bliain 's an lá amárach	67
O Breed, astore, do not marry the old man	160
O bright and welcoming mountain, I'm far from you now overseas	63
O Chrissey went up to Aunt Margaret's to get a loan of her dick	108
O, it was a fine and pleasant day	26
O it's one year tomorrow	68
O, Lukey's boat is painted green	18
O the grip, O the grip of irregular fields! No man escapes	275
O then, tell me, Shawn O'Farrell, tell me why you hurry so	72
Odysseus rested on his oar, and saw	505
Oh! a tall gangling lad had a boat on the Bandon	153
Oh it's hard and unforgiving work	24
Oh! this is the place where the fishermen gather	113
Oh were I at the moss house, where the birds do increase	50
Oh, youth whom I have kissed, like a star through the mist	162

'Oíche fhada gheimhridh	440
On a rock, Bishop of Cloyne	287
On Raglan Road on an autumn day I met her first and knew	279
on the bunk, behind the stove	414
One fine day I was going the Moyra pass	170
One frosty morning I roved out and a handkerchief was before	329
One heavy cloud held back the lifting sun	343
One pleasant morning in this new millennium	117
Our children have eaten supper	258
Out back of a house, the blue of a crib	430
Outside the boundaries of ancient and formica	299

P

Perhaps a maritime pastoral	461

R

Rachaidh mé amárach go haonach Chinn Trá	163
Remember that night	176
RosiaKKulak RosiaKKulak	234
Running the Quidi Vidi loop in mauzy weather	402

S

Samhradh buí 'na luí ins na léanaí	165
Saturday of an evening I beheld my strapping fellow	499
Seems I can mind them	290
She was standing by the dryer when the end-of-cycle timer went	484
She will have this memory of him	314
Shúd é an Domhnach a thug mé grá dhuit	171
'Siad mo chuid gamhna, na gamhna geala	167
Síleann céad fear gur leo féin mé nuair a ólaim leann	173
'Sin clábar! Clábar cáidheach	442
Sketches in the old mission letters suggested	392
'snowdrifts at my door . . .	272
Somehow, in Picasso's 'Madman'	292
Sound of a fragile moth, turning the page, bruising of small	333
'Speal mo sheanathar . . .	440
St. Ruth trots on a silver mare	348
Stand your ground, my soul	285
Sweeney kept going until he reached the church at Swim-Two	372

T

Tá jaicéid gairid á dhéanamh ó mhaidin dúinn, agus *trouser* dá réir	70
Tá siad á rá gur tú sáilín socair i mbróig	500
Tá sléibhte na leapa mós ard	330
Taisigh agad féin do phóg	503
Take me back to my western boat	27
Take it from us every grain	92

Index of First Lines 611

That great central bone of mountain	496
That is no country for old men. The young	253
That kitsch lumber-room is stacked	462
That was the Sunday that I gave you love: the second Sunday	172
That water-nipper hauled for us	309
'That's muck! Filthy muck, you little scamp	443
The arc of the yo-yo	320
The autumn days are here again, the night wind's chilly blow	57
The familiar pull of the slow train	466
The flag flat out	522
The light of evening, Lissadell	243
The *Montague* packet left Wexford at ten	20
The moon	313
The mountains of the bed are rather high and sickness a heat in	330
The new sled	408
The night before Larry was stretched	111
The Pope he leads a happy life	115
The shrubs on Frank's grave have withered	338
The shutters folded back in their frames	497
The trees are in their autumn beauty	252
'the village graveyard . . .	272
The year we plowed the river field, we found	288
The years spin quicker since that day I stood	457
'the young plum pickers . . .	272
There was a cook in a camp did dwell	101
There was my great-uncle Aaron Shale, one of the biggest fish	415
There'd seemed to be some justice	319
There's not a chance now that I might recover	454
they all save one last squirt	411
They are saying your little heel fits snugly in the shoe	501
They hate yellow blossoms	521
They never were part of a crew	306
This one spring an iceberg come and set right on top of Aaron	417
Those determined middle-aged	420
Three times we heard it calling with a low	232
Thumbing through your work tonight the aroma of memories came from every page	436
Tim Finnegan lived in Watling street	99
To Christ the seed, to Christ the crop	187
To still be driving the familiar roads	422
too bad you're not here	488
Tráthnóna an tSathairn sea chonacsa an strapaire	499
Trembling with engines, gulping oil, the river	189

U

UnikkausiKatlapungâli surutsiunigilauptaptinik	181
Up the hill	264
Uvanga uvanga piungitoalujunga	186

W

We are North Americans now	298
We came ashore	524
We hated them mad rocks, yes	308
'we return . . .	272
We watched it for ten days	301
We were bound home in October from the shores of Labrador	11
Well hell	517
We'll rant and we'll roar like true Newfoundlanders	21
What I know of you is only	511
What I remember of you	478
When Cook came ashore here, his heart rose	423
When he had made sure there were no survivors in his house	468
When the cliffs echo with shrieking, when fires hiss	308
when the rain comes and a cold wind	412
When the sun goes down on Cradle Hill	178
When they marched up from the cove to the Cross	306
When we came home from the Labrador in the fall, we'd take	400
While I keep my health, there'll be talk and discourse	40
Will went first	525
Willy-nilly, he comes or goes, with the clown's logic	229
Wujjiek Wa'so'q epin, ktuisunm mkite'tasij, ika'j kteleke'wa'kim	183

Y

Ye lads and lasses of Newfoundland, come listen to my sad tale	51
Ye people all both great and small, I hope you will attend	12
Yes, it's like that. Buffaloes whiten the moon	340
You may talk of Clara Nolan's ball	103

However Blow the Winds:
An Anthology of Poetry and Song
from Newfoundland & Labrador and Ireland

John Ennis is Head of School of Humanities at Waterford Institute of Technology. Winner of The Patrick Kavanagh Award, Listowel Writers' Week Awards and the Irish American Cultural Institute Award, he has been editor of *Poetry Ireland Review*. His latest book of poems, *Near St. Mullins*, was published by Dedalus Press in 2002. He is chairperson of the Centre for Newfoundland & Labrador Studies, Ionad Leinn Thalamh an Éisc agus Labrador, at the Institute.

Born in Vancouver, Randall Maggs has a PhD from the University of New Brunswick and has taught Canadian Literature and creative writing at Grenfell College in Corner Brook, Newfoundland, for 27 years. His poetry has appeared in many international journals and anthologies (including *The Backyards of Heaven*) and in a collection entitled *Timely Departures* (Breakwater Books, 1994). A visual artist as well, he had several pieces included in the 1999 collaboration of Irish and Newfoundland artists, *Wood: A Sculptural Investigation*.

Stephanie McKenzie is the editor of three other books of poetry (*An Island in the Sky: Selected Poetry of Al Pittman*, *The Backyards of Heaven: An Anthology of Contemporary Poetry from Ireland and Newfoundland & Labrador* and *Humber Mouths: Young Voices from the West Coast of Newfoundland & Labrador*). McKenzie received her Ph.D. in English Literature from the University of Toronto where she specialised in contemporary aboriginal literature.